Transition to an Industrial South

Transition to an Industrial South

ATHENS, GEORGIA 1830–1870

MICHAEL J. GAGNON

LOUISIANA STATE UNIVERSITY PRESS
BATON ROUGE

Published with the assistance of the V. Ray Cardozier Fund

Published by Louisiana State University Press

Manufactured in the United States of America
First printing

DESIGNER: Mandy McDonald Scallan
TYPEFACE: Whitman
PRINTER AND BINDER: McNaughton & Gunn, Inc.

All maps and graphs by Mary Lee Eggart

Library of Congress Cataloging-in-Publication Data
Gagnon, Michael J., 1957–
Transition to an industrial South : Athens, Georgia, 1830–1870 / Michael J. Gagnon.
p. cm.
Includes bibliographical references and index.
ISBN 978-0-8071-4508-1 (cloth : alk. paper) — ISBN 978-0-8071-4509-8 (pdf) — ISBN 978-0-8071-4510-4 (epub) — ISBN 978-0-8071-4511-1 (mobi) 1. Athens (Ga.)—History—19th century. 2. Industrialization—Georgia—Athens—History—19th century. 3. Cotton textile industry—Georgia—Athens—History—19th century. 4. Athens (Ga.)—Economic conditions—19th century. I. Title.
F294.A7G35 2012
975.8'18—dc23

2011048192

The paper in this book meets the guidelines for permanence and durability of the Committee on Production Guidelines for Book Longevity of the Council on Library Resources. ♾

To MariBeth

Contents

Illustrations

FIGURES

TABLES

Preface

As most historians publishing their first book will tell you, this is not the book I thought I would write when I first started down the academic road. Instead, it is a work that evolved as I learned more about the sources of my research and about myself as well. Upon entering graduate school in 1989, I originally intended to study early twentieth-century political radicalism in the United States; in particular, I wanted to know why America wasn't turning to socialism during the Progressive Era. In my first graduate seminar, however, I wrote a paper seeking to explain why Atlanta was not located a few miles east, in the pre-existing village of Decatur. In short, I discovered that the founding of Atlanta in the 1840s unintentionally resulted from industrialization in Athens, Georgia, in the 1830s. As a consequence of this seemingly minor insight, I spent the last twenty-two years researching, thinking, discussing, and writing about how the process of industrialization in antebellum America took place, who did it, why they did it, and why it all matters today.

Focusing on local sources proved my downfall. I always tell my students that history happens someplace, and to the people living it, it is their local history. Even important events occurring far away must be interpreted locally to make sense. Telling that local story to elucidate the national consequences of an event or process requires the use of analysis and of narrative, all the makings of good history. A local story almost always includes real people with human frailties, which is bound to raise reader interest much more than vague but powerful forces in history. However, finding those local sources to gain perspective on a national story, while always extremely rewarding, frequently proves extremely difficult. This book is filled with local sources, and I like to claim that my research took so long, indeed that nobody else attempted a book-length description of industrialization in Athens even though the town is the home of a major research university with a great history program, because the local sources proved so difficult to locate. But the truth is a bit more complicated.

The research proved more arduous than anticipated. Much of the research involved reading or taking notes from antebellum newspapers on microfilm, or from documents from the National Archives on microfilm, usually between 10:00 p.m. and 2:00 a.m., after already completing a day's work. I spent at least six months traveling round-trip from Atlanta to Athens nearly every weekday to find, read, and assemble data in numerous collections at the University of Georgia, at Athens/Clarke Court House, at Southern Mutual Insurance Company, and at the homes of some of the old families of Athens. All of this was incredibly rewarding but time-consuming. When not traveling to Athens, I regularly used the research facilities of my home institution, Emory University, or traveled to collections at Harvard, Duke, Chapel Hill, Wake Forest, Clemson, and the National Archives. As a result of my research, I assembled over ten thousand pages of notes in an electronic database called askSam, the same database used by the Iran-contra prosecutor to find sufficient evidence to bring to justice so many members of the Reagan Administration following the shredding of the main incriminating evidence by Oliver North. Thousands more pages of photocopies sit in my file cabinets awaiting inclusion in the database for use in future projects. It was this text-based database that allowed me to follow the story and make connections that I probably would have missed otherwise.

I attempt to fit the local into a regional explanation of a national process. Historians have already described the process of industrialization in the early nineteenth century in New England and the Middle Atlantic states reasonably well. We are only just beginning to describe the process in the antebellum South; in fact, previous efforts were devoted to convincing non-specialists that industrialization was even taking place there. So I have two main audiences to address in this work: economic and social historians of early industrialization, and southern historians. I trained as a social historian under a historian of early industrialization, but I never took a single southern history class (though I have taught southern history courses regularly since earning my doctorate). While I understood the issues of how to relate Athens's industrialization to the national processes taking place, I needed to learn the nuances of southern history to insure that I told the story accurately within its regional context. I am thankful for my dissertation committee and the many advance readers of this work, not only for their cogent remarks and adept editing, but also for requiring me to learn about the South. When now asked about how I describe myself, I proudly proclaim myself both a social historian and a southern historian, and I'm respectful of both.

Unfortunately, I failed to interest granting organizations in funding my graduate research, so I needed to work to help support my family. Fortunately, I started teaching at Georgia Tech, which treated me as a colleague rather than as some exploitable temporary worker. After earning my doctorate, I was blessed with a tenure-track appointment at William Paterson University in New Jersey, which provided release time for research and funded travel to conferences at which I gave papers. After returning to Georgia as a trailing spouse, I taught as either an adjunct or visiting professor for different durations at the University of Georgia, Georgia State University, Clemson University, and North Georgia College and State University. A new public college, Georgia Gwinnett College, hired me as their first historian on staff in 2007, and we have grown to seventeen historians and nearly eight thousand students in less than five years. While I enjoy both the service and teaching responsibilities of academic life in a new open-access institution, I am grateful to rediscover the joys of research and writing as part of the promotion process. In teaching history, I benefit because my students always challenge me to improve not only their understanding but my own as well. However, it is the research that drew me to the profession in the beginning; I am pleased to return to it.

All this is to say that I took my time, and that the journey has been as interesting as the destination. I enjoyed both the solitude and the fellowship. I discovered what I knew in the writing of my research. It sat fallow for many years, but I hope it will be worth your reading.

In the end, this study demonstrates a process of industrialization in the antebellum South. That process both mimicked and differed from similar processes taking place in New England and the Middle Atlantic states. Industrializing places in the antebellum South necessarily experimented with new forms of social organization, which created norms for later industrializing efforts following the end of slavery. Industrialization, everywhere, is a process that involves both continuity and change, which are not opposing ends of a dichotomy, but merely differing perspectives of the same complex phenomenon.

Acknowledgments

Scholarship involves much fellowship in addition to the solitude. We scholars regularly rely on the "kindness of strangers" to gain access to the data we desire to analyze, and those strangers then become our friends as we return to them time and again to gain more access. Nor do most of us work completely alone in thinking through the ramifications of our research. We rely on other scholars to help us through direct conversation, through online discourse, through organized presentations at conferences, through peer review of books and publication of articles, and through established lines of historiography. Without this interaction we would not be professional historians but merely enthusiasts or antiquarians, remaining largely ignorant of the important questions our works raise. Because we work in somewhat self-contained subfields, we get to know nearly all the other scholars who share our interests, and they too become our fiends. When we finally publish the results of our research and analysis, our publishers allow us to acknowledge that we did not produce our work entirely by ourselves. I will inevitably miss some important people in this brief acknowledgement; I do not mean to slight anyone's contribution, and I could not have done it without all the help I received. All that is right about this work is a result of the contributions of all those named or unnamed herein. Any mistakes are solely my own.

First of all, I thank all the people who shared their family information or information about their town. They invited me into their homes and shared precious time and secrets with me. In Athens this included Sue Fan Tate, Charlotte Marshall, Mary Claire Bondurant, Marguerite Hodgson, Lou De Vorsey, Milton Leathers III, Goodloe Erwin, and Rufus and Josephine Reaves. While the headquarters of the Southern Mutual Insurance Company in Athens was not a home, Carol Huber and Allen Green made me feel at home. Outside Athens, Monroe King of Douglasville, Georgia, and Lin Dearing of Clemson, South Carolina, likewise shared documents, stories, and fellowship. Others too numerous to name shared their stories and information through phone calls, letters, and emails. "I get by with a little help from my friends!"

Historians cannot work at all without the professional support networks of librarians and archivists. I specifically thank the entire staff of Emory University libraries, but particularly Marie Hansen, who handled so much of my interlibrary loan requests. At the Hargrett Library at the University of Georgia, the entire staff, but particularly its director, Mary Ellen Brooks, and manuscripts librarian, Chuck Barber, made certain I knew of every possible resource. In the course of my research, archivists at Georgia Archives, Georgia Historical Society, Atlanta History Center, Emory University, Harvard Business School, the University of North Carolina at Chapel Hill, Duke, Clemson, Virginia Tech, Augusta State, and Columbus State contributed time and effort to make valuable resources available.

Other historians contributed greatly to helping me clarify what I wanted to do. My dissertation director, Jonathan Prude, is simply the best editor a doctoral candidate could wish for. Bob McMath and Jim Roark read the entire work without complaint, and still continue to act as friends and mentors. Because this project gestated so long, I benefited from the comments of numerous scholars, including Susanna Delfino, Tom Downey, David Carlton, Peter Coclanis, Phil Scranton, Gavin Wright, Jim Cobb, Randall Miller, John Majewski, John Quist, Michele Gillespie, John Lupold, Joe Reidy, Randy Patton, Steve Reich, Sean Adams, Craig Pascoe, Louis Kyriakoudes, Pam Long, Jack Lozier, Jack Wynn, and Michael Bellesiles, all of whom read and/or discussed portions of the manuscript as it progressed. That I didn't always take their advice is my fault and not theirs.

I am especially thankful for the opportunities opened to me by Georgia Gwinnett College, the first public college created in the twenty-first century, as I took on service responsibilities I could hardly imagine the previous year. As an open-access liberal arts institution, my college is charged with taking our students from where they are to where they need to be, and so I spend a great deal of time in teaching my classes or in engaging with students individually. I thank my colleagues at Georgia Gwinnett for putting up with my vociferous opinions and for stepping in to help whenever the need arises. I also am thankful for the financial support from my institution to allow my attendance at scholarly conferences or to take undergraduate students to present their research at conferences.

Last but not least, my wife, MariBeth, made this all possible. She provided us with stable income, gave birth to our children, always gives wise counsel, and keeps us all on an even keel. Even though she sometimes wonders if she is not enabling my addiction to history, she supports and encourages me. She is my best friend, and I could not do this without her. That is why this book is dedicated to her.

Transition to an Industrial South

INTRODUCTION

Old England has her Manchester—New England her Lowell,
and why should not Georgia boast her Athens?
—*Southern Banner* (Athens, Georgia), May 11, 1833.

Just as Manchester did for industrialization in England, and as Lowell did for industrialization in Massachusetts, Athens served as a model for industrial manufacture in early nineteenth-century Georgia. After participating in discussions of the need for greater southern economic independence from the other sections of the country, in order to secure greater political leverage within the Union, entrepreneurs of Athens constructed a cotton factory and commenced business in 1830. Soon, other men of capital built two more factories within Clarke County, bringing the immediate area's industrial capital to more than $120,000 in less than five years. For the next forty years, these factories regularly provided profits for their owners, employment for at least three hundred people, a ready market for locally grown cotton, and inexpensive thread and fabric for local use. Immediately after building these factories, Athens' town fathers constructed railroads and created financial institutions to service the area's growing economy. Athens's textile industry later served and survived the Confederacy, and then it proved essential to the town's postbellum economy. While Georgia and other southern states boasted of many towns like Athens, historians know very little about the role such early industrial efforts played in the South's economy and how industry adapted to a slave economy.

While agriculture clearly dwarfed industry in the antebellum South, the eleven southern states that seceded from the Union formed the sixth most industrialized nation in 1861. Thus, a study of the process of early southern industrialization posses an interesting puzzle about the nature of the southern economy and about how southern society accommodated non-agricultural economic activities. After all, why would slave-holding southerners invest in textile manufactures when planting yielded both profits and status? And who actually built these factories? Were the industrialists artisans, who naturally altered their manufacturing modes as new technologies became available, or were they elites who imposed a new technology-based system for organizing labor on a slave-based society? Where would these industrialists choose to locate their factories, and why in those particular locations? How would they market their wares, and to whom? And most importantly, where would these entrepreneurs find workers for their factories? Would this new style of labor conflict with the needs of a slave society, and would the style of industrialization in a slave society dramatically differ from styles of industrial organization found outside the American South? The industrialists of Athens discussed many of these questions throughout the antebellum period.[1]

At the start of this process of industrialization, Athens's unique cultural and economic position as the seat of the state's university pushed the town to the forefront of Georgia's pursuit of economic development, both by introducing factory-style manufacturing and by developing other economic infrastructure that aided overall industrialization. Other aspiring Georgia towns emulated Athens's industrial experiments, and by mid-century, some surpassed its productive potential. But because Athens served as a central node of textile-related production in operating its cotton factories, bobbin mill, paper mill, gas works, foundry, banks, insurance company, and railroad, it remained competitive into the twentieth century, and it serviced nearby areas that similarly sought to develop their local economies. That Henry Grady, spokesman for a New South that embraced industrialization, grew up in Athens in the 1850s, highlights the importance of the process by which Athens's entrepreneurs created factory-based industry. By the early 1870s, two generations of the town's industrialists imprinted their enterprises with the character of a New South mill village, a character which others have successfully explored. Athens merits extended study because it served as an industrial and cultural center in Georgia beginning with the Lower South's earliest successful efforts at establishing industrial manufactures in the 1830s, and extending through the threshold of the New South era, in the 1870s.

Until recently, historians frequently misunderstood or overlooked the importance of early southern industrialization. Important dissertations on the subject never became monographs and thus deprived general historians of knowledge of the extent and effects of antebellum southern industrialization.

Journal articles in the era prior to the 1980s generally settled for describing social or business conditions rather than examining how industry fit within southern society. Those attempting analysis frequently relied on New South–era publications or essays written during the 1850s to document the growth of southern industry, without challenging the agenda of the original authors, who wrote their own versions of how industrialization proceeded in order to influence its continued growth and who downplayed previous industrial efforts. By uncritically adopting these perspectives, southern historians could not help overlooking the formative era and concurring with Broadus Mitchell that antebellum southern industry seemed neither extensive nor important to later industrial development. Thus as a field of inquiry, early southern industrialization failed to generate much interest for further investigation. As a result, the little discussion that did take place tended to minimize the importance of this sector of the southern economy and intended to use this understanding of it as an means of explaining other aspects of southern society, rather than exploring southern industrialization on its own terms.[2]

Until recently, general understanding of early southern industry derived from two classic interpretations. The first interpretation claimed early manufacturing faced ideological opposition from the planter class, which resisted the proliferation of cotton factories in order to preserve its own hegemonic influence over southern society. The second interpretation compared aggregate southern industrialization to that of the North and found that the South failed to fulfill its potential because slavery inhibited non-agricultural economic activity. Ultimately both analyses revealed little about early southern industrialization because they were more interested in developing general theories about southern society than in understanding how the South actually industrialized. Most analyses derived from these two approaches made claims of typicality by studying the entire South as a region rather than looking at industrial activity within a single state or locality. As a result, they missed the nuances of variation over time and between different places.[3]

More recently, however, historians began using case studies of states or localities to explore southern entrepreneurial activity in commerce and transportation, and a similar approach should illuminate the process of southern industrialization as well. These newer studies seek to understand the process of economic development within the context of a slaveholding society, and the effects of this process on issues of race, class, and gender. This study follows in that trend and seeks to demonstrate the concerted efforts of economic modernizers to formulate an economic network to support their efforts.[4]

State-level is more appropriate than regional analysis for understanding southern textile industrialization, which was the region's leading industrial sector. Individual states embody singular legal and public policy structures. Thus examination of process in one state may reveal the general contours for the region without making claims of typicality. Figure 1, Southern textile spindleage: 1840–1880, disaggregates regional data to state-level data and reveals variation among the six southern states with significant industrialization. Importantly, the trend in numbers of spindles, which is an important measure of textile manufacturing capacity, remained relatively flat up to 1870, after which no clear pattern emerged for state-level variation. However, for most of the nineteenth century, Georgia remained the leading textile state of the South, and thus an examination of the process of industrialization in Georgia may well serve as a starting place from which to explore the process throughout the region. But even this level of disaggregation proves insufficient, because entrepreneurs in the North pursued several modes

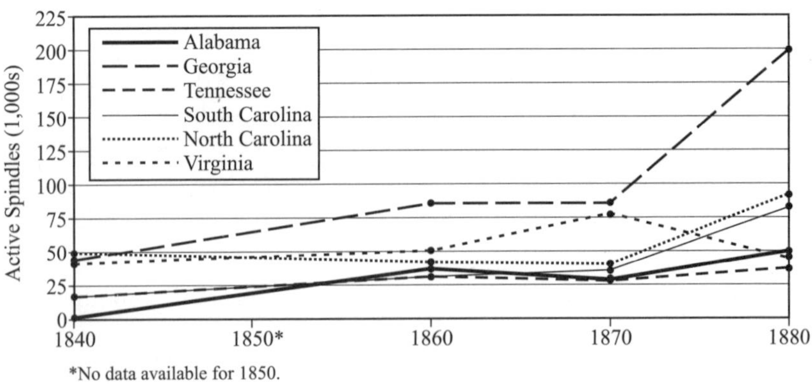

FIGURE 1. Southern textile spindleage, 1840–1880.

Sources: Alice C. Galenson, "The Migration of the Cotton Textile Industry from New England to the South: 1880–1930," "Table I.1: Number of Active Spindles, by State, New England and South, 1859 to 1929." Also *Report on Manufacturing Industries in the United States at the Eleventh Census: 1890,* part 3: 188–91.

of textile industrialization, and thus one might expect southern manufacturers to similarly seek a variety of means of pursuing their business. Since case studies of industrialization in the northern states demonstrate an uneven, segmented, and differentiated process, a similar case-study approach should be made of an important southern industrial site in order to identify at least one process by which southerners actually industrialized.[5]

A case-study of successful industrialization in antebellum Georgia merits closer scrutiny than previously accorded, not just because of what it tells us about the importance of one aspiring locality, but because of its implications for understanding economic development for the entire state, and perhaps for the region as well. Yes, Georgia, like most of the Lower South, was a land of cotton and slavery. But the State of Georgia encouraged manufacturing, as well as other forms of non-agricultural economic development. Planters not only engaged in the vicious cycle of purchasing-slaves-to-grow-more-cotton-to-buy-more-slaves-to-grow-more-cotton, but some also built factories, took risks in banking, and experimented with costly forms of improved transportation. Clearly not all planters tied themselves strictly to agriculture. While southern non-agricultural investments did not match those made in New England, most historical studies of early southern industry satisfied themselves to claim only that the South failed to replicate the northern experience. A case study of industrialization in the heart of the antebellum cotton belt will illuminate more than the fact the South was not the North; it will demonstrate the importance of ideology in mobilizing for industrialization, an ideology explained more forcefully at the start of this economic transition than at later times. Further, a case study of early southern industrialization demonstrates the process by which southerners came to understand their economic comparative advantages and their political disadvantages within the American republic, which in turn reveals the rationality of their sectionalism. Also, a case study deepens our understanding of the demography of class distinctions in the Old South, showing that slave-owning southerners fostered a free-labor industrial workforce that was not seen as a threat to the South's "domestic institutions." Finally, such a study highlights distinctions within the planter class, since owning the requisite twenty slaves to attain planterhood may not be a sufficient indicator of a planter's ability to diversify his investment portfolio beyond agriculture. Athens, Georgia, is a good candidate for studying these themes in a case study.

At the start of the first successful wave of industrialization in the 1830s, Athens's entrepreneurs looked to previous attempts in neighboring counties to understand the risks involved. Before 1820 all of Georgia's experiments in industrial manufacturing—the Bolton Factory in neighboring Wilkes County, Schley's Factory in Jefferson County, and Jacob Gregg's Factory in nearby Morgan County—had failed. One southern historian suggests that the two-hundred-mile distance of Georgia's fall line from its coast contributed to the delay in developing an industrial infrastructure, while New England's proximity between coast and fall line encouraged manufacturing. While details of the earliest industrial failures in Georgia remain fuzzy, the sparseness of the local populations, due to the proximity of the Indian frontier, probably proved too thin a market for profitable industrialization. Before industrialization could be pursued in earnest, the state needed to clear away its Native American populations.

Native American occupation of the Georgia upcountry prevented settlement of legal questions regarding ownership that necessarily preceded the development of water-power sites. Until 1818, the western border of Clarke County, which contains Athens, served as the boundary with territory controlled by Native Americans. After a series of treaties in the late 1810s and early 1820s, the frontier moved sufficiently west to organize counties in all parts except for the northwest corner of the state (comprised entirely of the piedmont and upcountry regions) which remained under Native American control until the late 1830s. Georgia politicians, particularly those later interested in textile manufactures, consistently championed the extension of Georgia's legal system over Indian territory, and the ultimate removal of the Indians, with or without federal acquiescence. The delay in acquiring control over its territory probably accounts for the postponement in developing the suitable water-power sites in the state. Still, Athens attracted a core population despite these difficulties.[6]

Although a relatively new town, Athens grew in population and in commercial importance prior to its citizens' experiments with industrial manufactures. The houses and shops that clustered around the University of Georgia soon after its founding in 1800 became a large enough collection to merit incorporation as the town of Athens by 1806. While it did not serve as the seat of county government, Athens attracted merchants and artisans to serve the needs of the college. Entrepreneurs erected stores, hotels,

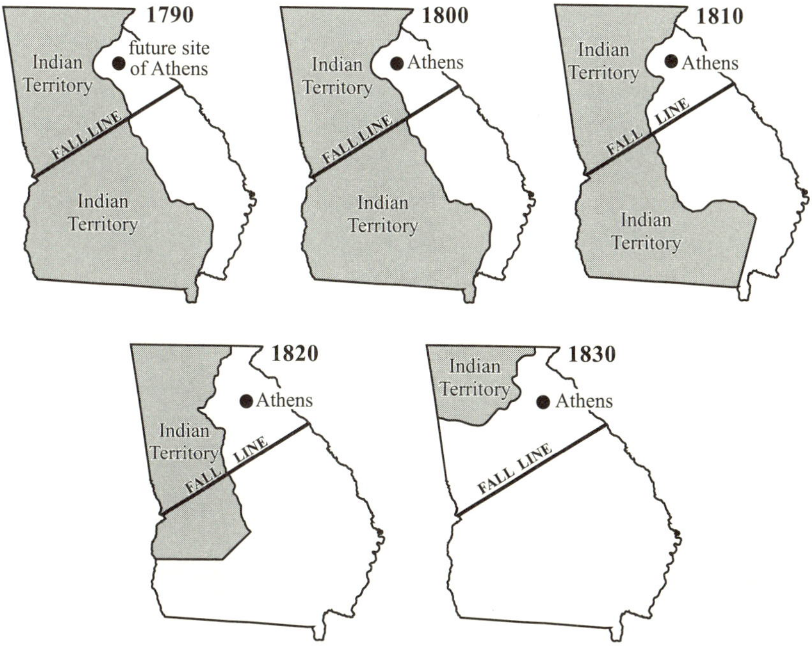

FIGURE 2. Map of Native American territory in Georgia, 1790–1830.

and boarding houses; speculators built homes for the town's potential population; and gentlemen purchased plantations near Athens in order to keep their families together as their sons attended the state university. Other families moved to Athens for the cultural ambience best exemplified by the university's annual commencement, which served as the social event of the year in antebellum Georgia. The commencement, the town's newspaper editor observed in 1832, "is to Athens what the carnival is to Rome or Paris. Here, in a few days, again will congregate the talented and the wealth[y], both real and pretended, of our state." While events surrounding commencement varied over the years, one could always count on the attendance of the state's elite for the staging of cultural and popular entertainments, for political meetings, and for works of economic or philanthropic development. With the concentration of a cultural elite, Athens frequently provided entertainments beyond what one would expect for a town of its size, located at the northern periphery of the cotton belt.[7]

By the town's third decade of existence, its growth increased at a perceptible rate, progressing from thirty-two houses and thirty university students in 1819 to seventy-two houses and one hundred students in 1827. As the university grew in reputation among the state's elite, people increasingly chose to move to the town. "Athens thrives very fast [with a] pop[ulation of] 1000," explained an observer in 1827. In 1828, a town census enumerated "583 Whites, and 517 Blacks, making a total of 1100," and the local editor set these numbers in context by explaining that the town possessed only 499 fewer people than the state capital at Milledgeville, and that no other village in the state could "boast as extensive improvements, as have been made with [Athens], in the last five years." The following year, the newspaper humorously commented on the recent growth of Athens, declaiming, "Athens is *more* than a *village*—is a town—has been laid off as such—is a mile square—has thirteen hundred inhabitants, a corporation, and will no doubt in good time have its lord mayor. A village! We flout the idea." Thus, with the movement of the Indian frontier beyond the county's western border in 1819, the university provided for the existence of a core of economic/urban functions that acted as a catalyst for Athens's continued growth. Before gaining this new threshold, Athens already engaged in using water-powered technologies for pre-industrial purposes.[8]

By the time Athens launched its experiments in industrialization, the settlers of the Georgia upcountry already employed water-powered technologies. Entrepreneurs occupied water-power sites in Clarke County before it separated from earlier counties. A grist and saw mill operated in the territory that would become Clarke County in 1791, and by 1799, entrepreneurs developed a similar mill on the edge of what would become Athens the following year. Citizens of Clarke County improved eleven water-power sites between 1800 and 1828 for processing agricultural products and for manufacturing iron products. After 1828, they developed eight more water-power sites for similar pre-industrial purposes while adapting some of the earlier-developed sites to textile manufacture, merchant milling of flour, paper manufacture, and eventually weapons manufacture.[9]

Industrial use of water power differs qualitatively from pre-industrial uses. "Industrial," "industry," and "industrialization" are all defined here as involving a system for producing goods for market exchange from a centralized productive space, equipped with labor-saving technology actuated by an innate power source. Primarily, in antebellum Georgia, this meant cotton factories. As relatively highly capitalized and centralized centers of production for market, water-power sites were utilized much more continuously than in pre-industrial uses. Industrial uses generally operated on a regularly scheduled basis in contrast to pre-industrial mills which operated only sporadically, when a need for their use arose, such as operating a grist mill when approached by a customer or operating a cotton gin following a harvest. Also, the industrial user proved less likely than a pre-industrial user to share with its neighbors the water resources during dry months and was more likely to flood neighboring lands during wet months. In both cases, the industrial user needed to maintain a constant supply of water because of this intensive use and therefore needed to redefine the law to obtain more control over its power source.

Similarly, industrial usage accelerated the extermination of common-law riparian rights of free passage, the right to use rivers and streams as common highways, as well as the requirement of providing a means for fish to pass upstream, in order to protect both its dams and its water sources. Keeping a portion of its dam open to allow the free flow of goods, and/or fish, reduced the power potential of the site and threatened the site's productivity. Thus the shift to industrial usage could cause disputes between the owners of dams and the users of the rivers, such as loggers, boatmen, farmers, and fishermen. But in Athens, the relatively recent white settlement of the area, together with the wealth of water resources, minimized such conflict. Since many more mill sites existed than were actually used in the nineteenth century, logging operations, which might have insisted on their common-law rights to float trees to distant saw mills, instead commonly used small mills on streams near cutting areas. When forced to flood neighboring lands, industrial water-power users generally bought or leased the inundated property and avoided extended legal confrontations. Thus Athenians kept these increasingly intensive uses of local resources from causing hard feelings, litigation, and social instability. But why industrialize at all, and why in the late 1820s, following the failures of the previous decade? A preliminary answer must take into account changes in the price of cotton.[10]

Cotton prices consistently affected southern industrialization efforts. Georgia planters, who normally carried a large debt load, constantly worried about changes in the price of their primary market commodity, over which they exerted little control due to the international nature of the cotton

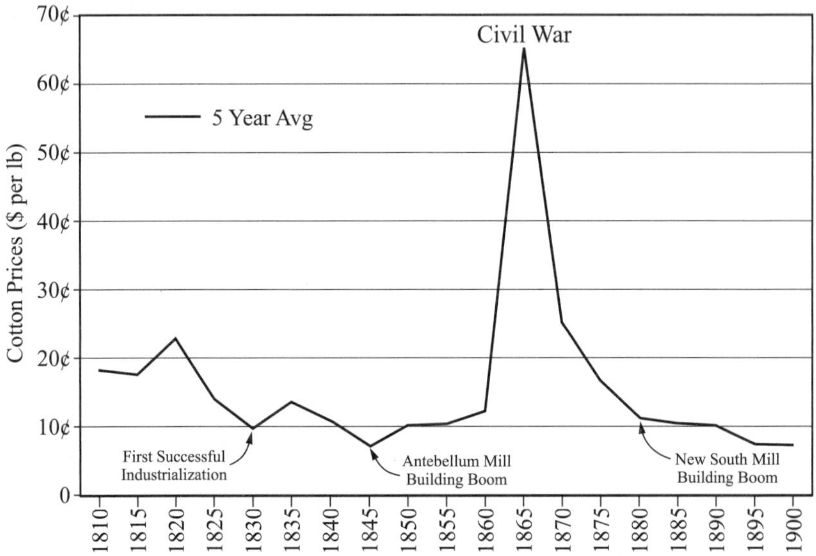

FIGURE 3. Cotton prices and mill-building cycles.
Source: James L. Watkins, *King Cotton; A Historical and Statistical Review 1790–1908* (1908; rpt. New York: Negro Universities Press, 1969), 29–31.

market. Classical economic theory suggests that a significant drop in a given crop's price should force its producers to consider alternate crops, or even to abandon agriculture for more lucrative profits elsewhere. However, a drop in the price of cotton reduced a textile factory's costs and therefore increased its profits proportionally. Also, since early southern industry bid against agriculture for labor, agricultural profits determined the availability and price of industrial workers, both free and slave. Thus, when cotton prices slumped long enough to alarm agricultural workers living on the margins, economic theory suggests they would consider other employment. Similarly, a master might move a portion of his slaves to non-agricultural endeavors (and/or refrain from purchasing additional land or slaves), as he perceived the possibility of poor profits from continued agricultural activity. Therefore, when cotton prices dropped, southerners should have shown greater interest in manufacturing, and when prices rose again, they increase their investments in agriculture. A comparison of the chronology of increased southern factory construction to changes in the price of cotton confirms economic theory: figure 3 demonstrates that the two cycles did roughly mirror each other.[11]

Cycles of interest in constructing cotton factories in Georgia bear an inverse relationship to the price of cotton. The initial interest in textile production in the 1810s developed from the effects of Jefferson's embargo and then the War of 1812. When these events prevented the United States from selling cotton to England, cotton prices plummeted. Exports of cotton dropped from over 228,000 bales in 1807 to approximately 38,000 bales the following year, and prices fell from nearly twenty-two cents per pound to only nineteen cents. Sinking to a low of ten and one-half cents per pound in 1812, prices only resumed their pre-conflict levels with peace in 1815. During the same period, entrepreneurs in Georgia built two cotton mills, but both failed with the resumption of prosperous cotton prices. After skyrocketing to more than thirty cents per pound in 1818, prices slumped steadily downward to less than twelve cents in 1824, due primarily to increased cotton production resulting from the opening of additional agricultural lands in Alabama and Mississippi. Spiking briefly to nearly nineteen cents per pound in 1825, the value of cotton fluctuated around ten cents per pound for the next eight years, roughly the same period as the first successful cycle of cotton-mill construction in the South. From 1833 to 1839, prices rose again above the ten cents benchmark, and agitation for more mill construction died down.

When prices nosedived from 1840 to 1849, the antebellum South experienced its largest mill-building boom, with the number of cotton mills in Georgia increasing from fourteen to approximately fifty-five. With the return of high cotton prices in the 1850s, many of the marginally managed mills failed or reorganized while others limped on, awaiting a better day. The Civil War years represent an exception to this analysis, because Confederate war policy artificially inflated the price of cotton, and because both Confederate and Union governments subsidized textile production through purchases of war materiel. Limited financial resources on the part of southerners, as well as the Union policy of destroying cotton factories, however, prevented an expansion of the number of factories during the war, although many of the southern factories that survived the war expanded their capacity during it. Following reorganization of the southern agricultural workforce, with the coming of emancipation and sharecropping, cotton prices remained inflated but uncertain through the early 1870s. During this time, established southern factories flourished, but limited funds and perceptions of the possibility of high profits in growing cotton kept southerners from expanding their industrial stock beyond prewar values. With the expansion of the British cotton supply from Egypt and India in the 1870s, U.S. cotton prices experienced a long depression, one that coincided with the cotton-mill movement that historians explain as instrumental in creating the "New South." While the economics of southern cotton prices explains much of the timing of the mill-building cycles, it proves insufficient in explicating the justifications for introducing a new system of production, one which Georgians understood could undermine the basis of their slave society. A case-study of successful industrialization in Athens, Georgia, provides the means of understanding the process in which local and regional efforts for developing an industrial infrastructure reinforced one another.[12]

1
COMMENCING SOUTHERN INDUSTRIALIZATION

> We notice this [factory groundbreaking ceremony as] . . . the first step towards a very important change in the productive industry of the country. . . . The experiment is an eventful one—the period, however, has arrived when no other alternative is left but to strike for commercial freedom.
>
> —*Athenian*, March 31, 1829

Only the worst weather entertained Athens and other localities in Georgia during the spring of 1829. In early March, severe rains flooded the rice fields around Savannah, delayed mail delivery on the Federal Road across the fall line, and destroyed the bridges, grist mills, and saw mills on watercourses throughout the state. Fortunately, Athens lay north of most the damage, losing only one bridge. Next, cold weather returned with snow reported on the ground in Athens in late March and with frost and ice still appearing there in late April. The low mountaintops of the ancient Appalachian chain, fifty miles to the north of Athens, continued reporting snow into May. Yet, amid all this unpleasant weather, a company of local notables broke ground on constructing a cotton factory. The local newspaper editor informed his readers that this was the beginning of a southern counter-offensive in the protracted struggle against the protective tariffs of Henry Clay's "American System." The report of the start of Athens's first factory also suggested that this experiment in industrial-style manufacture constituted a revolution in social organization: that reorganizing the basis of production was as inherently social as it was political and economic.[1]

After a decade lull, two related events reignited southerners' interests in textile manufactures. Cotton prices dropped drastically in the late 1820s due to reduced English demand following a correction from overproduction, while at the same time manufacturers in the northern states began lobbying for a protective tariff. As long as cotton prices remained high, southerners preferred the known risks of expanding their commercial agricultural production over the uncertain fate of industrial investment. With the reduced price for their primary staple crop, southerners called for diversifying their economy. More than merely desiring diversification for spreading risks and for increasing potential profitability, southerners noted their economic dependence on other sections of the country, notably on the Northeast for manufactured goods, and on the western states for foodstuffs. Anxiety over this situation manifested itself in resistance against anything new that seemed to increase southern economic dependence.

Southerners resisted protective tariffs as part of their opposition to Clay's "American System." Following the War of 1812, a faction within the Democratic-Republican Party pushed for a stronger central government in hopes of building a stronger sense of American nationalism. This National Republican plan, which took the name the "American System," proposed that the federal government should create a central bank, subsidize the construction of a national transportation infrastructure, and protect fledgling industries through a protective tariff. While the United States already enacted and enforced a tariff, these customs duties only generated sufficient revenue to pay the expenses of the federal government and were not intended to act as a barrier against importing foreign-manufactured goods. Using the power to tax, a "protective" tariff raises the price of foreign manufactures above the price of domestically produced goods, thus offsetting American disadvantages of higher-priced goods due to smaller economies of scale, and/or perceptions of the inferior quality of locally produced goods. If price proved the most important factor to consumers, a protective tariff would assure a market for goods manufactured at home.[2]

American manufacturers claimed they needed a high tariff barrier to compete with the more advanced foreign manufacturers. After the panic of 1819, British textile manufacturers "dumped" their goods on the American market for less than the price of production, destroying much of the fledgling American textile industry. Congress enacted marginally protective tariffs in 1816 and revised them slightly upward in 1824 with relatively little furor. However, in 1828, Congress enacted a genuinely protective tariff that raised the price of most imports by at least 50 percent. Called the "Tariff of Abominations" by those who opposed it, Americans not directly involved in manufactures organized themselves to seek relief from these new taxes.[3]

Athenians, like most southerners, confronted the tariff on a variety of levels, but understood it first as a pocketbook issue. Most importantly, they comprehended that increased customs duties raise the tax burden of consumers of imported goods. Since southerners imported more finished goods than did the rest of the country, they anticipated paying more of this new tax into the federal treasury than their neighbors. The tariff thus seemed unfair. Moreover, the new tax distributed benefits unequally as well, since the South contained the fewest factories, and the tax subsidized industrialization. Thus Georgians, like most southerners, believed they received little in return for their increased taxes. Then too, Americans from below the Mason-Dixon Line believed the tax redistributed national wealth. Popularly expressed economic theory explained that only the South created national wealth since it exported cotton in exchange for British specie. Southerners believed the other sections of the country simply rearranged existing national wealth because they did not increase the amount of specie in the country. Following this view, the tariff hastened the redistribution of wealth from the South to other sections of the country with more political clout.[4]

Put more starkly, southerners viewed the tariff as legalized theft. An editorial in the *Athenian* made clear both the belief system and the sense of grievance it generated, when it stated, "the *five* plantation States, furnish *more than half* of the *total* exports, and the *seven* Southern States, probably *three-fourths*. . . . What have the Northern States to give to Great Britain and France as an equivalent for the manufactures they send to the United States[?]"[5] Finally, southerners concluded the tariff could only hurt their section. Higher tariffs meant reduced imports, which in turn decreased the demand for British textiles, and thus lowered the price of cotton. A significant drop in cotton prices not only directly lowered southern standards of living by reducing their credit for consumption purchases but hindered their ability to pay debts previously engaged to increase cotton production. Thus the tariff affected both present and future prosperity. But arguments relying strictly upon the economic effects upon one's own section seemed inelegant. Hence, southern debate explained the effects of the tariff upon the entire nation, and upon civilized society in general.

Southerners opposed the higher tariffs as impractical and dangerous. They claimed the tariff caused social dislocation in England, as operatives thrown out of work relied upon government support for their sustenance. Dissatisfaction among the laboring classes would ultimately result in social upheaval, which might later be transferred to the United States. Editorials in the Athens newspaper also argued that higher customs duties endangered already poor international relations with Great Britain, and they expected the British to retaliate by refusing to settle national boundary questions between British North America and the United States. While these statements appear opportunistic (after all, why should southerners care about the details of the boundary between Maine and Canada?), they nevertheless summarized the fear that the new taxes would backfire on those they intended to help. Instead, southerners feared the tariff would encourage failure by rewarding inefficiency, and that both manufacturers and consumers would suffer the consequences.[6]

Underlying much of the southern analysis lay the issue of the age: monopolies. Editorials in the Athens newspaper explained that the tariff encouraged monopolies, which inherently favored a few over the many, and that the "American System" would create a sectional aristocracy of North over South. The tariff made privilege legal, just as the privileged distinctions between classes carried the weight of law in Old England. Furthermore, southerners failed to distinguish the ways of organizing a factory, and saw all textile factories as corporations. Again, corporations carried the taint of privilege, since a corporate charter usually conferred upon a business special conditions not available to the general public: for instance, limiting the liability of stockholders for debts legally incurred by the business. So it seemed to many southerners, in the Age of Democracy, that an aristocratic clique sought special status for their business, and for their section of the country. Southern acquiescence on the tariff would enable northern manufacturers to monopolize the nation's economic and political power. As southerners felt the whole situation to be vastly unfair, they proceeded to a fuller exposition of the evils of what they opposed.[7]

As a matter of general principles, the people of the South condemned the new economic programs because they felt the policies embraced a broad construction, allowing the federal government to expand its powers into areas not explicitly granted by the Constitution. If one assumes the editor of Athens's only newspaper likely reflected the views of most of his readers on questions of the greatest import, then most Athenians agreed with a strict interpretation of the Constitution, holding that the federal government could only exercise enumerated powers, and they supported reserving all other power to the states. Failure to oppose the centralizing efforts of tariff supporters would result in governmental "Consolidation and [ultimately in] Monarchy." Thus, raising the tariff beyond the needs of the government for operating revenue, seemed *prima facie* evidence of an unconstitutional extension of federal power since the Constitution made no provision for the uses of taxation for anything other than raising a revenue. Local editorials, editorials copied from distant (even northern) newspapers, and letters to the editor consistently called for bringing "the General Government back to the principles of the constitution" upon the tariff question.[8]

A "principled" debate necessarily invoked the rhetorical flourishes of republican ideology. Southerners, as reported in the Athens press, saw the new tariff as a conspiracy of northern merchants and manufacturers to rob them of their wealth and to strip them of the political power to resist the theft. So southerners felt oppressed, and they expressed their anger in an ideological language reminiscent of Revolutionary opposition to the Stamp and Sugar Acts. With the rising sectional debate, it seemed that a distant and increasingly hostile federal government, controlled by those bent on subverting the liberties embodied in the Constitution, was attempting to impose new taxes designed for a purpose never envisioned by the Founding Fathers.[9]

The people of Athens, of Georgia, and of the South reacted in much the same manner as their Revolutionary progenitors responded to a perceived governmental conspiracy. First, they held meetings to petition for redress of their grievances. Citizens wrote letters to the editor to proclaim their disapproval of the tax. People throughout the South promised to boycott northern-made goods and suggested wearing homespun clothing as badges to identify their non-consumption. Athenians and other Georgians toasted their own perseverance and railed against their enemies, whom they characterized as dark conspirators, at militia musters and at Independence Day celebrations. Athenians also kept track of similar anti-tariff activities of fellow southerners, noting the rise of committees of vigilance in South Carolina to enforce the boycotts. A few even questioned the value of the Union and called for the South to secede before submitting to the tariff. But then Athenians, and other Georgians, took an unexpected step; they called for severing their economic dependence upon the adjoining sections by diversifying the southern economy, an act which they hoped would strengthen their political leverage within the Union.[10]

Presaging dependency theorists by a century, Georgians began exploring how they could attain a greater degree of economic autonomy for their section. Southerners considered both the North and the West as fetters upon their independence, for they depended upon the North for manufactured goods and upon the West (today's Midwest combined with the western Upper South) for livestock and surplus foodstuffs. Repeatedly, they lumped the two sections together, claiming that southern property would be "sacrificed to the rapacity of the north and west"; that the tariff policies of "the North and West, [w]ould *force* the Southern [states] to become . . . manufacturers"; that southerners should boycott horses and hogs from the western states with the same vigor with which they avoided the manufactures of the northern states; and that, having been pressed into the "American System," southerners needed to forbear until they were "as independent of the north and west for clothing and food, as [they were] of the rest of the world."[11]

Having defined the problem, the people of Georgia proposed a solution at a statewide meeting held during commencement in Athens in August 1828. This meeting urged the expression of the citizenry's sense of oppression in "acts to evince their disapprobation of the tariff law, by making and producing every article of consumption within their power, that they may live independently of the supplies hitherto furnished by other States." Out of this sense of dependence, of being surrounded by those who would exploit them, came a determination to re-engage in manufactures that augmented their cotton economy. But what shape should this industrial economy take?[12]

One response to these calls for southern manufactures was to exhort southerners to greater domestic or home productions. Since most southern states possessed few if any factories, manufacturing in the late 1820s South usually consisted of household production or of production by local artisans according to their traditional arts. Fourth of July toasts reported by the Athens newspaper in 1828 indicate a continuation of these expectations of a republican resolve to wear homespun clothing in order to boycott goods manufactured under a system that oppressed their section's political rights. Similar sentiments also resounded directly in the press. For example, a letter to the editor of the Athens newspaper reiterated the same doctrine, declaring, "We of the South, have nothing to do but turn our attention to home productions. . . . Let us manufacture all our coarse woollens, cotton bagging, broad cloths, hats, shoes, boots, nay ever thing that is consumed by the South."

Other southerners also concluded that local production would lessen their dependence upon manufactures from outside the South. For instance, just prior to the Athens anti-tariff meeting, a similar meeting in South Carolina resolved to defeat the tariff by purchasing only goods manufactured by the artisans of their own state. Self-preservation, like charity, should begin at home. However, words alone would neither repeal the tariff nor make the South economically independent of the other sections of the country. Republican ideology required action as well.[13]

Almost immediately the people of Georgia applied their ideals. In Milledgeville, the July 3, 1828, Baldwin County anti-tariff meeting resolved to encourage textile manufactures by distributing premiums for superior specimens of cloth manufactured in the county. Following the example of South Carolina, the students of the University of Georgia resolved to wear homespun, and the college's trustees declared homespun the students' official uniform. Complying with this anti-dependency movement, the Georgia legislature allowed officers of the state militia to wear homespun as their uniforms as well. Also in early 1829, neighboring South Carolina ventured into artisan-produced textiles and beer, which Georgia editors proclaimed "the best *Anti-Tariff Argument*" to ever come from that state because it formed a "practical and efficient" solution to dependence upon imports from other sections. All these arguments and actions kept the idea of industrialization before the southern reading public, but none proved capable of changing the political economy that southerners perceived as detrimental to their rights. Unless they found a replacement for goods manufactured elsewhere, they would find themselves in continuing dependence when they resumed consumption.[14]

Home productions could not alter the South's dependence on the "tariff states." Despite the rhetoric and actions taking place, most southerners understood home production as a stop-gap measure that could not sufficiently supply all the manufactured goods they needed. Even while promoting home production, the newspaper editor in Athens hinted at these limits. A return to home manufactures in order to boycott imported goods required both the rebuilding of older technologies already discarded and the training of a new generation in the skills needed to operate them. All this would take time, time in which southerners would have to do without. Since long-term non-consumption seemed unworkable, they sought another means to supplement home production. So southerners proposed to operate cotton factories at home.[15]

Even before Congress enacted the new tariff, southerners publicly debated whether, and how, they should introduce industrial-style manufacturing to the South. Regional newsprints led the discussion when, in November 1827, Baltimore's *American Farmer* specifically invited an extended dissection of the topic of southern industrial manufacture. It suggested that a peculiarly southern mode of industrialization using slave labor could make the South independent of its oppressors. After making this call for a thorough investigation of this model of industrial manufactures, the *American Farmer* ran a lengthy series of articles over the next year, which other southern newspapers often reprinted or commented upon. Foremost of these articles was the Fisher Report.[16]

In 1828, newspapers throughout the South excerpted the Fisher Report, a document produced by a committee of the North Carolina legislature charged with investigating the viability of southern industrial manufacture. The committee calculated that a factory erected in the South could profit more than one of similar size erected in New England because of reduced transportation costs from the close proximity of cotton and also due to reduced labor costs from the proposed use of slaves. Not only would southern production cost less, but it would prove more efficient than northern production since an enslaved workforce could neither strike nor quit. Fisher predicted a victory for southern industry, in what appeared to be an economic war between the sections of the country. He concluded, "Let the manufacturing system but take root among us, and it will soon flourish like a vigorous plant in its native soil. . . . Nature has made us far more independent of [the North] than they are of us. They can manufacture our raw material, but they cannot produce it. . . . We anticipate the time, when the manufactured articles of the South will be shipped to the North, and sold in their markets cheaper than their own fabrics."[17]

The *Athenian* sometimes reprinted or more frequently echoed the ideas of industrialization contained in the *American Farmer* series. By January 1828, the Athens newspaper declared that southern people possessed sufficient capital and business sense, and it called for the immediate establishment of southern cotton factories to gain the desired economic independence from "Northern Harpies." Like the *American Farmer*, *Athenian* editor O. P. Shaw explained how the South could out-produce northern competitors. Raw material cost less in the South, and energy sources abounded. The South featured a superior topography for manufactures as well, since, unlike New England, snow would not prevent the use of water power in the winter. Similarly, underutilized southern forests could provide the fuel for steam-engine power. Clearly, southern supporters of industrialization believed they could undersell northern manufacturers, if only they tried. To convince southern cynics, a number of papers published financial calculations of what was at stake.[18]

Newspapers in support of starting southern industry frequently explained the advantages of local industrialization by enumerating its benefits to southern agriculture. In a primarily agricultural section of the country, southern industrial efforts should naturally focus first on reducing the costs of agricultural production, and/or increasing the market for southern produce. Therefore several newspaper editors suggested cotton bagging and rope as natural items for the South's first cotton factories. In August 1828, the *Athenian* commented that cotton bagging could replace the hemp bagging used to bind cotton bales, and it suggested converting Augusta's cotton warehouses (which would no longer be needed for holding cotton for shipment to northern and British manufacturers once the South began to manufacture textiles) into rope walks, in order to manufacture cotton rope as well. Thus, the newspaper calculated southern manufacture of rope and bagging would reduce Georgia planters' costs by $40,000. Further, production in Georgia would retain $160,000 within the state, thereby reducing the outflow of specie that normally would have paid for northern or foreign manufactures of hemp ropes and bagging. That specie would then be available to encourage further industrial and agricultural investment. Anticipating criticism from enemies of the tariff, the Athens newspaper argued that southern manufactures would continue to cost $80,000 less than comparable European manufactures even with the repeal of the tariffs. In short, southern fabrication of these agricultural items "would save the . . . planters of Georgia an immense sum of money."[19]

And so it did. When, in March 1829, northern prints announced the availability of at least four hundred tons of rope and cordage for southern use in the upcoming agricultural cycle, southern editors dryly commented, "We fear they are rather late; we begin to make these things ourselves now." Continuing the statistical approach, the Augusta *Constitutionalist* took the comparative analysis so far as to prophesy that the natural advantages incurred by southern industry would drain the North of its "surplus population" for employment in southern factories. Thus the business side of industry, the practical side of probable profits and risks, entered the debate. Opposition to the tariff originally seen as a pocketbook issue returned to pocketbook solutions, even as debate along lines of principle continued. For no newspapers went so far as to claim industrialization as a positive good in itself, but none condemned the concept of industrialization outright.[20]

While newspapers with an "ultra" disposition can be read as opposing industrialization, they really opposed protective tariffs, and they worried that changes in the southern political economy might reduce southern opposition to the tariffs. Before Georgia constructed any factories, the *Georgia Journal*, for instance, argued that "to be true to themselves" and "take the ground they ought to take in relation to the tariff," all southerners should "insist on the unconditional repeal of every law that has for its purpose the protection of manufactures." Taken out of context, one might presume this Milledgeville newspaper considered industrial society antithetical to southern ways. But on the basis of practical experience, the paper argued for expansion of domestic manufactures because previous southern factories proved unprofitable and new factories would require a protective tariff for survival. Later, when Athens constructed its first factory, the editor of the Charleston *Mercury* wrote, "We depreciate the introduction of the manufacturing spirit in the South, as calculated to diminish our strength in relation to the tariff, if not to fix the odious system upon us." Again, the opposition focused on the tariff, not on the factories, as the true point of contention. Despite this lack of an ideological opposition to industrialism, even the ardent supporters of industrialization attempted a fair representation of industrial society by informing their readers of the problems incurred under an industrial regime.[21]

Throughout the period of initial industrialization, the paper at Athens reported the social consequences of converting to an industrial society. Generally supportive of industrial efforts, the local newspaper constantly reported the financial interests of different cotton factories and explained the differing patterns of industrial organizing in the northern United States and in Great Britain. However, the *Athenian* also specifically reported the social unrest resulting from the depressed conditions of the international textile industry in the late 1820s. In January 1827, the *Athenian* excerpted a London

Times article explaining how protective tariffs strangled English industry, and concluded the column with British commentary on the effect of industrial unemployment upon society, that "means must be adopted to preserve the poor from misery and starvation." Two months later, the *Athenian* moved from general economic observations to more specific details related the conditions of child and female labor in factories in England. This reprint described the operatives as six- and eight-year-old children of both sexes who worked side-by-side with little relief from the work. The article further commented on how such a regimen imposed at such a young age permanently impaired the operatives' moral development and that such factories served as a schoolyard of loose habits. But these vices Athens already knew. Southerners understood the risks of grinding poverty. Children of landless whites already worked hard tending livestock while children of yeomen worked the fields. And even before becoming the Bible Belt, southerners feared that many of their neighbors led dissipated lives. Vice and loose habits already abounded. What struck them more powerfully was a discussion of how industrial society affected women.[22]

Factory work upset traditional gender roles. Women seemed to cease acting like women when they worked in factories. As they did with the children, the press worried about the morality of female workers. One article excerpted in the Athens newspaper claimed, "The women become men in the female costume." Not only did they lose their "domestic" virtue, but worse still, as wage earners, women exhibited an independence not expected in a patriarchal society like the American South. In one early example, the *Athenian* reported a strike by the women of the Dover Factory in New Hampshire. These New England women paraded through the streets with "great noise . . . and burnt several casks of gun powder." Once the factory agent surrendered to their demands, the women returned to the factory, which relieved the governor of calling out the militia to prevent the conquest of his state by this "gynecocracy." The event seemed comical to southern sensibilities because of what it said of men in New England more than how it implied factories affected women. But southerners also imbibed the subtext; southern men needed to plan their industrialization with care, least they find themselves as emasculated as they perceived New England's industrialists. Finally, the newspaper editor informed his readers of the direst possible consequences of manufacturing.[23]

Industrial society, as explained in the Athens press, could threaten

American political systems. Industrial manufacture undercut artisanal republicanism by denying mechanics access to learning their trades sufficiently to guarantee their economic independence, and hence undermined the guarantee of their political virtue as well. One reprinted article claimed that industrial laborers never became masters in their trades because they learned only a small part of the trade in the factories, and so the economic independence of self-employment, considered in republican ideology as necessary for individual political independence, always remained out of reach for factory workers. By reducing the possibility of independent artisan political participation, factory work lessened social cohesion, which could lead to class conflict, which could destroy the American republican polity, and which could conceivably lead to outright warfare. Athens's leading industrialist, Augustin Clayton, expounded on exactly this theme on the floor of the U.S. Congress, only a few years later. He declared he would rather live in the South with the anxieties of a possible slave rebellion than with endemic class rebellions that accompany the industrial societies of England and New England. With a republican flourish, he declared that England's government was "obliged to keep a standing force to overawe the turbulence of the manufacturing operatives" in order to protect property and order.[24]

But Clayton argued that, not only did factory-based manufacturing inherently inflame class differences, but it also enslaved its operatives. When one person owed his or her livelihood to another, as an employee of a cotton factory, the working person lost the liberty to act independently. Understanding slavery as the opposite of liberty, Augustin Clayton of Athens again explained, "A slave is a slave; the color of the skin does not relieve oppression; and depend upon it, white slaves are as dangerous as black ones, and all experience hath shown they are quite as ungovernable."[25]

Reporting the positive political and economic consequences of establishing southern factories alongside reporting the social disturbances in areas in which industrialization had already taken place obviously sent mixed signals to the general public. Southern economic independence might add to the South's political leverage in negotiating with other sections, but industrial manufacture might also change the acceptable parameters of society. Thus, since the South felt "compelled" to manufacture as a defensive measure against the tariff, supporters of southern industrialization sought to discover a method to minimize the anticipated social upheaval.

As an ideological device, industrial slavery appeared the ideal instrument for creating a non-threatening labor force for southern cotton factories. The *American Farmer* began its discussion of southern industrialization in 1827 based on the question of whether slaves could be usefully employed as factory hands. The Fisher Report, published nationally in early 1828, considered slave labor the capstone of the South's labor advantage over the free labor of the North, and provided calculations to prove its point. In May 1828, the Athens paper reviewed how hemp factories in Kentucky utilized the labor of slaves, and it concluded that factory work would prove beneficial for the slaves as well, since "the labor in the cotton factory is infinitely more easy than in a cotton field." By mid-1828, Tennessee reported the successful establishment of a cotton factory utilizing slaves. Although this factory employed a white superintendent, the notice, reprinted in Athens, declared that the factory differed greatly from northern counterparts because the laborers could not strike, and so the physical advantage of southern water power consistently unimpeded by ice would "*scarcely* be more steady than the slave power." Factories throughout the South utilized varying inputs of slave labor throughout the antebellum period, and as late as the early 1850s, manufacturers called for increased southern industrialization based on slave labor. Slaves, these writers all assumed, could be disciplined in ways that free labor could not, and therefore industrial slavery would deliver the benefits of an industrial society while ameliorating its social disruptions. Not limiting their plans to just utilizing a slave labor force, the nascent southern industrialists designed other features into their blueprint of acceptable industrialization.[26]

As an outgrowth of the practical business side of the debate, a southern model emerged that emphasized smaller rural factories. Early proponents originally opposed factory-style production due to Georgia's previous experience with cotton factories. If large cotton factories really needed the protection offered by the tariff, as Milledgeville's *Georgia Journal* argued, then southerners needed to engage in small-scale manufactures to reduce the risk of destroying limited southern investment capital when the anticipated repeal of the hated tariff took effect. Otherwise, the *Journal*'s editor, James Camak, charged, new southern industrialists would find "their buildings . . . unoccupied, and their spindles . . . all at a stand." The *Athenian* replied that great risks abounded if southerners imitated the large factories of the

North, but it continued that southerners need not emulate the large factories of Lowell. Small factories would suffice since the geographic advantage of locating factories in the South, close to the cotton supply, would offset the advantages of larger economies of scale held by the northern factories operating under the Waltham System. So, this pro-industrial editor advised: "Let us commence on a small scale, with caution, and [invest] such funds as we can spare . . . in small establishments; let them . . . look for their growth to the profits of the business." This advice became the essence of the Georgian model for successful southern industrialization. All fourteen factories enumerated in Georgia in the 1840 federal census followed this prescription. As a model, this counsel succeeded because it addressed both ideological concerns about the effect of industrial organization upon southern society, and practical problems regarding the insufficiency of southern investment capital.[27]

Once citizens of Georgia constructed and operated factories, opposition within the state vanished. Southerners began to "learn" to accept the change from a strictly agricultural to a mixed economy. By the early 1830s, an editorial in the *Georgia Journal* demonstrates this new but cautious acceptance of industrializing as a necessary evil. Never convinced that slavery would supplant free labor even in southern cotton mills, the editor of the state's Democratic Party organ explained his change of heart: "We were opposed, . . . to manufactories on a large scale, from considerations connected with the effect the business uniformly has on the character, and habits of those who work in them. . . . We are now, however, compelled, as a choice of evils, to congratulate our fellow citizens on the establishment of factories in our own state. It goes against the grain for sure." Although industrialists could have availed themselves of either large or small water-power sites for constructing their factories, they unanimously chose small ones in the first decade of industrial manufacture in Georgia. Smaller, mostly rural factories, in addition to requiring less startup capital, also resulted in more isolated social consequences, which limited their impact upon southern society in general. Having won the ideological battle in favor of industrialization largely with arguments of its political necessity, it was the practical admonition of starting small and enlarging only as profits allowed that created the first successful wave of industrialization in Georgia.[28]

Contemporaneous with discussions of the possibility and desirability of industrial manufacture, Georgians turned to specific plans for implementation. In several instances, experimentation stimulated both interstate and intrastate competition. As early as November 1827, John Schley, of the Augusta area, petitioned Georgia's legislature to provide seed money to begin constructing a factory. When the legislature refused the request because Schley associated with the political party out of power, the Athens newspaper scolded the action as short-sighted and claimed Schley's scheme would benefit the entire state, since his establishment would act as a model for others to follow. The following summer Schley raised some capital without the subsidy, and he went north to investigate the machinery he needed for the factory he planned to build ten miles to the south of Augusta. Simultaneously, Christian Breithaupt also journeyed north to shop for machinery for a factory in Edgefield District, South Carolina, fifteen miles northeast across the Savannah River from Augusta. During the two pioneers' absence, citizens of Augusta subscribed eight thousand dollars for a textile factory in Augusta, in the first hour its books opened. While Breithaupt constructed his Vaucluse Factory in South Carolina as a result of his visit to the North, neither of the Georgia efforts demonstrated immediate success. Schley postponed constructing his factory and again asked the state legislature, in November 1828, for a five-year, no-interest loan for a factory to manufacture "cotton bagging, coarse cotton and woollen cloths," but the Georgia General Assembly again declined his request. The Augusta speculation never materialized. But the Augusta area was not alone in promoting industry. At the same time as Schley's second petition, a legislator from Eatonton unsuccessfully proposed that the state encourage widespread small-scale textile production by purchasing patent rights to industrial machinery for use of all Georgians seeking to build factories. Clearly interest in starting to manufacture arose from many quarters, but capital for investment seemed wanting. Without inputs of governmental largess, Georgia's industrial activity shifted its focus to Athens.[29]

The announcement of the start of the industrial experiment in Athens, at the beginning of this chapter, demonstrates how the ideological and the practical strands of the debate on southern industrialization reinforced one another. In March 1829, upon the Georgia Factory's groundbreaking, the factory principals declared their opposition to federal subsidization through increased tariff duties while, at the same time, mentioning their sense of the opportunity to earn a profit. The newspaper reported, "A sense of safety and a feeling of independence, combined, doubtless, with an expectation of profit, have urged gentlemen to an undertaking, against which their political convictions are most unquestionably at war." Taken out of context, such a statement would seem schizophrenic, or at least an example of cognitive dissonance—the ability to hold two opposing ideas without discerning the contradiction. In essence, they declared they still opposed the "American System," but, in order to gain a degree of economic independence for their section, they would manufacture and earn a profit while doing so. Thus the experimenters gained societal permission to proceed, even though all professed a reluctance to do so. Whether they professed hesitation as an honest aversion to industrialization, or whether the protestations simply provided cover to engage in formerly questionable economic behavior, cannot be determined. However, since all those engaged in bringing factories to Georgia in the late 1820s had lived within fifty miles of one Georgia's three operating factories during the 1810s, they should have understood some of the social and economic effects of a factory. Thus they probably aimed their protests at the tariff and the American System rather than at factory-based production. But, whatever may have been their personal justification, such an experiment required the financial wherewithal to proceed.[30]

Setting up a textile factory in the Jacksonian South required a modest although not insubstantial initial capital outlay. The Athens Manufacturing Company, consisting of Augustin S. Clayton—one of the leading anti-tariff politicians of the state, William Dearing, John Nisbet, Abraham Walker, and John Johnson, built the Georgia Factory and filled it with machinery for about $35,000 in 1830. Clayton, Dearing, Nisbet, and Walker, who were planters and men of commerce, supplied the necessary funds, while Johnson, a textile man from Massachusetts, contributed his skill. After making the necessary financial and technical arrangements, deciding upon the mill site took next priority.

In February 1829, Johnson located Georgia's first successful industrial site about a quarter-mile downstream from Thomas Moore's grist and saw mill, on the shoals of the North Branch of the Oconee River, about three-and-a-half miles south of Athens. Combining creative financing with an anticipation of possible disagreement over riparian rights, the partnership convinced Moore to donate fifty acres for the factory, to repair and improve his dam, and to cease his use of the water power should low water occur. If the company abandoned the project, the land reverted to Moore. In the meantime, to reduce fire hazards to the planned factory, Moore also agreed not to construct any houses within a quarter-mile of the facility. No money changed hands, but Moore apparently saw the factory as an improvement that raised the value of his land, which surrounded the factory, and he expected to construct a mill village to supply housing for the factory operatives. Everyone seemed to benefit, and the partnership focused its financial resources on constructing and filling the factory building, without needing to pay for the mill site itself. The next step for the partners was to build their factory according to their political premise.[31]

This company built the Georgia Factory according to the prescription for success advised by the newspaper in 1828. Its dimensions remained small by Waltham/Lowell standards, its specifications being only "fifty-six feet long, forty-four wide, and four and a half stories high, [and] calculated for one thousand spindles, and thirty looms." By comparison, the first large American factory, built at Waltham, Massachusetts, in 1814, "measured 90 feet long by 45 wide and was four stories high above its basement." Thus, this early southern mill was only roughly half as big as the first of New England's earliest large mills. As with Rhode Island–style industrialization, the southerners utilized smaller, more rural sites. But unlike Rhode Island manufacturers, southerners combined spinning and weaving from the start. In the end, therefore, the company never intended to mimic northern practices. Instead it used northern technology and know-how for its own purposes.[32]

With the apparent success of the first factory, the same Athens company built a second mill, the Athens Factory, at the water-power site located at the edge of the town limits within two years of beginning operations of the Georgia Factory. On May 28, 1832, for $8,000, William Carr sold the fifty-five-acre site, which included an existing saw mill, grist mill, gin house, and other houses, and which straddled both sides of the North Fork of the Oconee River, to William Dearing, John Nisbet, Abraham Walker, and Augustin S. Clayton as tenants in common. (Johnson left the original company earlier that year, and returned north.) By September 1833, when the new factory began production, the machinery and improvements brought the value of the factory and mill site to $48,000. By August 1834, this factory became a separate firm from the first, when Augustin Clayton sold his share of the Athens Factory but retained ownership in the Georgia Factory.[33]

A third company formed in May 1833 under the guidance of James

Camak, a former college professor and the retired editor of the *Georgia Journal*, who previously expressed his reservations about large-scale southern manufacturing. Under the name Camak Manufacturing Company, it obtained a corporate charter from the state legislature in December 1833 to build a cotton factory and issued equal shares of stock to its ten incorporators. Following incorporation, the firm paid $2,500 to Noah Prince and Noah F. Prince for a sixty-two-and-a-half-acre mill site on the Middle Fork of the Oconee River, one-and-a-half miles southwest of Athens, on January 1, 1834. Although the tract bounded the river at its high-water mark, this deed reflected a concern for riparian rights by allowing the new company to increase the height of the dam by two feet or "to any height necessary for manufacturing purposes." The ten incorporators assessed themselves $3,000 each to acquire this and adjacent land and to build the factory and fill it with equipment. By December 1834, however, many of the original investors sold their shares in order to purchase shares in another Camak project, the Georgia Railroad. In December 1835, the company obtained an amended charter, renaming itself the Princeton Manufacturing Company, and its factory finally began operations. By September 1836, Athens newcomer William Williams, a banker who moved to Athens from Eatonton, Georgia, bought all the shares of the corporation.[34]

Between 1829 and 1835, not counting expenses for purchasing material or labor, Athens's industrialists spent approximately $110,000 for constructing and fitting out the three factories for operation. This amount represents a modest but reasonable beginning since Athens remained isolated from outside markets due to poor roads, and since success in industrial manufacture previously eluded the people of northern Georgia. However, compared to investments in land or slaves—traditional agricultural expenditures in Georgia—the amount of $110,000 is quite significant. In April 1835, William Lumpkin, an incorporator of the Princeton Factory (and brother of the sitting Georgia governor, Wilson Lumpkin), sold his plantation lands adjoining the Princeton Factory—a sixty-one-acre tract and a two-hundred-nine-acre tract—for $225 and $836, respectively. (The more expensive tract included a mill seat that Athens's industrialists developed into another manufacturing site in the late 1840s.) One could also purchase slaves as prime field hands for under $800 each in the early 1830s. Thus one could purchase a modest plantation for about the same price as purchasing partial ownership of a factory, in the range of $5,000 to $10,000. But most southerners continued investing in the known perils of commercial agriculture; few southerners risked the unknown challenges of industrial investment.[35]

Factory production entailed great risk to investment capital. Fire posed a constant threat to cotton-factory investments. In 1831, the cotton factory in Edgefield District, South Carolina, burned with a loss of $20,000, only half of which was insured. The Athens Factory burned in 1834, costing its proprietors $40,000. Fire destroyed the Eatonton Factory in 1840, with estimated losses of $60,000. Scull Shoals Factory burned in 1845; the Mars Hill Factory met a similar fate in 1850; and the Athens Factory faced total destruction by fire again in 1857. Other factories in Georgia suffered only partial damage from fire during the same time, some of which the industrialists recovered from their insurance companies. Flooding also posed a significant hazard to these water-powered enterprises. Severe rains swelled the rivers and destroyed mill facilities throughout northern Georgia in May 1840, July 1852, and April 1854. The fear of risking limited investment capital probably best explains the lack of industrial investment after initial efforts demonstrated the possibility of profits. But southerners also anguished over the risks incurred to their industrial enterprises when the firm dissolved due to the death of a partner.[36]

In the initial phase of industrialization in Athens, and in Georgia, manufacturers increasingly chose to organize their businesses as corporations, to minimize disruptions by death of a member of the firm's leadership. The Princeton Factory began its existence as a corporation with ten equal shareholders. By contrast, the Georgia Factory and the Athens Factory started as partnerships, with five and four partners respectively. The last two factories operated smoothly, and even the first death of a partner, Abraham Walker, produced no ill effect until the Athens Factory burned. At that point, however, Walker's heirs obtained an injunction to slow the liquidation of part of the firm's assets, in order to get a better accounting of what the firm owed Walker's estate. Once rebuilt, the Athens Factory continued its partnership form of organization, but death also continued to play a role, forcing payment of dividends to aid in settling the deceased partners' estates. Retaining their portions of the company, the addition of heirs as fractional partners must have created difficulties in managing the firm's business. The Georgia Factory also exhibited a period of unwieldy ownership: Partners sold their portions of the company, or assigned the control of their portion to others, or administrators of a deceased partner temporarily inserted themselves into the company's affairs. In 1839, the Georgia Factory received a special incorporation act from the Georgia legislature in order to systematize the transfer of ownership, as well as to limit the debt liability of its shareholders. In 1848, the last of the original partners of the Athens Factory sold his portion of the company to the heirs and relatives of previous owners, and these new owners incorporated under the general incorporation law recently enacted specifically for manufacturers. Although incorporation introduces an element of democracy into the administration of a business, each factory in Athens experienced consolidation of leadership as specific families purchased controlling shares of stock. Thus, incorporation limited risks from disagreements among partners, as each factory became a family enterprise. One could not control fire, flooding, and other acts of God. But human transactions could be made less perilous.[37]

As they contained the risks involved in the transfer of ownership, southern industrialists also sought to limit interfirm competition to reduce the risks to their capital. In the first decade of textile factories in the Athens area, each of the three firms produced similar lines of course yarns and cloth in a market relatively isolated from outside competitors. Until completion of the railroad to Athens in 1841, Augusta, the nearest urban area to Athens in the 1830s, lay a week's wagon ride away. During the 1830s, the transportation barrier to importing goods from outside the region created a large enough local market for all the factories to survive while "learning" the business of textile manufactures.

Given the relative proximity to one another, and the isolation from outside forces, one cannot help but suspect that the social connections of the factory owners limited the degree of destructive competition between firms. While the boards of directors and the partnerships did not "interlock" in the formal sense of partners serving as board members of "competing" firms, the directors of the factories in Athens collaborated on outside projects quite frequently. Like the "shared" boards of the textile factories of New England, the directors of the three cotton factories in Athens acted as leaders of the community and thus participated together directly in the civic, religious, political, and philanthropic life of Athens. Town meetings consistently called upon them to serve as officers. After saturating the local market, they also invested together in founding the Georgia Railroad to broaden their markets. The officers of the textile mills served as officers of the railroad: James Camak and William Dearing served as the first and second presidents of that enterprise; William Williams served as its secretary; and Augustin Clayton, Thomas W. Baxter, John Nisbet, and Alexander B. Linton, as well as others associated with the three factories served on the board of directors of the railroad. With interlocking industrial investment in Athens, cooperation rather than commercial rivalry served community interests best. Working together, they understood their capital as a limited resource, whose use benefited the entire community.[38]

Industrialization served to develop the community, not just to enrich a few investors. Town boosterism played a major role in the economic expectations of the early southern industrialists, just as it would for New South entrepreneurs. But to serve the community and to provide work for the indigent, manufactured goods for consumers, and a degree of political independence for all, financiers sought projects that promoted local unity rather than local conflict, at least among the elites. Runaway interfirm competition would foster conflict and damage overall community development goals. When Albon Chase, a local newspaper editor, noted an insufficient market for yet another newspaper in northern Georgia in the late 1840s, he expressed a general belief held in Athens that southern markets possessed limited elasticity and that a surplus of manufactured goods would not create greater demand for them. Instead, excessive competition from oversupply destroyed investment capital needed to advance the economic development of the community, and destroyed shared financial resources used to build factories, construct the railroad, and finance banking and credit schemes. Thus, maintaining small factories with circumscribed output, as prescribed in 1828, reduced the risk of rampant competition. The second half of the editorial prescription for industrial success proved equally important: that Georgia industrialists should expand their facilities out of their profits.[39]

The Athens textile firms reinvested their profits into their companies. In some instances the manufacturers reinvested to recover from disaster, while in better years they expanded and diversified their facilities. The example of the Athens Factory demonstrates both approaches to reinvestment. In 1836, two years after fire destroyed the factory, the firm valued its assets—the factory buildings and land, smith tools, wagon and team, stock of wool, seven slaves, land, mill, machinery and appurtenances—at $30,250. The next year, the same company valued itself at approximately $60,000, nearly doubling its value, after an additional capital outlay of only $11,500. Rather than issuing a dividend, the partners of the Athens Factory reinvested their profits in the business, and, in 1839, they added a brick-drying house, and another stone mill, and then converted the new stone mill to a merchant flour mill. Not only did the firm expand its productive capacity but it also diversified by using more of the motive force of the water-power site for other purposes—as a saw mill, a grist mill, a cotton gin, and now a merchant flour mill. However, when spring floods demolished much of the factory in May 1840, the company spent $28,000 to repair the buildings, machinery, and facilities and to order sixteen new looms. Between 1829 and 1841, the Athens Factory partners invested over $90,000 in renewing or expanding their facilities. The costs of starting and then continuing industrial operations proved high, but the yield on the investment proved equally high.[40]

Both direct and indirect measures of profits of the early industry of the South indicate high returns on investment. First, we should try to take the industrialists at their word when they described their profits as "excessive." Augustin Clayton, in a speech on the floor of the U.S. House of Representatives, asserted that his factory doubled its capital in two years. In an isolated market lacking an adequate transportation system to facilitate commerce, he claimed his factory earned $30,000 on an investment of $30,000. Confusing his northern antagonists with seemingly anti-capitalist language aimed at defeating the tariff, Clayton claimed his factory "soaked up, as with a sponge," all the capital from his immediate neighbors. While Clayton did not explain the rationale behind his figures—leaving ambiguous whether his numbers reflected gross receipts or net profits—his factory supplied a sufficiently large local demand to continue operations. Clayton's adversaries plainly thought he exaggerated, and they interpreted his comments as inconsistent with his actions. Nathan Appleton, of the Boston Associates, contended Clayton's profits in the Negro cloth trade exceeded those of northern manufacture, and that Clayton's statements "only went to show . . . how much advantage the South might engage in manufacturing, if they were so disposed. If anything like such profits should be made at the North, they would instantly be brought down by competition."

Southerners like Clayton expected repeal of the tariff once he revealed the degree of his profits, indicating that political consequences as much as personal gain motivated his industrial activity. In reply to the debate on the tariff, however, the New York *Journal of Commerce* concluded that the tariff produced the desired effect; it encouraged manufactures where none previously existed. Meanwhile, the southern press used the same data to discuss the perceived cupidity of northern industrialists, as an *Athenian* editorial claimed that the local factory's profits would aid in defeating the tariff, for when northerners discovered that southerners "*share* in the *profits* as well as the burthens, the system will not find such zealous supporters." Such attitudes appeared to mystify northern manufacturers, for surely, Appleton seemed to ask, if industry earned such profits, then why did not more southerners engage in it? To Appleton's credit, his implied question became prophecy. Within ten years of starting the first factory in Athens, Georgia boasted fourteen factories with an investment of over $500,000. But was Clayton exaggerating his claims of southern industrial profits in the early 1830s, or can confirmation be found outside the rarefied rhetoric of national politics?[41]

High industrial profits in Athens can be discerned from a number of indirect sources. For example, internal estimates of the value of the factory facilities indicate high earnings. In its reinvestment, the Athens Factory doubled its estimates of its own value from $30,000 to $60,000 from 1836 to 1837 with only 50 percent of the increase coming from additional inputs of capital. The increase in the resale value of company stock or property can also be interpreted as a sign of financial health. William Dearing and Thomas Hamilton purchased the Princeton Factory for $36,000 at the death of its previous owner, William Williams, paying $16,000 and $20,000 respectively for their shares. Before completing the transaction in 1845, however, Dearing resold his stock for better than $20,000, gaining over $4,000 from a short-term speculation. Probably the most compelling indirect indicator of positive returns was the desire of the industrialists to continue in the business, despite the hazards of fire and flood during the era of extreme economic uncertainty of the 1830s. Whenever disaster struck the Athens Factory, the industrialists found the necessary money to continue, regardless of the economic environment. When the Athens Factory burned, cotton prices were beginning to rebound, so a return to agriculture would have constituted a rational response to the disaster, yet the surviving partners rebuilt. Following the 1840 flood, with economic depression bankrupting many planters, one could purchase agricultural lands or slaves at bargain prices, yet the Athens Factory partners rebuilt again. These industrialists knew exactly how much they reinvested in their firm and authorized specific sums for facility improvements or repairs. One would not expect such commitment for a failing business. Responses to the financial needs of the industrialists during personal crises also point to respectable profits.[42]

Dividends paid as emergency funds in the event of a death of a partner provide more evidence of high profits. When a partner died, the heirs requested the company to pay a dividend in order to settle the partner's estate. For instance, following John Nisbet's death, the Athens Manufacturing Company declared a 6 percent dividend in February 1844 to aid his heirs. An emergency 24 percent dividend, declared to aid Thomas Baxter's family immediately following the company agent's death the same year, amounted to $22,224. Twelve thousand dollars of this second dividend came from cash in the local branch of the Georgia Railroad Bank, and the rest came from outstanding notes, most of which were held against the surviving partners. In 1845, a U.S. Treasury Department report noted the 1844 Athens Factory dividend, commenting that the profits were made, after expending only $19,500 on raw materials, "from an increasing demand in the States of North Carolina, South Carolina, Alabama, and Louisiana." Between the two separate dividends declared in 1844, the Athens Factory released $27,780, only three years after investing approximately the same amount to rebuild after the mill was destroyed by flood. While these records do not indicate the details of overall remuneration, when combined with the other indications of yields they amount to an indictment of extreme profitability.[43]

High profits required the combination of a successful marketing strategy, the appropriate technology for that strategy, and the correct mix of skilled and unskilled labor to effectively operate the machines. Since all three factories engaged in both spinning and weaving, the Athens industrialists adopted two marketing strategies, one for yarn and another for cloth. For yarn, the entrepreneurs sought a limited versatility for their output. For cloth, the Athens textile mills produced coarse durable cloth. Both strategies demonstrate an awareness of their markets and dictated the technology chosen and the labor mix used.

Before developing a marketing strategy, entrepreneurs necessarily considered the terms of exchange they wanted to employ to maximize their market penetration. Since, even in the "good" times of the 1830s, Georgians complained about shortage of circulating specie, the factories sought to trade in a variety of forms of exchange. Certainly, they accepted cash. Yarn sold for twenty to twenty-five cents per pound in 1830, and the carding of wool cost ten cents per pound for plain and twelve and one-half cents for mixed wools (which produced stripes). In addition to cash, in 1831 the Athens Factory granted six months' credit to western merchants for up to a hundred dollars without special arrangements, which would "enable them to regulate their prices and credits, to suit their own convenience." In addition to credit, the factories gave discounts for volume purchases. They also exchanged finished goods for cotton and wool in lieu of cash, "at the Augusta price, with the freight deducted." By 1836, the Princeton Factory advertised "the highest prices for cotton," adding that they were "at all times in the market for cotton of good quality." In the early 1840s, the severity of the depression made the barter economy a substantial mode of exchange. By trading in barter, as well as in credit and cash, the factories penetrated as many sectors of the market as was possible, and obtained raw materials in the process. While this flexibility in media of exchange dealt with both cloth and yarn, other aspects of the marketing strategy differed with respect to the output.[44]

The Athens industrialists sought to maximize the market for yarn. They expressly marketed a variety of the coarser yarns in order to attract as much local business as they could. In February 1830, the Athens Factory advertised "yarns of any number" for sale, specifying prices for numbers five through eight, but advertising that they could produce yarn qualities up to number sixteen. Although systems of grading the fineness of yarn could associate lower counts with lower quality, or reverse the order, with higher numbers representing coarser grades, the early factories in Clarke County increased prices for the higher numbers, indicating use of the first system. Under this system, yarns graded under number thirty were considered coarse; numbers thirty to sixty constituted the middle grades, and everything over number sixty sold as fine yarns. For comparison to the output of early industry in New England, the first factory at Waltham, in 1814, produced a coarse yarn, graded at number fourteen, for weaving into heavy sheeting. So southern manufacturers in the initial years of production sought the market for the most course yarn grades, but with the ability to produce the most popular grades produced by the largest northern factories. However, despite the emphasis on coarser, stronger grades of yarn, the factories still emphasized versatility within those grades. William Williams, of the Princeton Factory, advertised that he kept a large supply of cotton yarns on hand "embracing in suitable proportions all the different [numbers] that are in demand, and can supply orders to any extent, at a moment's notice, and on as good terms as can be had anywhere in the State." Williams's marketing strategy therefore must have been similar to that of a small textile "factory" in Philadelphia: to produce only small quantities in order to quickly alter output to suit a change in demand. So although the factory embraced modern notions of industry with centralized production and labor-saving devices driven by a power source, the output seemed to imitate the non-continuous character of artisan production. The technology for yarn production also bridged the gap between artisan and industrial modes.[45]

The technology for yarn reinforced the marketing strategy by stressing versatility within the cruder ranges and by stressing technical sophistication. While the record does not state what equipment actually filled the original facility, the Athens Factory hired a mule spinner in the late 1830s, which indicates a desire to market multi-quality output. As a highly skilled, non-continuous process, mule spinning could produce many grades of yarn, both coarse and fine. Claiming quality and versatility, the Princeton Factory in December 1835 advertised "cotton yarns of all sizes, which the proprietors [war]rant to be of the very best quality." While their technology supported their claims of versatility, they stayed within the coarser ranges, for which there was greater demand among non-elite Georgians. The elites continued to purchase the fine cloth and thread from area merchants who imported the goods either from the North or from Europe.[46]

However, the local factories also varied their yarn output by altering the content of the raw materials. Almost immediately after they commenced production, the textile mills of Clarke County, Georgia, added wool to their manufacturing repertoire. Indeed, as early as October 1829, even before the textile factories started production, Noah Phillips set up his equipment at the edge of town, opposite the future site of the Athens Factory, to card wool for spinning. The following April, Phillips moved to the Georgia Factory and advertised his capacity to spin both woolen and cotton yarns and to mix other materials into yarns as well. The woolen yarn constituted a seasonal variation in demand; the industrialists combined it with cotton, both to create desired winter clothing called linsey-woolsey for their slaves and in the spring as the sheep were sheared. When the Athens Factory first opened in 1833, its owners specifically called it a "Cotton & Wool Factory," and they bragged about its versatile production and technical capacity by advertising the technology to spin "cotton yarns from numbers 5 to 18," as well as sporting a new "48 inch double wool carding engine with tube condensers (nothing like it in Georgia), also 150 wool spindles." In January 1836, Daniel Mack advertised the sale of his wool carding machines, used the previous season at the Athens Factory's grist mill. Production of wool yarn continued well beyond the antebellum period, as is demonstrated by the Athens Factory's purchase of seven thousand wool jack bobbins in 1875. Cotton was king, but wool yarn continued to have its place in northern Georgia as well.[47]

The early southern factories in Athens imported standard machines emphasizing versatility from areas more familiar with textile production. During construction of the Georgia Factory in 1829, John Johnson, the factory superintendent, returned to Massachusetts in March to obtain the necessary equipment while local mill wrights built the facilities to house the machinery. The Princeton Factory reportedly ordered its machinery from England in 1834. When the Athens Factory expanded in 1837, it ordered equipment including "4 throstles of 132 spindles each, 6 cards, 1 drawing frame with 3 heads, 1 speeder with 12 strains, 4 pullers of 25 inches for throstles, and pullers for drawing frame and speeder" from Rogers, Ketchum and Grosvenor, a locomotive and machine works in Paterson, New Jersey. Standard technology for the day, the machines demonstrate a versatility and technical sophistication in yarn production. A throstle was an advanced version of Arkwright's water frame; a drawing frame produced fine even slivers of yarn; and a speeder twisted the yarn to add strength. The yarn technology reinforced the marketing strategy: quality, versatility, and technical sophistication. The technology and marketing strategy for cloth would similarly augment one another.[48]

Unlike the yarn-marketing strategy, the marketing strategy for cloth was concentrated on a specific market: the upcountry trade. The Georgia Factory in 1831 advertised for the wagon trade around Athens, stating, "The country dealers will have an opportunity of supplying their customers with goods made of the best materials, and manufactured faithfully at lower rates than can now be obtained at the north." An 1838 Princeton Factory advertisement specified its intended customers as "the merchants and planters . . . and especially [the] merchants in the interior and up-country of Georgia." From the start, the factories in Athens saw the retail and wholesale merchants servicing Athens's extended economic hinterland—northern Georgia, eastern Tennessee, and the western portions of the Carolinas—as their principal market for cloth. They intended to sell the upcountry yeomen a crude grade but appealed to the merchants' sense of patriotism and profit. William Williams, president of Princeton Factory, described the rough-grade cloth he intended to sell in the hinterland as "Georgia Nankeens," Oznaburgs, and "Kentucky Jeans," which he claimed improved the profit margin over northern-made cloth, because he cut his in lengths of thirty-two yards rather than the northern standard of ten-and-one-half yards. The longer length, he said, reduced losses from waste by producing fewer remnants. Williams also guaranteed the Princeton Factory's products against fading, indicating that the mill dyed its cloth. Other sources demonstrate that all the factories pursued the ability to dye cloth as a marketing strategy. By planning the strategy before purchasing the machinery, the factories locked themselves into a particular range of production, with a specific market.[49]

The market strategy reveals underlying assumptions about the market for southern-produced goods. First, directing a portion of their output toward the planter class, as cloth for slave clothing, implied that the planter class held no ill will against southern manufacturers for bringing industry to the South. Historians sometimes repeat a litany of anti-industrial sentiment among the planter class, stemming from political opposition to protective tariffs. If the planters opposed the corporate nature of northern industry (reflecting anti-corporatism in a Jacksonian sense), rather than opposing industrialization per se, then the industrialists' strategy made cultural sense in the agrarian South. While some early southern factories organized as corporations, their small size and limited influence probably counteracted any sense that they could develop into a large-scale Waltham-style system of production, which the southern press characterized as typical of northern industry. Instead, all the southern factories competed with the northern "monopolists," and local editors encouraged patronage of the firms as a means of breaking free of the South's dependence on the North. Rather than acting as a means of oppressing southerners, these new factories intended to increase southern liberty by decreasing the section's economic dependence. But the Athens industrialists wisely did not expect patronage from patriotism alone; they also priced their products lower than northern goods in order to attract business from planters.[50]

Beyond the planters, however, the Athens industrialists also directed a portion of their output toward the upcountry merchants. The industrialists appealed to the merchants through higher profit margins due to less wastage, and they diverted a portion of their limited capital to establish sufficient credit so upcountry merchants could peddle their goods without requiring cash. Underlying these actions, the industrialists assumed that the yeomen, who demographically dominated the upcountry, would purchase manufactured goods. Market participation, of course, is not the same thing as fully embracing notions of a capitalist money economy. However, an extended market for cloth and yarn in the upcountry forces us to revise some of our ideas about the degree of self-sufficiency of the yeoman household. Yeomen resisted the commodification of labor, and they valued exchange within the communitarian context of friends and neighbors. But they did not limit their purchases just to items they could not produce themselves.[51]

In the 1840s, changes in the market, attributable in part to economic conditions generated by an extended depression, in part to penetration of the upcountry by the railroad, altered some of the details of the cloth-marketing strategy, albeit without changing its general tenor. With the drop in the price of cotton in the early 1840s, cotton bagging, for shipping cotton bales, finally became an attractive alternative to the hemp bags previously used. Forty-four inches wide, the bagging contained one-and-a-third pounds of cotton per yard, and each yard cost the planter twenty cents. One could stuff 450 to 500 pounds of cotton into five yards of the cotton bagging. In contrast, hemp bagging cost about the same, held less, and was generally considered inferior as a packaging material because it quickly rotted when wet and easily tore when manipulated by the hooks used in the warehouses. In 1842, the Princeton Factory sold 20,000 yards of cotton bagging to planters in neighboring Morgan and Putnam counties. The same mill planned to manufacture bagging exclusively the following year. With an expected production of 70,000 yards, the Princeton Factory owners anticipated gross receipts of $14,000 for a factory capitalized at $36,000. With raw cotton locally priced at six cents per pound that year, the value added in the manufacturing process, including profits, came to nearly nine cents per pound of cotton. However, unlike the market of the 1830s, when only a handful of factories operated in Georgia, and when completion of the railroads was still a distant dream, manufacturers expected competition from the other factories to drop the price of the cotton bagging below fourteen cents per yard. But as the price of cotton rebounded in the late 1840s, its use became prohibitively expensive as a shipping material and the factories returned to other "coarse" goods—osnaburgs, sheetings, stripes, bed-ticking, checks, jeans, and linsey-woolseys. With the completion of the railroads to Athens, the factories also began sending their products outside the local area, beyond the upcountry "wagon trade" to urban markets in Savannah, Charleston, Mobile, New Orleans, and even Philadelphia.[52]

The technology for cloth reflected a more focused marketing strategy. Standard looms, such as those probably imported by the early southern textile industry, wove cloth within a limited ranges of grades. The records do not indicate the types of looms used in the factories, but again the output gives clues. Only coarse cotton and woolen cloth was advertised, not fine woolens, nor stockings, nor rugs. Since the mills did not advertise other grades of cloth, they presumably lacked the technology to produce anything else. In 1839, James S. Buckingham, a British visitor to Athens, confirmed the factories' output as limited to "cloth of coarse qualities, for local consumption only." Since success in business required coordination of many factors, the technology and market strategy necessarily enhanced one another in order to turn a profit. Given the success of initial industrialization, and the professed desire to gain political leverage through lessening economic ties to the other sections of the country, one would expect southerners to quickly create ancillary industries to support their industrial efforts. Unlike the earlier infant industries of New England, however, southerners failed to create a machine-building sector to support their factory production.[53]

Historians often note the lack of local production of textile equipment as a sign of the "backwardness" of the southern textile industry. While backwardness is not exactly the same as inferiority, failure to replicate the stereotype of the northern experience is taken as evidence of irrational economic behavior rather than as a sign of divergent goals. But, if we accept that the South began with markedly different goals, and that it started with a factor endowment distinctive from that of the North, is it any wonder that the South's experience deviated from the northern "standard"? With the South's limited liquid capital, and its late start in introducing industrialization, which affected the reproduction of skilled labor from which to draw a workforce, southerners jumped into the transatlantic textile trade in much the same way many third world countries forced the introduction of semi-skilled industrial labor in the late-twentieth and early twenty-first centuries.

None of the southern textile industrialization grew organically from southern artisan or home manufactures. Instead, similar to industrial development in early New England, southerners imported managers who built ready-to-operate factories for them, managers who would train workers in industrial culture as well as inculcating needed skills. But, unlike the experience of the early textile industry in New England, southerners were not excluded from technology purchases from existing industrial centers. Since a machine-building sector already existed in the North, southerners purchased standard equipment without the added expense of developing this ancillary industry. So, southern manufacturers did not need to steal industrial secrets, like the early New England industrialists had done from England from the 1790s through the 1820s. Why pay for research and development, or for industrial espionage, when one could buy a broad range of standard industrial machines at low cost? Southern industrial backwardness made complete sense in an era of industrial experimentation, since seeking technological as well as economic independence from the North would have added to the risks of production. After the South more fully adopted the idea of an industrial economy, as it did by the time of the New South, the establishment and expansion of machine shops followed. Until then, southern industrialists obtained the majority of their equipment from the established machine shops outside the region.[54]

One New Jersey machine shop deserves special notice for providing textile machinery "southward." The Paterson, New Jersey, machine-building firm of Rogers, Ketchum and Grosvenor played a central role in supplying equipment to the southern textile industry. As early as February 1833, William Dearing, the president of the Athens Factory, received a letter from Paterson manufacturers asking his help in resolving the Nullification Crisis, indicating previous correspondence between Athens and Paterson. In 1837, the Athens Factory directors' minutes specified purchasing equipment from Rogers. An 1849 survey of manufactures in Georgia stated that the Athens Factory's machinery came from New Jersey. The pattern continued well into the late antebellum period as the Athens Factory's agent, John S. Linton, visited Paterson, as well as Philadelphia and New England, in 1853 and in 1858, in order to purchase equipment for the factory.[55]

But the Athens Factory was not alone in pursuing a strategy of generally purchasing technology from the North, and of specifically obtaining it from Paterson. Roswell and Barrington King built the Roswell Factory in 1839 according to plans drawn by Thomas Rogers of Paterson and filled their factory with his machinery. Henry Merrell, a New York native, who superintended the Roswell Factory from 1839 to 1844, and who built the Curtright Factory in the mid-1840s in Greene County (which was adjacent to Clarke County, where Athens is located), long regretted that he did not purchase his equipment from Rogers. Merrell chose a different tactic, purchasing older machinery from defunct southern factories, and he attributed his later business failure in the 1850s, in part, to this cost-saving decision.[56]

Just as southern strategies for obtaining technology proved economically rational, so did its experiments with various forms of labor. Athens's industrialists experimented with the composition of skilled workers as well as the makeup of its unskilled workforce. For factory superintendents, the Georgia Factory and Athens Factory imported experienced textile men from outside the region, offering them minority shares in the factory to retain their loyalty. As the experience with John Johnson, the first factory superintendent in Athens, demonstrates, it did not always work out. Johnson determined the location of the factory, built it with the help of local millwrights, and oversaw its operations for two years. However, he apparently clashed with the other partners over the rules of running the factory. Augustin Clayton, the factory's founder, declared the rules—like fines for infractions, long winter workdays, and short breaks, as well as corporal punishment—unfit to southern culture, as "the free people of the South would not bear that kind of regimen." When Johnson left the company, presumably because the investors interfered with his management of the factory, the other partners complained that he overestimated his contribution and required the intercession of an arbitrator to determine the fair value of the superintendent's share of the establishment. During Johnson's tenure, he remained an outsider, hired for his technical expertise. The factory company hired subsequent superintendents as minor partners who clearly were expected to defer to their superiors.[57]

Advancement for superintendents beyond the status of minority shareholder proved unlikely for most. The superintendent worked in tandem with the mill agent, a senior partner who also acted as the secretary of the partnership. As the real power in the factory, the agent contracted all of the firm's business: the buying of raw materials, the selling of the finished product, and the contracting of repairs. At the Athens Factory, any questions directors had about the state of the factory were addressed to the agent and the superintendent, together. Despite his subsidiary role, the superintendent managed the day-to-day work within the factory. And he frequently performed many of the skilled jobs himself. Compared to later, and larger, factories proposed in the South, the smaller mill superintendent's job combined many jobs that would have required hiring additional skilled help: machinists, carpenters, engineers, etc. After the first generation of industrial textile manufacture in the South, some of the firms in Athens expanded their personnel to include these positions.[58]

Early southern textile factories hired a second tier of skilled workers, beyond the superintendent. Thus each factory hired overseers for most departments within the mills. At the start, just as with the factory superintendents, factories filled these lower-level skilled positions with personnel imported from the North or from Europe. With an approximate salary of $100 per year, the Athens Factory's overseers in the 1830s came cheap. An 1851 estimate of southern textile-industry labor costs in Tennessee proposed paying each overseer $600 annually. The lowest tier of labor at the mill performed semi-skilled tasks in spinning and weaving under the direction of these more skilled overseers.[59]

The development of early southern industry in Athens demonstrates an attempt to rationalize ideology and practical concerns. Athens led an active campaign of industrialization as a reaction to perceived political subordination of the South within the Union. Creating industry relieved the South of its economic dependence on other sections, which all hoped would translate into greater political leverage. Home productions could not fulfill all southern desires for manufactured goods, so southerners necessarily built factories. They focused their energies on small factories, because previous experience demonstrated factories constituted a high risk endeavor, and southerners believed their capital to be a limited resource to be utilized for the entire community. Profits necessarily played a major factor in planning the new industrial enterprises, and so the industrialists were forced to mold their output to fit their market. Since standard equipment could be purchased "off the shelf" to manufacture coarse yarns and cloth, and since a ready market existed in the South for these products, southern industry wisely filled that niche. In the start-up phase, poor transportation protected southern factories from northern competition as well as from competition from other southern factories. Technical skills could be hired from abroad, and its loyalty was guaranteed in the short run by offering a minor share in the enterprise. Only the question of people, of who would work in the mills and who would run the mills, remained unanswered during the initial phase of Athens's industrialization.

2

THE PEOPLE OF INDUSTRIALIZATION

Recurring for a brief moment to past associations and recollections connected with our late honored fellow-citizen, we call to mind his unceasing efforts to advance the interests of Athens, and set it forward on an active career of commercial prosperity, to increase its facilities for trade, to enhance the value of private property, and to render it permanent as a place of business. In calling up and passing in review before us the respected names of the generous foster-fathers of our present prosperity, we can bring to mind few . . . who draws more largely upon our gratitude for past exertions to serve us.

—*Southern Banner*, June 9, 1853

Every enterprising town possesses a corps of boosters. The above 1853 memorial of the Athens Town Council paid tribute to the passing of the final member of the city's first generation of industrialists and reminded the town's citizenry of how the efforts of a small cadre of like-minded capitalists transformed the town's economy in the previous twenty years. A similar group promoted Athens in its second generation of industrialization, lasting from 1845 to 1870. But successful boosters usually represent or aspire to membership in the town's elite. Typically, therefore, the newspaper failed to mention the efforts of less elite folk in Athens that enabled the elite's successes. In contrast, this chapter will also explore the lives of those who played the supporting roles in developing Athens's industrial economy, especially the mill managers and workers. An investigation of the lives of non-elites suggests the advent of a New South–style mill village culture in Athens, by the 1840s, with skilled labor imported from outside the local area. By the late 1850s, however, Athens sustained its industrial endeavors with a home-grown workforce that routinized the life-cycle of textile employment. Also, an explication of the elite's industrial participation suggests a common life-trajectory, similar to the life-cycle of the planter parvenu. As with the workers, the elite's participation changed during the second generation, with "new" men taking an interest in forwarding the industrializing process in the South just prior to the Civil War.[1]

Before proceeding to decipher the lives of southerners involved in early industrial efforts, I should clarify the periods of generations of industrialization used throughout this chapter. Since industrial workers left few accessible records of their lives, the periodization is based on the lives of the industrialists. However, even when considering only the industrialists, this typology is imposed somewhat arbitrarily on the data, and the start and end dates of each generation need not be considered fixed or impermeable. While industrialization continued unabated in Athens throughout the nineteenth century, many industrialists participated to some degree in a period other than in the one in which they are placed here. For instance, while John White began purchasing the Georgia Factory in 1839, he is placed in the second generation because he did not consolidate his ownership until 1846, and he became economically and socially powerful only after he completed that purchase. White also continued his ownership into the third generation, after 1870, but, by then, he passed much of the management of his industrial enterprises to his sons, and focused his own efforts in banking.

Despite such apparent capriciousness, this generational typology can be justified. For the first generation (1830–45), all those who began the industrialization of Athens either died or abandoned those concerns in the 1840s. Also, the introduction of a general incorporation law for factories in Georgia in 1847 regularized the rules for incorporating a cotton factory and thus altered the manner in which first- and second-generation industrialists participated in manufacturing. For the second generation (1846–70), the death of leading industrialists or their abandonment of industrial pursuits in the late 1860s and the early 1870s resulted in similar changes in personnel guiding the future of the factories in Athens. For the workers in the factories, the periodization mattered less than the nature of the cotton economy and the duration of the industrial enterprises.

THE INDUSTRIAL WORKERS

In accordance with the political prescriptions for starting southern industry discussed in the last chapter, the Athens textile mills originally planned to use slave children as the lowest tier of labor in the factories. The local newspaper reported the Athens industrialists' attempt to follow this plan in 1830, with "small slaves" as the factory's workers. Further, the men running the factory "consider[ed] the matter as settled that these hands will do as well if not better than whites." Without resorting to a "positive good" explanation that later pro-slavery theorists employed, the argument for industrial slavery relied upon a practical yet ideological base. They believed slave labor would protect southern factories from shutting down due to labor shortages, a fear that permeated American business in the antebellum period. In New England or in the Middle Atlantic states, operatives occasionally struck for better wages or for better conditions. Alternately, needed workers left after they simply saved sufficient money to head west and buy a farm. Slaves obviously lacked this mobility. Fortuitously, the factory partners were major slaveholders seeking to use more of their slaves' time in the early 1830s. But matters did not quite work out as they hoped.[2]

Industrial slavery proved less desirable than initially anticipated. One indication of the industrialists' early negative expectations can be discerned from a favorable editorial comment that slaves engaged in factory work learned readily and gave "their instructors little or no trouble." Clearly this comment reflected the anticipation of productivity or workmanship problems from the slave labor force. A later critique of using slave labor in cotton mills elaborated exactly this same point, that "slaves . . . have not the necessary incentives to improvement. They reason thus: 'What advantage will it be to me to become a good mechanic? My master feeds me, clothes me, pays my tax and doctor's bills and supports my children, and he would do no more, or not much at most, if I become ever so expert.'" Although slaves never constituted more than half the factory workforce of Athens, and usually a significantly smaller percentage, the dissatisfaction with slave labor is also indicated by the propensity of the Athens Factory to sell the slaves it owned anytime it experienced a major setback—such as fire, flood, or the death of a partner. After the Athens Factory's destruction by fire in 1834, one of the partners, John Nisbet, offered for sale several "likely Negroes, some of which are good Factory hands" who he previously rented to the factory. The Athens Factory partnership proved Nisbet's move to be a trend by always immediately voting to sell the factory's few slaves following any of the disasters.[3]

Still, the Athens Factory continued to own a handful of slaves until the middle of the Civil War, so they must have had at least limited utility. Most probably, slave operatives performed the dirtiest work of the mill, such as transporting and breaking up the bales, work considered too degrading for white operatives. While the racism of the day always intruded in questioning whether slaves possessed the intelligence or the mechanical abilities necessary for employment as factory operatives, the historiography of industrial slavery repeatedly demonstrates that factory owners resorted to slave labor whenever it proved more profitable than free labor. In the early 1850s, the widely read J. B. D. De Bow reported, "Mr. Deering [*sic*], of Georgia, has employed slaves in his cotton factory for many years with decided success," as an example of the effectiveness of industrial slavery in the textile industry. Other factors, such as William Gregg's desire to bind the poor whites to the elites in order to deter class warfare over the existence of slave property, helped to exclude blacks from the factories in the long run. But undoubtedly problems with slave resistance existed in the mills. Had slaves appeared efficient, productive, motivated workers, their owners would not have been so quick to use them as a form of liquid capital when faced with adversity. But the most important determinant of industrial slavery's efficacy was its cost.[4]

Slave labor simply cost more than free labor. By 1840, all three factories in Athens used a combination of slave and free-white labor for their semi-skilled mill work. In 1839, a visitor recorded that the factories paid each worker the same amount: seven dollars for a monthly wage for whites, or seven dollars monthly rental for the slaves. The directors' minutes of one factory confirms the visitor's estimate of unskilled wages. In 1836, the Athens Factory paid Abraham William Royal, a worker not indicated as skilled, an annual salary of eighty-four dollars, which equals seven dollars per month. Slave labor in agriculture determined the base pay of factory work, but slave rental agreements usually required the factory to provide food and lodging for the slave, so slaves ultimately proved the more expensive form of labor. While one mill owned its slave-labor force, the others rented their slaves. The largest detriment to hiring free labor, however, was simply the lack of availability. Thus one Athens industrialist, in considering his labor costs, hoped that "the progressive increase of white population by immigration, would enable him to employ wholly their free labour." Even at a time when depressed cotton prices diminished the cost of renting slave labor, a slave's work cost the industrialist more than that of a free white. So, as employers, the industrialists preferred less expensive white labor. At the same time, however, the owners also rejected the anticipated social dislocations that attended both the Waltham and Rhode Island systems of manufacturing. How, then, did free white labor become the standard in early southern mills?[5]

White labor supplanted slave labor without an outburst of ideological opposition because local elites already considered the poor whites engaged in manufacturing as a dependent class. From the beginning, the factories in Athens rented slaves and hired poor white children, women, and even men who already lived in town as dependent classes. For example, when one adult white male worker suffered the first "industrial" accident in Athens in 1834, the paper described him as "an elderly man in low circumstances and has a wife and family of children dependent upon him for support. He is worthy of the kindness and attention of the benevolent." The man deserved the town's charity, not just because he was injured but because he was a member of the working poor, a person who deserved charity only because of his demonstrated work ethic. The upper classes considered factory work the means of identifying those who attempted to assist themselves but could not do it. Throughout the 1830s and 1840s, Athens's town fathers instituted philanthropic drives to help the town's poor, but they also explicitly delimited whom they expected to help: the industrious poor of good character. So the town instituted a system of district matrons and overseers to exclude the undeserving—that is, those who refused work in the factories—from the additional aid they extended. Athens did not invent such justifications; its town fathers simply adopted notions common throughout the nation, as did other Georgia communities.

An 1844 editorial reported a similar rationale for Augusta's creation of a work house for poor white women: "The poor of every city have to be sustained. . . . [B]y setting them to work, they soon become a source of revenue, instead of a burden, and industry, self-respect and virtue are the pleasing results." In Athens, the elite believed the deserving poor primarily preferred charity "extended in the form of employment." Such solutions to dependency were not limited to Athens. The poor and powerless in other industrializing towns in Georgia demonstrated similar dependence upon factory employment, which is why women and children alike despaired when the Eatonton Factory burned in 1840. The slaves were rented; the white workers—women, children and men—had no other place to go. They worked alongside each other in the 1830s and 1840s, when cotton prices remained depressed. A visitor to the town commented that in these racially integrated mills, "There is no difficulty among them on account of color, the white girls working in the same room and at the same loom with the black girls; and boys of each color, as well as men and women, working together without apparent repugnance or objection." Like the original operatives intended to run Alexander Hamilton's factory, in America's first planned industrial town, Paterson, New Jersey, all shared in dependency upon the good will of the factory master.[6]

Whites performed manual labor much more commonly than we are led to believe from the writings of planters. Plain folk—poor whites who frequently owned livestock, although no land, as well as landowning yeomen and other small farmers—almost universally performed manual labor alongside their wives, their children, and any field hands they may have owned.[7]

The poverty that forced poor whites into dependence upon factory work also placed them in the care of the factory owners. Since factory owners also owned and supplied slaves to the factories, they understood factory work as an extension of how their families, black and white, related to one another on their plantations. While incorporating whites into the factory system, southerners believed they could ameliorate the system's worst aspects and head off the potential of class conflict arising from factory work by introducing a paternalistic system of management. While paternalism existed in all early industrial endeavors, North and South, historians have commented on the strength of paternalism in the southern textile industry. That this industry began its learning process while slavery defined the nature of dependency causes one to consider its long-term impact on labor relations. By the late 1840s, when prosperity returned to cotton culture in the South, masters logically chose to maximize the profits of cotton production by keeping as many slaves as possible working in the cotton fields, rather than risking damage to their valuable human property in the potentially dangerous environment of a cotton factory for only marginal profits. Thus, contemporary apologists for expanding southern industry, like William Gregg, may have been trying to deflect attention from the failure of planters to rent their slaves to the factories by arguing that factory work would bind poor whites to the elites in support of slavery. As cotton prices rose, with coinciding increases in the price of field hands, slaves simply became too valuable to work in factories in the Deep South, except for jobs that whites could not be induced to take.[8]

By the late 1840s, agriculture rebounded and drained surplus white and slave labor away from manufacturing. Since agricultural wages determined the lowest scale of factory wages, the rise in agricultural opportunities raised manufacturing wages. In the cotton prosperity of the 1850s, Henry Merrell, the president of a cotton factory in neighboring Greene County, sadly explained that only the worst workers remained in his employ for any length of time. While no direct indications point to recruitment problems in Athens, some Georgia factories experienced labor shortages in the 1850s, and the increasing cost of local labor forced others to seek operatives at a distance. Henry Merrell's Curtright Factory recruited Irish laborers (including homeless orphans) from New York in the early 1850s. Others sought more experienced labor, as Frederick Law Olmstead reported that the Augusta Factory recruited New England mill girls. In neither case, however, did those recruited remain in southern factories, for agricultural and industrial opportunities lured them elsewhere. To add to the shortage, another factory in Greene County advertised its desire to hire enough operatives to staff the entire factory after its previous workforce left while it rebuilt following a fire.[9]

Although hopelessly flawed for depicting the structure of Athens society, the federal census can still suggest a limited impression of what life might have been like for factory workers. Unfortunately, the census prior to 1850 did not identify occupations in the population schedules, so information about labor remains anecdotal for the first twenty years of industrialization in Athens. Clearly, census data is frequently incomplete, or in error. For instance, the census consistently undercounted industrial workers in Athens from 1850 to 1870, generally failing to count women and "youths" (however defined). In 1850, although the manufacturing schedule reported 105 males out of the county's 230 factory workers, the manuscript population schedules of the census enumerated only 54 factory operatives, all male. The manufacturing schedules can be assumed to be more accurate since factory owners or their representatives probably provided the information from their records. Thus a comparison with the manufacturing schedule demonstrates that the population schedule enumerated 51 percent of the male workers in Athens's factories in 1850, but only 23 percent of the county's textile mill hands. The 1860 census appears more accurate than the previous one because it enumerated 66 percent (150 of 227) of the reported factory workers in Clarke County, including 96 of the reported 125 (77 percent) female operatives, and 54 of the reported 102 (54 percent) male operatives. The 1870 enumeration proved almost as defective as the 1850 census, since it enumerated only 42 percent (186 of 440) of the county's textile workers. Of the 186 textile workers enumerated in 1870, women accounted for 106 cases (57 percent), and men accounted for 80 cases (43 percent), while children, of both sexes, age thirteen and under, accounted for 33 cases (18 percent).[10]

Researchers inevitably desire to extrapolate from available data. However, one must understand the data sufficiently to create testable hypotheses. For instance, since only one child under the age of fourteen was enumerated as a factory worker in the 1860 census, we might hypothesize that all the uncounted operatives were children. By inference, we would conclude that 23 percent of all female factory workers in 1860 were children under the age of thirteen, and that 45 percent of all male textile workers belonged that age group. These conclusions are doubtful, however, since children fourteen and under tended to be the tail of the curve, exhibiting no modality. That means more fourteen-year-old children should have been enumerated in order to expect larger numbers of children under that age. Alternately one could apply the larger percentage of children under age fourteen, enumerated in the 1870 census, to extrapolate for other census years. However, the 1870 compendium of manufacturing information failed to delineate the sex of factory workers, so we have no clue how to correct for gender and thus check on the accuracy of the assumption. We cannot assume the undercounted prior to 1870 were children, and for 1870 we have no idea how to gender the percentages of child workers. As one can see, comparisons over time are difficult because different marshals collected data differently, different censuses asked similar but different questions, and finally compendia aggregated the data differently. Yet, for all its systemic unreliability, the census population schedules, starting in 1850, contain much rich information. Thus, in order to use census data to explore the identity of factory workers, one must ask limited questions, and one must also understand that the answers divulged by manipulating the data are only suggestive and impressionistic rather than definitive or causative. So let us ask some simple yet illustrative questions.[11]

What occupations did factory workers list? In 1850, 43 men listed the generic "factory operative" occupation, while 9 others listed some other factory job, including a carder, a dyer, a machinist, 2 mule spinners, a weaver, and 3 overseers. In 1860, when women were first enumerated by occupation, 127 people, 42 men and 85 women, listed their occupations as either factory operative or factory laborer. Additionally, 22 individuals, 11 women and 11 men, listed specific job titles that included a drawer, a spinner, a presser, a ruler, a machinist, 4 weavers, 2 reelers, 3 bosses, a supervisor, 2 overseers, and 2 superintendents. Since many of those specifically listed job titles supervised other workers, one can aggregate them as managers for separate analysis from those with undesignated job titles. Obscuring the clarity of such a simple device, however, census marshals in 1870s failed to differentiate among factory occupations, with the exception of enumerating 2 factory superintendents and 1 factory salesman. All the rest, 176 souls—106 women and 70 men, including some previously sporting managerial titles of "boss" or "overseer"—were reduced to "works in factory." Rather than second-guess the 1870 census, I accepted its listing and categorized the jobs as I had in the two previous censuses, as either managers or workers. Excluded from this analysis were the industrialists and those affiliated with them, those who identified themselves as manufacturers, factory clerks, or factory bookkeepers. Also excluded were the factory guards, because their jobs did not contribute to factory productivity, but instead provided service to the factory. With the understanding that most workers held undifferentiated jobs, and that a few held managerial, or technical support jobs, we can now explore the demographics of the industrial cohorts.

Age is a primary category of analysis for understanding Athens's textile workers. As might be expected, the factory managers were generally older than the rest of the workforce. In 1850 and 1860, the mean age of managers exceeded the mean age of workers by ten years and eight years respectively. Median ages of managers and workers reflect a similar split with managers exhibiting a median age of 25.50 years for the two decades while workers exhibited a median age of 18.75 years for the same period. The workforce became even younger in 1870, even with possible inclusion of most of the managers within the worker cohort, with a mean age of 20 years and a median age of 18 years. A look at modality reinforces the sense of the youthfulness of the factory workers.

Teenagers made up a majority of the factories' workers. In 1850, 22 of 42 enumerated workers were teenagers (ages eleven to nineteen), with the largest single aggregation (6) at age seventeen. In 1860, teenagers made up 74 of the 127 enumerated factory workers, with 35 reporting their ages as either fifteen or sixteen. In 1870, 96 of 176 workers reported ages between eleven and nineteen years, inclusively, with almost equal numbers (either 12 or 13 workers) in each year of age, from twelve through seventeen years old. Children under age thirteen were probably under-reported but may not have been used very extensively either. No children under age thirteen were reported for 1850; only 1 (age eleven) was enumerated in 1860, while 21 children under age thirteen listed textile mill employment on the 1870 census (of the 21, 13 listed their age as twelve.)

While older groups also participated in factory work, the workforce itself

TABLE 1
Clarke County Textile Worker Demographics

Population	Number	Age		% Skilled	% Nativity[b]				% Literate[c]
		Mean	Median		Ga. Born	Other South	Other U.S.	Non-U.S.	
1850 Total	54	24.9	22.0	18.5	65.0	26.0	2.0	7.0	63
1860 Total	152	22.9	19.0	16.4	73.7	23.7	0.7	1.9	80
Male	56	25.6	20.0	25.0	76.8	16.1	1.8	5.4	82
Female	96	21.2	19.0	11.5	71.9	28.1	0	0	78
1870 Total[a]	186	21.5	18.5	. . .	94.1	5.4	0.5	0	44
Male	80	23.8	20.5	. . .	93.8	5.0	1.2	0	48
Female	106	19.7	17.5	. . .	94.3	5.7	0	0	41

[a] 1870 Census did not differentiate occupations among textile workers for Clarke County.
[b] Percentages may not total 100% due to rounding.
[c] Literacy measures changed each census.
Source: 1850, 1860, and 1870 Clarke County Manuscript Census, National Archives.

did not significantly age from one census to the next. Twenty-something-year-olds comprised a respectable portion of the factory workforce, with 15 between age twenty to twenty-nine in 1850, 39 in the same age group in 1860, and 53 in 1870. This steady increase for each succeeding census did not translate into an aging workforce, however, since the median age (approximately eighteen), as well as the mean age (approximately twenty), for the cohort remained nearly unchanged for the entire period. Long-term youthfulness of the labor force may indicate that factory work represented a stage in the life-cycle, to be fitted in between childhood and further adult experiences. To understand the intersection of the age of workers and the geographic persistence of workers remaining in Athens, we should begin by examining how gender affected the long-term participation of workers in the factories.

The census suggests that in Athens, as elsewhere, women performed most of the labor in the textile mills. While the 1850 population schedule did not enumerate occupations for women, the manufacturing schedule, as compiled in the census compendia, reports that women comprised 54 percent of the textile-mill workforce. In 1860, when the census began reporting women's occupations, the census compendia reported women worked 55 percent of the jobs in Athens's factories, but population manuscript schedules enumerated women as 64 percent of the local industrial workforce. The 1870 compendia failed to delineate a gendered breakdown of Athens's industrial work, but women filled 57 percent of the town's factory jobs as enumerated for that year's census. So women and girls probably comprised between 55 percent to 60 percent of Athens's textile workers. Men and boys made up the remaining 40–45 percent.[12]

A breakdown of the age distribution of female workers is particularly instructive for understanding how Athenians fit factory work into their lives. In 1860, female operatives enumerated an average (mean) age of just over twenty years, a median age of eighteen-and-a half, and exhibited a mode, meaning a primary spike, at age sixteen (with 12 of 85 female operatives in that age group.) For the teenage years, the curve forms a right-leaning bell as the mode is less than both the mean and the median ages. In the twenty-something age group, the curve becomes relatively flat with between two and five cases for each year of that group, except for a trough of one case each for ages twenty-six and twenty-seven. Above age twenty-nine, the curve diminishes to singular sporadic cases, and finally disappears at age thirty-seven. In 1870, the same-shaped curve appears. In that year, the enumerated factory women and girls in Athens averaged just under twenty years of age, and they registered a median age of seventeen-and-a-half years, with the mode of eleven cases at age sixteen. The distribution curve is again right leaning, sharply curtailed on the right at age eleven, but gently sloping from five and six cases per year of age from age eighteen to twenty-two. The curve from ages twenty-three to thirty-three is flat with two to three cases per year of age, with two exceptions. Age twenty-five spikes to seven cases while age twenty-eight drops to zero cases. The 1870 age distribution for women trails on longer than the 1860 curve, terminating at age forty-two. The two similar distributions suggest similar patterns of work participation by women in their early teens followed by a falling away from factory work, at a time when girls in Athens were likely to marry and raise children. Despite the small aberrations in the mid-twenties, it does not appear that women who left the workforce returned at a later time. If they had, then the age distribution curve would demonstrate bimodality (two main spikes) with many more female operatives over the age of the thirty. So one might assume that women worked to support their parents' household until they married. Unmarried women continued to work.

An examination of persistence among Athens female factory workers demonstrates that unmarried women pursued textile careers after married women quit the mills. Because the 1850 census marshals did not enumerate women's occupations, one must look for family connections to factory occupations in the 1850 census in order to sense how women might have persisted during the 1850s. Fourteen female factory workers, aged fourteen to thirty-three in 1860, persisted from families which reported a male factory worker in the 1850 census. Some of these women probably worked in the factories at some time prior to 1860, particularly the five women aged twenty-five or older in 1860. Of the fourteen, only one appeared married, and she, Beckey Allen, lived with her husband in a household headed by her aged mother-in-law. All the rest lived in households headed by one of their parents. Like Beckey Allen, other household members worked in the factories at the same time as the fourteen persisting women workers.

A similar pattern emerged in 1870 when eleven women, aged twenty-five to forty-two in 1870, persisted as factory workers through the 1860s. (Two more listed a factory occupation in 1860, and while each listed "at home" for their job descriptions in 1870, both lived in a household in which another member listed a factory occupation that year.) Of those 1870 female persisters of factory families, aged twenty-five or older, only one did not list factory operative as her occupation in 1860. In 1870, the mean, median, and modal age of this cohort was twenty-five years, so we can assume those below that age could consider marriage a possibility, while those over twenty-five were probably considered over the hill. Importantly, none of the persisting factory women were married in 1870. All but one of these operatives lived in a household headed by one of their parents, or headed by a sibling. The one who headed her own household included her sisters as her dependents. Since the number of cases is very small, a review of the manuscript data of a few of these women will confirm this trend.

Parmelia A. Smith persisted in a factory household for all three censuses. In 1850, twenty-year-old Parmelia and her eight-year-old sister, Melinda Smith, belonged to a household of nine in which their elder brother, Pinckney, reported factory employment while their father and another brother listed themselves simply as laborers. The following two censuses reported Parmelia

TABLE 2
Clarke County Textile Worker Persistence

Persisters	Number	Age		% Skilled	% Nativity[c]				% Literate
		Mean	Median		GA Born	Other South	Other U.S.	Non-U.S.	
1850–60	31	24.4	20.0	16.1	90.3	6.5	3.2	0	77
Male	13	28.5	20.0	38.5	84.6	7.7	7.7	0	69
Female	18	21.6	19.5	0	94.4	5.6	0	0	83
1860–70	35	27.6	25.0	8.6[b]	85.7	14.3	0	0	43
Male	16	29.3	26.5	18.8[b]	93.7	6.3	0	0	56
Female	19	26.2	25.0	0[b]	78.9	21.1	0	0	32
1850–70[a]	5	37.0	40.0	. . .	80.0	20.0	0	0	60
Male	4	35.8	35.0	. . .	100.0	0	0	0	75
Female	1	42.0	42.0	. . .	0	100.0	0	0	0

[a] 1870 Census did not differentiate occupations among textile workers for Clarke County.

[b] Used 1860 occupation to determine skill level.

[c] Percentages rounded.

Source: 1850, 1860, and 1870 Clarke County Manuscript Census, National Archives.

as an undifferentiated factory operative. Not only did Parmelia enter and maintain a long career in the mills, but she also lived with other operatives. In 1860, her sixty-five-year-old father maintained householder status but then identified himself as a farmer with personal property valued at $130. The 1860 household contained Parmelia's mother, her three younger sisters, who were all factory operatives, and another factory operative, thirty-two-year-old Mary Williams (probably a relative, but the relationship is not discernable from available data). By 1870, with her parents apparently dead, forty-two-year-old Parmelia, now the householder, maintained two sisters, one of whom continued as an operative while Melinda "kept house." The household still also contained Mary Williams, now forty-two and still a factory operative. With no children listed, this was a house of independent women, albeit a poor one which listed neither real nor personal property in the 1870 census. However Parmelia's household did not have to maximize the work potential of all dwelling within to survive but kept one out of the factory so the other three could pursue an income without having to keep house themselves. Similarly, the housekeeper needed the income provided by her working "sisters" in order to stay out of the mills. The other working women who persisted in Athens's factories led similar lives.

In 1870, Athens's persisting factory girls always worked with the support of someone to keep house for them. Generally either an aged mother, or a sister or sister-in-law with small children, would take care of the household's business, leaving the rest free to earn an income to support the household. Lucinda Burger lived with her mother, sister, and brother-in-law, but only she and her brother-in-law worked in the factory. The other two women kept house. Twenty-five-year-old Lucy Bailey appeared to have worked along with her younger brother, George, in the mills, while George's wife, Arminta, kept the house and raised the children. Nancy and Amanda Peck worked in the factory alongside their thirty-nine-year-old aunt, Artimesia Smith, while the girls' mother kept house for all three operatives. As most of the female operatives came from a household headed by a woman, factory work provided a means of survival for the entire household without working everyone beyond the point of exhaustion. Not all were completely without means, as one householder of a persisting factory family, Biddy Porterfield, reported one thousand dollars in property, but this was a singular exception. Instead of wealth, factory work provided for survival. While we do not know about the private lives of Athens's women operatives nor about their public lives between censuses, their responses as recorded in the census replicate much of northern textile experience for women—although not the lifestyle made famous at Lowell. While at least one factory owned a boarding house for its workers, there is a great probability that it was reserved for single male workers, and the female operatives generally boarded with some extension of their families. Clearly the newspapers would have reported in great detail had the factories in Athens instituted a system of female boarding houses similar to that used in New England. But they were silent on all aspects of factory boarding houses. What then was the place of the male factory workers in Athens?

The workingmen also seemed to divide into those who made factory work a career and those for whom it served as a temporary stage in their lives. The demarcation, however, is not as clear as it was for the women. Like the women, those who listed their job as just an operative tended generally to be younger. In 1850, male operatives averaged twenty-two years, with a median age of nineteen, and a mode of seventeen. In 1860, a similarly defined group averaged twenty-two years, with a median age of eighteen, and a mode of fifteen to sixteen, with six teenagers in each of the modal age groups. For 1870, textile workingmen averaged nineteen years, with a median age of eighteen, and a mode of seven cases of twelve-year-olds working in the mills. So, like the women, men generally began leaving factory employment in their late teens and early twenties. For example, in 1870, roughly 80 percent of the enumerated fifty-nine male factory operatives were less than twenty-five years of age. Seventy-five percent of the male workers ranged in age between eleven and twenty-four, inclusively. Thus, similar to the experience of Athens's working females, textile work generally proved a stage in a male's economic life.[13]

Very few men persisted within the factories, unless they moved up the career ladder to take on a more managerial job as an overseer, boss, or superintendent. From 1850 to 1860 only three male factory operatives enumerated in the 1850 census still listed their occupations as operatives in 1860. Additionally, four younger brothers of Benjamin Davis, who was enumerated as a factory operative in 1850, emerged as operatives working alongside their brother in 1860.

The example of the Davis family is illustrative of the form of upward mobility offered by factory work. In 1850, seventeen-year-old Benjamin Davis worked as a factory operative at the Georgia Factory but lived in his sixty-three-year-old father's household with seven others, none of whom enumerated an occupation. In 1860, twenty-seven-year-old Benjamin now headed his own household with his wife and listed a specific job within the factory—a presser. At the same time in 1860, four of Benjamin's siblings now enumerated factory jobs as well. Longevity within the factory granted Benjamin limited status above the group of poor whites, to which he had formerly belonged. More importantly, the income that accompanied his titled job appeared to provide him the means of marrying. None of his younger brothers had married, and all still lived in his father's now ten-person household. Others moved out of factory work without increasing their status or property holdings.

Members of the Pledger family of Athens demonstrated upward mobility by pursuing factory work as a career while others experienced downward mobility by leaving mill work. In 1850, the twelve-member household that contained five-year-old Marshal Pledger enumerated factory-operative jobs at the Georgia Factory for Marshal's father, forty-seven-year-old Isaac Pledger, and for two of Marshal's brothers, twenty-five-year-old John Pledger and fifteen-year-old Isaac Pledger. In 1870, twenty-six-year-old Marshal recorded personal property of $100 as he was listed as a factory operative at Princeton Factory, probably one of the jobs with a higher status since he was able to accumulate some capital, despite supporting his wife and his one-year-old child. Marshal's brother John, however, gave his occupation in 1870 simply as a day laborer in the town of Athens, and he recorded no property with which to support his family of six. The Pledgers probably maintained close ties to, if not careers in, the factories. Marshal may have found some success in his career as he seemed able to support a nuclear family on his own salary. John's fortunes seemed more dismal since his finances required the labor of two minor children and one adult child to support his family. Movement from factory operative to day laborer was apparently a downward social trajectory, but the census is silent on what happened to John in the twenty years between enumerations. We can only speculate as to why John Pledger did not accumulate property or move into a higher level of management. It may be that he chose to leave the factory for opportunities elsewhere that did not work out, or perhaps the Civil War affected his ability to perform mill work, or alternately, perhaps some form of age discrimination derived from environmental health problems factored into his removal from the factory. Despite John's failure to earn a living wage to support his family, some operatives succeeded in moving into a lower level of the managerial class.

SKILLED OPERATIVES AND OVERSEERS

Athens's factories could not operate without the small group of workers who filled the ranks between the undifferentiated operatives and the factory superintendents. The many skills listed for these upper-level workers included carding, drawing, dying, pressing, reeling, ruling, spinning, and weaving. Although rarely tabulated as "skilled" workers for enumeration purposes, these workers trained and supervised those with less experience at the job they performed. One can conflate these skilled workers into a class of lower management since the factory contained few skilled laborers, and many of them took the title of overseer or boss for their particular department. Longevity within the factory system, in addition to experience and "skill," obviously played a role in the promotion to factory overseer or boss, and the promotion entailed increased pay and status within the factory, as well as added duties. As early as 1836, the Athens Factory specified extra pay for two of its overseers.[14]

While little is known about the overseers prior to the time when the census began tracking occupations, evidence points to their origins outside Athens for the first twenty years of industrialization. Since few factories existed in the South, most experienced workers necessarily came from the North or from Europe in the early years of industrialization. Before 1850, clues to their origins can be found in newspaper social notices. In 1839, Jeremiah A. Fairfield, of Boston, married Jane Close at the Princeton Factory. While Mr. Fairfield's occupation was never discussed, one can assume the happy couple found some attachment to the factory, and that he was probably a manager of some sort, brought to Athens for his knowledge. Athens attracted journeyman artisans in many trades, artisans who took temporary jobs as they traveled around the country before ultimately settling down to become a master. Perhaps Athens became a way station for similarly footloose textile workers as well. Or perhaps, as with the factory superintendents, Athens's industrialists actively recruited the needed experienced labor.[15]

With time to learn, local folks increasingly filled these "lower managerial" jobs within the factory. The census data bolsters this claim. In 1850, of the nine men in Clarke County who listed a factory job title other than "factory operative"—one dyer, two overseers, one machinist, one carder, one weaver, and two mule spinners—the two overseers reported European origins while the machinist reported New England nativity. The weaver came from South Carolina; the others came from Georgia. By 1850, therefore, a few operatives had learned their jobs sufficiently to rise to the next level within the factories. In 1860, of the eighteen cases in which someone enumerated a specified factory job—boss, drawing, overseer, machinist, presser, spinner, reeler, ruler, or weaver—two came from South Carolina, one from North Carolina, and the rested reported Georgia as their birthplace. Of these eighteen, none of the ten women included in the cohort rose to the level of boss, machinist, or overseer. The 1870 census failed to enumerate specific jobs within the factories, so a similar analysis is not possible for that decade. However two men who persisted from the 1860 census to the 1870 census had listed their occupation as either boss or machinist in 1860. A third male "operative" in 1870 had been reported as an overseer of carding operations in a factory in another county in the previous census. All three of these management persisters were Georgia born and raised. None of the eleven female persisters from 1860 to 1870 listed a job other than operative for either of the censuses.

With increased experience as textile workers in the local community, some male factory workers began to rise out of the working class. William Center and F. Marion Williams both listed their jobs as factory operatives in 1850, but in 1860 Center reported his job as overseer and Williams as a factory superintendent. Henry Lovern, too, progressed from operative in 1850 to carding-room overseer for the Sweetwater Factory in Campbell County in 1860. One must wonder how such a small number of promotions affected a worker's chance for economic success. Anecdotal evidence suggests that promotion within the factory increased one's chance for accumulating property but did not necessarily guarantee a large enough wage to support a family.

Factory work provided some means of upward mobility for William Center. A South Carolina native, Center apparently began working at the Georgia Factory in the early 1840s, and he married his wife, Mary Lee, at the factory in 1844. In the 1850 census, he was enumerated as a factory operative with six dependents (including his sister and his sister-in-law), but he reported owning $600 in real estate, despite the size of his family. Probably the two older siblings worked in the factory, although the census did not record their occupation, and they probably contributed their wages to the maintenance of the household. In 1860, however, William Center listed his occupation as an overseer, with seven dependents, no longer housing his wife's and his own siblings but now including more children and his aged mother. Center's holdings reportedly dropped to $62 in personal property, probably due to the difficulty of supporting such a large family on one salary; nobody else in the household reported an occupation. Center dropped out of my census tabulation in 1870 because he no longer engaged directly in a manufacturing job. Instead he became a minor merchant in the firm of Center and Reeves, acting as an agent for the Athens Factory in selling its yarn and cloth. William Center died in 1876 after a life of work in textiles, but he had raised himself out of the working class and entered the commercial class. Other persisters' dossiers were not as complete as Center's, nor were they as clearly successful.[16]

Twenty-seven-year-old Georgia native Green Connell reported his occupation as a factory machinist in the 1860 census. His Georgia Factory household contained five dependents (his wife and four young children), and he reported only $90 in personal property. In 1870, Green and his two eldest children, sixteen-year-old Alice and fourteen-year-old Elizabeth, supported an enlarged household of eight through their factory work. Despite needing the help of his children to support the household, the family now reported property of $250, and the three middle children attended school while the youngest remained at home with her mother. Clearly this was a family who exceeded mere survival. Others were not quite so lucky, despite upward mobility within the factory ranks.

Economic success eluded Grandison "Henry" Lovern despite his many years of work as a carder in textile factories in Georgia. A lifelong textile worker, Georgia native Henry Lovern reported himself as a factory operative in Athens in both the 1850 and 1870 censuses. Between those dates, Lovern moved to Campbell County, Georgia, in 1858, where he worked as the overseer of the card room of the Sweetwater Factory. After the factory's destruction by the Union Army in 1864, Henry returned to Athens with his family. In 1870, forty-year-old Henry Lovern reported no property in the census, and three of his six children, aged nine to fourteen years old, worked in the mills, while the three under the age of eight stayed home without receiving schooling. Lovern's career seems not to have improved his financial status nor position in the community. Instead, the survival of his household required maximizing his household's work potential. Given the experience of these factory households, it appears that by 1870 factory-work longevity, even with some upward occupational mobility, did not necessarily create financial security if one did not simultaneously control the size of one's family.[17]

Factory households consistently shrank in Athens from 1850 to 1870. While dependents in these households generally included spouses, children, parents, in-laws, boarders, and other relatives, households headed by a factory worker took on a nuclear composition over the course of industrialization. The seventy-five householders who reported working in the factory sometime between 1850 and 1870 averaged 4.5 dependents. During the same years, the 117 families in which someone (not necessarily the householder) took factory employment averaged 7.8 dependents. The thirty-four households in 1850, in which someone worked in the factory, enumerated an average of 6.2 dependents. For the 16 families, in which the householder listed a factory occupation in 1850, the average decreased to 5.63 dependents. By 1860, the average number of dependents for the sixty-six households that contained a factory worker dropped to 5.6, while the twenty-four householders enumerating factory jobs averaged only 4.7 dependents. The average number of dependents decreased even further to 3.9 people in 1870, for households headed by a person reporting a textile factory as their employer, while households listing a factory worker averaged 4.6 dependents. In each decade, the average number of dependents in households containing factory workers possessed at least one more dependent than households headed by a factory worker. Family size shrank across the board, but families more firmly integrated into the industrial order shrank at a faster rate than those only marginally connected to it. From the census data, one cannot tell if factory workers consciously limited their family size, or if factory work increased mortality rates or decreased fertility rates, either one of which limited family size, perhaps more effectively than rational planning.

SUPERINTENDENTS

Just as Athens's textile factories could not produce without adequately trained workers and overseers, neither could they operate without superintendents to manage the entire works. Like a master artisan, a superintendent generally served a lengthy apprenticeship learning his trade before taking on his duties as a master. Henry Merrell, a factory superintendent imported from New York to run the Roswell Factory in Georgia in 1839, spent seven years learning his trade. Since Georgia lacked factories in which to train factory superintendents before 1830, the factories in Athens necessarily imported its managers from elsewhere.[18]

Prior to establishing a supply of home-grown technical managers in the postbellum years, most factory superintendents in the Athens area came from the Middle Atlantic states, New England, or the British Isles. Athens's first factory superintendent, John Johnson, came from Massachusetts. He constructed and operated the Georgia Factory from 1829 to 1832. Robert and John White, father and son, came from Larne, Ireland, near Belfast. Robert White superintended the Athens Factory from 1836 to 1845 while John supervised and then purchased the Georgia Factory. Johnson Garwood, originally from Pennsylvania, probably worked at one of the outlying factories around Athens in the late 1830s and then superintended the small Mars Hill Factory in western Clarke County in the early 1840s until he sold his share of the business to

Henry Merrell in 1844. Garwood later returned to Athens in the early 1860s to superintend the Georgia Factory. Prior to Garwood's return, the 1860 census listed Jonathan Francis, of Ireland, as superintendent of the Georgia Factory. The census also enumerated William Mason as Princeton Factory superintendent in 1850 and 1860. Born in Nottingham, England, Mason emigrated to New Jersey soon after his birth, when his father established a cotton-spinning factory at Nutley. By the late 1850s, the pattern of hiring outsiders was broken when Athens native Francis Marion Williams became superintendent of the Athens Factory, a job he retained into the 1870s. Non-southern-bred superintendents still ran factories in the Athens area after Marion Williams's employment, but clearly the learning curve for southern mill hands advanced sufficiently to enable a limited number to become superintendents in southern factories. As confirmation of this alteration, Georgia native Edward Russell superintended the Princeton Factory in 1870. Also evincing the difference, Russell's brother, William J. Russell (the father of a Georgia Supreme Court justice, and grandfather of legendary Georgia Senator Richard B. Russell) served as factory agent, a role usually requiring ownership in the factory.[19]

Experience in Athens suggests that financial success for a superintendent required a small investment in the firm that grew with one's tenure. Since no official record was left of the superintendents' salaries, one must look at the census for indications of wealth or capital accumulation among superintendents. John Johnson, Athens's first factory superintendent, invested $4004.98 in the Georgia Factory in 1830, either in cash or through his work, and netted a profit of $4,182.78 in only two years. After quickly earning that large sum, Johnson could afford to disagree with the senior partners in the firm, sell out, and return north. William Mason reported no property in 1850, but the 1860 census enumerated his property at $6,765. Mason may have hidden his property in 1850. Alternately, he may have saved the entire amount during his tenure in Athens. Or the census marshal simply may have asked the wrong person to evaluate Mason's wealth in 1850. As a younger son of an established New Jersey manufacturer, Mason probably arrived in Athens with a small amount to invest and improved upon his capital over the years. As confirmation of the small but not inconsequential capital of these factory managers, Georgia Factory superintendent Jonathan Francis reported $1,200 worth of property in the 1860 census. And finally, Athens native F. Marion Williams rose from reporting property of $65 in 1860 to $750 in holdings in the 1870 census. Unlike previous superintendents, who were imported because of their knowledge, and who could bargain for a share in the stock of the factory, Williams lacked both the capital to invest and the prestige of someone hired as an outside expert. Thus, rising within the local factory system meant starting with fewer financial resources and lengthened the time it took to accumulate a competency. However, those who earned enough to allow them to invest frequently moved into the ranks of the industrialists. The experiences of Robert and John White, factory superintendents in Athens in the 1830s and 1840s, are instructive.[20]

Robert White superintended a factory in Athens for nearly a decade as he improved his financial resources, and then he moved to a nearby location in Georgia to build and manage his own cotton factory. Born April 1, 1776, in Larne, County Antrim, Ireland, Robert White probably learned the textile business as a linen weaver at Cairn Castle, in Ulster. However, White was no impoverished weaver but an owner of a linen mill and one of sixty investors in an Irish savings and loan in 1816. After immigrating to Charleston, South Carolina, in late 1828, with most of his immediate family, White bought into a partnership running a small cotton mill on Hurricane Shoals in the Abbeville District, where he remained until the factory burned in 1832. He moved to Athens by 1835 with the $4,000 left from a lifetime of work, and he invested the small fortune in the Athens Factory as a minor partner while he worked as superintendent. Supplementing his factory income by making small loans, White left Athens in the mid-1840s, and ultimately ventured his accumulated $10,000 in a factory in Newton County to the west of Athens in 1846. Robert White operated small factories with his son Hugh in Newton and Butts County from that time until his death in the late 1850s.[21]

John White, Robert White's son, managed the Georgia Factory near Athens from the mid-1830s to the middle 1860s and slowly amassed a large estate. Legends diverge as to how John White came to settle in Athens. A memoir, written by one of White's grandsons, claims White had been in New Orleans, selling linen cloth manufactured by his father in Ireland, and while traveling overland to Charleston, to avoid the rough water of the Florida straits, he took ill in Athens and remained there until nourished back to renewed health. An alternate family tradition maintains Congressman Augustin Clayton, the instigator of industrialization in Athens, met John White in Alexandria, Virginia, when White visited his fiancée at the house of her uncle, who was an Irish political émigré. John White then moved to Athens but returned to Ireland to marry and to bring the rest of his family to Georgia. A third report contends John White journeyed to Australia when his parents and siblings moved from Ireland to South Carolina in the late 1820s. John reputedly rejoined his family about the time they moved to Georgia, after he survived a bout of smallpox, which forever soured him on Australia. Whichever legend contains the most truth, John White became the superintendent of the Georgia Factory by 1836, and both he and trustees of his wife's estate began purchasing portions of the factory's stock, along with farmland surrounding the factory, soon thereafter. John White purchased his first shares in the company in 1839, and he finally consolidated control of the factory in 1846.[22]

John White's possession of the factory became the engine for amassing his fortune. Without explanation, he attempted to sell the Georgia Factory in the late 1840s, but found no takers. In the 1850 census manufacturing schedule, White reported that his "New Georgia Factory," capitalized at $75,000, with 1,500 spindles, 100 looms, and 48 cards, employed seventy-five "hands" to consume $60,000 worth of cotton annually and produce goods valued at $120,000. In the late 1850s, John White reinvested his capital in his factory and made money when others could not. R. G. Dun called John White a "hard driving Irishman" who "d[id] not speculate," and spoke glowingly of his business acumen, commenting that he "commenced with nothing and now owns the whole factory," and that he "made money faster than any man in the country." Throughout the late 1840s and early 1850s, these credit reporters variously estimated his worth at $30,000, $50,000, and $100,000. They further noted, in 1854, that White "built a large brick factory and bought new machinery very cheap" from the defunct Charleston Factory. Although encumbered with a $30,000 debt to pay for these improvements, the reporters expressed confidence in White's ability to avoid financial embarrassment. During the Civil War, White sent a portion of his funds to an Irish bank, and immediately re-established his economic clout in Athens by retrieving more than $60,000 in cash once hostilities ended. Turning the management of his factory over to his sons James and John R. White, John White now played the role of bank president and financier as he expanded his industrial investments by purchasing Georgia factories experiencing cash-flow problems in the 1870s. Before his death in 1881, credit reporters repeatedly called John White one of Athens's "few rich men."[23]

Despite the long-term rewards of superintending, Georgia's manufacturers could not always recruit or retain trained supervisory staff to operate their factories. Promoters in the 1840s believed they could always recruit factory superintendents and departmental overseers from the North or from England with the promise of high wages. However, some of those recruited lacked adequate skills or temperament to manage a southern factory. The Roswell Factory's owners hired a northern man named Cheever to act as factory superintendent but found him lacking in practical ability, despite his technical knowledge. Others, such as the first agent of the Macon Factory, lacked the temperament to encourage the best work from southern laborers. Henry Merrell, at the Roswell Factory, for instance, insulted his southern employers and alienated his workers for not accepting his northern-bred sensibilities about manual labor. Owners and stockholders also alienated their managers when they interfered with the efficient management of the factories. For example, a stockholder insisted on a monopoly for provisioning the Curtright Factory, in the county adjacent to Athens, and he charged more than the factory master would have paid elsewhere. To make matters worse, when factories experienced severe setbacks, particularly in the early 1850s, they sometimes jettisoned their managers in a cost-cutting effort, and then attempted to run the business themselves, usually without success. Fortunately, Athens did not need to participate in these trends because its tenure as a manufacturing center created a supply of locally raised managers trained in the business even before the coming of the Civil War.[24]

Starting in the 1830s, factory masters in Georgia worried about their ability to attract and train sufficient local talent to create a pipeline of future southern factory superintendents. Roswell Factory Superintendent Henry Merrell complained when he could not attract the sons of the local gentry to sign on for extended apprenticeships to learn to become factory superintendents. But Merrell also despaired when he realized he would never progress beyond superintendent at Roswell Factory, because the same boys who resisted his offers of "honest" manual work were being trained to purchase the factory's supplies and sell its manufactured goods. Thus, these young men were groomed to become factory agents, which put them on the path to becoming gentleman industrialists. The more elite young men had more options available to them: college, commerce, and even agriculture called to them. Without a supply of higher-status trainees, Athens, like the Roswell Factory, taught the technical end of industrial production to non-elite youths such as

Marion Williams instead. Thus, while upward mobility proved possible for factory superintendents, as the lives of Robert and John White demonstrate, by the 1840s clerking in the factories had become a better vehicle for improving one's financial and social position in the community.[25]

CLERKS

Clerking in Athens, like clerking in the North, designated which young men would find a fast track for social and financial advancement within the community. Local studies of aspiring towns in New York—Rochester and Utica, for example—explain the advantages, freedom, and anxiety experienced by the numerous clerks of those towns. Athens, although a center for trade in northeastern Georgia, provided fewer such opportunities because the population that supported trade was much smaller. The small-town setting did not offer the anonymity of larger northern towns that enabled the development of a young white male culture that encouraged clerks to rebel against community standards of dress and deportment. Instead of releasing young men from social constraints, clerking in the South inculcated country boys in the urbanizing norms of gentlemanly behavior and commercial culture. Thus when young southern non-elite men with few opportunities took clerking positions in the early 1840s, they worked hard to create the opportunities that previously eluded them.[26]

The life of John W. Nicholson serves as an extreme example of the transformation of a country lad into a southern gentleman of commerce and connections. In 1843, at age nineteen, Nicholson moved to Athens from neighboring Oglethorpe County, Georgia, where he had worked as an agricultural laborer and as an unskilled worker in a carriage-building shop. Nicholson entered Athens's commercial culture as a post-office clerk but had switched to clerking in William S. Grady's store by December 1849. By 1852, he had married Grady's sister-in-law and had become Grady's partner, which led to his rise to respectability. During William Grady's two-year absence in the California gold fields (which the credit reporters of R. G. Dun considered suspect at best), all responsibility for success of the firm devolved upon Nicholson. Throughout Nicholson's tenure as Grady's partner in the 1850s, R. G. Dun's credit reporters expressed their respect for him and frequently commented that he would do much better if he jettisoned his partner. Although the junior partner,

Nicholson seemed more respectable and cautious than William Grady's go-for-broke risk-taking style of business. But Nicholson never abandoned his partner, and in 1857 he followed Grady's lead in purchasing ten shares of the High Shoals Factory on the western edge of Clarke County. Following Grady's death during the Civil War, Nicholson continued William Grady's investment strategies by purchasing the local paper mill (which had suffered total destruction several times in the previous decade), as well as an interest in Grady's gas works. By the early 1870s, as one of the town's leading men, he successfully headed a new railroad promotion to free Athens from domination by Augusta's economic elite. Thus, in the space of twenty-five years, Nicholson moved from country bumpkin, to clerk, to junior partner in a minor mercantile house, to industrial investor, and finally to full-fledged industrialist. Other clerks found similar, although less meteoric, success in linking their commercial careers to industrial endeavors.[27]

All of Athens's factories hired clerks to balance accounts, but these differed greatly from clerks in merchant houses. The factories wanted older, stable men, already educated in commerce, and immediately capable of performing their tasks. When John White sought to hire a clerk for the Georgia Factory in 1847, he advertised for "A Married man, who has some knowledge of accounts and can write a good plain hand, industrious and willing to make himself generally useful. He must be of steady and sober habits—none others need apply." Similarly, the clerks the southern factory owners desired deviated from the norm for northern factory clerks. Henry Merrell's description of his tenure as a factory clerk, learning the mechanics of the textile business as well as how to keep accounts, sounds like the typical experience of a schoolboy, an apprentice or a young clerk learning his business. In each of these environments, teenage boys rebelled periodically against the discipline necessary to learn a specific body of knowledge by playing pranks against their teachers. This background contrasts markedly with the experience of Moses E. McWhorter and Edmund Palmer when they served as clerks for the Athens Factory. Both appeared to be older men with previous experience in commerce and a knowledge of bookkeeping. Especially different from the northern factory clerk, McWhorter and Palmer served the company agent rather than learning the business from the factory superintendent. A quick summary of each of their lives is again illustrative of clerking in an early southern factory.[28]

Moses E. McWhorter, a South Carolina native, clerked for the Athens

Factory before 1844, when Thomas Baxter was its agent. After Baxter's death, McWhorter joined in a retail partnership with Baxter's son Andrew, and when that firm dissolved a few years later, he bought out the president of the factory's share in the grocery firm of Dearing and Son. From the 1830s to 1850s, McWhorter paid taxes upon wild lands in distant counties, upon an increasing number of slaves, upon sporadic loans made at high interest, upon occasional ownership of breeding stock, and upon town lots. Although Moses McWhorter enumerated only $650 in property for the 1850 census marshals, credit reporters placed his worth between $4,000 and $10,000 at about the same time. Starting as a factory clerk with an annual salary of $600, McWhorter then shifted to a life of commerce in partnership with A. P. Dearing, agent of the Princeton Factory. When Dearing retired from being factory agent in 1856, McWhorter purchased a minor sharehold in the Princeton Factory in order to take on the job of factory agent. Listed as a manufacturer, he enumerated more than $19,000 in property in the 1860 census.[29]

Forty-year-old Connecticut-born Edmund Palmer succeeded McWhorter as the Athens Factory's clerk in the late 1840s. Credit reporters claimed that Palmer failed at business prior to taking the job at the Athens Factory, but that he was hard working and honest. To supplement his income for keeping the books of the factory, Palmer occasionally purchased a few goods from the North and sold them from the factory office. As with McWhorter, the reporting of Palmer's fortunes grew from $300 in the 1850 census to $4,500 in the 1860 census. The latter figure is confirmed by R. G. Dun estimates of $4,000–$6,000 in property at the same time. Palmer transformed his job title from "clerk" to "bookkeeper" during the same period, indicating that he saw the position not as a stepping stone to other business but as a career in itself. After Palmer died in the early 1860s, the local insurance company sold his estate an $1,800 policy on his house, $1,200 on the building itself, $500 on furniture, and $100 for the kitchen. While Palmer was not impoverished, neither did his occupation make him wealthy. However, by the end of the antebellum period, in addition to becoming a service position in the company or a ladder to other industry-related careers, clerking in a factory also became a path for training younger members of the factory owner's family as future management.[30]

James White grew up as a member of the industrialist class and learned the textile business from his father, John White. Although the census enumerated him as a factory clerk in the 1860 and 1870 censuses, his life experiences diverge greatly from the lives led by McWhorter, Palmer, or even Nicholson. When his father took an extended trip to retrieve his funds from Irish banks, he elevated James to factory agent in his stead. This third-generation member of Athens's industrial class spent his entire business life up to that point within the Georgia Factory. Unlike Palmer or McWhorter, he was still young, only about twenty-five years old, when he was given responsibility of managing the factory. James White, unlike the others, more closely resembled the clerks of northern factories, even more so since he would inherit the entire works when his father decided to focus his energies on creating the Athens National Bank. Thus, by 1870, James White could report property holdings of $5,000 in real estate and $12,000 in personal property. By the 1890s, he took over as president of the bank, bought the Princeton Factory when it went bankrupt, and bankrolled other industrial and commercial endeavors. Clerking, for James White, served as the school in which he learned how to run the family enterprises.

THE INDUSTRIALISTS

Before exploring commonalities among the lives of Athens's industrialists, one must understand that entrepreneurs participated in industrial endeavors in varying degrees. Entrepreneurs, labeled here as "major industrialists," directly managed and promoted multiple industrial enterprises. Industrial enterprises are defined somewhat broadly to include not only manufacturing but also the ancillary enterprises without which those primary categories could not have sustained themselves. These include railroads, banks, and insurance companies as well as the construction and operation of municipal infrastructure such as street railways, and gas and water systems. For the first generation of industrialization in Athens, William Dearing, Augustin Clayton, William Williams, and James Camak fit into the first category. Dearing served simultaneously as president of both the Athens Factory and the Georgia Railroad, and he successfully instigated a series of southern commercial conventions seeking greater economic independence for the South by eliminating northern middlemen from the cotton trade with England. Augustin Clayton precipitated Georgia's entrance into successful industrial manufacture by starting the Georgia Factory, and he served as an active director of the Georgia Railroad. James Camak built and incorporated the Princeton Factory (but sold it before it went into operation), presided over the Georgia Railroad in its first two years, and then served both as an active director and as the principal employee of the railroad. William Williams purchased the Princeton Factory from Camak's investment group and operated it for ten years, while proving instrumental in the formation of the Georgia Railroad. Major second-generation industrialists included Dr. John S. Linton—who served as agent of the Athens Factory until 1863, and who helped establish the local foundry and paper mill—and Albon Chase, co-founder and agent of the town's paper mill, who also served as secretary and general agent of the town's insurance company.

Others can be classified as "industrialists" since they participated in more than one industrial endeavor, but not as actively as the major industrialists. For Athens's first generation, Alexander B. Linton, John Nisbet, and Thomas W. Baxter all served as directors of the Athens Factory and the Georgia Railroad. While Baxter was also agent of the Athens Factory, none of them promoted the advance of industry with the same prominence as the major industrialists. Filling this category in the second generation were Thomas N. Hamilton, owner of Princeton Factory, William P. Talmage, president of both the foundry and the paper mill, and William S. Grady, an investor in the High Shoals Factory, and operator of the Athens gas works.

The third and final category of participation contains the "industrial investors." Investors purchased stock and took dividends but did little else in the way of promoting industrial endeavors. Abraham Walker, who participated in the Georgia Factory, and whose death precipitated the reorganization of the Athens Factory, qualifies as such an investor. Others who belong to this first-generation cohort include the original investors in what became the Princeton Factory, and the changing membership of the Georgia Factory. All these tended to be short-term investors. For the second generation, the liberalization of incorporation for factories in 1847 caused this category to explode, but within specific enterprises one can usually arrange investors into family groupings.

While the eulogies of Athens's industrialists frequently incorporated a southern version of the nineteenth-century self-made man, individuals rising from poverty and obscurity to die rich and prominent, the lives of these figures can be best understood within the life-cycle theory of the planter parvenu. The largely accepted life-cycle theory advanced by James Oakes explains that planters rarely possessed enough slaves to establish each of his male children as a planter upon attaining the age of majority. Instead, a planter developed his son's ability to earn a living outside agriculture, usually by financing an education in the professions of medicine, law, or commerce, so that, through a slow accumulation of capital earned at his profession, and through non-agricultural investments, the young man eventually could purchase the requisite number of slaves to rejoin the agricultural elite. Increasingly, the planter parvenu would abandon his profession as planting took up more of his time, until finally he left the profession completely in order to pursue his agricultural and political pursuits full-time. The following summary biographies confirm a similar process, but with three major differences. First, not everyone who became an industrialist, or a planter-industrialist, originated in the planter class. However, they experienced a life trajectory that seems to mimic the planter-parvenu life-cycle, even if missing planter origins. Second, nearly all who initially followed the life-cycle of the "industrial" planter parvenu failed to abandon the non-agricultural financial pursuits upon attaining "planterhood." Third, some industrial-parvenus avoided the denouement of the cycle and only dabbled in agriculture after gaining an estate from their non-agricultural investments.[31]

Augustin Smith Clayton, who began the process of industrialization in Georgia when he founded Athens's first factory in 1829, fits the life-cycle of a planter parvenu. A memoir of one of Clayton's sons claimed his father "was very poor when he commenced life." Another son remarked that his grandfather provided his father with an education but left his small estate to his only daughter. Even were this true, Augustin Clayton experienced privilege and distinction at an early age when President George Washington presented the eight-year-old with a copy of Sallust as a prize for his oratory when Washington visited Augusta in 1791. Yet the promise of his intellect did not bring wealth for many years. When Clayton graduated in the first class of the University of Georgia in 1804, he was obsessed with his poverty and strove to better himself.[32]

Like a character in a Horatio Alger story, with a peculiarly southern twist, Clayton used his education to find a profession to give him income and status, and then worked diligently in that profession to accumulate sufficient estate to establish himself as a planter. Thus, with the connections obtained from his university education, Clayton read law under the judge of the Western Circuit of Georgia. He married the judge's daughter and then eventually returned to Athens, set up a law practice, and engaged in politics. Slowly he acquired wealth through his law practice, his political offices, and his farm, and by the early 1820s he possessed enough slaves (twenty or more) to be considered a planter. In his spare time he wrote poetry, a novel, and a political satire but was best known for his numerous political essays, written under the *nom de plume*, "Atticus."

Augustin Clayton first came to national attention in criticizing the John Quincy Adams administration in an Atticus essay attacking federal reticence in accepting an illegal treaty Georgia negotiated with a minor group of Creek Indians in 1825. He gained further notoriety as the judge of original jurisdiction in the *Worcester v. Georgia* case, in which Georgia ultimately resisted a U.S. Supreme Court decision regarding the Cherokee Nation within its borders. As a congressman in the early 1830s, Clayton remained in the national limelight by opposing high tariffs, national banking, and, eventually, Andrew Jackson. In 1829, Clayton started the Georgia Factory, ostensibly as a political device to prove that the high profits gained from manufactures did not merit a protective tariff, but he remained a partner in the firm until his death, long after the tariff faded from the forefront of national politics. He served in the state legislature, on the bench, and in the U.S. Congress, but after failing to gain the gubernatorial nomination of Georgia's nascent Whig Party in 1835, he retired from partisan politics. By the time Augustin Clayton died in 1839, at age fifty-five, he possessed 820 acres of farmland, $2,500 worth of town lots, sixty-seven slaves, and at least $12,000 invested in the Georgia Factory. Although clearly a planter (though from questionable class origins), Clayton continued his non-agricultural investments—in urban real estate, in factories, in railroads, and in banking—until his death. Athens's elite considered Clayton so socially important that the town fathers celebrated his funeral as a community-wide event and then published the funeral eulogy.[33]

William Dearing fits a similar pattern. While we know little about Dearing's early years, his later life shows the constant activity of a well-connected Jacksonian era promoter who worked very hard to increase both his wealth and his social status. Born in 1785 as the son of a North Carolina Revolutionary War veteran, William Dearing moved with his family to Rappahannock County, Virginia, while still quite young. By 1809, he moved to Wilkes County, in northeastern Georgia, as a merchant. He married there in 1813, and by the mid-1810s he operated a plantation and was speculating in real estate around Georgia. By 1820, he reported taxable property of thirty-six slaves, $16,000 in town lots, and $14,000 in stock in trade. However, by the time he appeared in Athens in 1829, he reported only twenty-five slaves, $4,050 in town lots, and no stock in trade, and the following year he reported no taxable town lots. In moving to Athens in 1830, he apparently liquidated much of his slave property and town lots to invest in both the Georgia Factory and the Athens Factory with Augustin Clayton. Dearing soon sold his portion of the Georgia Factory to concentrate on managing the Athens Factory. While in Athens, he also speculated in developing town lots and served as a partner in several retail stores.[34]

Dearing's relations with his slaves did not evince the planter ideal. At his entry into Athens, William Dearing owned twenty-five slaves, which he increased to forty-seven by the time he rebuilt the Athens Factory in 1835, after it had burned in late 1834. The year following rebuilding, his taxable slaves decreased to twenty and then slowly increased to thirty-five at the time he left Athens in 1841. Thereafter, this number of slaves fluctuated, probably the result of moving slaves between households in different states. While Dearing clearly rates a planter designation from his ownership of slaves and agricultural land, one must question whether his apparent sale of slaves when faced with adversity met with the supposed planter ideal. If such an ideal amounted to self-delusion, then Dearing fit within the class of planters around him. If there is more truth to it, then such an aberration from planters with diverse investments needs further exploration.[35]

William Dearing gained statewide, regional, and national renown from his public activities in the 1830s. He acted as a commissioner in selling stock in and promoting the concept of the Georgia Railroad in 1833 and 1834. After organizing the railroad, the stockholders elected William Dearing one of their directors, and when the railroad expanded into banking he took over as company president in 1836. Dearing built much of the road during his tenure, until Augusta bought control of the railroad's stock in the early 1840s and moved the home office to Augusta. William Dearing also gained national recognition when he initiated a series of southern commercial conventions held between 1837 and 1839, and he served as an officer in each of the four conventions. So important was his contribution to the organization of the conventions that the third one presented William Dearing with a silver cup.[36]

Dearing ultimately left Athens, but the town always considered him one of its own. In 1841, Dearing moved to Charleston to pursue business there, though he remained an absentee president of the Athens Factory until he sold his stock in 1848. He moved to Savannah from Charleston in December 1852, seeking a better climate for his failing health. After he died, his body was returned to Athens for internment. The tribute from the Athens Town Council confirmed Dearing's life as a prototypical planter in noting that he rose "from comparatively humble life, [but] by the most assiduous attention to business and his duties as a citizen, [he] reared for himself and family an honored and exalted position, amongst the foremost of the land."[37]

James Camak, another first-generation major industrialist in Athens, also fits the planter parvenu pattern. Born in Fairfield District, South Carolina, on February 1, 1795, of allegedly humble origins and supposedly "without the aids of wealth or patronage, . . . [Camak] worked his way through South Carolina College." (The claim of doing so without assistance should be doubted, given the nature of scholarships to southern colleges at the time, and given Camak's later use of patronage.) Camak graduated in 1814 and served as a tutor in South Carolina College until 1817, when he moved to Athens to become professor of mathematics at the University of Georgia. Two years later, after marrying the college president's daughter, he moved to the Georgia state capital at Milledgeville and for thirteen years served as the co-editor and proprietor of the *Georgia Journal*, which was the official organ of the Troup Party. During his years in Milledgeville, he received numerous government sinecures, including the responsibility for surveying the state's boundary, overseeing the state penitentiary, and running the state's central bank. He almost rejoined the faculty at the University of Georgia in 1829, but Baptists' complaints of the university's trustees appointing yet another Presbyterian to the faculty prevented his acceptance.

After gaining a competency from his business, civic, and political pursuits in Milledgeville, he retired to Athens in 1833. Almost immediately he was elected a director of a new bank in that town, and he headed a group seeking to construct a second factory in the Athens area. While in the process of seeking a corporate charter for the factory, Camak helped organize the Georgia Railroad Company to connect Athens to Augusta, and he lost interest in the cotton factory. After obtaining the corporate charter and purchasing the factory site, Camak and most of his co-incorporators sold their shares in the manufacturing enterprise in order to concentrate on organizing the railroad. Camak held the first organizational meeting of the Georgia Railroad Company at his federal-style home in Athens in March 1834, and the organizers elected him president and general agent. When the Georgia Railroad received banking privileges two years later, Camak resigned the presidency of the railroad to become the cashier of the company's bank, a position he held until 1842, when the bank was closed in Athens following the hostile takeover by entrepreneurs from Augusta. He then engaged in promoting scientific agriculture and edited a regional agricultural newspaper from 1845 to his death on June 16, 1847, at the age of fifty-two. During the time Camak paid taxes in Athens, he never listed more than four slaves of his own, although a complete accounting is impossible since he remained delinquent in assessing his taxes from 1840 to the end of his life. However, his estate paid tax on ten slaves in 1848. Unlike Clayton and Dearing, therefore, Camak remained a man of limited means in terms of slave ownership. Notwithstanding his deficiency in owning human capital, one must question whether his contemporaries would have withheld the title of planter from him, given his social standing in Athens. The public accolade at his death explained that "In the various and responsible stations and duties in life to which he was called, he acted with an ability and honesty but rarely equaled."[38]

William Williams, the proprietor of the Princeton Factory from the start of its operations in 1833 to his death ten years later, pursued a banking profession as well as his factory and planting interests. Since the record is silent on most of Williams's early life, one cannot determine if he followed the life-cycle of the planter parvenu. However, he was born in 1786, married in 1811, and resided in Eatonton, Putnam County, Georgia at least as early as 1818. Sometime after 1829, "Money" (as he was known) Williams transported $60,000 in gold to Florida to help establish the Bank of Florida in Tallahassee, and he was elected president of the bank after his large investment. When the Florida Territorial Assembly established a powerful rival to his bank for political reasons, the upstart bank drove Williams's bank nearly insolvent and purchased its stock. At the age of forty-seven, William Williams returned to Georgia, and, within a few months, by June 1833, he participated in meetings in Athens to promote the incorporation of the Georgia Railroad. By November of the same year, he began purchasing the Princeton Factory and a plantation adjacent to the factory, two-and-a-half miles from the town limits of Athens. At the same time, he announced his availability to make private loans at interest. When Athenians organized stock subscriptions to secure the railroad's charter, Williams served as one of the commissioners responsible for the subscription books in Athens.

In the process, he loaned the company enough to meet the legislative requirements for stock sales prior to legal incorporation, and since he owned most of the stock, the company subsequently elected him its secretary and treasurer. After the company obtained banking privileges, however, Williams's participation fell off. In addition to his factory and planting, William Williams continued his private banking, and although a Democrat, he advised Clarke County's citizenry to support general incorporation laws for banks in the early 1840s. Surprisingly, Williams never paid taxes on more than five slaves during his tenure in Athens, despite owning a plantation in Clarke County that varied in size from 300 to 550 acres. Unless he simply enumerated his slaves in another county, historians would not consider him a planter, although most certainly his contemporaries would have. Williams died April 15, 1843, a deacon in the Baptist church, a banker, and a manufacturer. His children married well and rose to prominence as professional clergy and educators.[39]

The life of John Nisbet, a lesser industrialist only in his notoriety, demonstrates a long trend in risk taking, similar to what one would expect of the planter parvenu, except he ultimately failed to engage seriously in planting. Born the son of a wealthy merchant and politician of the same name in Rowan County, North Carolina, in 1781, Nisbet operated a store in Statesville, North Carolina, until 1821, when he moved to Eatonton, Georgia. Two years later, he joined his brother, James, who was a prominent doctor and planter in Athens. However, John Nisbet did not close his store in North Carolina but left an agent, Joseph Davidson, who reputedly sent $120,000 to him in Athens. If John Nisbet continued as a merchant in Athens, he either acted as a silent partner in someone else's firm or served as a cotton merchant since he possessed no stock in trade upon which the county could levy taxes.[40]

John Nisbet primarily invested his funds in real estate which he then rented out, offering plantations, houses, stores, warehouses, taverns, and hotels for sale or rent in Athens and Macon from 1828 through 1840. Nisbet's tax records demonstrate a focus on urban real estate, with taxes paid on town lots valued at an average of nearly $7,700 for a sixteen-year period. Although the aggregate value of his town lots tended to rise over the length of his career, he reduced his town real-estate holdings in 1826, 1832, and 1834. Significantly, Nisbet invested in construction in the Athens Factory in 1832 and 1834, which means the "dips" may represent a diversion of funds into other forms of capital. Given his propensity for real estate, Nisbet also foreclosed on the real estate of those who owed him, particularly when it possessed development potential. For example, in 1833, he foreclosed on five thousand acres of Madame Gouvaine between Trail Creek and Sandy Creek, which included the mineral springs known locally as Helicon Springs, which out-of-towners frequently visited to take the waters. Additionally, Nisbet purchased out-of-state property and resold it. In short, he made money the old-fashioned way: he speculated in real estate.[41]

Despite John Nisbet's wealth and community standing, it is difficult to determine whether he merited planter designation. Interestingly, Nisbet did not own the number of slaves one would expect of a man of his wealth. He averaged only eight slaves for his entire time in Athens, with a slow rise from seven in 1826 to fifteen in 1834. When the Athens Factory burned in September that year, he sold his excess slaves within weeks of the fire in order to raise cash to reinvest in rebuilding the factory. Thus in 1835 he paid taxes on only eight slaves, and this figure decreased until the county taxed him for only three slaves during the last three years of his life. Yet, even when not faced with adversity, John Nisbet showed a willingness to part with his human property, as, in 1831, he advertised the sale of two young slave girls, as a seeming afterthought in an advertisement for his rental property. Unlike the planter ideal, John Nisbet clearly viewed his chattels as capital and not as "family." During his life in Athens, Nisbet also owned thousands of acres of agricultural lands throughout Georgia, including at least fifty or more acres in Clarke County. Apparently he engaged in agriculture more as a speculation than as a way of life, but he would probably still rank as a planter among the elite of Athens.[42]

Overall, John Nisbet invested as much as his co-industrialists in Athens, albeit Nisbet preferred to take greater risks than did the others. In addition to his share in the Athens Factory, Nisbet continued as a partner in the Georgia Factory long after William Dearing sold his share in the enterprise. Nisbet served on the Georgia Railroad's board of directors from its founding, and, by 1840, state documents record his investment of over $40,000 in the railroad and banking company. He invested in banking, made private loans, and discounted notes at usurious rates. While Nisbet operated a plantation in Clarke County, he bought special stud animals as investments, gaining profit both from their stud fees and their resale value. Like his fellow industrialists in Athens, when John Nisbet died, in 1841, he earned an obituary labeling his numerous business activities as positive developments affecting the community. Like the obituary of Dearing and others, the newspaper claimed that "few men have contributed more to [Athens's] prosperity, or been more efficient in promoting its welfare" than John Nisbet.[43]

Dr. Alexander B. Linton, the lone medical doctor of the cohort of lesser, first-generation industrialists, served as a partner in the Athens Factory and on the board of directors of the Georgia Railroad in the 1830s. The son of a Scots tanner, born in upcountry South Carolina circa 1780, he migrated to Georgia by the early 1810s. Linton married in 1811 in Greene County, where he lived, and owned a plantation in adjoining Taliaferro County, both of which were less than fifty miles to Athens. He moved to Athens in 1829, reputedly to educate his five children. Athens may have also been a destination to give his wife opportunity for diversion as her health continued to fail, and she died of tuberculosis within months of relocating there. Once arrived in Athens, A. B. Linton ran his medical practice much like a business, frequently changing partners and locations, and adding a pharmacy as a sideline, in which he sold chemicals and dyes, paints, oils, and glass as well as medicine in conjunction with his son-in-law, William Bacon (who also was brother-in-law to another doctor in town, Dr. Henry Hull), in an upstairs office adjacent to his medical practice. In addition to the diversity of merchandise, the firm also advertised wholesale business to out-of-town doctors and merchants, which indicates the status of Athens as a regional trade center at the time.

In the eight years Dr. Linton reported his taxable property in Clarke County, he averaged forty-one slaves, with the only great change being a reduction from forty-five to thirty-five between 1835 and 1836, roughly at the same time as he invested in the Athens Factory. Like the reductions evidenced by Dearing and Nisbet, this may represent a diversion of his capital from slaves engaged in agriculture to a more liquid investment in industry. Throughout the same time, Linton maintained his 1,200–1,300-acre plantation in Taliaferro County and invested in smaller parcels of agricultural lands in southwestern, central, and northwestern Georgia. Unlike the other industrialists, Linton did not speculate in as diverse investments as banking and distant undeveloped agricultural lands; however, he did win a drawing in the lottery for land lots in the gold area taken from the Cherokee in 1832. Because his interests were not as broad ranging as those of the other industrialists, Linton was not identified in the community's mind other than as a doctor, and so his obituary failed to highlight the industrial and commercial aspects of his life, although the Georgia Railroad's board of directors published a special notice of bereavement.[44]

Like others, the record is silent on the early life of Thomas W. Baxter, another minor industrialist, so one cannot determine if he fit within the parameters of the parvenu-planter life-cycle. But his pattern of non-agricultural investment that supplemented his planting activities matches precedents established by other Athens industrialists. Baxter, born in 1787, probably originated in Hancock County, Georgia, but can be found in Milledgeville, Baldwin County, Georgia, by 1830. By 1832, Baxter worked as a retail merchant in Macon in the firm of Baxter, Fort & Wiley of Macon. He apparently already received public notice when he publicly defended the actions of his partner, Robert W. Fort of Macon, at a time when Fort, the president of the failed Bank of Macon, was accused of bank fraud. Baxter was not implicated in the banking fiasco, nor did his connections to Fort hurt him politically, since in 1835 at least one Democratic newspaper editor suggested Baxter as a dark-horse gubernatorial candidate. But, by June 1836, Baxter removed to Athens, possibly in order to educate his sons at the University of Georgia. He invested in the Athens Factory and became its agent. While in Athens, Baxter continued to pay taxes on town lots owned by his Macon and Milledgeville businesses, demonstrating his continued close connection to them. However, since he did not pay a tax on a stock in trade, those firms probably engaged primarily in cotton speculating rather than retail. Continuing a close business connection to cotton factors made sense while Baxter simultaneously served as the Athens Factory's agent, since such an arrangement would amount to an informal version of vertical integration. But Baxter engaged in other business pursuits as well. He invested in banking, with $20,000 invested in 1837, and by 1840, after three years of depression, his investment principle rose to $22,500.

As the economy turned downward, he privately loaned over $12,000 and increased the amount loaned at usurious rates by $6,000 by 1842. In 1840 he and other Athenians served as commissioners to subscribe stock for the Augusta & Waynesboro Railroad, a feeder to the Georgia Railroad, of which Baxter had been a director since 1838. When William Dearing moved from Athens to Charleston, in November 1841, Dearing appointed Baxter his agent for the rent and sale of his real estate and slaves in Athens. Like Linton and Nisbet, Baxter's slave holdings show signs of speculation with a one-year spike of forty-three slaves in 1843, an increase of thirty over his average holdings of only eleven slaves taxed per year while in Athens. Although generally owning an insufficient number of slaves to be considered a planter by historians, Baxter paid taxes on approximately 250 acres of diverse agricultural lands in southwestern Georgia, and he may have owned distant speculative lands in Mississippi and Texas as well. Like other Athens industrialists, Baxter also developed town lots, paying taxes on lots averaging a value of $5,000 from 1837 until his death in 1844. Baxter frequently traveled to attend to business for the Athens Factory, travel which would have limited direct oversight of his planting activities. However, despite all this non-agricultural activity, when Thomas W. Baxter died of tuberculosis in 1844, his obituary took pains to mention his public character and specifically noted that his business dealings were not of the variety one would associate with a "fast" businessman, as "he was scrupulously exact in all his dealings, and in the various communities in which he resided, acquired a character for honor and punctuality which commanded the confidence and esteem of all who knew him."[45]

Ignoring for the moment the industrial investors, the first-generation industrialists of Athens shared much in common, although they varied as well. Augustin Smith Clayton started Athens's industrialization in 1830 at age forty-six. William Dearing was approximately forty-five years of age when he invested in the Georgia Factory. William Williams moved to Athens in his forty-seventh year and immediately began purchasing the Princeton Factory. James Camak was the youngest of the major industrialists at his entry into industrial investment at age thirty-nine. John Nisbet entered into industrial investments at the age of forty-nine in 1830, when he invested in the Georgia Factory. Dr. Alexander B. Linton joined the Athens Factory partnership with in April 1835, at age fifty-four, two years after he invested $10,000 in the Georgia Railroad. Thomas W. Baxter filled out the list of industrialists, serving as agent of the Athens Factory from the time he joined it in 1835, at age forty-eight, until his death in 1844.

Like parvenus, all engaged in a profession: merchant, lawyer, doctor, banker, and newspaper editor. The average and median age of this cohort was forty-seven years, indicating that all seven industrialists were in the prime of their lives, and, according to the planter-parvenu life-cycle, they should have moved beyond accumulating capital through practicing a profession into a life strictly circumscribed by slave ownership and agricultural pursuits. The four major industrialists differed from the lesser industrialists by achieving statewide or national prominence through their public activities. While all seven achieved social prominence as community leaders, and all seven owned slaves, only three possessed enough slaves to be considered a planter. Like planter parvenus, the entire group evinced a propensity for geographic mobility. None originated in Athens, and most moved several times before settling in Athens. Once invested in Athens, the cost of removal, the age of the industrialists, and the possible need to rebuild social standing in a new location probably contributed towards the group's remaining in the town after other communities started to surpass Athens in commercial, cultural, or industrial promise. Only William Dearing left the town alive, and his relatives returned his body to Athens for its final rest.

A continuing propensity for risk-taking is the defining characteristic of the first-generation industrialist cohort, which makes them very different from what we know of planters. Planters were supposed to be conservative, not risking anything that might jeopardize the opportunity to buy more slaves, land, and cotton. However, the industrialists made many decisions that had nothing to do with raising, shipping, or selling cotton. Nearly all made taxable private loans at some time. All engaged in speculation in town lots, and in distant undeveloped agricultural lands as an investment vehicle for securing long-term wealth. Ownership in slaves varied on an annual basis, and shifted significantly for three of the cohort when pressed for funds for industrial investment. Rather than necessarily leading to slave ownership, then, the pursuit of wealth for Athens's industrialists proved a goal in itself. Clearly the major industrialists were "movers and shakers," men who enjoyed using their accumulated wealth and prestige in shaping the economic and social landscape, in making a difference for the future of their community.

Since the lesser industrialists also acted as community leaders, only at a lower level than the major industrialists, they probably pursued risky investments with the same end in mind. An 1839 letter from the youngest of the cohort, James Camak, to his friend Mirabeau Lamar, the second president of the Republic of Texas, situates this risk-taking propensity, which included industrial activities: "You recollect my love of change. Tho' things are going as well with me here as I could reasonably expect, yet I am getting tired of my situation; and would like to change it, principally because of the want of excitement in the pursuits in which I am engaged. Suppose I come to Texas, what prospect would there be for me in that region to get into some exciting and profitable business?" Industrialization was not the end toward which they worked; it was but one exciting tool utilized in the economic development of their region. While each of the major industrialists lived with a degree of controversy surrounding his public actions, the community never considered any of them a social pariah for bringing industry to the South. Nor did it consider any of the industrialists less elite due to an interest in non-agricultural economic activity.[46]

The lives of Athens's industrialists make evident the need to reevaluate the definition of a planter as merely involving owning more than nineteen slaves. While slavery may have conferred social standing independent of wealth, how much of the standing was based on the value of the slaves, and how much was based on mere ownership of any kind of property? To define a region's elite in such terms prevents clear discussion of variations within the elite, variations based on factors other than slave ownership. Clearly southern industrialists such as these belonged to the town's, to the state's, and to the region's elite. Their lives demonstrate that many sorts of wealth in antebellum Georgia, not just slave ownership, worked in conjunction with public perception of a person's integrity and intellect to form the basis for public authority. Finally, their lives demonstrate that participation in industrial activities did not decrease social standing; rather, public economic activity designed to expand the potential for wealth accumulation, without directly undermining the existing economic substructure of slavery, enhanced social standing, particularly as their locality increasingly meshed with emerging regional and national economies.[47]

The lives of second-generation industrialists demonstrate how these endeavors became routinized among a portion of Athens's elite, with three important changes in the mid-1840s. First, for some, inheriting an interest in the industrial concerns not only conferred a sense of tradition and longevity upon the enterprises, but also short-circuited the parvenu life-cycle. Thus a few needed not pursue a profession to accumulate capital in order to invest in non-agricultural interest. Of those inheriting industrial stock, A. P. Dearing and John S. Linton merit full investigation to discover how continuing their industrial legacies altered the life-cycle. Secondly, as industrial activity became less novel with the passage of time, it took less wealth and social standing to start new industry-related firms. Some of this new, but less prestigious, manufacturing aided the established textile industry—for example, the foundry and the bobbin mill. Others created non-textile manufactures, either as a local source for a needed product—such as the creation of a paper mill, or as a new technology not previously used in Athens—such as the gas works. Albon Chase, William P. Talmage, and William S. Grady serve as good examples of both sorts of industrialists. Finally, the second generation experienced an explosion of investment in industrial activities: investment made possible by routine expectations of dividends from manufacturing enterprises, as well as by the routinization of legal incorporation. With the expansion of ownership, as one might expect, industry became less elite in its breadth, but paradoxically became an avenue for upward social mobility as well.

John S. Linton and Albin P. Dearing became factory agents through family inheritance. Dearing did not directly inherit his appointment, however. In 1845, his father, William Dearing, and his father-in-law, Thomas N. Hamilton, reported to be the richest man in Georgia, purchased the Princeton Factory from William Williams's estate. William Dearing, then a resident of Charleston, however, never became involved in the management of the factory, and sold his 45 percent interest in the $36,000 factory to Hamilton and Asbury Hull. Both Hull and Hamilton preferred to take a back seat in managing the factory's affairs, and they made A. P. Dearing their agent. At the same time, Albin P. Dearing also acted as William Dearing's agent in Athens. However, as late as 1851, A. P. Dearing possessed no taxable property, although he paid the taxes as agent for his father's property in Athens and on the Princeton Factory. Thus credit reporters considered him a risk because the wealth he controlled really belonged to his wife. Through much of the 1850s, he engaged in the grocery business, became an agent of the Athens-based insurance company, and worked as the agent of the Princeton Factory. Eventually he either earned enough, or his father's estate brought him sufficient wealth, to retire from manufacturing (in 1856), and he was elected cashier (the equivalent of agent) of a newly formed Bank of Athens. Following the Civil War, credit reporters considered him worth $250,000. He was elected a director of the Southern Mutual Insurance Company in 1867 and remained a salaried employee of banks in Athens until his death in 1885.[48]

John S. Linton began as a planter parvenu until he came into his father's industrial estate, after which he rose as a major industrialist in Athens. Born in 1813, Linton studied medicine in Philadelphia in the 1830s, but never practiced. Instead, he attempted to establish a plantation in Alabama. After his father's death in 1839, Linton returned to Athens and discovered that little was left him other than the factory stock. Having served as secretary of the Athens Factory partnership in the absence of the company agent, Thomas W. Baxter, Linton became the agent of the Athens Factory upon Baxter's death in 1844. Only after earning a $1,500 annual salary in that position did Linton's wealth increase to taxable levels. John Linton was taxed on his first slave in 1845 but reported no other taxable property. However, the lack of taxable property did not mean he was poor. By 1847, credit reporters estimated his worth at $15,000, invested in agricultural lands, a house, slaves, and factory stock, as he started a new paper mill in partnership with Albon Chase. In the 1850s, Linton continued as the Athens Factory's agent but decreased his involvement with the paper mill to an investment of only $7,000. In 1850, Linton also helped launch a foundry in Athens, but no evidence exists to show that he continued the investment for long. In 1863, he sold his portion of the Athens Factory, roughly three hundred shares, to Robert L. Bloomfield, and he retired from running the factory. After the war, Andrew Johnson's reconstruction plan required that he apply for a special presidential pardon because he owned more than $20,000 in property. He supposedly lost $20,000 in burned cotton during the war, another $100,000 through the emancipation of his slaves, and then he lost the remaining $60,000 of his fortune when he endorsed a note for a friend who failed to pay the note when it came due. In genteel poverty, he sold his town property and retired to his farm. Although no longer an economic power in Athens, Dr. John S. Linton continued to be active in the Grange, in the Presbyterian Church, and in the local agricultural society. Like the industrialists of the first generation, he was memorialized for his industrial and business pursuits. His obituary claimed he "was a potent factor in the upbuilding of the town, and full of public spirit always responded with time, talents and money to every worthy enterprise."[49]

Albon Chase, William Talmage, and William S. Grady represent a change from people with professions as the driving forces behind creating Athens's new industries to individuals with more modest origins in the second generation. While each of them ultimately became an industrial proponent in Athens, none started out that way. Chase came to Athens as a printer, Talmage as a blacksmith, and Grady as a minor merchant. Of the three, Chase probably commanded the most respect since he served as editor and proprietor of the Democratic Party–affiliated *Southern Banner*. Talmage probably rose the least, never really joining the "elite" of the town, and continued to work with his hands even after he became a respected industrial investor. Of the three, the town fathers suspected William S. Grady's character the most, as he was early associated with gold mining in northern Georgia, but Grady ultimately rose to elite status at the same time as he became interested in industrialization.

Albon Chase rose to ranks of industrialist and financier after retiring with a competency from a career as a printer and newspaper editor. Unlike first-generation editor-cum-industrialist James Camak, Chase sported neither a college degree nor a southern pedigree. A native of New Hampshire, Chase probably came to Athens via Columbia, South Carolina (his wife's hometown), as part of his printer journeyman's sojourn. Only arriving in Georgia during the fall of 1830, the twenty-two-year-old took over running the printing business of the local paper, the *Athenian*, in 1831. The following year, he became co-editor and co-proprietor of the *Athenian*'s successor, the *Southern Banner*, which was decidedly Jacksonian in its politics. By 1836, his partner sold out, and he managed the paper alone until he retired in 1846. While Chase frequently chose to moderate the intensity of partisan debates, he remained an ardent Democrat, was elected to town offices on the party's ticket, and to numerous positions within Georgia's Democratic Party as well. But he did not forget his artisan roots, as he helped found the Athens Mechanics Mutual Aid Association and served as its secretary for many years.

Nonetheless, Albon Chase sought to profit from many business opportunities, forming partnerships with carriage builders, book binders, and book sellers, sometimes as a general partner in equal shares, and sometimes as a limited partner, risking only five hundred dollars in the venture. In his stationary shop, he sold textiles in Athens for the Princeton Factory, and when he sold his interest in the newspaper in 1846, he helped found and then ran the Pioneer Paper Mill, which produced newsprint and wrapping paper. The next year, 1847, when Athens stole the Southern Mutual Insurance Company away from another Georgia town, Chase became a director of the company, and, by 1852, he became its secretary and general agent as well. Whenever a new idea created the possibility for profit, Chase was involved. At various times, he promoted devices and medicines as an authorized agent for the out-of-state patent owners. He attempted to publish a newspaper to cater to enthusiasts of growing silk in 1839. Chase was appointed a member of the executive council of an anticipated telegraph company in the early 1850s. He also represented out-of-town firms selling insurance in Athens to supplement the coverage given by the town's insurance company. When he died in 1867 at age fifty-nine, although still the paper mill's agent, the town considered him primarily an insurance man, and the insurance company he served for sixteen years paid him tribute, claiming Albon Chase possessed "all [the] qualities of a good and useful citizen—Sound in judgement, Public spirited and of liberal practical views."[50]

New Jersey native William P. Talmage also pursued numerous lines of profit in Athens, including promoting manufactures after 1850, but found it did not move him into the ranks of the elite. Talmage first arrived in Athens at age twenty-one, in November 1834, and worked as a blacksmith at the forge of his brother, John Talmadge (who spelled his name differently), who had moved to Athens in 1820. William moved around during the 1830s, returning to New Jersey as well as tramping in Georgia and Alabama as a journeyman blacksmith. When John was declared insane in 1841, twenty-eight-year-old William took over John's shop, married the daughter of a local tradesman, and settled in Athens permanently. By the 1850s, William Talmage began to diversify his business enterprises by investing in the foundry started by John Linton, as well as purchasing stock in the paper mill run by Albon Chase. By the 1860s, he also ran the "People's Saw-Mill" on Sandy Creek, to the north of town. From the mid-1860s to mid-1870s, Talmage paid taxes on only about $400 worth of furniture and $4,000 in real estate. Just before his death in 1877, estimates of his real-estate holdings rose to about $8,000. Despite assuming the office of president of the paper mill in the 1850s and 1860s, William P. Talmage remained an artisan all his life. He never joined the elite nor became very wealthy, but he lived reasonably well, despite the periodic propensity of his properties to burn down.[51]

William S. Grady, Henry Grady's father, found a correlation between his industrial activities and his slow rise to elite status. Grady moved to Athens in the early 1840s from North Carolina via the gold fields of northern Georgia, where he operated a small store in conjunction with his brother, John Grady. From the time he arrived in Athens to open an outlet of his brother's store, until the time he abandoned his dry goods business in order to purchase and operate the local gas utility in 1859, credit reporters always worried about William Grady's character and his chance for business success. In short, they thought he took too many risks. He speculated too heavily in cotton, and he gave too much credit. He shifted partners too frequently, often forming a partnership that lasted for just one business venture. Worst of all, in 1852, when Henry Grady was still a toddler, William appeared to have abandoned his wife, his family, and his business to seek a fortune in the California gold fields, and remained out of Athens for two years.

William Grady always seemed to make a buck, to succeed at his risky ventures, and to plan sufficiently for contingencies so that no one could make the accusations of bad character stick. For instance, he paid off any creditor who would not sanction his California sojourn before he went, and he left his business in the hands of his new partner, John W. Nicholson (who married his wife's sister while Grady was in California). When William Grady returned, credit reporters argued whether he had turned a profit or lost it all, but Grady remained solvent despite their doubts. In the late 1850s, he took a risk that paid off; Grady and Nicholson invested in the stock of the High Shoals Factory at the western edge of Clarke County, at a time when such risks looked foolhardy because of the poor receipts of textile factories in Georgia during the 1850s. Soon afterwards, Nicholson's nephew, Rufus Reaves, married the daughter of the factory's president and major stockholder, Isaac Powell, a maneuver which cemented the relationship between Grady's firm and the factory. In conjunction with investing in factory stock, Grady sold most of his business to Nicholson but remained a silent partner in the firm. He then purchased the floundering Athens Gas Works, which had incorporated in the mid-1850s but had not yet found solid financial footing. William Grady turned the firm around, employing his wife's brother, Henry Gartrell, as the gas works superintendent.

At the time of his industrial investments, William Grady found doors to the elite opening for him, doors he had found shut while working simply as a merchant. His wife's distant connection to the elite Cobb family of Athens made some of these social opportunities possible, but his new "conservative-for-Athens" investments in industry probably made him seem less chancy as well. William was elected to local office, remaining until June 1861, when he decided to raise a company of volunteers. Again, his less-than-elite origins may have caused him problems as he could not find enough men to volunteer for his company in Athens (but also in part because everyone so inclined had already volunteered). Not only was he forced to go back to North Carolina to find men for his company, but Georgia refused to sanction the company, and so it took a North Carolina designation. William Grady may have earned elite status in Athens, but he apparently did not command respect at a distance from the town.

After William Grady's death during the war, his brother-in-law, Henry Gartrell, continued to run the gas works for his estate, and his wife ultimately sold the business to the heirs of Howell Cobb, who operated it in the 1870s. However, in the mid-1860s, Henry Gartrell purchased a gas works in Rome, Georgia, and almost disrupted Henry Grady's schooling so that the family could run gas works in both towns. Following his death, William Grady's estate paid taxes on $4,000 in furniture and $50,000 in real estate. Such financial success in his life probably contributed to his moving into more elite circles. William Grady's life demonstrates the potential for social advance through appropriate industrial investments, but it also demonstrates the importance of information networks developed through family connections.[52]

During the first forty years of industrialization in Athens, the demography of its industrialists changed. Founded first by the town's leading men, who had some form of profession and a planting background even if they chose not to pursue it. These were older men who were generally well known in the locality, if not in the state. By the 1850s, smaller enterprises were formed that required more modest, although still significant, sums. Thus, in the second generation, the professions gave way to artisans and minor merchants, men of lesser means who generally invested in an ancillary industry rather than focusing their capital in large enterprises such as railroad, textile factories, and banks. What the two generations of active industrialists shared, despite their class differences, was their propensity to take risks in seeking non-agricultural profits. Yet the descendants of the first-generation industrialists did not pass away from the scene. A few abandoned industry entirely to pursue financial careers, both as private and as very public bankers. But most, with a few important exceptions, formed a broad base of industrial investors, which meant they passively awaited the dividends of their factory stock, becoming active only during annual stockholders' meetings or during special meetings called to respond to a disaster.

INDUSTRIAL INVESTORS

The cohort of first-generation industrial investors echoed the composition of the first-generation industrialists, but with several differences. First, the investor cohort contained more planters than did the cohort of industrialists. Second, the first-generation investors generally risked much smaller sums, averaging only three or four thousand dollars each, rather than the seven to fifteen thousand the industrialists ventured in the factories. Third, the investors tended toward shorter-term investments, although their investment strategies sometimes were simply shortened by an untimely death. Finally, and unsurprisingly, the investors generally seemed much more passive about the management of the business and left the details of running the factories to the industrialists. Thus, while still perhaps members of the local elite for other reasons, most industrial investors cannot be considered members of the industrial elite, except when viewed as an extended family, not as individuals.

A brief sampling of summary biographies of the first-generation industrial investors demonstrates these points. Abraham Walker, who invested with Augustin Clayton in founding the Georgia Factory in 1829, and as well as with Dearing and Nisbet in founding the Athens Factory in 1832, was a lawyer, a planter owning more than seventy slaves and $6,000 in town lots, a major of the local militia, an energetic elder of the Presbyterian Church, and a dutiful trustee of the University of Georgia. He suffered a very public divorce in 1832–33 and died after a short illness in February 1834, at the age of forty-one, which required the surviving Athens Factory partners to dissolve the partnership and liquidate the property in order to satisfy his estate, when the factory burned later that year.[53]

Many of the stockholders who initially incorporated the Princeton Factory followed the same pattern as Walker. Daniel Grant owned a plantation and more than thirty-five slaves in Greene County, as well as town lots in Athens, and ran for election as a local official in Athens several times in the 1830s on the Democratic (Union) Party ticket. He may have been related to Thomas Grant of Columbus, who also invested in the endeavor, as well as to Dr. A. B. Linton, who later joined the Athens Factory. Lawyer William Lumpkin, the brother of the sitting governor of the state (Wilson Lumpkin), owned a plantation with more than fifty slaves in Clarke County and helped found the Georgia Railroad before divesting himself of his Georgia property and investments in order to move to Mississippi. Asbury Hull, a banker, a planter averaging about thirty slaves in the 1830s and forty in the 1840s, was a Whig politician who was already elected the speaker of the Georgia House of Representatives by the time of his initial investment in textiles. Hull continued such investments throughout his prominent life, being active in organizing the Georgia Railroad, investing in the Princeton Factory in the 1840s, serving as chair of the last Southern Commercial Convention before 1840, and as the president of the Southern Mutual Insurance Company, from its inception in Athens until his death in 1866. Dr. Edward R. Ware, a brother-in-law of Asbury Hull and a medical doctor, who, after his short factory investment, served as president of the Athens Branch Bank of the State of Georgia, as a director of the Southern Mutual Insurance Company, and as a municipal elected official. E. L Newton, a minor merchant with a college education, stands out as different from the other Camak Factory investors since his tax assessments rarely declared more than ten slaves, but his town property seemed to increase exponentially with time, and he held at least one hundred shares of Georgia Railroad stock. More importantly, Newton came from a prominent Athens family, and he frequently served as a local elected official, as well as a director of the Southern Mutual Insurance Company.[54]

The second-generation industrial investors differed from the first generation through their inheritance of their stock, but more significantly through their use of family networks to control corporate industrial enterprises. Not only did Athens industrial families intermarry among themselves, they also married into industrial families of other Georgia towns. The children of Thomas W. Baxter married into two other industrial families, one distant, the other local. Baxter's daughter, Mary, married John J. Gresham, who was then mayor of Macon and would become one of the founders of a steam-powered cotton factory in Macon. Baxter's son, Andrew, married Martha Williams, the daughter of the Princeton Factory owner, William Williams, after the deaths of both their fathers. While eschewing direct involvement in running the factories to focus on planting and the retail trade, the Baxter clan continued to receive dividends from their Athens Factory stock well into the postbellum period. In addition to these direct vertical links to industrialization, of one generation to another, the Baxters made horizontal connections as well. Thomas Baxter's wife's brother, Leroy Wiley, of Macon, who was Baxter's partner in their firms in Milledgeville and Macon, invested in Mark Anthony Cooper's iron works in Cass County, after which the firm operated under the firm name of Cooper & Wiley. Congressman M. A. Cooper was brother-in-law to John Nisbet, the Athens industrialist who owned stock in both the Athens Factory and the Georgia Factory. Thus two of Athens's leading industrial families, the Nisbets and the Baxters, after the deaths of the two patriarchs, found family connections through third parties outside Athens.[55]

The Linton and Hull families found a similar industrial investment information network through intermarriage. Dr. John S. Linton, the agent and driving force of the Athens Factory from 1844 to 1863, was already related to the Hulls prior to his inheritance of his father's factory stock. Linton's sister, Mary Cordelia Bacon, was sister-in-law through her husband's sister, Mary Agnes Bacon Hull, to Dr. Henry Hull. Although John S. Linton had already invested with his Hull kin in business ventures in Athens, he created a second stronger link when he married Dr. Hull's daughter, Lucy Ann Hull, in 1849, soon after the Athens Factory reorganized under a corporate charter and the Hull Family bought a large share of the stock. But the Hulls were related to owners of stock in other local factories. Widower Dr. Henry Hull married John Nisbet's daughter, Mary, in 1846, which associated this influential family to both the Baxter and the Williams families. Also, in 1844, Henry Hull Jr. (son of Asbury Hull) married Anna M. Thomas, daughter of Stevens Thomas Sr., and Peninah Thomas, which linked the Hulls to the Thomas's investments in the Scull Shoals Factory in neighboring Greene County. Thus a network, or at least a coalition of influential families, saw industrial investment as a vehicle for securing their financial futures. Therefore, of the twenty-two stockholders listed in the publicly announced incorporation papers of the Athens Factory in 1848, at least eighteen were attached to the Baxter-Nisbet-Linton-Hull-Thomas network of industrial families. Nor did the connection go unnoticed. One credit reporter observed that John S. Linton, as agent of the Athens Factory, "with some relatives [was] controlling the corporation." Similar connections can be seen in other factories, such as the Grady-Nicholson-Reaves-Powell network involved in financing the High Shoals Factory starting in the late 1850s.[56]

Clearly, there are implications from all this intermarriage among manufacturing families prior to 1850. Within just one industrializing community, one can easily see the formation of an intermarried business cohort whose industrial and financial interests lay throughout the state and was connected to other community elites. This enterprising elite can be extrapolated across the boundaries of localities with the passing of only a generation or two. Clearly, intermarriage reduced the risks in pursuing industrial investment strategies, since working within an extended family reduced the investment risks to limited capital caused by poor information flows, and since family connections encouraged the exchange of investment information and restrained some from purposely perpetrating frauds. Although no evidence suggests that these families self-consciously pursued a marriage strategy to link with other industrial families, they nevertheless did intermarry and then used the new relations to form business alliances. The extended family connections had another effect on industrial organization as well.[57]

The corporate form of business has frequently been noted for its democratic possibilities, which at first glance seemed to be the case for the textile industry under Georgia's relaxed charter laws in the late 1840s. Corporations, the theory goes, allow many investors, some with smaller amounts to invest, to share in the risks and profits, giving all a collective stake and a voice in the business of the firm. The diversity of class representation in ownership of the firm moderates the conduct of the firm's business and promotes social responsibility for the actions of the firm, avoiding the sort of profit-mongering that might negatively impact a community. But when viewed from the standpoint of an extended family, the corporate format differed little from the partnerships, other than from the limits of debt liability. Instead of spreading risks and opportunities about, a corporation composed of extended family groupings concentrated them in the hands of the heirs of the first-generation industrialists. Thus, if viewing extended-family investments as aggregates, investment in and control of industrial enterprises during the second generation of southern industrialization tended to replicate the investment-and-control patterns of the first days of industrialization: participation was limited to a wealthy few. But now the links between families concentrated the control into fewer groups, even though many more individuals were represented.[58]

By the close of the antebellum period, Athens developed the human capital needed to sustain industrialization. A sufficient number of laborers worked within the system to make industrial work routine for non-elite Athenians. The town began training a technical managerial staff to supplement its homegrown business office staff. Industrialists learned that less was needed for start-up capital for ancillary industries, and that family-dominated corporations made best use of limited capital for larger enterprises. Within Athens, therefore, workers, managers, industrialists and investors all learned what to expect from industrial enterprises, and how to work with them. But learning does not just apply to individuals. Athens's society also learned how to interact with manufacturing as a new form of social organization, and to make it productive enough to sustain investors' interest. To understand the full extent of this learning process, therefore, we must evaluate how local culture made industrialization respectable.

3

THE CULTURE OF INDUSTRIALIZATION

As this is the age of improvement . . . all appear anxious to husband the resources of the country and to develop new ones.
—Augustin Clayton, *Southern Banner*, August 3, 1833

The advent of cotton factories was but one of many forms of "improvement" in Athens before the New South era. This broad impulse to improve arose from an indigenous culture and demonstrates, contrary to popular scholarly belief, that the reform movements evident throughout the antebellum North and West played significant roles in the antebellum South as well. Unlike the situation in the North, however, industrialization did not prove the motive behind the desires for improvement. Instead, industry and other improvements experienced parallel development because they sprang from the same source: a population increasing in both size and respectability. In the end however, the Athens elite found support for their improving agenda only within their own town, and even then other forces within southern society forestalled carrying the reforms to the same level of completion as one would have found in the North.[1]

Athens's reform impulse emerged from a growing population seeking to retain or enhance its respectability. Because the town possessed the state's university, Georgia's elite congregated there at least once per year to celebrate commencement and to partake in a variety of popular and intellectual entertainments. But the town also lured monied and enterprising people who desired to participate regularly in the kind of culture offered during commencement. As a result, popular and elite forms of entertainment were promoted regularly. But town members also cultivated a local version of the wave of change that they perceived as engulfing the entire nation. Thus they experimented in opening educational opportunities, in establishing institutional religion, in creating institutions of mutual support, in adopting scientific agriculture, in promoting temperance, in providing for poor relief, and even in exploring what might be misconstrued as a form of abolitionism. Unsurprisingly, the same cast of characters that introduced industrialization participated in these other forms of improvement as well, not because their industrial background privileged them, but because they led the town in nearly every civic endeavor. However, just as these town leaders participated in industry in varying intensities, they also devoted various levels of time and resources to promoting these other reforms. Thus, understanding how the community engaged in improvement reveals variations among the elite and illuminates some of the class, gender, and racial dimensions of the culture that sustained industrial efforts. These cultural activities created an aura of respectability that acted as a social portal for upwardly mobile members of the lower classes in Athens.

Respectability, of course, is a slippery concept. However, in Athens, the term was frequently used in a fashion similar to its use in the North. The respectable sorts of all classes of society worked hard at their immediate tasks to improve their own lot in life, and to improve the world around them. Similar adjectives as northerners would use to describe the respectable of their society—punctual, forbearing, honest, charitable and thrifty—all seemed applicable to the responsible in Athens. In the business life of Athens, variations of these attributes included declining to seek excessive profits at the expense of one's neighbor and refusing to disrupt established patterns of doing things. In short, a respectable person understood the fine line between working toward improving their town, state, and region and upsetting the social order. A respectable southerner did not rock the boat and acted neither unpredictably nor rashly. Instead, the respectable of Athens exuded a confidence that came with working within the comfortable limits of extending their existing world.[2]

"Improvement" also needs clarification. Why use the term instead of the more common idea of "progress" when discussing reform movements, particularly since the two seem very similar? Historians have previously demonstrated that southerners embraced progress and modernity on their own terms. Southerners desired the rewards of material and technological advances but worried about their political and moral ramifications. Most of all, they saw material progress as the handmaiden of moral reform. Improving the physical environment not only increased general prosperity but promulgated moral uplift. "Improvement" better captures the correlation between material life and uplift because, unlike "progress," it is not laden with the ideological ambiguities of an intervening 150 years of definitions. But also, "improvement" is the term Jacksonian Americans—North, South, and West—would have used to describe the material and social experiments taking place.[3]

Americans in the 1830s usually talked of improvements as embodying material advances. For instance, they called railroads, toll roads, and canals internal improvements. The facilities of factories they considered industrial improvements. New warehouses and stores constituted municipal improvements. Each type of physical change advanced the enterprise of community building, binding different geographic areas or social classes together in common endeavor. But the proponents of improvement clearly understood the political and social effects of the introduction of these material changes and so connected the idea of improvement to altering social and cultural mores. More importantly, they believed that, to benefit from one area of improvement, one must pursue change across the board, simultaneously.

Athenians of the Age of Jackson accepted improvement as a regional as well as national spirit and envisioned it as an interlocking set of relationships that worked for the betterment of all. Augustin Clayton, founder of manufacturing in Athens, explored the meshing of these connections in a speech promoting educational reforms at the time that he constructed Athens's first factory. Clayton explained, in 1829, "We constitute one of a sisterhood of States, all laudably ambitious to excel in everything which will ameliorate the condition of the people. In all the great purposes of Internal Improvement, Education and Domestic Manufactures, there is rivalship between [the States], and a strong continued effort to produce some happy consequence upon the state of society. Shall we decline to enter the lists of such a grand and spirited contest?" Improvement, therefore, is grounded in, but includes more than, economic and physical advances. Besides creating prosperity and uplifting the morals of local society, it also includes a sense of competition among familiar equals.[4]

Athenians were not atypical southerners in their understanding of improvement as an interlocking series of reforms requiring simultaneous adoption. Other Georgians accepted similar conceptualizations. For example, the state legislature's Committee of Finance declared that its policy priorities for spending the tax turn-backs from the federal government on education and transportation reforms in 1836 were not only expected by their constituents, but were required to "preserve unimpaired, our political influence in the Union" as well as the state's status in agriculture and commerce. Thus the committee stated the negative implications of the concept, as well as exposing the breadth of public acceptance. Failure to improve at the same rate as other states would ultimately result in political suicide within the Union as other states improved their societies and attracted greater populations, while Georgia did not.

Another editorial used both carrot and stick to urge Georgians to support internal and other improvements, arguing that, if Georgians failed to promote them, "we must soon sink far below the station assigned us by a beneficent Providence among our fellows." However, the spirit of improvement "promises to give a new and profitable impulse to the energies of the farmer, the planter, the mechanic and the capitalist" alike. Thus like Lewis Carroll characters, Georgians in the Jacksonian Era believed they must remain in constant motion in order to hold their current place. To retain its political equality among the states, Georgia (and by extension, the South) needed to pursue improvement—physical, economic, moral, intellectual, social and cultural—with a vengeance. Athens uniquely provided a suitable environment in which to test the compatibility of these improvements with southern sensibilities.[5]

Culture was Athens's reason for existence. In many ways, Athens was the university and the university was the town, so interlaced were their identities. Unlike northern college towns, wealthy and ambitious families relocated to Athens while their sons attended college. An advertisement of the sale of one plantation aptly demonstrates the centrality of education to in-migrating, as the seller stated "the situation is healthy and sufficiently near . . . the College for all the advantages of the schools." Such comments were widespread, but the schools created an intellectual culture not found elsewhere in the state. Thus people chose to locate in Athens because it already contained so many other people with desires for living in a cultured town, and this cultural corps "forms a powerful attraction, and brings people in from the plantations of the interior, to make [Athens] their permanent home." While Athens's citizens primarily concerned themselves with the education of their sons, the town also provided cultural resources for the finishing of their daughters and the educational entertainment of their families. An exploration of the institutions of formal education provides a window into the social imperatives of Athens.[6]

INSTITUTIONS OF EDUCATION

At the center of the movement for improvement was institutional education, and the foremost educational institute in Athens was the University of

Georgia. Without the college, Athens would not have existed, since the town did not even serve the function of a county seat. Many of the town's industrializers found themselves in strong association with the school at some point of their lives, as students, as faculty, or as parents of students.

In many ways, it appears that the degree of identification with the university contributed to the definition of one's social standing in the community, and so many of Athens's industrialists remained connected to the college throughout their lives. Augustin Clayton received his baccalaureate degree, as the class poet, in the college's first graduating class in 1804, and he helped found the school's first literary society, the Demosthenian Society, of which he remained an honorary member thereafter. After graduation, Clayton served as secretary to the school's board of trustees and was later appointed to the board himself. He served on the college's Prudential Committee, and was renowned for mediating any difficulties among faculty, administrators, and students of his alma mater.[7]

Other community leaders maintained similar lifelong connections to the college. James Camak carried on a long relationship with the University of Georgia, serving as a professor of mathematics for two years. Later, he too was appointed a trustee and, like Clayton, served in that position for the rest of his life. Other industrialists serving on the board of trustees included Abraham Walker, Thomas N. Hamilton, Stevens Thomas, and Asbury Hull. Still others associated with Athens's industrialization—including Stevens Thomas (who invested in Scull Shoals Factory in neighboring Greene County), Ephraim Hopping (a native New Yorker who tutored the university students in the early 1830s before he started a cotton factory at High Shoals), and William L. Mitchell (an attorney who briefly served as the Athens Factory's president in the 1850s)—served on the school's board of visitors, examining students before approving their advancement or graduation. Some acted in various ad hoc capacities, such as when Alexander B. Linton advertised for bids to construct the new Phi Kappa Society building on behalf of the committee of student members. The industrialists also sometimes lodged students, either for profit or as a favor to friends. For instance, Dr. A. B. Linton boarded several students in different years, probably for profit. Alexander H. Stephens (future vice-president of the Confederacy) resided for a while with William Dearing due to their families' relationships in Wilkes County. Nearly all the industrialists' sons attended the school, and thus all wished the university success.

The industrialists' interest in the university's appearance is illustrative of their continued association with the school, as well as the ongoing interconnections between the university and the improvement of the town.[8]

Several times in the antebellum period, leading townsmen noticed the unkempt grounds of the university and called for their transformation. In 1830, an anonymous group of the town's elite issued such a call to rehabilitate the dilapidated grounds of the college and then nominated a committee, which included Augustin Clayton, to oversee the efforts. Significantly, this notice called the beautification of the campus a "species of internal improvement" and requested friends of the project to donate the labor of their slaves and mules as well to provide equipment or trees. In 1847 and 1859, similar projects improved the campus's appearance again. Clearly, the university functioned as the center of the town's economy, its culture, and its aesthetics. It played a similar role in developing the town's other institutions of education.[9]

Throughout the antebellum period primary and grammar schools in Athens started elite boys on their way to gaining entrance to the university. Primary schools, according to one alumnus of the system, taught basic literacy and numeracy while grammar schools, which were also called academies, occupied the niche between the primary schools and the university by introducing students to the basics of Latin and Greek. An advertisement for the Parley Place Primary School in 1839, sponsored by Athens Factory agent Thomas W. Baxter, indicates that the primary schools operated co-educationally, accepting both boys and girls. Basic literacy and numeracy skills proved so important to the commercial and industrial improvement of Athens that the town's newspaper editor suggested the citizens of the state voluntarily select impoverished but promising students from their midst and provide them with a college education, in exchange for a four-year commitment to teaching primary school in the community that sponsored them. Among other benefits, the author thought his plan would reduce class antagonism, as "the benefits of the College be extended to the poor as well as the rich." The population of Athens increasingly utilized these basic educational facilities with on-going industrialization. Although no data exists for 1830, when industrialization originated, the 1840 census enumerated five primary schools with 170 students in Clarke County, and the 1850 census counted seventeen such schools with 482 students. The grammar schools demonstrate a comparable increase.[10]

Athens promoted the equivalent of a high-school education from the time of the town's creation. The university operated its own grammar school, from 1808 to 1829, after which William L. Mitchell ran the academy as a private business from 1829 to 1831. When it looked as if the Athens Grammar School would close in 1831, a town meeting appointed a committee that included Asbury Hull and William Dearing to petition the academy's trustees to re-establish the school, to guarantee payment to the teacher, and to relocate the facility to a more convenient location in upper-town Athens. When successfully re-established, the academy promised a salary of one thousand dollars annually, plus whatever amount above one thousand dollars that the academy might earn through tuition, to a teacher who could give instruction in the standard texts needed for gaining college entrance, including: "1. English Grammar, 2. Arithmetic, including fractions, and . . . [square] roots . . . 3. Caesar's Commentaries. 4. Virgil. 5. Cicero's Orations. 6. Greek Testament. 7. Graeca Minora." During the time that the school offered these terms, the instructor, Granby Hillyer, supplemented his income through an appointment as a tutor to the college students. Just as those who supported industrialization served in higher education, they also aided institutions of preparatory education, with E. L. Newton (an investor in the Camak Factory) acting as secretary of the school's trustees, and William Dearing (of the Athens Factory) serving as the board's president. At the same time that these agents of improvement provided for various levels of education of Athens's boys, they also educated their girls.[11]

Citizens of Athens also supported a girls' school from the 1820s onward. The Athens Female Academy combined the functions of the primary and grammar schools for boys, advertising for students aged five to fifteen years. It also combined the curriculum of both male institutions with its 1828 courses consisting of "Spelling and Reading, Grammar, Arithmetic, Geography, Chemistry, Rhetoric, Logic, Philosophy, Chronology and History." A few years later, the school added Latin, Greek, and mathematics, and students could purchase art and music instruction for an extra fee. Like the boys' schools, the girls' school publicly examined the knowledge of its students to ensure the quality of their education. Also like the boys' schools, the girls' school did not last. In 1836, another town meeting decided to reopen the school "upon a more extensive scale and more durable basis" than previously. Augustin Clayton served as the chairman of the new school's board of trustees, and the meeting elected industrialists William Williams, Asbury Hull, and Thomas N. Hamilton to the board. Later still, in the 1840s, the town opened yet another facility, the Athens High School for Young Ladies, which may have usurped the grammar-school functions of the Athens Female Academy. The inability to consistently remain open did not drastically interfere with the education, and status, of the female children of the most elite in Athens, who could find a place in one of the small primary schools run by widowed European aristocrats, such as those provided by Madame Gouvaine before the Civil War, or by Madame Sosnowski after the war. With the founding of the Lucy Cobb Institute in the late 1850s, the town gained a permanent girls' high school which would survive well into the twentieth century. Despite their high-minded intentions of providing an education and a social finish for their girls, the facilities served practical purposes in city-building as well.[12]

The girls' schools in Athens attracted patrons from a distance. The parents either moved to Athens to educate their daughters, or they boarded girls at the school. Either way, Athens gained from the situation. Parents chose to educate the girls there for practical reasons. One letter to the newspaper explained that people moved to Athens in order to educate both sexes of their children, because, as the university would provide the future legislators of the state, the town's girls' school would provide the wives and friends of those future legislators. That is, a girl could find a better mate through courting the young men attending the university than she might catch if attending school elsewhere in the state. The curriculum and the connections, Athens's town fathers hoped, would convince "parents to send their daughters to this place in preference to one more remote and possessing less advantage." Thus the parents formed a symbiotic relation with Athens; both parents and the local practical culture profited from one another, and education from an early age delimited social status in the town.[13]

Athens's lower classes also found access to improved status through education. In the years accompanying early industrialization, the churches instituted Sabbath or Sunday schools designed both to increase the literacy of the lower orders in town and to inculcate moral values in them. Originally only the Presbyterian Church offered a Sunday school, purportedly because its facilities were located on college property, and because it offered a non-denominational version, under a union Sunday school plan. In offering this sort of public service, those who attended could obtain some literacy and arithmetic skills, while neither paying the tuition of the private schools, nor subjecting themselves to the indignity of attending the chronically underfunded poor schools for the indigent of the county. In return, the Presbyterian Church—which represented most of the town's elite—probably recruited more of the school's scholars than did the other churches in town. As other denominations became better organized, they initiated their own sectarian Sunday schools to pre-empt the Presbyterian recruitment efforts.[14]

Athens's churches also used the structure of the Sabbath schools to bring religious instruction to the town's slave population. One Presbyterian report evaluated the law forbidding the teaching of literacy skills to slaves and decided that the church could (and must) give religious instruction to them, even if the teaching of reading and writing was proscribed. However, not all slave owners approved of their slaves' participation, and some sought legal recourse to forbid their slaves' attendance, specifically requesting "those who have charge of the Sunday School in Athens, for the instruction of the coloured people, to prevent his Negroes in future from becoming members of that school—and [to] dismiss those . . . who have already joined." Some slaves in Athens clearly participated in literate culture, even if they could not themselves read, since they received instruction in Sunday school, which must have included the reading of scripture. Also, one cannot review the monthly notices of letters in the post office awaiting retrieval without periodically noticing letters addressed to slaves. One cannot assume that slaves read the letters, but they did participate in the culture of improvement by receiving the written word from a distance. Notwithstanding sectarian differences and opposition to instruction of slaves, by 1844, over three hundred students attended the town's various Sunday schools, which in itself is an indication of the increasing value placed on education by the underclasses of Athens.[15]

In addition to indirect indications of possible literacy among slaves, there are occasional direct references. One narrative from a former slave of Thomas R. R. Cobb suggests the resources for slaves to learn to read were not too difficult to obtain in Athens, claiming that more than one of "Marse Tom's" slaves were literate and that "Aunt Vic" read the Bible regularly. The case of Lucius Henry Holsey exemplifies the potential for the improvement of the enslaved. In the late 1850s, Holsey, a teenaged mulatto carriage driver owned by a college professor, sold rags to the town's paper mill in order to surreptitiously purchase books with which he taught himself to read. But he did not quite do it all on his own. The white children of his household took pleasure in reviewing his lessons from time to time. The experience created a "burning desire" to learn in Holsey and set him on a path to becoming a national leader of the Colored Methodist Episcopal Church following emancipation. Holsey is particularly illustrative of how the various strands of improvement in Athens held the potential for catalyzing all segments of society, and for opening doors for upward social movement within specified hierarchical paths. Industrialization here combined with educational opportunities. Had the paper mill not existed, Holsey might have found other options for earning his book money, but as it was, his chance came because slaveholders apparently overlooked rag collecting by slaves, and because they ignored how their children flouted the laws regarding slave literacy. Holsey's first steps toward social advance were taken during slavery, and his social mobility, even after emancipation, was circumscribed by the racial context of the times in which he lived. But slaves were not the only underclass desiring improvement, nor the only ones directed toward specific paths of social respectability.[16]

The upper classes of Athens attempted to encourage, and possibly to co-opt, the opportunity for formal education of the white underclass. For a year the Presbyterian Educational Society of Georgia experimented with a manual labor grammar school which they opened adjacent to Athens. In October 1832, this society held a conference in Athens specifically to devise the experiment, and then it publicized plans to purchase the 450-acre plantation of the son of Athens industrialist John Nisbet (who also served as one of the secretaries of the conference). The idea of moral improvement is clearly demonstrated by the order in which the society listed the admission of potential candidates for the school: poor boys who desired to study to become Presbyterian ministers were given top priority; other Presbyterians desiring to prepare for college would be considered second; third and last, members of other orthodox Protestant denominations would be admitted as space allowed. This school project thus served more than one goal as it sought to improve class relations while providing more ministers. Industrialist William Dearing, as chairman of the school's trustees, published the official prospectus of the school later that year; and the school began operations in January 1833 under the tutelage of W. W. Waddel, son of the previous president of the University of Georgia. During the year, letters in the local newspaper commented on the workings and benefits of the general scheme of manual labor schools, with which many communities around the nation were experimenting. The annual report—attested to by Athens Factory partners William Dearing and John

Nisbet—at the conclusion of the first year indicated that the school raised sufficient crops to support itself, without impeding the education of its scholars. They declared the school a success and fully expected other denominations and communities in Georgia to emulate their work. The following August, however, the state Presbyterian Education Society, which met again in Athens during commencement, decided to move the school and appointed prominent Athens Presbyterians William Dearing, William L. Mitchell, and E. L. Newton to dispose of the school's property near Athens. Exactly why they abandoned the school's first site is a matter of speculation.[17]

This shift can be interpreted in two ways. First, there may have been something dreadfully wrong with the site near Athens. One historian ruminated that Athens was too cosmopolitan for such an endeavor, but given the improving milieu of Athens prior to the school's inception, this interpretation is unlikely. Early reports indicated the farm to be profitable enough to support its charges, so the economics of the situation probably had negligible effect as well. The choice of the school's new site suggests that church politics rather than the school's profits or morals proved the deciding factor. In December 1834, the Presbyterian Education Society announced the creation of two new branches of the manual labor school; the society would build a literary school at Midway, about two miles from the state capital at Milledgeville, and construct a preparatory school, like the one previously operated near Athens, in Gwinnett County, near Lawrenceville. The literary school soon became Oglethorpe College, the Presbyterian Church's entry into the denominational college competition of the 1830s. In essence, the society decided that Athens already possessed sufficient advantages over other aspiring towns in Georgia, and so it moved the manual labor school "to a more suitable location" in order to transfer the economic advantages of having an educational institution of statewide importance to another deserving community. By dividing the efforts to two locations, the society could please several groups at once. Athens, in the minds of most Georgians in the Age of Jackson, needed no such help.[18]

Rather than submit to the charity of, and control by, the elite, Athens's skilled working people, its mechanics, established a school of their own to teach their children what they thought important, and to start them on a path of respectability. Throughout the 1840s, Athens's mechanics operated a school for their sons to receive the "English education" acquired by the younger children of the town's elite at their academies. Significantly, the specification of an

"English education" seemed to ignore the study of the classic Greek and Latin as non-essential subjects for practical people, as unnecessary for those not expected to attend the university. Why did the mechanics choose to operate their own school, rather than attend schools frequented by children of the elite? While the costs of these elite schools and the probable discrimination against admitting less-than-elite scholars obviously played an important role, so did the extent of class conflict between elites and non-elites in Athens.[19]

CLASS CONFLICT, CLERKS, AND MECHANICS

Athens was never an undifferentiated mass of gentility. By the 1840s, the town possessed a growing class of clerks who rose from humble origins and sought to prove themselves worthy of becoming a partner with a man of capital who would finance their retail ambitions. It also boasted a large coterie of mechanics who provided essential services for the community and jealously guarded their dignity against comparison with slave labor. Not surprisingly, the town demonstrated evidence of class antagonism between those who worked with their hands and those who did not.[20]

Articles in the Athens newspapers suggest a problem of class antagonism in the industrializing town. From the late 1820s to the 1840s, Albon Chase, the editor who operated the *Southern Banner* as a master printer, frequently published articles dwelling on the dignity of labor and on the prevailing prejudices in all sections of the country against the working classes. In an article reprinted from a Massachusetts newspaper, and published in Athens about the same time local elites began discussing building textile factories in the area, the author asserted the equality, if not superiority, of mechanics to the upper classes because mechanics produced tangible things. He argued that the artisan who understands both the theory and practice of his craft possessed more intellectual capacity "than twenty of those minute philosophers who spend their time in the world with empty metaphysical speculations." The statement reveals a cleavage between those without classical education and those possessing one, or more aptly, a battle between town and gown. Other articles revisited the same theme by comparing the useless but highly educated fop to the manly mechanic wrongfully considered inferior by a society resting on pre-revolutionary aristocratic prejudices. Finally these articles injected issues of gender and class reproduction by discussing how a mechanic's daughter or son would serve as the perfect spouse for all upwardly mobile Americans since they understood the work ethic, while the child of gentility would flounder in dissipation.[21]

Athens engaged in its own battles between social classes, which explains why the local editor considered the reprinted northern articles relevant to his readers. The message intended for southerners, however, differed slightly from that received by northerners reading the same tract. Rather than deriding the dress and manners of the fop as an emerging group, the message here aimed at class relations. In one telling example, a letter to the editor expressed regret that young women exiting church on Sundays were forced to transit through the stares of the crowd of "rude boys and unpolished mechanics" always gathered at the church's doors. "A Mechanic" replied to the insults to his class, and took the original writer, "Friend of Virtue," to task, explaining, "It is easy to perceive from your writing to what class of society you belong. You are, no doubt, one of those young men who have just broke from the leading strings of the Professors and Tutors of College." The "Mechanic" verbally boxed the ears of the "Friend of Virtue," explaining that no mechanics belonged to the crowd outside the church and that the writer needed to learn a little more about life before insulting useful citizens. But the problem of differentiation was not limited to jibes between mechanics and college students.[22]

Class resentment against the upper classes of Athens by the agricultural class of laborers from whence the mass of clerks in town arose also is also evident in the press. Another letter to the editor explained the difference in manners between country folk and their city brethren in church. The writer questioned why the young men of Athens took seats reserved for women, why they did not relinquish them for late-arriving females, and why church attendance appeared primarily an opportunity to demonstrate one's wealth and social standing. The country writer "thought every body was looking at my homespun suit, and listening to my heavy tread, and laughing at my awkward gait." He railed against Athens's society and sarcastically claimed he would eventually know what qualities constituted urban "politeness," only after he had abandoned his background, his friendships, and his freedom to act as he chose. While one cannot discount that this may simply be a jeremiad against the sin of pride, its author clearly seemed unhappy with the urbanity of his surroundings. And the discomfort fits within a framework of class differentiation and resentment in the urban South. Descriptions of Athens's municipal geography similarly demonstrate class differentiation and antagonism.[23]

In 1836, a visitor commented at length about the sectional rivalries that existed within Athens. Members of both sections, "upper town" and "lower town," suggested he avoid the other section as an unpleasant place. Yet the writer found that persons in both parts of town were equally attentive to his needs and equally friendly and intelligent. He finally commented, "This sectional feeling or spirit is unfortunate, and if not checked, is sooner or later to do harm. Pity that in a community so intelligent as that of Athens, such a foible should be suffered to exist. And I am told that it did not exist a few years since." Others used similar geographic bounds to describe portions of Athens. Professor Charles F. McCay, while developing actuarial statistics in the 1840s, divided the town in three parts: upper town, middle town, and the factory village. In effect McCay split "lower" town in two, while leaving upper town intact. The differing death rates he evaluated sprang from class and occupational differences between the sections. Lower town contained the textile factory and housed its operatives, while middle town billeted the clerks and petit merchants of the town. Not surprisingly, as a result of class-based occupational differences, lower town's death rate routinely exceeded upper town's. That Athens only recently developed the geographic split along class lines indicates the confluence of the town's accelerating discomfort about disruptions in its sensibilities about hierarchy as the factories attracted a growing population of the landless and the desperate. After 1830, the town's most respectable families increasingly lived in upper town, and they worked to move their children's schools nearer to them.[24]

Relief for Athens's poor demonstrated similar geographic divisions. Athens's systems of providing for social reciprocity reflected the same class-based geographic divisions as used by the actuary. At the same time the county government constructed a work house for the county's poor at the county seat in Watkinsville, the elite of Athens organized the town's Benevolent Society in 1838. The society's constitution divided the town into three districts for the visiting committees to inspect the needs of the respectable poor and to dole out charity to them. The committees divided the established part of town into northern and southern districts, and established a third district for the newer sections to the west of the longer-established sections. The Southern District embraced the middle and lower towns described above, and the Northern District contained the upper town.

While local institutionalized charity grew out of efforts to provide relief for disaster victims at a distance, namely after fires swept Charleston in 1838 and Tallahassee in 1843, the philanthropic organization delineated the respectable members of the upper crust and of the impoverished of Athens. As exemplars of respectability, Athens's industrialists served as officers of the new society. William Dearing, president of both the Athens Factory and the Georgia Railroad, as well as James Camak, cashier of the Georgia Railroad Bank, served on the Prudential Committee. Thomas W. Baxter, agent of the Athens Factory and a director of the Georgia Railroad, served on a visiting committee. The elite did not intend to assist able-bodied mechanics and clerks as objects of their charity, but only the poor they considered "deserving." As in northern industrial towns, the poor in Athens merited charity only if they failed to sustain themselves despite making efforts to raise themselves up. The poor who worked were respectable, and thus deserved the support of the community to revitalize their own efforts to improve their situations.[25]

Athens intended its middling sorts to set an example for the poor that a work ethic equated to personal independence. Positive newspaper articles presented successful mechanics (and by extension in Athens—successful clerks) as the perfect representation of the American ideal, fulfilling the spirit of an age of improvement. One such article in the Athens papers claimed not only respectability for laboring to improve oneself, but also that "industry and virtuous ambition are seldom exerted in vain." The self-made man, the icon of Jacksonian democracy in the North, was thus touted as the ideal in the South as well. That all white men could rise to a station in society according to their talents, unhindered by their humble origins, was the moral repeated in this organ of the Democratic-Union Party in Georgia. Performance within the bounds of accepted society provided the ladder of success to all. Poor performance of one's social tasks could result in downward mobility, just as easily as exceeding society's expectations could move one upward. The mechanic who took the college student to task for insulting all mechanics attempted to explain that "college learning is the mere working tools of your future profession; and that as you use them skillfully or unskillfully, you will, like the mechanic, either be set down a jack-leg or skillful workman."[26]

While Athens's society saw clerks and mechanics as agents for determining their own future through their individual merits, as a group these young men received unsolicited notice from the public that they must seek self-improvement. Respectability for these groups came from concentrating first on improving their literacy and numeracy. Failure to pursue intellectual improvement would cripple a promising clerk or mechanic with bad habits, expensive tastes, and a poor choice of friends. The author of this passage, writing under the pseudonym Senex, seemed intent that the rough-and-tumble popular culture of mechanics and clerks in New York should be avoided in Georgia, and he assumed that all sought the same end of material advance. Some of the town's mechanics explicitly understood the culture against which Senex wrote since they had come to Athens from places in which a clerking culture dominated. For instance, Robert Hodgson, one of the brothers who came from Troy, New York, to start a carriage-building shop in Athens in the 1840s, was critically reported to have been "rather wild," and "fond of fun and frolic," before he settled down as a respectable artisan in Athens. But unlike those who tried to rein in cultural rebels in New York, Senex did not promote forcing "twenty-something" journeymen and clerks to join churches to enforce their good behavior. Instead he merely suggested they could voluntarily modify their behavior to their advantage by partaking of the prevailing culture of improvement in Athens. The town already provided at least one vehicle for mechanics to alleviate their class resentment through programs of self-improvement.[27]

The Athens Mechanics Mutual Aid Association worked to establish mechanics as a respectable class in antebellum Athens. This mechanics society came into existence by 1832 and published its constitution in 1836. The association rejected simple trade unionism and claimed its place among Athens institutions of respectability, explaining, "The Society deem it of importance that the true objects of their Association should be understood by the community, particularly as they have learned that an impression exists in the minds of some, that it is a trade combination to regulate the prices of work. This idea they utterly repudiate. Their object is mutual improvement, and they hope through the facilities afforded by their Association, to become better mechanics and more useful and intelligent citizens."[28]

Acting to fulfill this pledge, the mechanics society became a microcosm of Athens's larger plan of improvement. Through its burial insurance and widow's pension policies it attempted to provide charitable relief for its own deserving poor. To deserve this relief, the mechanic must keep his dues current. While these services comprised its primary benefit, the Athens Mechanics Mutual

Aid Association moved to consummate its plan to improve its members. The society sponsored orations and debates of current topics as well as educational lectures at its monthly and annual meetings. Their constitution provided rules for operating a library, and the society soon began acquiring books through donations. By 1844, they owned sufficient books to open a reading room, and the association invited public subscriptions that enhanced their collection, so that by 1850 the reading room contained fifteen hundred volumes. And of course, the mechanics opened a school for their children. In the process of fulfilling their pledge of self-improvement, the mechanics acquired a Mechanics Hall that served as their meeting place, functioned as their library, and housed their school. By the 1850s, several of the master mechanics who served as officers of the society in the 1830s and 1840s (Albon Chase and William P. Talmage, for example), graduated into industrialists and merchants, and thus they not only imbibed the improving spirit that abounded in Athens, but used it to move entirely out of their class.[29]

The Athens Mechanics Mutual Aid Association, despite being a vehicle for class improvement, never evolved beyond its original intentions. No workingman's party emerged from its confines. Neither did it call for the abolition of slavery, nor for a revolution of the working classes. Embedded within a hierarchical society, the association provided space for venting frustration without rupturing existing social norms. One had to be a workingman to become a member, and only members could attend and vote at the association's meetings, but it also invited non-workingmen to attend as honorary members, and frequently asked members of the elite to provide the lectures by which the mechanics improved themselves. In short, the master mechanics were petty businessmen who relied upon the patronage of the elites. So the master mechanics, those who were the most permanent members of their class in Athens, participated in maintaining the hierarchy of Athens society, despite their statements of support of the equality of all classes of citizens. For Athens's mechanics, respectability meant becoming more like the elite. Improvement alleviated conflict by raising a few men out of their class, rather than reducing barriers between classes. Given the culture of improvement and its links to respectability, Athens's mechanics did not find an alternate path to prosperity though their association. Instead, like the town's clerks, their route was already established. Those seeking respectability could not create institutions with truly independent agendas; they could advance only by participating in the informal institutions elite Athenians created to promote mental culture in the 1830s.

CULTURAL ENTERTAINMENTS AND EDUCATION

Improvement frequently clothed itself in the guise of popular entertainment in industrializing Athens. Throughout the Jacksonian Era, the town's newspapers announced the arrival of musical troupes, the staging of theatrical and minstrel shows, as well as the procession of circuses and freak shows. Many of these entertainments came around the time of the college's commencement, but some also appeared in the winter months when a southern tour proved more congenial to traveling shows. Because the number of such entertainments exceeded what one would expect for such a small town, the upwardly mobile were frequently advised to avoid the more vulgar of these entertainments, like attending circuses. Instead, one could enhance the prospects of gaining respectability by attending "entertainments" which inculcated cultural skills. Athens became a standard stop for traveling cultural entertainments, and some of these became somewhat permanently installed within the town.[30]

All sorts of lecturers entertained and educated Athenians in the antebellum period, and topics varied as frequently as someone new entered town. Traveling musicians added lectures about their music to the staging of musical entertainment. Science proved popular, particularly if assisted by experimental apparatus or if the topic addressed fads such as ventriloquism, hypnosis, or phrenology. Another favorite theme consisted of travelogues of the Holy Land, or of lectures on biblical topics. Reformers advocated temperance, colonization of free blacks, public education, and agricultural improvements. Lawyers and doctors engaged in discourse about their professions. Lectures became so common that the town council decided to grant such educational entertainment explicit exemption from town taxation, lest they be linked with lower forms of entertainment—billiards and circuses, for example—which required regulation.[31]

Organizing lectures by local notables as a lyceum also became a permanent feature of cultural education in Athens. In January 1834, some of the town's elite met several times at the house of the college's president to organize a lyceum for spreading useful information. Following the planning sessions, the newspaper ran a two-week promotion regarding the importance of a lyceum to awaken Athens's citizens to implement the plan, the most important part of which was directed toward women of the town. By March, the lyceum became a reality with James Camak, who just finished erecting the Princeton Factory and begun work as president of the Georgia Railroad, elected as the lyceum's president. In April, William L. Mitchell presented the first of the Athens Independent Lyceum's lecture series, speaking on the history of lyceums. By July 1834, the faculty of the college asked Congressman Augustin Clayton to attend the annual meeting of the American Lyceum in New York and report its methods and intentions, which he published in the local paper.

After this initial flurry of activity about the intention of this institution for the mental improvement of women at Athens, the newspapers did not report any more activity until 1837. This three-year period of silence does not necessarily imply that the lyceum had died. Instead, if those it wanted to attract already attended, it may have simply operated without further public notice. However, in 1837, the paper announced "the Young Ladies Lyceum of Athens," established, in conjunction with a ladies literary magazine, "for the promotion and advancement of science and literature, where knowledge is dispensed gratis, sociability encouraged, and a tone and character given to the manners and customs of thy citizens." The paper again fell quiet on the subject for several years afterward but resumed notice of the institution in the 1840s under the new title of the "Athens Independent Lyceum." In the 1840s, the lyceum appeared to be a strictly male organization, sometimes called the "Young Men's Independent Lyceum of Athens," which frequently entertained with debates as well as orations and lectures. Occasionally, however, the lyceum advertised lectures directed at both the "Ladies and Gentlemen of Athens." So women, as well as men, participated in this form of cultural improvement, albeit passively rather than actively. However other institutions also arose to transfer knowledge and inculcate speaking skills.[32]

Athenians could partake in at least four debating societies in order to improve their oratorical skills. At the start of industrialization, Athens already possessed two debating clubs associated with the university—the Demosthenian Society and the Phi Kappa Society. Students founded the former in 1803, while students excluded from it formed the latter as a competing society in the early 1820s. Each literary society (as they styled themselves) invited students from the college and its grammar school to join and allowed graduates of the university to participate as honorary members in the years immediately following graduation. Both societies intended their members to develop the intellectual prowess, rhetorical skills, and logic "so as to fit them for the active duties of life." One joined a debating society in order to improve the chance for success as a lawyer or a politician later in life. These were elite professions, to be sure, and the students commanded respect as members of the upper classes of the state.[33]

In the 1830s, a third such organization arose for those not associated with the university. Meeting in General Edward Harden's law office in 1834 and 1835, the Citizens Polemic Society of Athens heard lectures and debated current political and social issues. The club continued to meet into the late 1830s, when a British visitor chronicled one of its meetings. This visitor characterized the club's participants as "resident gentlemen of the town, not connected with the University." He described one orator as a "man of fortune and leisure, not engaged in any business or profession." The club's president, General Harden, had been the law partner of Augustin Clayton's in the early 1830s, until they differed over nullification, with Harden becoming a leader in the state Democratic organization and Clayton becoming a leading Whig politician. These were not ambitious clerks, seeking to upgrade their oratorical skills for future advancement, but instead respectable members of the town's elite who entertained themselves by discussing political issues in a forum divorced from partisanship. One can only speculate that this club allowed some of its members the nostalgia of again participating in their college debating clubs. In addition to weekly debates, which routinely met on Thursday afternoons from three to seven o'clock—four hours filled with speeches from six orators (three per side of the debate) and a summation by the club's president—the society also provided a reading room stocked with newspapers from all over the country. Thus Athens possessed four debate societies, these three plus the debating done by the mechanics' society, all of which were exclusively part of male culture, even as they crossed a wide spectrum of classes. Other areas of cultural improvement were open to the ladies as well.[34]

Music instruction became permanent fare for both sexes in Athens. For example, the town supported several music schools during this period, some paid and some voluntary. In 1830, voice teachers led two classes per week for the improvement of church music. From 1835 to 1842, John F. Goenke operated a music school in conjunction with his musical instrument store and associated concert hall. In keeping with his job as superintendent of the town's female academy, which was located across the street from his concert hall, Goenke maintained the respectability of both his schools by segregating his music classes by the gender of the students. In 1846, O. B. Rice proposed that members of all the church choirs in town organize a school to promote training in sacred music. Other schools of culture operated even less formally than those of music, in that they relied upon traveling instructors rather than local residents.[35]

Itinerant instructors operated less formally as inculcators of culture throughout the Age of Jackson. Dance masters came and went with such frequency that they rarely rated public notice, but many considered them agents of possible immorality since distant dance masters were rumored to seduce their female students, particularly in teaching waltzes. Other courses offered to educate their students in masculine culture but included women as passive participants. When a French fencing-master named Bauge operated his gym in 1837 and 1838, he advertised for younger students and specifically claimed that exhibitions of his students' proficiency were suitable for viewing by the ladies. Clearly he intended to solicit the boys and young men at the college, who imagined that fencing might be useful at some point in their future to uphold their honor, and, perhaps, to sway a potential spouse. To claim gentility, respectability, and local acceptance, Bauge included the names of prominent locals who sponsored his endeavors. Given the cost and the expected benefits of such a regimen, there can be no doubt that the fencing master expected high social rank among his initial students, and they anticipated elevated social prestige in return.[36]

Other itinerant instruction promoted less romantic but respectable skills needed for business and middle-class life. Courses offered in double-entry bookkeeping and penmanship offered upward mobility for ambitious men, but women practiced penmanship as well, in order to round out their education. Interestingly, these penmanship classes attracted confidence men who posed as instructors. Athenians warned neighboring communities to beware of one imposter who skipped town without paying his bills, after he was discovered as a result of his "ungentlemanly conduct." The charlatan apparently proved unable to mimic the proper class pretensions associated with those who usually taught the courses. This episode makes clear that recipients of cultural instruction expected narrowly defined environments and curriculum directed at improving their chances for upward mobility within an established system of social relations. They did not intend to challenge that system, nor is there evidence of any unintentional social confrontations arising from such instruction. Other cultural institutions with the potential for promoting radical social change had similar results.[37]

RELIGION AND IMPROVEMENT

Institutionalized religion came to Athens at about the same time as the industrial order. Before 1820, Athenians worshiped privately or journeyed outside town to attend an official church. The Baptists built the first church a few miles to the east of town, up Trail Creek, but only a handful of its members actually lived in the town of Athens. The Methodists also started early with meetings held in a rough log house of townsman Hope Hull, who had introduced the denomination to Georgia as a circuit rider in the 1790s under orders of America's first Methodist Bishop, Francis Asbury. The formal organization of Presbyterian and Baptist congregations in Athens were the result of the hiring of a minister of each sect as a college professor, with the installation of Presbyterian minister Moses Waddel as president of the University of Georgia, in 1820, and the employment of James Shannon, a Baptist minister, as professor of ancient languages in 1830. Prior to completion of the new church buildings, the three major denominations met, at times, in the chapel on the college campus. The pace of institutionalization increased in the next decade, and all three denominations constructed church buildings: the Methodists in 1825, the Presbyterians in 1827, and the Baptists in 1830. Although individuals may have belonged to other denominations, no other churches were built until the Episcopalians and the Disciples of Christ built their respective churches during the 1840s. Also by 1828, the town built an African Church for the slaves and free people of color to enjoy segregated worship under the guidance of a white minister, although people of color could also continue to attend the three major churches as well.[38]

The rise of institutional religion in Athens preceded industrialization only slightly, but one cannot attribute causality from one to the other. Although Athens industrialized and gained the institutions of evangelical Christianity at about the same time as the same thing occurred in northern rural communities undergoing industrialization, it would be wrong to assert a causality between the quickening of the religious impulse and industrialization in Athens.

Instead, by 1830, the two movements arose relatively simultaneously, more the result of the town's increased population than from forces arising from imminent industrialization. Rather, the improved standing of the university in the state led the town to achieve the critical mass of population necessary to support a complex social and cultural infrastructure. Thus organized religion proved incidental rather than essential to creating the manufacturing facilities of Athens. The example of Augustin Clayton serves as a point of clarification.[39]

Augustin Smith Clayton, the first industrialist of Athens, was a life-long religious skeptic, yet his infidel beliefs did not noticeably affect his standing in the community or in the state. Clayton rose to political prominence from the 1810s to 1830s, having been elected a superior court judge, state senator, and congressman. He also considered a bid for the governorship. He led a number of political meetings on the important issues of the day, including nullification (which he supported). The local elite repeatedly gave him a place of honor, electing him an officer of many civic meetings, or an administrator of the town's many benevolent causes. Yet he turned down only one position publicly proffered him. When a meeting elected him *in absentia* to help distribute Bibles to the needy of northern Georgia, Clayton quietly declined without real explanation, claiming "not being present at that meeting so as to fully know its objects, I must beg to decline the service confided to me." Starting in the 1820s and escalating in the 1830s, religious revivals began to sweep Athens, yet Clayton remained unmoved. Only after suffering a paralyzing stroke in 1838, a year before his death, did Clayton recognize his own mortality, and he began inquiring into his wife's Methodism. Once converted, Clayton, as in so many other of his endeavors, chose to publicize his change of heart so that others might emulate him, "to undo the evils of his former life" in spreading his skepticism to his friends and colleagues. All three churches took turns officiating at his funeral, primarily to celebrate his conversion, but they also honored the life he had led before his eleventh-hour change of heart. None of Clayton's political opponents ever attacked him for his lack of religion. And Clayton's experience was not unique.[40]

James Camak, who built the Princeton Factory, also probably did not affiliate with any church. He lost an appointment as professor of mathematics at the University of Georgia in 1829, not because of his lack of religion but because the state's Baptists feared domination of the institution by Presbyterians, and his wife belonged to that denomination. But even after he lost the appointment, Camak did not join the Presbyterian Church with his wife. Sectarian differences proved much more important during this time than did lack of formal ties to any denomination. So Camak, like Clayton, suffered no ill effects from his reluctance to join a church; he too served on numerous boards and committees throughout his life.[41]

For the less politically prominent, the choices of Clayton and Camak may not have been so easy. Notwithstanding the lack of evidence for causality between industrialization and the institutionalization of religion, nearly all of the other industrialists belonged to organized religions, and most of them participated in the various endeavors for moral uplift promoted by those churches. Almost the entire first generation of industrialists were Presbyterians: William Dearing, John Nisbet, Alexander B. Linton, Abraham Walker, and Thomas W. Baxter all served as ruling elders of the Athens Presbyterian Church. John White, who purchased the Georgia Factory from Clayton and company, also belonged to the Presbyterian Church, but did not become a leader until he came to economic prominence in the 1850s. Clayton, as mentioned above, was the only Methodist in the first generation, and his conversion came after the end of his industrial activity. William Williams proved the lone Baptist, serving as deacon and secretary of the Athens Baptist Church until his death. In the second generation, after 1845, the town's leadership still seemed dominated by Presbyterians; William L. Mitchell, John S. Linton, Stevens Thomas, Ephraim S. Hopping, and E. L. Newton all belonged to the Presbyterian Church. But Athens's elite now included an increasing number who were not Presbyterians. Albon Chase, Asbury Hull, and Young L. G. Harris, who all associated with the town's insurance company as well as with industrial enterprises, were devout Methodists.

Despite the affiliation of this economic elite with organized religion, few stressed the importance of an "industrial Christianity" as hypothesized by social historians of the industrializing North. William Williams provided a chapel for his operatives, but there is no indication of his mandating attendance. From the 1840s through the 1860s, the Methodists provided special missions to factory operatives, just as they did to slaves. Clearly church membership rose throughout the antebellum period, and more members of all social classes joined them. But institutional religion did not play a central role in organizing factories, nor is there any evidence of coercion of the rising classes to join a specific church. In fact, joining the Presbyterian Church would seem the most advantageous choice for the upwardly mobile, since it would give the ambitious contact with the cream of Athens's elite, but census records indicate that the Baptist and Methodist churches grew at a much faster rate than the Presbyterian. However, Athens's industrialists, as members of the town's elite, generally participated in improvement campaigns associated with religious activity—Bible distribution, temperance, and even a reform that could be construed as limited abolitionism—to promote the moral uplift, and to increase the social respectability, of the Georgia upcountry.[42]

Athens took a lead in attempting to distribute Bibles to all families in northern Georgia that did not own one. As early as 1826, Moses Waddel, the president of the University of Georgia, presided over the founding meeting of a local chapter of the American Bible Association. The chapter met at least annually for many years, on the anniversary of its founding, although it may not have actually made much headway in distributing Bibles to the needy of the twenty-one counties of northern Georgia. By 1830, the society reorganized itself at a meeting chaired by industrial investor Abraham Walker, and it appointed a committee of fifteen to use any expedient method to achieve its goals. This committee included all the local industrialists operating in Athens at that date: Augustin Clayton, Abraham Walker, John Nisbet, and William Dearing. But the society proved moribund, neither meeting frequently nor raising much money. In 1839, the society reconstituted itself yet again, emphasizing a narrower geographic scope by calling itself the Bible Society of the Western Judicial Circuit of Georgia. This time the notice explained that the Bibles were not to be distributed for free, but at cost. Again the officers included most of the town's manufacturers, with William Dearing serving as the society's president, William Williams and Asbury Hull as two of its three vice-presidents, and John Nisbet and Thomas W. Baxter on the board of directors. The British travelogue writer James S. Buckingham attended this meeting, as did a representative of the American Bible Society. Buckingham explained that this northern society had learned to use southern agents to quiet southern fears that northern philanthropy secretly promoted abolitionism. Yet, unlike the contemporary disengagement of philanthropy in Charleston from national philanthropic societies, Athens chose to affiliate with the northern-controlled "benevolent empire." This Bible society reorganized once more in 1842 by again reducing the number of counties it served, because new societies arose in some of the more rural counties previously served from Athens. Again resident manufacturers Asbury Hull, William Williams, and Thomas W. Baxter served as officers. Other future industrialists—Albon Chase, William L. Mitchell, and Dr. Henry Hull—also served as officers of this not-quite-successful society.[43]

The repeated failures of the Bible societies seem not the direct fault of the efforts of the town's industrial elite, but more a result of lack of interest among the elites in the counties the Athens groups hoped to help. The leaders of these distant communities apparently opposed the control of the moral improvement agency by Athens. In the earliest stages, the distant counties refused to contribute their share to pay for the efforts spearheaded by Athens. Later they simply ignored the city's leadership and launched their own county-level societies. The prestige of the town's most respectable sorts did not carry much weight outside Athens, at least not when interfering with the social order of other communities without first gaining the full support of the more directly connected local elite. Like Bible distribution, the cause of temperance frequently allied itself with increased religiosity.

Newspaper reports in Athens about temperance seemed to indicate a greater popularity for this moral reform. As early as 1829, the town newspaper reported that the legislature felt "the free use of intoxicating liquors [to be] . . . the greatest evil that afflicts the country," but the Georgia General Assembly would not suppress alcohol consumption through prohibitive laws because of the difficulties of enforcement. (Banning militia musters seemed a practical first step toward decreasing alcoholism, but the legislature did not implement the idea.) Another article in 1831 proposed that the South find alternatives to alcohol as an entertainment for the state's youth, just as New York had instituted soda fountains for that purpose. In the same year, the Clarke County grand jury suggested the county needed to regulate the sale of alcohol. By 1835, the local paper published temperance tracts that frequently relied on the sentimentality of the day to make their point. One work of fiction adopted the perspective of a woman with five children, whose drunken husband could not support his family, to demonstrate how alcohol destroyed one's respectability. Another article used a statistical approach and claimed the United States had 300,000 drunks, and if they all died at once, their graves would stretch 3,409 miles or require a cemetery of 680 acres. But these sorts of publications waxed and waned. By 1839, however, a new cycle of interest arose, and the paper again printed discussions of the need for suppressing the sale of alcohol. In 1842, it reprinted an article from a New York paper that combined humor with technological enthusiasm in claiming that electrical shocks could cure alcoholism. On a more serious side, another article blamed a disastrous fire on the railroad from Macon to Savannah on the intemperance of the railroad's employees. At other times, the grand juries of other counties in northern Georgia commented on the success of their efforts to eliminate alcohol, suggesting a sales tax as an effective measure. Many Athenians considered alcohol a national curse, and they did not merely expect to talk about the problem. Instead they waged their local "war" against liquor with nationally, regionally, and locally sanctioned weapons.[44]

Over a twenty-year period, reformers in Athens developed an arsenal of institutions with which to attack the problem of drinking. Students operated a temperance society on the campus of the University of Georgia. The local Presbyterian Church prohibited the drinking of alcohol by its members, upon pain of expulsion. Local temperance organizations arose and changed as the needs of the times changed. A local "Clarke County Temperance Society" met semi-annually in the Presbyterian Church to promote abstinence from drink in the early 1830s, and a chapter of the Baltimore-based Washingtonian Temperance Society met in the Methodist Church to hear lectures in the early 1840s. Prominent locals filled the ranks of the Sons of Temperance in the late 1840s. State temperance conventions frequently met in Athens, particularly around commencement. "Cold Water" replaced alcohol at some official functions, with a smattering of temperance militia musters, barbeques, festivals, and Fourth of July celebrations. One businessman even opened a coffee house (which offered food twenty-four hours per day) as a culturally condoned alternative to a tavern. In the middle of one recruiting drive in 1842, organizers announced the addition of "47 names to the pledge—28 gentlemen and 19 ladies," bringing the total pledged in Athens to abstain from drink to 222.[45]

While the reform seemed popular, Athens's industrial leaders failed to fully embrace temperance. Only three industrialists assumed leadership roles in local temperance organizations: William Dearing, William Williams, and Asbury Hull. All served as Athens delegates at Georgia Temperance Society annual meetings in the 1830s, and Dearing chaired an occasional meeting of the Clarke County Temperance Society during the same time. Given the longevity of this reform campaign, these leadership roles seem minimal, and the names of Athens's other industrialists cannot be found among the reform's active leadership. Thus it seems they stood divided, or only minimally interested. This lack of interest put Athens's manufacturers at odds with trends in other parts of the country engaging in manufactures, which considered temperance a central element of moral reform and upward mobility. Since most of Athens's industrialists belonged to the Presbyterian Church, which required teetotalism, one can assume they did not actively oppose the cause. But neither did they actively promote it, like the industrialists and businessmen in the North. Perhaps, in their hierarchical society, they felt other devices better exposed a person's character to the community to provide an indication of who among the lower orders deserved to be lifted up to a higher station, and sobriety was the *a priori* moral condition they expected for all applicants. In a small town like Athens, only a few would make the cut and move beyond their origins. The small size of the town and its other measures of respectability may have removed temperance as a movement from the highest priority of Athens's elite.[46]

More to the point, the industrialists may have simply felt that zealotry about temperance caused unnecessary division within their town. From the start, temperance efforts garnered active opposition. At the same time that the Clarke County Temperance Society organized, a few Athenians (one a nephew of John Nisbet, the industrialist) announced the formation of an "anti-semi-temperance society." The instigators of this new society claimed the high-handedness of the county's temperance leaders disparaged reputable members of Athens society just because they drank, regardless of the degree of their consumption. This new group argued that moderate consumption of alcohol endangered neither the individual nor society, and thus occasional tippling did not merit censure. Further, unlike the temperance organization, the semi-temperance group invited the truly intemperate to join their organization, in hope of reforming them, rather than merely organizing the temperate to impose new standards of normative behavior on the rest of society. In the final analysis, it is difficult to assess the representativeness of this opposition to teetotal temperance since the paper printed no more notices of the semi-temperance group after its initial proclamations.[47]

Opposition to temperance operated in the same cycles as the reform movement's advocacy. In 1839, when temperance reform reignited in Athens, Albon Chase indicated the divisiveness of the topic on the readership of his newspaper when he stated that he only reluctantly reopened discussion of the pros and cons of the subject (although he ardently took the side of temperance), when others suggested petitioning the legislature to prohibit the retailing of all ardent spirits. These prohibitionists (who included Joseph H. Lumpkin, brother of former governor Wilson Lumpkin and an important Georgia jurist in his own right, as well as Josiah Flournoy, an industrialist and state senator from Eatonton) acknowledged resistance to their suggestions when they advised the public that those opposed should send their own petitions to the legislature so that body could evaluate both the number and character of the names of supporters of each position, in order to make a fair determination of public opinion. Again, as the cycle of reform peaked later that year, the reporting of support and opposition disappeared, but the legislature did not pass this measure either.[48]

In the mid-1840s, opposition to temperance by student pranksters rapidly dissipated the activity of the local chapter of the Washingtonian Temperance Society. The society's influence peaked with a well-attended temperance barbeque on the Fourth of July in 1843, but attendance dropped soon after. By early 1844, an editorial suggested the lecture by a founder of the first chapter in Baltimore reinvigorated the society with another forty-four citizens taking the pledge. Almost immediately, however, the Augusta chapter reported that Athens's citizens purposely insulted the speaker by allowing students to disturb his lecture. While Albon Chase, editor of the *Southern Banner,* expressed his dismay over the disruption, he felt that the entire town should not be held responsible for the actions of the six college students who caused sneezing fits by dropping snuff on the audience. But, following this, the newspapers reported no more activity of the society in Athens.[49]

Disruptions, such as that of the Washingtonian temperance meeting is 1844, indicate the limits of social reform in the South, and why the town's industrialists chose not to fully embrace this movement, as well as others. In 1839, Eatonton industrialist Josiah Flournoy found himself systematically harassed for his anti-alcohol efforts, suffering the demolition of his buggy and the public humiliation of having his mule shaved and painted, as well as having his temperance meetings disrupted. Historians argue that temperance failed to achieve the same success in the South as in the North because the planter elites preferred to maintain the convivial lifestyle by which they purchased their political power (by supplying alcohol at most public events, particularly militia musters and court days), and because the upcountry plain folk felt their economic livelihood threatened by the potential loss of a market for selling their surplus corn as liquor. The North, they argue, abandoned such pre-industrial agricultural-based folkways as increased industry required greater social discipline, and as new immigration caused members of more established ethnic groups to react by supporting temperance and prohibition. If true, the South possessed none of the motivation for accepting such radical changes. The industrial population remained a minor portion of the population, as did the percentage of non-Protestant immigrants in the South.

Had southern industrialists wanted to champion the cause more strongly, they lacked the economic and political clout of their northern industrial brethren to enforce their desires upon the lower classes. Indeed, the very notion of imposing new patterns of behavior upon the society would have struck the southern industrialists as contrary to their very notion of respectability, that social changes needed to proceed in an orderly fashion, and along established paths, lest they subvert the establish social and economic systems which sustained their wealth and social status. Thus temperance reform in the South never became an active agent for change. Instead, southern temperance worked toward voluntary self-improvement, but without the policing mechanism adopted in the North. So, in the late 1840s, middle-class professionals in Athens started the Father Mathew Division of the Sons of Temperance, which resembled a Masonic fraternity. But, after a few years, notices of this largely self-contained group also ceased. In fact, national politics thereafter pushed temperance entirely out of the news in Athens, which reinforces the historiographic contention that antebellum reform impulses in the South only gained momentum during lulls in sectional conflict. However, a reform movement involved in the animosity between North and South did have adherents among those connected to Athens's industrial elite.[50]

Like most southerners, Athenians generally opposed abolitionism, but versions of the reform occasionally arose in the town. As early as the 1820s, the college president, Moses Waddel, privately confided to a visiting dignitary of the American Missionary Association that he opposed slavery and would leave the South if he thought his health could stand the rigors of the North's climate. In the next decade, a future Georgia Supreme Court justice with Athens connections, Joseph Henry Lumpkin, made a slightly abolitionist speech while in Boston to raise funds for a theological seminary in South Carolina, claiming the "interests of the owners, and the slave, were alike identified with emancipation, and the time was rapidly coming on, when [slavery] would be abandoned." But most Athenians actively opposed northern efforts to impose abolitionist solutions on the South. They generally supported the "Gag Rule" in Congress, which suppressed the readings of abolitionist petitions, without congressional consideration, although some like Judge Clayton wanted Congress to reject the memorials outright. In 1835, an Athens town meeting, in which industrialists Augustin Clayton, William Dearing, John Nisbet, and Stevens Thomas all played official roles, formally protested allowing abolitionist material in the mail as incendiary to the peace in the South. And the town ran one editor out of town for receiving abolitionist mail.[51]

Despite local congruence with the regional trend against abolitionism in the late 1830s, a few Athenians gave succor to a reform that could easily be misinterpreted as a mild form of abolitionism. In the 1830s, respectable Athenians supported national efforts for colonization, which advocated transporting freed slaves back to Africa. In August 1837, R. R. Gurley, secretary of the American Colonization Society, addressed a meeting in Athens, and the local paper dedicated four columns to publish the address. The society collected a hundred dollars in donations, which was as much as was donated to many of the town's other philanthropic events. In this case, thirty dollars came from an anonymous donor, but the rest came from a small cohort of the town's most respectable citizens, including five dollars from the wife of industrialist Thomas W. Baxter, and ten from Professor Charles F. McCay, the future son-in-law of industrialist William Williams. Further, the society directed any future donations to be paid to lawyer and future Athens industrial investor William L. Mitchell. Mitchell played an interesting role by serving as secretary both to the colonization meeting in 1837 and to the 1835 town meeting protesting the mailing of abolitionist tracts. For insight as to why elite southerners might have supported colonization, contrast the 1837 meeting with the activities of John Jacob Flournoy—the deaf first cousin of Athens's notables Howell and Thomas R. R. Cobb, who was the town's leading eccentric.

Flournoy publicly proclaimed his opposition to slavery based on his racist views that contact between the races would only lower the whites to the level of blacks. Consistent with his stated ideals, Flournoy supported colonization in order to deport African Americans and thus eliminate that contact. Yet, in the year following the colonization meeting in Athens, Flournoy attempted to start a local chapter of the colonization society but found no support. The differences between Flournoy's attempt to encourage colonization and the success of the other meeting is telling. The few who donated to the society after the lecture were respectable members of Athens society while Flournoy was considered by most to be the town's crackpot. While the brevity of the event indicates no long-term commitment to the cause, it is likely the elite initially supported colonization for motives dissimilar to Flournoy's (although the effect would be the same). They likely wanted to eliminate the quiet but visible challenge to the institution to slavery represented by free people of color, for the existence of such people in the South, however circumscribed their freedom may have been, always served as a reminder that African Americans need not always be enslaved, that freedom remained a possibility. So colonization did not equal abolitionism in their minds; instead they saw it as reinforcing the South's existing domestic relations. However, once Flournoy took on the cause, the more respectable citizens abandoned it. In Athens, respectability proved more important than any outcome that might have resulted from their support of a dubious "improvement."[52]

The growth of institutional religion and of movements commonly associated with the expansion of the religious sphere in the North neither contributed directly to industrialization efforts nor directly toward the increased respectability of its adherents. Clearly, Athenians desired moral uplift of their fellow southerners, but they never seemed willing or able to assemble the permanent institutions necessary to carry forward their work in the long run. Colonization proved to be a single episode in the town's cultural life. Enthusiasm for temperance ran in cycles in which each new cycle created new but equally impermanent and ineffective organizations. Bible distribution efforts could not overcome opposition from the very communities Athens intended to help. Only organized religion proved permanent, but even for this "improvement," lack of church membership did not impede the livelihood of entrepreneurs or workers. In this college town, education of all sorts influenced respectability more than moral reforms did. Practical improvements also proved respectable.

PRACTICAL IMPROVEMENT

Agricultural improvement may be considered the pinnacle of respectable reform in Athens. Unlike other improvements, this series of reforms did not focus on the placement of the individual within society; instead it simply intended to make life better for all. At the center of this movement for Athens, and for the entire state, stood James Camak. Camak constantly experimented with different species of plants he thought capable of advancing Georgia's agricultural output. In August 1833, he forwarded his first letter to the local paper reporting the yields of a new grass bred for consumption by livestock, following two years of experimentation. Prior to Camak's research in potato cultivation in 1835, Georgians did not routinely raise them and considered potatoes a cold-climate crop. But after adopting his techniques, potatoes became a staple of Georgia food production by 1850. Also in the mid-1830s, James Camak tested different methods of corn cultivation to produce seventy bushels per acre by abandoning plowed fields and using a mulch to retain moisture and to reduce weeds. He announced his findings in regional agricultural journals, but not at home, so his advanced corn-raising techniques were not immediately well known. In 1839, Camak advertised seeds of a new strain of multi-bolled cotton for sale and explained his own efforts to grow the seeds, attaching a tract discussing its success in areas where cotton culture was more predominant. The newspaper commented that Camak was "always foremost in encouraging whatever pertains to agricultural advancement," and he did not limit his discussions to his own experiments. When he found a specimen of merit in someone else's garden, as with the "mammoth strawberry" in fellow industrialist Thomas W. Baxter's, he brought those to public notice as well. His disinterestedness, his civic-mindedness, and his continuous efforts filled this reform with respectability, both in the content of a traditional way of life and in the method promoting changes.[53]

Camak combined his background in journalism with his agricultural pursuits in 1844, when he took over as editor of the *Southern Cultivator.* Begun in 1842, this regional agricultural journal had been attempting to find its niche and was on the verge of collapse when Camak assumed its editorship. Under his guidance, the paper finally began consistent monthly publication and earned a high reputation for its content. One Athens newspaper endorsed the appointment of Camak to the post, noting, "To his high literary and scientific attainments, he adds great practical knowledge, the result of many years experience in agricultural and horticultural pursuits." Along with this editorial post, Camak continued his own investigations and agricultural promotions, frequently using the paper as his pulpit to promote agricultural diversification for the South. In February and May 1845, he purchased seeds for new varieties of wheat from the U.S. Patent Office and donated them to the local newspaper for dissemination among its readers. Finally, in 1846, he began promoting viticulture in Georgia as a substitute for importing the "rot-gut" sold in Georgia as "foreign" wines. Throughout the last two years of his life, he attempted to revive interests in Georgia fruit production.[54]

While he stood as the primary impetus for scientific agriculture in the state, Camak was not alone in Athens for his enthusiasm for improving cultivation. Albon Chase, then still the editor of the *Southern Banner,* also contributed to movement for agricultural improvement in Athens. In 1839, Chase proposed a new agricultural journal specializing in the cultivation of silk to ride the crest of the renewed interest in the material. Although insufficient subscriptions halted his proposed regional monthly journal, he and others continued to attempt to grow silk in Athens. However, the 1840 census enumerated only twelve pounds of silk reeled in the town. It further estimated its value at fifty-eight dollars and reported that nine men had been employed in its production. Undeterred, E. L. Newton, one of the minor original investors in the (Camak) Princeton Factory, operated a facility which housed fifty thousand silk worms in 1842, with the intent of carrying the experiment in southern silk to its conclusion. No other notices of silk production were mentioned in Athens after that date, so one may assume the experiments proved unsuccessful.[55]

The culmination of these individual pursuits of scientific agriculture resulted in local and statewide institutions for advancing the field. As early as 1834, editorials proposed forming an agricultural society to improve the provisioning of Athens with fresh food. However, nobody acted upon the proposal until 1842, when locals created the Clarke County Agricultural Society. Even this society, however, did not last. Its constitution required only annual meetings, and its initial project of convincing a prominent politician of South Carolina to lecture during the university's commencement on the improvements he made to his plantation was rebuffed. Camak and others created a second society of the same name in 1845 and associated it with a new organization, the Central Georgia Agricultural Society, which acted as a statewide clearinghouse for agricultural information. The local organization in Athens elected Camak its president during the last few years of his life. By 1846, the Clarke County Agricultural Society organized a county fair and awarded premiums to members of the society as prizes for the best specimens of their agricultural productions. The next year, the state organization created a state fair, which promoted not only agriculture but also artisan and industrial manufactures.[56]

The movements for improved agriculture and for manufacturing were believed to be connected means of retaining population in the state, which would in turn raise the value of land and improve the standard of living. For instance, throughout the 1850s, the Manufacturer's Association met at the state fair at Stone Mountain to issue premiums for textile production, as well as to attempt to set a minimum price level for textiles manufactured in the state. Similar events promoted agriculture and manufactures elsewhere in the South. Many of these events encouraged textile manufacturers from all over the region, including Athens, to compete for prizes for the best quality output. The connection of industry to agriculture through these fairs intended increasing manufacturing's prestige and acceptability, thereby adding to its respectability as well.[57]

The milieu of cultural improvement played many roles in Athens. It enabled the young elite to progress in polite society. Elite boys and young men attended school and made the sorts of connections that would give them social advantages for the rest of their lives. Debate and declamation in the school's literary societies provided the basis upon which they would build their professional and political careers. Extracurricular courses in music, business skills, and fencing taken in town, enhanced the connections made at school and, likewise, perhaps aided in securing a profession or a spouse. Attending lectures and orations, as well as adult attendance in the elite debate club independent of the college, enabled elite males to not only take in new information but also to develop ideas in a non-partisan forum, providing sanctuary from the highly charged partisan political environment of the day.

Non-elite males—the petty merchants, clerks, and mechanics of Athens—partook of some of the same improvements as the elite. Many attended schools that focused on conveying basic literacy and arithmetic skills. The town's educational opportunities encouraged them to pursue mental improvement as a means of embracing elite culture. And the elites advised them to avoid endangering friendships that frittered away their spare time and money in simple working-class entertainments when they could more wisely invest in upward mobility. Skilled workingmen took control of their own advance by organizing a mechanics' society to protect their claims to respectability, despite their non-elite status, but they never challenged the social order. Master artisans might find a way to advance beyond their class origins, but most mechanics simply wanted recognition as upright members of a hierarchical society who performed their tasks well and who contributed to the good of society. Clerks adhered to the prevailing business culture of Athens and could only hope to advance to elite status by becoming a partner with an established merchant. Thus, more than any others, they must have deeply imbibed in the improving spirit to prove their respectability, lest they lose an opportunity for advancing themselves.

Women, too, partook in the cultural improvement activities in Athens during the early years of industrialization. Lyceum lectures, literary magazines, debates and orations, as well as fencing demonstrations encouraged passive participation by females. Women's education also proved an important concern in Athens at the time, with a variety of levels of schools for women or girls of varying social status. Like the boys, they took extracurricular courses in art, music, dance, and even penmanship. But women operated in the popular culture as well. The ladies performed ceremonial roles in militia celebrations on Independence Day, and they held fairs to raise money for relief for the poor, as well as for additions and repairs of their churches. Not to be outdone by the young men, the young women of Athens also demonstrated their oratorical skills at a May Day festival one year. Elite women served actively on the visiting committees of the Benevolent Society as it examined families to determine their need and worthiness of charity.[58]

Visitors noticed the coeducational nature of intellectual prowess that set Athens apart from many other places in America. James Silk Buckingham, the British diarist who like Alexis de Tocqueville published a journal of his travels through America, generally found parties in America to be very boring because married women usually excluded themselves and married men usually talked business among themselves. Parties thus left most of the merry-making to teenage men and women who lacked the education and sophistication to rise above inanity and gossip. The fete Buckingham attended in Athens proved very different. There women and men talked freely and warmly. Unlike ladies of similar social rank in the North, he explained, the young ladies in Athens possessed "more resources for conversation, and more power, as well as ease or freedom of expression." Buckingham attributed the intellectual vigor of the party to its host and attendees. The professors of the university, with their wives as well as members of the senior class of the college, together with their relatives, formed perhaps one-half of the body of the party. Over two hundred attended the affair, in a town with scarcely over one thousand whites (although some may have ridden in from their plantations, outside town). Because of the general intelligence of the culture, Buckingham rated his time in Athens as some of the most agreeable time he spent in America.[59]

For slaves and the poor, improvement also offered a chance for some advance to respectability within their own sphere. Both could gain limited literacy through Sabbath schools, and opportunities abounded in Athens for those who took it upon themselves to go beyond the most rudimentary improvement. If they demonstrated their efforts to advance themselves through work, the poorest whites could qualify for charity from the town's elite. But the elite also attempted to direct the poor with the highest promise of intellect and energy into elite-sponsored activities, such as the manual labor school or the Sabbath schools. Poor schools never obtained enough local financial support through county government to operate regularly, or even to pay the teachers for the schooling already provided. Thus the lowest classes could not co-opt their own education for purposes independent of elite desires. Slaves could only hope for real change when emancipated, but like Lucius Holsey, they could gain access to instruments of improvement through their own efforts. Only future research will show whether those slaves who provided for their own improvement fell under elite white hegemonic understandings of their options for respectability following emancipation, or if they defined improvement differently from polite white society. Certainly, leaders of the freedmen understood how education affected their chances for improving their social and economic positions. Thus, immediately upon emancipation, they clamored for the establishment of schools for improving all levels of their education—primary schools through colleges.[60]

Finally, Athens's milieu of reforms had mixed results in a changing society. The elite did not compel the ambitious lower-class youths to join any specific church, nor did they consider public support of temperance a top priority. Rather, upwardly mobile clerks and mechanics probably embraced sobriety, and voluntarily may have joined a religious denomination, as *a priori* proof of their merit to seek the limited number of jobs that would allow them to move to higher status in the town. However, despite serving as a powerful attraction for culturally minded members of the state's elite, Athens found its influence for projecting social reform to be limited. Outside its immediate sphere of influence, the Athens elite failed to convince leaders of smaller communities to follow its lead in supporting the distribution of Bibles as the first step toward remaking the social relations of those villages in Athens's image. Nonetheless, some of those villages adopted more limited versions of the town's cultural institutions. For instance, the village of Clarkesville operated a "literary" lyceum in the 1830s, which seemed to compress lectures, writing, and oration into one organization. Athens's greatest success came from the improvement which completely avoided altering class, gender, and race relations: scientific agriculture. By the end of the 1830s, other larger towns in Georgia sought to mimic Athens's prosperity by obtaining denominational colleges, supporting improved transportation facilities, and building factories. Thus Penfield, Macon, Milledgeville, and Covington all began to compete with Athens for the interest of the state's elite, which ultimately reduced Athens's hegemony as Georgia's cultural center. Athens faced a similar cycle of increasing and declining importance as a center for promoting internal improvements.[61]

4
THE NETWORK OF INDUSTRIALIZATION

Like a Northern manufacturing town, [Athens] has her rail road, and her factories in full operation, and like them, her condition is flourishing, amidst the decline and dilapidation of other places.
—Milledgeville *Federal Union* April 1, 1845

Athens led the industrial revolution in Jacksonian Georgia by putting three textile mills into operation between 1830 and 1833. Also in the 1830s, it successfully led a renewed campaign for internal improvements to open the Georgia upcountry to market penetration that resulted in a statewide rail system with direct state participation. Despite such active leadership, and the many successes enjoyed by Athens's industrialists as they sought to enrich themselves and Georgia's economy through diversified entrepreneurial activity and increased market participation, Athens itself would reach a limit to what it could accomplish due to the limits of its geography and financial resources. Nonetheless, the town's entrepreneurs diversified their manufacturing activities in order to supplement their investments in textiles, with the result that Athens became a node of commercial and industrial activity for an extended economic hinterland as the region became more embedded in an emerging national and international economy.

In 1840, Clarke County's factories led the state by any measure of industrial production. Factories in the county employed 5,630 spindles. No other county in the state operated more than 3,000 spindles, while most worked less than 2,000. Athens utilized more industrial labor and produced a higher value of cotton goods per year than any other manufacturing setting in Georgia. And the federal census undercounted Clarke County's output when it failed to enumerate a fourth small mill started in late 1839. But most importantly, Athens largely missed the most serious pratfalls of the depression of the 1840s, which greatly affected other locales, because it pursued a broad vision that developed both manufacturing and transportation.

TABLE 3

Measures of Textile Production of Georgia Counties, 1840

County	Factories	Spindles	Employees	Output	Capitalization
Clark	3	5,630	220	120,000	$200,000
Greene	1	2,700[a]	. . .	. . .	. . .
Putnam	1	2,200	111	50,000	$75,000
Richmond	2	2,000	100	50,000	$81,000
Upson[b]	2	1,720	76	52,400	$74,000
Warren	2	1,125	125	. . .	. . .
Cobb	1	480	28	6,000	$45,000
Newton	1	396	36	. . .	$30,000
Henry	1	384	17	5,700	$8,500
Carroll	4	74	6	233	$335
Total[c d]	14	16,635	713	284,100	$513,500

[a] Manuscript census lists 27,000 spindles in Greene County—an apparent error of magnitude.

[b] Union County returns excluded because of identical duplication of Upson County returns.

[c] Carroll County excluded from total because of pre-industrial form of manufacture; Greene County corrected.

[d] Missing values not included in total.

Source: Schedules of Mines, Agriculture, Commerce, Manufactures, etc. (1840), Georgia vols. 16 and 17, entry 322, Records of Census Bureau Record Group 29, National Archives.

Other places in Georgia surpassed Athens in commercial status, but none outranked Athens in industrial endeavors. Savannah and Augusta remained Athens's commercial superiors. Savannah, in Chatham County, reported more manufactures than did Clarke County, but artisans rather than operatives fabricated Savannah's manufactures. By 1840, Augusta, in Richmond County, reported two factories in its environs, each with 1,000 spindles, but several counties commanded larger factories than Augusta. Macon and Columbus surpassed Athens in population and in capital engaged in commerce. But Clarke County surpassed those places, too, in terms of economic stability and sustained growth, by pursuing a vision of growth that married industrialization to commercial development through participation in regional and national projects that promoted economic improvement.

A few other Georgia towns in the 1830s pursued industrialization in a fashion similar to Athens. The Eatonton Factory in Putnam County contained 2,200 spindles. Poullain's Scull Shoals Factory, which sat across the county line from Clarke County, in Greene County, probably contained 2,700 spindles. Industrialists in Upson County operated one factory with 1,320 spindles and another with 400. Warren County possessed two factories with an aggregate of 1,125 spindles. Cobb County's Roswell Factory operated only 480 spindles in 1840, although this number would greatly increase within a few years. Newton County enumerated one factory with 396 spindles. A Henry County factory listed 384 spindles. Carroll County's cotton mills, in the western end of the Georgia upcountry, can be assumed to be primarily artisan in nature, since its largest worked only 36 spindles, and its other three operated 6 spindles each. The factories of Athens operated more than double the spindles of their nearest rival, the mills of Greene County. But the factories of that county should be considered to be in the economic sphere of Athens. While the list of factories would grow in the 1840s as prosperity returned in the latter half of the decade, several proved to have direct ties to Athens.[1]

Athens served as the commercial center for the counties of eastern Georgia that bordered on the upcountry. While each of the surrounding counties contained small towns—Oglethorpe County had Lexington, Wilkes County had Washington, Greene County contained Greensboro, Jackson County contained Jefferson, and Madison County contained Danielsville—Athens served as the emporium for more diverse tastes and for transshipment of goods into or out of the region. The other towns served more as court towns than as places of business or refined entertainment. Athens attracted visitors for both cultural and business opportunities.

Through family and personal connections, Athens in the 1830s and 1840s became a node of manufacturing activity for the surrounding countryside. In the 1830s and early 1840s, additional factories arose at the periphery of Clarke County, generally with a direct connection to Athens. In September 1832, Stevens Thomas of Athens, Thomas N. Poullain of Greene County, Ephraim Hopping of Wilkes County, Thomas Wray of Greene County, and Albert Wray of Oglethorpe County invested $45,000 to construct the Scull Shoals Factory on Poullain's plantation on the south side of the Oconee River, which separated Greene and Clarke counties. Each invested $10,000, except for Thomas Wray, who only put up $5,000. Not only did Athenians invest in the firm, but most of the factory's operatives lived on the Clarke County side of the river and "commuted" to work using Poullain's bridge to cross the river each day. When the factory burned in 1845, Stevens Thomas's heirs (including Asbury Hull's son, Henry Hull Jr.) contributed to building a more substantial brick edifice, and the corporation continued to operate until after the Civil War.[2]

After serving as a tutor at the University of Georgia in the early 1830s, New York native Ephraim Hopping operated a plantation and flour mill at High Shoals, at the extreme western edge of Clarke County (about thirteen miles from Athens), while acting as a silent partner in the Scull Shoals Factory run by his wife's kinsmen. By the early 1840s, Hopping started the High Shoals Factory, adjacent to his plantation in Walton County, just across the Apalachee River from Clarke County. By 1849, the High Shoals Factory incorporated with a stated capital of $44,000 and a number of lesser investors with Clarke County addresses.[3]

Within Clarke County, about 1840, James Allen and Johnson Garwood began operating the small Mars Hill Factory on Barber Creek, about midway between High Shoals and the town of Athens. While never enumerated by the census, this textile mill contained only 350 spindles and twelve looms, and it experienced frequent shut-downs. After changing hands several times in the 1840s, it burned in 1851 and was never rebuilt. Also in the 1830s and 1840s, Robert White, son of the Athens Factory superintendent of the same name, operated a small wool factory in Jackson County, on Mulberry Creek, about fifteen miles from Athens. Like Mars Hill, this mill proved transitory, and after marrying well, the younger Robert White abandoned manufacturing for planting and politics. Less directly connected to Athens, the elder Robert White moved fifty miles west to Newton County in the mid-1840s, and invested in the already operating Newton Factory, but after a falling out with its senior partner, he started a small mill across the Alcovy River with his son, Hugh. Hugh and Robert Senior continued their contact with John White, who finished purchasing the Georgia Factory in Clarke County in 1846.[4]

Thus, not only did Clarke County contain more spindles in 1840 than any other single county, but if one counts the spindles of factories in other counties known to be affiliated with the entrepreneurs of Athens, the number soon grows from 5,630 to more than 8,700 spindles. The exact number is unknown since there may be connections between other cotton factories in Georgia, and since the number of spindles for the Mars Hill Factory in Clarke County and of

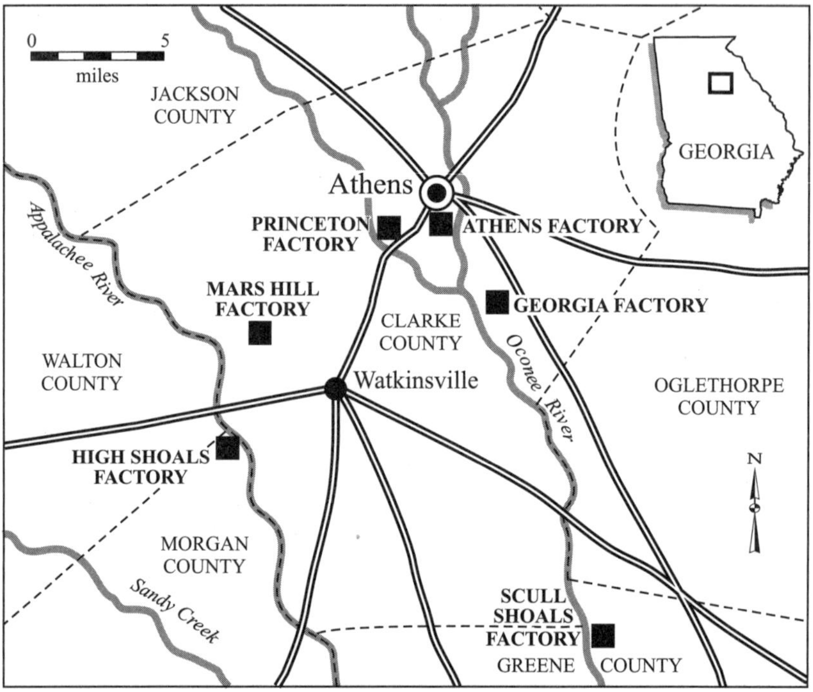

FIGURE 4. Map of factories adjoining Athens (greater Athens).

White's Factory in Jackson County was never enumerated. However, it is clear that Athens entrepreneurs commanded perhaps as much as two-thirds of this measure of the state's textile production in 1840. The number of factories affiliated with Athens grew in the 1850s, with the establishment of Hopping's factory in Walton County, and of the White family's factories in Newton and Butts counties, while the smaller factories in Jackson and Clarke counties disappeared. To be sure, by the 1850s, other locales, with superior water power and financial resources, outpaced Athens, and the community fell behind Augusta, Columbus, and perhaps even Atlanta as a node of industrial activity. But such an increase in activity required greater market penetration to create sufficient consumers for the factories' industrial goods. Thus southerners, those of Athens and elsewhere, adopted the transportation revolution as a means of negotiating the market and industrial revolutions on their own terms.[5]

THE TRANSPORTATION REVOLUTION

Southerners fully participated in the transportation revolution of the first half of the nineteenth century. Within a year of New York's completing the Eire Canal in 1825, Georgia surveyed its mountain passes in the hope of connecting the Tennessee River to the rivers of Georgia in a great system of inland water transportation connecting the Ohio River to the Gulf of Mexico. The surveyor, Wilson Lumpkin, realized that the Appalachian Mountains represented an insuperable obstacle to canal feasibility and suggested construction of a railroad as an alternative. But Georgia hesitated, since the Cherokee Nation occupied and controlled the northwest corner of the state, through which this improvement must pass. In the meanwhile, South Carolina leapt ahead of Georgia by constructing the Charleston and Hamburg Railroad to connect Charleston to the upcountries of South Carolina and Georgia. The Charleston promoters of this railroad initiated their project specifically to siphon off Savannah's cotton trade, which then floated down the Savannah River from Augusta. At its completion in 1833, the 136-mile Charleston and Hamburg Railroad constituted the longest railroad in the world, under a single company's management. But Georgia did not long remain in South Carolina's shadow.[6]

As early as 1829, the Georgia upcountry clamored for improved transportation connections. Commonly throughout the nineteenth century, local grand juries lamented the state of county roads and asked for legislative intervention. Just before the meeting of the 1829 legislature, the Walton County Grand Jury noted the desperate state of the road from Augusta to Athens, which it called "the most important market road to the up-country," and called for the state legislature to provide for construction of a turnpike to relieve the situation. During the legislative session that year, one wag joked of the road from Athens to Augusta, "This Road is not passable. Not even Jackassable."[7]

But the politics of Georgia's legislature twisted the upcountry's attempt to improve its major market road. Merchants in Savannah feared improved roads to the upcountry would divert to South Carolina the produce normally destined for their port, and the representatives of the western counties proved indifferent to northeast Georgia's problem. So the final legislation assigned the state-owned slaves used for clearing rivers and road building to the city council of Augusta. But since Augusta already considered northeastern Georgia its economic hinterland, the council focused on expanding Augusta's market share by building a new road to Milledgeville, and it provided only minor improvements on roads to nearby towns. So letters to the Athens newspaper advised the upcountry not to count upon the generosity of Augusta. As long as the cotton merchants there obtained cotton, they cared not about the obstacles upcountry farmers overcame to deliver their produce. More than anything, the planters of the interior desired cost-effective transportation for marketing their agricultural products. Against this backdrop, the citizens of the upcountry began to organize rail transportation.[8]

The people of Georgia's upcountry very quickly sought ways to bring improved transportation to their communities and formed a network to coordinate their activities. As early as 1831, the town of Eatonton attempted to extend rail connections into the Georgia upcountry and called for a convention to form a railroad from Augusta to Eatonton. Influential people from all over the state attended this convention, which resolved to promote state-supported transportation improvements to connect all the major population centers of the state, but failed to specifically call for chartering a railroad to Eatonton. So, as soon as the convention adjourned, its originators called a second meeting, composed only of the delegates from the immediate vicinity. These delegates, who after extensive debate as to the location of the western terminus, narrowly voted to ask the legislature for a charter. Eatonton's entrepreneurs knew what they wanted to do, but, without the support from surrounding communities, they lacked the capital. When it became clear that several of the upcountry's other towns desired to become competing endpoints to the railroad, the project floundered for want of stock subscriptions, until new agitation in Athens broached the subject again. The timing for renewed interest was perfect: Competition between Savannah and Charleston increased as construction of the railroad in South Carolina approached completion, which reduced Savannah's opposition to rail links to the interior. Simultaneously the public groused about the competition among the upcountry towns attempting to monopolize the advantages everyone assumed would accompany becoming a railhead. Hogging the area's limited financial resources to boost a single town seemed excessively lacking in public virtue. So when Athens entered the fray, most northeast Georgians felt the area needed a rational plan to lessen the cost of moving goods and produce, but that the plan needed to benefit the entire section of the state, not just a single community. All this propelled

Athens to the forefront of promoting a railroad as a means of restoring the harmony of interests in the Georgia upcountry.[9]

As the Charleston and Hamburg Railroad neared completion in early June 1833, Athens's capitalists initiated public ruminations about the idea of rail connections, both in general and specifically between Athens and Augusta, and they floated a plan that would eventually become the Georgia Railroad and Banking Company. First the local paper began by ridiculing those who previously thought of railroad projects as visionary enthusiasms. Then it suggested that prominent and stable men had investigated the topography between Athens and Augusta and declared it suitable for rail connections. Within two weeks Athens's citizens called two meetings for interested parties to start the process of organizing a railroad. Two days after the second meeting, they gathered again to adopt a lengthy report containing three resolutions: First, that they should request a corporate charter from the legislature. Second, that they should correspond with other railroads to obtain information about how best to organize and construct a railroad. And third, that they should organize similar meetings throughout their section of the state to promote the railroad and to establish grounds for soliciting subscriptions. The last two resolutions necessarily preceded successfully pursuing the first. In order to successfully start the project, the industrialists understood that they needed to create a network of active support as well as an information network to learn what they must do.[10]

But why should the Athenians think success a possibility when Eatonton's attempt, using many of the same tactics, generally languished? The answer has many parts, which were summarized in a newspaper editorial,

> We have long been satisfied that a rail-road from Augusta to Athens, would not only be a feasible undertaking, and one that could be completed at a reasonable cost, but of incalculable benefit to the State, and a profitable business to any Company. . . . Athens is flourishing, and rapidly increasing in wealth, population, and respectability. . . . Factories are springing up in its vicinity with astonishing rapidity, and supplying with their treasures the wants of the needy, and the demands of the wealthy. Athens is indeed the centre of attraction; and all that is necessary to make it to the upper country, what Augusta is to the middle counties, are facilities in the transportation of the Planter's produce, and the Merchant's merchandize.[11]

First, the project expected reasonable costs and a reasonable profit. Second, Athens already existed as a substantial community with a firm economic base. Hence potential investors could look at what the town already accomplished in order to determine whether a track record of success accompanied rhetorical forecasts of prosperity. Third, Athens's educational facilities and factories maintained a cash economy for the town, creating a worthwhile destination for a railroad that desired consistent freight and passenger traffic in both directions, rather than just seasonal traffic from the interior to the cotton merchants following the annual harvest. Nor did it hurt that a large population surrounded Athens; that prominent men with extensive financial resources promoted the project; and that the approaching completion of the railroad in South Carolina piqued public interest. All of these points proved advantageous, but similar points could be made by every railroad promoter in the country. Even if we accept that the public seemed more favorably disposed to supporting a railroad from Athens, such an attitude was by itself insufficient to secure the monetary loyalty of the surrounding countryside.

One must note the connection between the factories of Athens and the creation of railroads in Georgia. In the first meeting, on June 27, 1833, Asbury Hull chaired the meeting, James Camak acted as the meeting's secretary, and Augustin Clayton delivered its inaugural oration, exhorting the benefits of a railroad to Augusta to his fellow citizens. Two of the three "officers" of this first meeting possessed ties to industry: Clayton and Camak operated the Georgia Factory and the Camak Factory, respectively, and Hull eventually became an investor in factories as well. The town's industrialists also dominated the committee that drafted the company's plan of action at the second meeting. Moreover, seven of nine committee members—Judge Clayton, Asbury Hull, William Dearing, James Camak, John Nisbet, William Williams, and Stevens Thomas—already invested, or would soon invest, in industrial endeavors. The roster of commissioners who collected the stock subscriptions always contained the Athens industrialists as its core, as did the directorate of the corporation following the legal organization of the company, until Athens lost control of the railroad during the banking crisis of 1839–40. But more than mere leadership, the very idea of a railroad to Athens originated from the needs of the town's industry.[12]

Athens started agitating in earnest for a railroad in order to solve distribution problems associated with its factories. Local legend holds that plans for the railroad arose after wagons carrying the machinery James Camak imported from England for his new factory bogged down on the muddy roads from Augusta to Athens in early 1833. The machinery allegedly remained stuck for several months, delaying completion of Camak's factory. This event certainly struck a chord with the manufacturers and helped propel them to action. But factories purchase capital equipment only infrequently, and such delays need not produce agitation for constructing a railroad.[13]

Instead, the Athens industrialists' concern about the size of their local markets stimulated their interest in the railroad. They now operated three factories in a county with a population that never exceeded twelve thousand (half of whom were slaves) in the antebellum period, and they worried about survival in a limited market. Thus, the Athens railroad promoters anticipated expanding their industrial markets as well as their immediate area's agricultural markets. In the first report of the committee proposing the railroad from Athens to Augusta, the industrialists argued that decreased transportation costs allowed local goods to compete with those imported from the North, since they claimed that only the costs of the goods distinguished those produced in the two places. With reduced freight costs, Georgians would no longer be "excluded from our own Markets in [the] many articles of similar northern produce," meaning that Georgians could compete in the markets for their industrial production. Once the railroad construction began, the railroad's chief engineer, J. Edgar Thomson, also embraced the goal of enlarged markets as benefiting the quality of life at both ends of the railroad, that "articles which have heretofore not been deemed worth the expense of transportation, will then be exchanged for others from the sea-board, which are now, from their cost, dispensed with." Clearly with the majority of the state's industrial potential already located in Athens, better transportation should increase markets that benefited the town's manufacturers more than it would increase the possibility of competition that might hurt the factories.[14]

Athens's industrialists already considered expanding their markets as the key to survival. Soon after purchasing the Camak Factory, in an advertisement of the output of his factory, William Williams asked the people of Georgia to buy a sufficient amount of local industrial production in order to create a "home market" for his goods. In short, he co-opted a variation of the nullification arguments for seeking economic independence from the North, and claimed supporting locally manufactured goods profited suppliers of raw materials, manufacturers, and consumers alike. To achieve these benefits, Williams promised reciprocity in his industrial transactions. He desired constancy in patronage from local and regional buyers while he offered a form of stability in terms of quality products and fair business practices in return. By enlarging the market for manufactured products at home, industrialists like Williams also argued that they created new markets for local agricultural products, since the manufacturing process consumed cotton as its raw material. Thus expanded markets not only directly benefited manufacturers and consumers but also created a cycle of growth through backward ties to agriculture.[15]

The Athens railroad promoters went beyond the claims of mere merchant capital that improved long-distance trade guaranteed existing social relations, suggesting that improved transportation integrated less-developed markets into their sphere of influence. As such, the back countries of the Carolinas and eastern Tennessee seemed ripe for increased market penetration since Athens merchants already supplied some of their needs, albeit inconsistently. The advent of rail links, however, would bind those peripheral markets more tightly to Athens as the metropole of southern Appalachia, as they expected a portion of the existing and future trade "of North and South Carolina, and particularly of Tennessee," to use the Athens railroad to ship goods to other Georgia towns for immediate use, as well as to port cities for transshipment to other states.[16]

Previous experience with upcountry trade persuaded the Athens industrialists of the potential of this market. Probably because the Federal Road from Augusta to what would become Chattanooga went through Athens, entrepreneurs in the university town routinely traded with peddlers on their way to the upcountry. Again, because of the existing road, citizens of the western part of the Carolinas and eastern Tennessee occasionally drove horses and hogs through Athens to provide a burgeoning market in Georgia. Sufficient corn and wheat grown by upcountry farmers also moved through Athens's merchants in trade with the coast to affect prices offered in Athens. While we do not know the social origins of the farmers involved in this market trade from the upcountry, it is clear that enough agricultural trade took place between the market town of Athens and areas of the back country to call into question the historiographic contention of the near self-sufficiency of these people. These routine transactions seem to indicate a greater degree of existing commercial relations than a "safety-first" mode of agricultural production should maintain.

With such apparent readiness for market relations, the industrialists/railroad promoters of Athens considered improved transportation the catalyst for even greater penetration of an area they already considered part of their economic hinterland.[17]

Finally, the Athenian industrialists expected improved transportation to allow manufacturers to export their excess industrial production to out-of-state markets once they saturated local and regional markets. By the early 1840s the factories of Athens shipped their textiles to a variety of out-of-state clients, both throughout the South—to Charleston, Mobile, and New Orleans—as well as to the northern markets of Philadelphia and New York. Production beyond the consumption capacity of local markets need not require lowering prices in order to encourage greater demand. One informed writer explained the operations of Georgia's factories to readers of the Athens newspapers: "When our cotton spinners in Georgia have supplied the market here with twist, they export to the North the excess, and the profits upon what is sent off, is about as large as upon that consumed at home. The amount of twist sent to the North, is believed to be at least equal to that consumed at home." Thus, for Athens boosters, railroad promotion remained a means of expanding industrial markets, regardless of how they sold the program to others. But, of course, the influence and backing of local manufacturing magnates need not result in a successful railroad project, although it proved helpful.[18]

The entrepreneurs of Athens succeeded after Eatonton's boosters failed because the Athenians used an inclusive rather than an exclusive approach to organizing. Athens's rail promoters offered compromise and coordination of efforts rather than rigidly insisting upon going it alone. Instead of forcing a solution that satisfied only a small portion of those interested in building a railroad into the Georgia upcountry, as the Eatonton meeting had done, boosters in Athens created a cooperative network of investors among the communities that hoped for rail connections. In order to convince those communities, the Athens projectors sought to show that their railroad stood to benefit everyone along its route, and the region generally. The editor of the Athens newspaper explained why the railroad would prove a boon to all. Capitalists would find it a profitable investment. Planters would benefit from lower costs of transporting their produce. Merchants and artisans would find an enlarged market for their goods and services. Property owners would profit from increased land values. But the projectors knew they could not raise sufficient funds to finance such a large undertaking solely within Clarke County, so they began appealing to potential investors in neighboring communities. The same editorial further expounded that the railroad afforded advantages "to the whole North Western portion of the State" as well as to the portions of northeastern Georgia adjacent to the project. Thus they claimed all northern Georgia should support their cause because the railroad benefited the region as a whole by integrating the Indian frontier counties with the state's core. But in addition to generating favorable opinion, the Athens projectors needed to find an immediate means of eliminating competition from the Eatonton railroad proposal for the limited financial resources of the Georgia upcountry.[19]

The Athens railroad project needed to secure cooperation from the Eatonton company that already gained a legislative charter for a portion of the route that Athens needed to make its line viable. Only a month after the Athens industrialists initially met to promote a railroad to the Georgia upcountry, the renewed interest in railroads enabled the Eatonton company to subscribe the minimum amount of stock required to organize as a legal corporation. Meeting the minimum, however, did not guarantee the future sales of stock to actually build the project on its own, particularly when competing with such a prominent group as the Athens boosters. When the Eatonton company formally organized at a meeting on July 26, 1833, a consensus emerged to contact the Athens projectors about uniting the two projects. The meeting then assigned a committee of correspondence, which included Mark A. Cooper, a kinsman of Athens industrialist John Nisbet (who was a member of the committee organizing the Athens railroad project). Like the Athens meeting, this Eatonton meeting proposed seeking subscriptions from other communities and called for hiring an agent to solicit subscriptions.[20]

The Athens promoters expanded their local network by actively encouraging nearby counties to participate in the railroad promotion. Just prior to the Eatonton company's formal organization, an Augusta newspaper editor suggested that Athens work with the surrounding countryside to determine the extent of support for the project. Given Augusta's later coolness to the project, the Augusta editor may have hoped to derail the project by including too many interested parties with divergent goals, but his advice proved practical for organizing an extended support network. While the Eatonton projectors finally found sufficient subscriptions to organize its corporation under the terms of its 1831 charter, many expressed reservations about Eatonton's ability to complete the project and to place the good of the region before its own local interests. Thus, despite the need of the financial support of the surrounding countryside, all expected the Athens elite to lead in promoting the project because only they possessed sufficient enterprise and prominence to ensure completion.[21]

Soon the counties in northeastern Georgia held their meetings to consider which project to support. Meetings held in Oglethorpe, Taliaferro, Greene, Morgan, and Newton counties supported the idea of a railroad but called for cooperation between the Eatonton and Athens projects so as to not waste a propitious opportunity to improve the economy of the upcountry, an opportunity they feared would be squandered if the two projects diluted the efforts and capital of the region. Most of these meetings also clamored for the inclusion of their locality in the final route. For instance, the Greene County meeting expressed concern over the competition of routes and appointed a committee to correspond with both projects to determine "the direction of the railroad" as well as to press for a route favorable to itself. Letters to local newspapers followed the same line; for example, an Oglethorpe County correspondent urged "an union of the two routes" since he thought it "not probable that sufficient capital can be procured to extend both roads separately" to Augusta. He further argued that a single route to that city "will answer all the purposes of two, for a great part of the way."[22]

Such strong public opinion made the notion of union irresistible, but the question of which route would prevail remained undecided. Both the Eatonton and Madison routes considered by the Eatonton company still found support in the countryside while the market towns along the direct route from Athens to Augusta supported a more northern route. By September, public discourse seemed to have arrived at a consensus to build a common trunk line, accessible to all three towns in contention for the railhead. This proposed common trunk headed west from Augusta to a place in Greene County, just east of the county seat, which then allowed the construction of branches to Athens, Eatonton, and Madison. Even with a consensus on this compromise route, financing the branches still remained undecided. As one solution, the Athens editor suggested that each branch from the trunk line might incorporate as a separate entity. However, by building the first seventy-five miles of the line as a joint project, the Athens and Eatonton ventures would unite "both their influence and patronage."[23]

Finally, organizers of the competing railroad projects in northern Georgia met in Greensboro on October 21, 1833, to formalize the details of the compromise that had been working itself out in the press. The thirteen delegates (with two representing Athens, two representing Madison, one representing Eatonton, three from Greene County, two from Taliaferro County, and three representing Augusta) agreed to pursue the project as a single entity, to build the common trunk line from Augusta to eastern Greene County, and then to construct branch lines to Eatonton, Madison, and Athens. Interestingly, the resolutions called for possible extensions of each of these three branches: the Eatonton branch to go southwestwardly to Macon and thence to Columbus, the Madison branch to head west to the Alabama border, and the Athens branch to reach northward towards Tennessee. Despite the local interests, which were largely limited to boosting the importance of each separate community, the meeting affirmed the idea that long-distance trade would soon supplant the short local branches in importance.[24]

Still, none of this explains why Athens succeeded while others had not. An important further ingredient in the success in starting the Athens project was the rapidity with which its promoters implemented their plan. Within two months of the Greensboro Conference, the legislature met, considered the bill to charter the railroad, and with minor changes regarding taxation of the corporation, granted the charter along the lines requested. The Georgia Railroad, as the project was now properly constituted, announced the names of its commissioners in the towns of northern Georgia, along with the amount of stock available for subscription in each place. Connected to the speed with which the company organized was the depth of financial resources available to Athens. As such, the allotment of the lion's share of available stock subscription went to Athens and Eatonton for 2,500 shares of stock each. Commissioners for Madison, the other terminus, received 2,000 shares to sell, and the remainder of towns along the line generally received either 500 or 1,000 shares. The subscription books opened only for ten days, starting February 3, 1834, and the company needed 5,000 shares subscribed in order to organize under its charter. Although each share cost $100, an investor needed only a down payment of $5 to subscribe. So the company needed subscribers to pledge to purchase $500,000 worth of stock, with an initial payment of $25,000 going towards that sum. Augusta, with its large population and great merchant wealth, received only 1,500 shares because the city saw the railroad as a threat to its future prosperity and thus was not expected to participate with enthusiasm.[25]

Augusta opposed the railroad for many good reasons. With the advent of "easy" transportation via the railroad, upcountry planters could take on some of the duties of Augusta's cotton factors for themselves, thereby saving transaction and storage costs on the sale of their cotton. Also, the railroad enthusiasts claimed their project would facilitate commercial penetration of the upcountry and aid in town development by relocating the wholesale trade from established trade centers like Augusta to the interior towns. One letter to the Athens paper argued that, if steamboats allowed Augusta to supplant Savannah as the commercial entrepôt for the interior of Georgia, then a railroad would have the same effect on the relationship between Athens and Augusta. Not surprisingly, opposition to the rail project immediately arose in Augusta. One Augusta editorial claimed that the Georgia Railroad would "annihilate" Augusta. To assuage such fears, the Athens entrepreneurs explained that a similar commercialization of the countryside in New York resulted from construction of the Erie Canal. Rather than destroying the commerce of Albany in favor of Buffalo, the canal increased the business of all the towns. Using New York towns as a metaphor for the future of Georgia, they argued that Athens would always stay a Buffalo to Augusta's Albany, while Augusta would remain an Albany to Charleston's New York. They expected the details of the towns' relationships to change while the overall schema remained the same. Furthermore, the Athens promoters continued, the railroad project would go on, with or without Augusta's aid. When Augusta's leaders saw they could not influence the future of the project without purchasing stock in it, they chose to invest modestly.[26]

To secure the charter, the Georgia Railroad used a ruse to overcome the obstacle of obtaining sufficient subscriptions in the extremely short period the legislature authorized at the behest of Augusta's representatives. William Williams, an Eatonton native who had operated a bank in Florida before moving to Athens, purchased 4,125 of the 6,015 shares subscribed, during the ten days that subscription books were open. Although the charter prevented excessive purchases of stock by an individual in any one place during its first days of offering, it opened up the subscriptions to manipulation if the purchaser bided his time or traveled to each of the communities with subscription books. Thus Williams traveled on behalf of the company and bought a majority of the stock needed to overcome the legislative requirement of subscribing 5,000 shares. Williams did this with the understanding that the company would repurchase his stock after securing the charter and before issuing any more shares. Without this gambit, the project probably would have floundered since less than 2,000 other shares were sold during the allotted ten days. That William Williams could afford to loan the company $20,625 through down payment on his stock subscription without gaining any interest, even for a short time, is very interesting. That he possessed that much loose cash is not doubted; he reportedly hauled $60,000 in gold to Florida only two years earlier, when he established the Bank of Florida, at Tallahassee. But as a banker, he surely thought purchasing that much stock constituted a sufficient risk to require remuneration. Perhaps his reward came with his election as secretary and treasurer when the company organized. Williams clearly deserved the treasurer position since most of the money in the company's coffers belonged to him.[27]

In accordance with the breakneck pace already set by the project, the company formally organized and elected officers in Athens on March 10, 1834. Therefore, in under eight months, between June 1833 and February 1834, the industrialists of Athens conceived, promoted, and brought to fruition a plan to improve the future markets for their textiles by improving the transportation facilities of the region. That this scheme ultimately involved millions of dollars and required considerable public relations skills only serves to show that these men seemed to operate in a more modern world than commonly assumed.

In the long run, Eatonton lacked the clout to require a branch line and received short shrift in the union with Athens. The portion of the route originally chartered by Eatonton constructed as the common trunk line became known as the Union Railroad, but Eatonton soon found that the union was not based on equality. Within the united company's directorate, only one director, Josiah Flournoy, came directly from Eatonton (although a few relocated there from Athens). Apparently investors considered Eatonton a focal point of regional interests rather than a worthwhile final destination. Thus when the railroad was actually built, the investors found places along the line as amenable to them as Eatonton would have been. The new charter that merged the Eatonton project out of existence also worked to Eatonton's disadvantage. When the Georgia Railroad's charter finally passed the legislature, it contained a provision that required construction of the Union Railroad before building the branches to the three towns. The new charter presumed that, after finishing the trunk, the united company would build the three branches simultaneously. However, it also allowed the company to build them one at a time and use the profits of one branch to finance the construction of another. The directors of the Georgia Railroad ultimately chose that second option, and they focused on constructing the Athens and Madison branches. Thus, in the 1830s Eatonton still expected to receive a branch line. The company initially preferred the branches to Athens and Madison over the line to Eatonton due to events related to the long-distance trade, but the economic depression of the late 1830s and early 1840s sealed the fate of the third branch, and the Georgia Railroad never connected to Eatonton in the antebellum period.[28]

Although the Athens projectors of the Georgia Railroad achieved their objective of organizing and maintaining control of the project, they still needed to sell enough stock to finance constructing the railroad. The corporation elected industrialist James Camak its president; chief investor and future industrialist William Williams to the dual posts of secretary and treasurer; and the partners of the Athens Factory, William Dearing, John Nisbet, and A. B. Linton, to its directorate. To encourage investment, despite meeting the initial stock subscription, the Athens industrialists again took their project directly to the public, this time in face-to-face meetings in the smaller towns of the upcountry, including those not normally associated with the plantation economy. For example, the railroad's officers, Camak and Williams, attended a meeting in neighboring upcountry Jackson County on May 27, 1834, to encourage subscriptions in the market town of Jefferson. To entice the county's cash-poor yeomen to subscribe, they advertised they would accept notes, payable January 1, 1835, in place of the standard five-dollar initial payment per share of stock. In creating this investment network, the Athens industrialists rubbed shoulders with planters and yeoman alike, much as they might in a political campaign.[29]

Industrializing Athens looked for much from this extensive network of diverse investors. Clearly first and foremost, the industrializers expected the network to raise funds to build the railroad, and the investors in the network anticipated a return in the form of regular dividends. But everyone also expected the network to function as a conduit to rationalize developmental impulses throughout the state, at least the northern portion. Here again, the Athens editor argued that the project should influence Georgia's economic development by harmonizing the "collision of interest and effort." The editor probably thought of the opposition of Augusta and Savannah toward railroad development when he wrote the passage, but he rightly anticipated that creating the Georgia Railroad would systematize the disparate efforts of extending market relations and that the creation of such a system would determine the path for future economic development in the state. Developing transportation for the Georgia upcountry near Athens forced middle Georgia, the area around Macon, to promote its own railroad project to connect with Savannah. Within three years of gaining their railroad charters, the two competing areas, middle Georgia and northeast Georgia, began to coordinate their efforts into a state-wide system, with the creation of the Western & Atlantic Railroad as an enterprise of the State of Georgia. This investment network therefore succeeded as the impetus for further development.[30]

The formation of the railroad investment network produced an important secondary effect: the network of railroad investors served as a pool for recruiting investors into industrial efforts. At the start of creating the network, three of Athens's four subscription commissioners already participated actively in manufacturing: James Camak (president of the Camak Factory, which received a corporate charter from the legislature during the same session as had the Georgia Railroad), William Dearing (president of the Athens Factory), and Stevens Thomas (an investor in the Scull Shoals Factory in neighboring Greene County, which also incorporated in December 1833). The fourth commissioner from Athens, William Williams, began purchasing the Camak Factory the following November, and renamed it the Princeton Factory. Of the other forty subscription commissioners, representing ten communities, two became outright industrialists: Thomas N. Hamilton, of Appling County, purchased the Princeton Factory in Athens in 1845 for $36,000. Josiah Flournoy, of Eatonton, served as the Eatonton Factory's president in the late 1830s and early 1840s and owned half the $60,000 factory's stock at the time it burned down in 1840. Flournoy had been a leader in the original Eatonton railroad project and was the only Eatonton delegate at the Greensboro conference. A. B. Linton and others in Athens moved from investing in railroads to investing in factories as well. Thus, the railroads not only existed as an adjunct to plantation agriculture, but they also formed the nexus from which industrial developmental activities in Georgia continued to spring. The network ultimately succeeded because it offered goals that promised something for everyone: industrialists, planters, small town merchants, and merchants of the larger trade centers. In the process of delivering on the goals, the network of support expanded further, although complications would arise from its size.[31]

The Georgia Railroad Company started much like the developmental corporations described by historians of northern railroads and canals. In the formulations about how northern transportation systems grew, the historiography explains that many early transportation companies failed to return a profit to their investors in the form a dividend, but did profit the investors by increasing the value of their real estate and by quickening the trade of the area. Essentially the promoters of the Georgia Railroad promised a branch to any town near its projected route that pledged substantial stock subscriptions. But more importantly, they merged the interests of the groups intent on bringing a railhead to their own town. Individual stockholders quickly discovered the lie in the promise of immediate, continuous, and large profits. In the long run, however, the areas that the railroad served found increasing prosperity as a form of indirect profits for participating in the project. Unlike the development of transportation projects in Virginia, however, the Georgia Railroad survived as a private enterprise and ultimately become profitable because shareholder expectations always included the indirect profits for the region.[32]

Although manufacturing interests played a central role in creating the Georgia Railroad, the railroad's developers envisioned a larger set of goals that benefited many other segments of society as well, particularly for those involved in commerce and agriculture. First, they believed that railroads should link the state's interior to the coast to increase the profitability of agriculture. The railroad boosters argued that since one-third to one-half of the proceeds of the sale of cotton went to pay for its freight to market, a railroad would greatly reduce this cost, providing greater profits to the planter, who could then afford to purchase more goods from local and regional merchants, who would use the railroads to more efficiently transport their increased volume of merchandise. All this increased commerce would then guarantee profits for the railroad, allowing it to operate more efficiently. Thus, they argued that reduced transportation costs due to construction of the railroads would act as a multiplier for increasing the general prosperity in the area through which the railroad would pass.

From the beginning of the Georgia Railroad, Athens's entrepreneurs plugged into a national network of railroad enthusiasts to keep abreast of new developments. The very first meeting of the promoters of the Athens rail line organized a committee to correspond with other railroads in order to learn from their experience and to coordinate future business with them. Almost immediately after securing the company's corporate charter, proposals for regional trunk lines from the Mississippi River and Ohio River valleys entered into the discussion of where and how to build the Georgia Railroad. By becoming a part of a system for shipping long-distance freight, the promoters hoped to rationalize the cost of shipping both directions on their railroad. However, the pull of these emerging systems required transforming the company from one strictly linked to developing the local economy to one that facilitated interaction between local and regional economic interests. As such, connecting to one or another trunk line entailed varying financial and political costs to the corporation. With both types of costs in mind, the board of directors of the Georgia Railroad finally decided to construct their main rail line through Madison rather than through Athens, and this decision ultimately limited the scope of Athens's antebellum economic development while creating the potential for a new entrepôt to arise at the juncture of the rail lines of this emerging network.[33]

Starting in 1834, even before meeting the charter's subscription requirements for organizing, the Athens-based railroad project repeatedly considered including itself as part of a regional trunk. In that year, U.S. Army General Edmund P. Gaines proposed an east-west railroad to connect Memphis to the South Atlantic coast, and he dispatched a noted topographical engineer, Stephen H. Long, to survey the route. Colonel Long included the Georgia Railroad as an integral part of his proposed route, which started in Memphis and then ran along the northern portions of Mississippi and Alabama and entered Georgia through the state's Indian country before joining the Georgia Railroad at Athens. Connections with the Georgia Railroad would then allow freight to be shipped to either Charleston or Savannah from Augusta. James Camak, the Georgia Railroad's first president, predicted this trunk would transport the agricultural, mineral, and industrial production of the Georgia, Tennessee, Alabama, and Carolina upcountry to the coast, all of which would undoubtedly "find its way to New York" via Georgia's ports. If true, this outcome ought to reduce the antipathy towards railroad development by the established commercial centers. However, this line was not formally organized as a single system in the 1830s, and the ultimate completion of the route occurred too late to have a significant impact on the antebellum economy.[34]

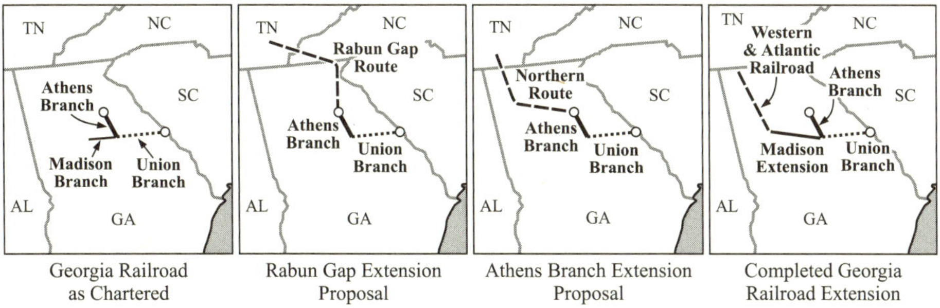

FIGURE 5. Map of Georgia Railroad expansion options.

A second trunk project, directed from Cincinnati this time, proved much more influential. Starting in late 1835, Georgia's merchants anticipated the success of a projected Charleston-to-Cincinnati railroad to funnel the long-distance trade of the Ohio River Valley to Savannah and other South Atlantic ports via a north-south trunk line. Although Georgia's legislature failed to charter this interstate corporation within its borders, as the other states had done, the Georgia General Assembly nonetheless funded surveys of Georgia's mountain passes to entice the project into the state. Reports of these surveys at the trunk's organizing convention at Knoxville in July 1836 convinced the convention to authorize a branch, called the Hiwassee Railroad, through eastern Tennessee to connect the main trunk at Knoxville to the emerging system of railroads in Georgia. The proponents of the Hiwassee Railroad planned to meet the Georgia Railroad through a short but rugged route through the Great Smoky Mountains and enter Georgia at Rabun Gap, near the intersection of Tennessee and North Carolina.[35]

Although the Georgia Railroad eagerly sought inclusion in the Cincinnati-to-Charleston project and gave an early commitment to the Rabun Gap route, it continued to consider other options. Seeking the best route for the Athens-based railroad to pursue, the Georgia Railroad's chief engineer, J. Edgar Thomson, investigated an alternate route through northwestern Georgia to McNair's Gap, near the midpoint of Georgia's border with Tennessee. Wilson Lumpkin's survey of possible canal routes through the mountains of Georgia in 1826 included portions of this northwestern route, as did Colonel Long's survey of an east-west trunk in 1834, making the investigation worthwhile.

Despite already promising to connect to the Hiwassee Railroad through Rabun Gap, and despite expecting higher construction costs in the McNair Gap route, the Georgia Railroad's board of directors leaned toward adopting this alternate route due to its potential for links to other commercial centers at Memphis and Nashville. So the Georgia Railroad hoped to keep its options open.[36]

The competing lines in Georgia quickly realized their disadvantage if the Georgia Railroad pursued the Rabun Gap line and lobbied the legislature to forestall Athens's ambitions. As part of a national chain of internal improvements, the Georgia Railroad could anticipate higher stock values, as well as faster subscription of stock offerings, due to its visibility outside the state. The Georgia Railroad could also anticipate easier terms for construction bonds from New York or London lenders since it expected to offer sustained income from profits due to long-distance freight traversing its rails as part of a national system as collateral. Given the perceptions of limited financial resources within the state, the other railroads feared loss of the financial allegiance of their investors to Athens should the Georgia Railroad appear too successful. Almost immediately after the July 1836 convention held in Knoxville to plan the Cincinnati-to-Charleston route, another convention called for Georgia's railroad enthusiasts to meet in Macon at the beginning of November to plan Georgia's response to the Knoxville Convention.[37]

In the interim between railroad conventions, the Georgia Railroad's competitors mobilized public opinion to persuade the Athens-based company to renounce its direct route to Tennessee. In short order, the Athens railroad found itself charged with many of the evils that Jacksonian Americans frequently accused corporations. Essayists opposed to extending the economic power of Athens argued that the Georgia Railroad conspired with other corporations, primarily the South Carolina Railroad, to abuse the commonweal of the people for usurious ends. Again, their republican ideology conflated economic and political subservience, and so ultimately the polemicists accused the Georgia Railroad Company of seeking to dominate Georgia's economy in order to gain political rule over the entire state. These essayists claimed that the Rabun Gap line intended to turn Georgia into an economic satellite of Charleston's wild-eyed nullifiers because it crossed only a small corner of the state before immediately funneling all the traffic to the South Carolina Railroad across from Augusta. Thus they feared Georgia would become a "colony" of South Carolina, dependent upon that state for its prosperity. As they argued in the discussion about tariffs, they commonly feared that a loss of economic independence necessarily surrendered one's ability to act independently in politics as well. Thus one essayist in Macon claimed the plan of the Georgia Railroad intended to "draw off the wealth and trade of Georgia to Charleston," making the citizens of Georgia mere "hewers of wood and drawers of water" in service "to the more proud and talented Carolinians, and their interested coadjutors in the North-east part of Georgia."[38]

These essayists improved upon the fear of domination by outsiders in order to explain the corrupting ability of the economic power of a large corporation at home. Polemicists in middle-Georgia newspapers argued that, if the Georgia Railroad controlled the trunk line, even under the McNair's Gap proposal, the corporation would become an economic monster which the state could not hope to regulate. Thus the railroad would determine who would benefit from improved transportation connections by deciding where to direct the freight it carried. A new class of railroad industrialists was rising as a secret faction to dominate and corrupt the political process within the state. Under either form of economic domination, foreign or domestic, the people of Georgia would lose their political as well as their economic independence. The Macon essayist further explained that the Georgia Railroad already acted as a secret faction lobbying to subvert the good of the people before the legislature. If the citizens of Georgia failed to convince the legislature to control this monster, they would soon find themselves "under the control of a foreign joint stock company."[39]

Unsurprisingly, the Athenians recognized the sensitivity of their position and attempted to compromise in order to blunt the attack upon their company. The Georgia Railroad initially calculated its costs on the basis of going alone, but the political pressure from the rest of the state forced it to seek a third alternative: a route that reduced the financial burden of constructing through mountainous terrain, that limited the political liabilities of economic development, and that ultimately limited the vision and scope of Athens's railroad. When J. Edgar Thomson submitted his report analyzing the first two routes, he only mentioned in passing that the railroad system that connected Savannah to Macon (the Central Railroad) could link to the northwestern route at the point at which the McNair's Gap route turned northward. However, the Georgia Railroad's cost calculations, combined with its reading of public opinion, soon overrode the desire to "monopolize" the trunk. With surveys before them, the Georgia Railroad's directors understood that a more southern route than the one proposed from Athens to McNair's Gap entailed lower construction costs because of the southern route's less difficult terrain. And a more southern route also reduced both fiscal and political costs in other ways. A southern route extending from Madison, rather than from Athens, allowed other railroads to join the northward trunk sooner, resulting in a trunk that could be built as a joint project, thus reducing the financial costs to the Georgia Railroad, and engendering a cooperative spirit among the rival coalitions building the railroad system in Georgia. Given Athens's experience in uniting with and then ignoring its Eatonton partners, however, the middle-Georgia proponents of building the trunk line to Tennessee persuaded the legislature to construct the trunk as a state-owned and -operated project, and thus deny the potential for competition between powerful corporations. Operating the trunk as if it were a common road would join the interests of all the economic factions within the state and eliminate the possibility of political domination by a clique from any part of the state.[40]

So was born the Western and Atlantic Railroad of the State of Georgia in December 1836. This state enterprise is still owned by Georgia, and it connected what would become Atlanta to what would become Chattanooga, neither of which existed in 1836. The Georgia Railroad agreed to extend its Madison Branch as its new main line, and Athens remained quietly at the end of a feeder to the main branch of its own railroad.[41]

Although now relegated to the end of a branch line and frozen out of the long-distance trade, Athens nonetheless continued to seek its share of increased commercial activity generated by the railroad. However, the town's boosters found the potential to expand Athens's markets much more limited because their town no longer lay on the main line. So they refocused their efforts on tying the surrounding countryside more securely to Athens's economy. Thus, in December 1841, with the completion of the railroad to Augusta, the merchants of Athens immediately began agitating for improved transportation connections into the higher regions of the upcountry, specifically to expand sales in order to increase the town's prosperity. Economically sophisticated, Athens's citizens now understood that transportation facilities alone would not guarantee continued prosperity. To sustain the town as the center for trade in the Georgia upcountry, Athens's merchants needed to provide upcountry citizens with the means of buying supplies that came to Athens by rail, by first purchasing goods from them for transshipment to Augusta and beyond. Again, a newspaper editorial cogently summarized the arguments by claiming that, while many in the upcountry to Athens's north wanted to use the town as their principal market, "many are deterred, in consequence of the . . . bad roads." Thus Athens found itself in the position Augusta had held prior to the coming of the railroad, but with a smaller and poorer hinterland, requiring significantly more work to guarantee prosperity through expansion of its markets. In many ways, Athens's physical and financial limits ultimately prevented its merchants from stealing the wholesale trade of Augusta in the 1840s. Thus Athens failed to transform itself into a Buffalo to Augusta's Albany, despite its heady success in initial railroad promotion.[42]

Athens's compromise with the realities of state politics regarding the extension of rail facilities proved only one cause of the town's loss of influence in determining its economic future. More significantly, Augusta's financiers outmaneuvered Athens's industrialists. After petitioning for and receiving banking privileges from the legislature in 1836, the Georgia Railroad nearly doubled its stock offerings to capitalize its two banking branches, as well as to extend the Madison line (which it initially called the Middle Branch Railroad) to join with the state's proposed trunk line. Several Augusta banks, along with Augusta's Town Council, immediately bought up 2,000 of the proffered 7,500 new shares of stock, while private citizens of Augusta bought a large portion as well. The Augusta newspaper reported its delight in such a large taking of the Georgia Railroad & Banking Company stock. The editor then advised Augusta to wait for a propitious moment for taking full advantage of its nearly controlling share of the stock, arguing that, "if we are not too eager to enjoy before the fruits of our industry are ripe and fully matured . . . , we cannot fail in accomplishing . . . the prosperity . . . of our own dear Augusta." The merchants, bankers, and the corporation of Augusta reserved their increased stock holdings as a Trojan horse; they waited, ready to co-opt control of the railroad they previously opposed. During the Panic of 1837, the Athens industrialists overextended themselves, which forced them to sell enough of their railroad stock that the Augusta stockholders took control of the board of directors and voted to move the company headquarters to Augusta. Athens's newspaper correspondents noted how Augusta's financiers subscribed to the stock in the Georgia Railroad only "to obtain the control of the institution." Unflatteringly, the Athenians compared the financial establishment of Augusta to a "wily serpent" which "first charms and entertains, then swallows her victim." But turnabout was fair play. Just as Athens's industrialists neutralized the proponents of an Eatonton line, the balance of power within the corporation depended on the financial resources available to each coalition of stockholders, and Athens lost its influence to Augusta to determine the railroad and banking company's future.[43]

Part of Athens's problem of retaining control of the company arose due to the profitability of the company's banks. Initially, the railroad company located its main bank in Athens with a directorate (independent of the railroad's directorate) composed largely of the town's industrialists. Meanwhile the railroad allowed the Augusta branch of its bank to operate independently of the main branch with its own directorate, which consisted mainly of financial officers from other banks in Augusta. While the Athens Branch of the Georgia Railroad and Banking Company catered to financing smaller merchant houses, planters, and the industrialists, the Augusta branch counted not only on income from similar borrowers within its immediate area but also upon profits from loans to cotton factors and shippers as well. Therefore, the main bank at Athens made fewer loans than the Augusta branch, and it earned an insufficient profit with which to weather the long depression of the late 1830s and early 1840s. With the removal of the company's offices to Augusta, the new Augusta-dominated Georgia Railroad directorate ordered the main bank at Athens to close its affairs. The independent branch bank in Augusta remained solvent, however, and citizens of Augusta remained in control of the company until the 1980s, long after losing interest in railroading.[44]

With Athens's loss of control over the railroad, the merchants and financiers of Augusta reasserted their town's economic hegemony over the upcountry of northeastern Georgia. Despite the howls and lamentations of Athens's citizens against the favoring of through freight over local freight, the Augusta-controlled railroad instituted discriminatory freight rates against the upcountry to reduce market development with the potential to disrupt the economic supremacy of Augusta's merchants. Under Augusta's rule, the railroad also instituted unfavorable schedules for the Athens branch line, forcing passengers from Athens to board in the middle of the day (every other day), and depositing them in Augusta too late in the day to do business. This schedule forced Athenians conducting business in Augusta to remain in that town several extra days before they could return home. Clearly the Augusta stockholders took to heart all of Athens's earlier arguments that rail connections enabled upcountry planters to eliminate the Augusta middlemen from their business transactions. The railroad's rates and schedules for the upcountry henceforth ended all movement toward such economic empowerment. Similarly, passengers headed toward Atlanta from Athens frequently waited for hours for connections at Union Point, where the Athens Branch connected to the main line. The directors of the Georgia Railroad and Banking Company guaranteed that the Athens branch continued to serve the interests of the Augusta elite that now controlled the corporation.[45]

The reversal of fortunes for the Athens industrial elite over control of the railroad highlights the tension between local boosterism and the supra-local nexus of antebellum business activities. Despite the connections and prestige of Athens's elite, they needed the financial resources of the surrounding countryside to implement the scale of their economic dreams. Once the railroad began to pay dividends, however, the countryside chose the promise of continuous profits over loyalty to those who initiated the successful transportation project. With the leadership of the town's elite called into question because of their failure to adequately manage their bank, the majority of the Georgia Railroad's stockholders, who generally resided between Athens and Augusta, voted for Augusta's leadership. Had the Athens industrial elite maintained the support of the countryside, they could have overcome the hostile takeover despite the strength of stockholding in Augusta. Furthermore, despite the newspaper rhetoric about Augusta's profligacy, the citizens of both towns routinely worked with each other. Three of the four southern commercial conventions organized by Athens in the late 1830s were held in Augusta. Moreover, Augusta always controlled the means of transshipment out of the upcountry by providing facilities for barges on the Savannah River and by refusing to allow the South Carolina Railroad to connect directly with the Georgia Railroad. Finally, citizens of Athens and Augusta maintained strong personal relations throughout the period. For example, William Dearing's son, Dr. William E. Dearing, served as mayor of Augusta in the 1850s. And family members of several directors of the Georgia Railroad resided in both towns as well. In the creation of the railroad, the supra-local business network proved superior to local interests. With Augusta's takeover of the Georgia Railroad, local boosterism won out. Such relationships would prove contingent upon events in the future as well.[46]

Ultimately, geography worked against Athens. Augusta's discriminatory policies contributed less to Athens's failure to gain ascendancy over the upcountry's economy than did Athens's location at the end of a branch line. Authors forecasting future prosperity for Athens always tempered their prophecies with acknowledgments of Athens's geographic limits, that "her position is a little remote from the cotton region." This location off the beaten path limited the town's growth after 1835, and Atlanta became the commercial metropolis of the upcountry. Located at the intersection of the Georgia Railroad, the Macon and Western Railroad (which was the northernmost portion of the system that connected Macon to Savannah), and the state-owned Western and Atlantic Railroad, Atlanta grew from a tavern named Whitehall at the edge of the Cherokee Nation during initiation of Georgia's rail system in the 1830s to a real town in the late 1840s, to a major place of commerce in the 1850s. After 1850, Atlanta's continuous campaign of self-promotion proved effective in extending its economic reach, but the town originated from Athens's efforts. Had Athens built its line to Rabun Gap to connect with the Hiwassee Railroad, Athens might have grown to be the city that Atlanta later became. But topography and politics worked against Athens. Therefore, what seemed reasonable for the future expansion of the Georgia Railroad in the 1830s, when Athens controlled it, ultimately worked to the town's detriment. By agreeing to run its westward extension from Madison rather than either westward or northward from Athens, both of which the original Georgia Railroad corporate charter allowed, the company relegated Athens to becoming a regional market town, important only within a limited area of the Georgia upcountry.[47]

Despite the loss of leadership by the Athens industrialists, the Georgia Railroad largely succeeded in promoting its initial goals. It reduced transportation costs for agricultural products and made the slave regime more efficient. It encouraged the growth of markets for local manufactures and the penetration of markets into nominally self-sufficient areas, and it promoted the growth of upcountry market towns. The railroad's efforts clearly stimulated systemizing Georgia's transportation network, while avoiding costly and disastrous state-sponsored projects like the canal systems of Indiana, Pennsylvania, or Virginia. The Georgia Railroad succeeded while contemporary projects in other states failed because the Athens leaders placed the profit potential of the long-distance trade ahead of their own local boosterism. Of all its promises, the Athens-led initiative delivered best upon its goal of improving markets, which increasingly brought more southerners into commercial society. An 1847 letter by a young Charleston merchant in commenting on his commissions on net sales of fifty thousand dollars of northern Georgia produce emphasizes this success, that "as the [Georgia Rail] Road progresses into Turnpikes our business will continue to increase." Continued market penetration into the upcountry as a result of the railroad, he felt, would extend his business "to an almost indefinite amount." Thus, the network the Athens industrialists built produced lasting effects on Georgia's economic development, but the choices the network made left Athens behind as other parts of the state chose to increase their industrial activities in the late 1840s—particularly Augusta, Macon, Columbus, and Atlanta, which drew entrepreneurs and financial resources away from Athens.[48]

INDUSTRIAL ATHENS IN THE 1850s

Despite twenty years as a leader in bringing the industrial and transportation revolutions to Georgia, by 1850, Athens began experiencing both real and relative decline in its economic significance. The merchants of Augusta now controlled its railroad, which limited Athens's commercial possibilities. When the depression ended in 1846, other Georgia cities lurched ahead of Athens by experimenting with larger factories, with steam power, and with greater industrial diversification. Thus, by 1850, the three Clarke County factories enumerated by the federal census accounted for only 12 percent of the state's official capitalization in textiles, 17 percent of the value of its textile output, and 11 percent of the state's factory operatives (down from 38 percent of the capitalization, 42 percent of the value of the output, and 30 percent of the factory operatives of the state's totals in 1840).[49]

While still strong, Athens's industrial economy no longer served as the dominating model for the state. Yet the perception of the town's successes with its factories, in the eyes of the rest of Georgia, set off a mill-building boom for the state in the late 1840s. An 1846 U.S. Treasury Department circular on tariff reform, commonly called the Walker Tariff Report, acted as the catalyst of this boom. Federal Treasury agents in Georgia held the Athens Factory up as a peculiarly profitable manufacturing firm because of its 24 percent dividend in 1844. (This was actually a deceptively high figure since the firm declared an excessively large dividend that year to expedite settling the estate of the company's agent to preclude his heirs from demanding the dissolution of the partnership.) Other manufacturing firms in Georgia, the Walker Tariff Report noted, declared similar although not quite as spectacular dividends, averaging 18 percent from 1842 to 1845, when agriculture and commerce experienced severe depression. None of the Georgia manufacturers who corresponded with the Treasury Department expected diminished returns in the near future. In fact, Henry Merrell, who the report referred to as Georgia's "shrewdest northern manufacturer," and who operated textile factories near Athens for ten years, expected to retire with a fortune before "competition could bring [his profits] down to twelve per cent." The Walker Report encouraged further industrial investment by forecasting an "[i]ncrease of profit aris[ing] from an increasing demand in the States of North Carolina, South Carolina, Alabama, and Louisiana." This expanding market would provide profits for all who invested, rather than increasing competition for existing firms.[50]

Seeking to emulate the profitable experience of the Athens manufacturing firms, cotton-factory projects along the Georgia fall line attracted investors at a frenzied rate during the peak years of the mill boom, 1845–50. Henry Merrell explained the fevered pitch. After losing on investments in railroads, in banking, and in businesses ancillary to commerce (such as marine insurance) during the depression years of 1839–45, persons of wealth in Georgia sought remunerative safe havens for their funds by investing in textile factories as a sure thing. Unfortunately, poor accounting practices in starting up these factories often confused the collection of factory capital with profits from the sale of its production. So while a company continued to collect its subscriptions, like a modern Ponzi scheme it declared a dividend on its "profits." After a few years, however, investors came to understand the overvalued nature of the stock, as factory directorates either ceased or drastically cut dividends while contemplating means of avoiding bankruptcy. However, to make matters worse, stockholders already invested additional funds in yet another factory project based on the early dividends gained from the first factory. When the first factory failed, factory stock (and manufacturing in general) became an object of derision in the eyes of investors. While not all factories started during the mill boom failed, sufficient numbers went bankrupt that southern manufacturing developed a poor reputation in general, despite later successes enjoyed by those who purchased the failed factories at deep discounts. The "sour grapes" about poor investments combined with an occasional outburst against the corporate form by which most of these newer firms organized themselves to contribute to a general sense that southerners in the antebellum period universally opposed instituting a system of industrial manufactures.[51]

During the boom years, before the factories failed, nothing could have been further from the truth. In fact, in 1847, the Georgia legislature enthusiastically encouraged the construction of additional textile factories with the state's first general incorporation act, requiring factory companies to file papers only in their local courts to incorporate, rather than requiring individual legislative acts for each factory. Some of the mill-boom projects followed the Athens model of modestly sized, community-based, water-powered factories. Others, like those built in Augusta and Columbus, used the Lowell model of large-scale water-powered enterprises, complete with independently incorporated power-canal companies. Still others—in Macon, Milledgeville, Greensboro, and Madison—experimented in steam power when town fathers decided they lacked sufficient water power to run a factory.[52]

Unfortunately, the mill-building boom proved a bust for most of the Georgia factories as well as for the state's corps of investors. Rather than creating market niches for themselves, nearly all the factories produced the same lines of course yarn, and, after quickly saturating their local markets, they used Georgia's new railroads to market their surplus in the North. Georgia factories routinely sent goods to New York, Philadelphia, and New Orleans as wholesale markets for further transshipment, as well as selling directly to merchants in the upcountry of the Carolinas, Georgia, Alabama, and Tennessee. But the increased competition drove prices down and further depressed public expectations of the profits to be made in southern textile manufacturing.[53]

But new competition came from other sources as well. Northern manufacturers understood that the same forces that opened new southern markets to southern factories opened them to penetration by northern firms, too. Henry Merrell explained that northern mills crushed infant southern industry once the "[r]ailroads . . . brought the Southern manufacturer . . . into direct competition with . . . the Northern manufacturer, with none of that protection from government which the Northern manufacturer enjoyed . . . in his infant struggle against foreign competition."[54]

And compete they did. Northern companies soon reportedly copied the styles manufactured in southern factories and sold them in Georgia at lower prices than local factories could charge and still survive. One cannot say if this constituted "dumping": the sale of goods at prices lower than the cost of production by well-financed firms in order to temporarily undercut their competition and drive them out of business. Clearly northern textile manufacturers saw the nascent southern textile industry as competitors for the same business, since both North and South felt the reduction in prices for finished textiles as part of an increasingly cohering global market. But a combination of greater economies of scale enjoyed by the largest northern firms and the reduced transportation costs gained from using the new southern railroads probably undercut prices offered by Georgia factories. Thus northern factories competed head-to-head with southern firms in the southern home markets.[55]

While weathering the storm of increased competition better than the newcomers, Athens's industry participated both in the mill boom of the 1840s and in the industrial downturn of the 1850s. Sometime during the 1840s, the Athens Manufacturing Company purchased a water-power site in neighboring Jackson County with the intent of expanding its productive capacity by constructing another factory there. Retrenching from low profits in the early 1850s, the Athens Factory sold this potential manufacturing site and abandoned further discussions of building a second factory across the river from its current facility. Moreover, the company only episodically issued dividends during the remainder of the 1850s. Twice during that decade, disgruntled stockholders forced votes to liquidate the company's assets rather than continue such a meager business. In each vote, the factory company narrowly followed the lead of its agent, second-generation industrialist John S. Linton and, both times, decided to update its facilities instead. Thus, in 1853 and 1858, the Athens Factory sent Dr. Linton north to purchase new machinery. Such action was economically rational because, even during hard times, factories needed to reinvest in equipment and facilities in order to remain competitive in a stiff market. To be sure, each vote to continue the business met with resistance from the minority block of stockholders that advocated liquidation, particularly after the factory burned to the ground in 1857.[56]

Other factories in Athens also vacillated about continuing the textile business. John White seemed ambivalent about keeping his Georgia Factory running. In 1849, without explanation, he put his cotton factory up for sale but apparently found no satisfactory offers. But in the mid-1850s, White updated his factory by purchasing the equipment of the defunct Charleston Manufacturing Company and expanding the size of his factory facilities. While most considered upgrading equipment and expanding production during a down market to be a risky venture, R. G. Dun's credit reporters acknowledged White's business acumen and expressed confidence in his ability to pay off his thirty-thousand-dollar debt. Less aggressively, the Princeton Factory rebuilt and improved only after floods destroyed its dam in 1852 and 1854. However, all of these expenditures proved essential to the survival of the firms. As one informed source explained, since the textile industry in Georgia possessed insufficient labor to staff all its factories in the 1850s, "only those factories which had the most improved machinery in the place of manual labor could hope to succeed—the rest must go under." Following this prescription, all three textile firms in Athens survived the shake-out of the industrial depression of the 1850s.[57]

Stymied by the relative unprofitability of the textile industry, and shut out of control of the railroad, Athenians interested in non-agricultural investments in the 1850s developed other industrial ventures, some directly connected to the town's existing industry, and others which supplied specialized niches of consumer demand in an increasingly sophisticated town. From 1848 to 1852, Athenians started a bobbin factory and a foundry to service the cotton factories around the town. During approximately the same time, Athens enjoyed the additions of a paper mill and a gas work (neither of which constitute industrial usages as defined here, but each added to the town's "manufacturing" stock, nonetheless). Additionally, entrepreneurs augmented the physical facilities of an increasingly diversified industry by creating new financial institutions to enhance their control over their local economy. In 1848, the town fathers captured control of the board of directors of a new insurance company (reminiscent of the manner in which Augustans gained custody of the Georgia Railroad) and moved its headquarter to Athens. In 1856, the town started a second bank to replace the financial institution lost by Augusta's takeover of the Georgia Railroad. By the end of the antebellum period, Athens presciently positioned itself to profit from the industrial needs of the Confederate military.[58]

During this new direction of investment, however, Athens's industrialists remembered how their efforts in railroads in the 1830s, and in textiles in the 1850s, failed to meet their expectations. Thus profits mattered, and they minimized the size of these new investments to limit the possibility of losses. However, an editorial about starting a telegraph line to Athens makes clear that these profits could be counted when either paid directly to the investor, or when indirectly received by the entire community, by making existing business arrangements more profitable: "We are aware that the first and essential inquiry is will the stock pay? We think it will, if not interest on the capital invested by way of dividend, at least in the increased value thereby imparted to town property, and in the general commercial prosperity of our place." Enhancing existing business proved to be the impetus of most of the new "industries" of Athens.[59]

Although Athens had long supported many forms of artisan manufacture—from cobblers to carriage makers—the existence of three successful cotton mills within the county, two more on its borders, and several more within a single day's travel created an opportunity to service the needs of the mills. Textile manufacture requires a constant supply of wooden bobbins and spindles since they wear out with great frequency. As such, local manufacture of bobbins and spindles prevents the factory downtime that would result from awaiting shipment from the North. Thus, in the late 1840s, entrepreneurs in Athens erected a water-and-steam-powered facility to produce various sorts of bobbins. Federal census marshals enumerated the firm of E. J. McCall & Company on June 1, 1850, reporting a three-person workforce in a company capitalized at only three hundred dollars but capable of producing 50,000 bobbins annually (which meant a per capita production of 66 bobbins per workday). In addition to bobbins, these wood turners produced custom orders of bedposts and wagon axles as needed by the community. While the exact date of the bobbin mill's origins remains unknown, it probably began operations prior to 1850 since an 1849 advertisement in the Athens newspaper sought to sell goods to manufacturers of heddles, bobbins, spools, and reeds.[60]

Although manufacturing a needed industrial item, the bobbin mill frequently changed hands. Following enumeration in the 1850 census, the next notice of the bobbin mill occurred in 1854, when P. A. Summey & Brother, of Athens, advertised taking custom orders for all sorts of spokes for wagons and carriages, as well as for bobbins for cotton factories. A North Carolina native and a tinner by trade, Peter Summey failed at business several times prior to manufacturing bobbins and he did not last long at that either. Two years later, Harmon Schevenell and Company (owned by John H. Newton) took over the operation in 1856, relocated the business to a creek three miles west of town, enlarged the facility, and reinstalled a steam engine. Explaining the custom nature of bobbin manufacture, they requested that customers send them a sample bobbin of what they wanted, or, at least "a description . . . when a sample cannot be sent." Originally German master cabinet makers, Harmon Schevenell and his brother, Richard, specialized in carriage manufacture prior to producing bobbins. John H. Newton, one of Athens's major merchants since his arrival in the town in the early 1830s, surfaced several times as an owner of the bobbin mill, owning all or various shares of the business in the 1850s, 1860s, and 1870s. Another seemingly permanent fixture, Pennsylvania native Edward McCall acted as the master wood-turner in charge of the bobbin mill throughout the 1850s and 1860s. In 1858, McCall bought out the Schevenells' one-third share of the firm for $250. Although never terribly prosperous, the bobbin mill continued as an essential adjunct to the area's textile mills.[61]

Like Athens, other textile centers in Georgia operated bobbin mills, the larger of which they called "novelty works," or a "variety works," in the antebellum period. In 1848, the Columbus Variety Works, which served a much larger manufacturing center than the bobbin mill in Athens, operated with a capital investment of $30,000, employed between forty and one hundred hands, and produced an assortment of "buckets and bobbins." However, most variety works, such as those in Marietta, Thomasville, and Americus, probably produced bobbins on a smaller scale, similar to the production pattern of the Athens bobbin mill.[62]

Athenians started a foundry just before 1850, both to supply the needs of local industry and as means of diversification. On January 22, 1849, the unnamed partners of the Athens Steam Company obtained a bond to purchase land for the company. In June 1850, federal census marshals reported that the company invested $15,000 in facilities that included a steam engine for its source of power. The following month, Richard S. Schevenell, Peter A. Summey, Rufus L. Moss, and John S. Linton incorporated the Athens Steam Company as a multi-purpose company with a capital of $5,000, under the provisions of the general incorporation act, to manufacture any article composed of wood or metal, as well as machinery. Carriage maker Schevenell quickly quit the company, advertising his stock as a bargain to anyone seeking "to invest money in a profitable speculation." Blacksmith William P. Talmage purchased Schevenell's stock for $1,500 in February 1851, and seven months later, he bought $500 of the company's stock from Edmund Palmer, the clerk of the Athens Factory, who probably obtained his stock from R. L. Moss sometime soon after the firm's incorporation.[63]

The steam company continued business despite setbacks. In November, the Athens Steam Company announced its main focus as pouring castings, and as building and repairing machinery. Its advertisement no longer mentioned manufacturing wood products. Soon afterward, a fire broke out in the foundry at 10 p.m. on February 23, 1853, burning the foundry, the machine shop, the blacksmith shop, the coal house, and a new building recently completed as a warehouse and office. The company saved only their patterns and some of the machinery. Talmage, then president of the firm, estimated the uninsured loss at $4,500, and the members of the company assessed themselves in order to rebuild. In February 1854, the company incorporated again, with a capital of $15,000, this time by special legislation that named the company's stockholders as William P. Talmage, John S. Linton, Edmund Palmer, and Peter Summey. This special legislation then identified the firm's manufactures as "hollow ware, castings, gearing, tools, machinery and other articles of which iron or other metal constitutes the whole or a component part." The following month, the company proudly displayed the first steam engine built in Athens, which was rated at only twenty-five horsepower. Despite this limitation, the company boasted that it could build such steam engines as cheaply and as well as any northern firm and thus could save southern buyers significant freight costs. Other works of the foundry included circular sawmill blades, mill wheels, shafting and gearing, mining machinery, pumps, firefighting equipment, and the decorative fence surrounding the University of Georgia. Given the range of uses of steam engines resulting from the increase of mills and factories in Georgia, these product lines seemed wise choices. Still, the foundry did not find financial success in the antebellum period. Throughout the 1850s, R. G. Dun credit reports consistently doubted the ultimate success of the company, claiming that its indebtedness always equaled its capital and that it survived only because of the skillful management of its agent, Reuben Nickerson, a machinist from Maine.[64]

Despite the small number of such machine-building businesses in the antebellum South, one should not underestimate the importance of this growing industrial sector. In the 1850s, cotton factory agents routinely went north to purchase equipment with which to make their factories competitive during the international slump in textile profits. John S. Linton, agent of the Athens Factory and a stockholder in the Athens Foundry, made two such trips, in 1853 and 1858. Enoch Steadman's 1858 manual for southern factory managers listed the lack of southern machine shops as the first of six disadvantages under which the southern textile industry operated. Southern industrialists thus logically promoted the establishment of small machine shops. Entrepreneurs in Augusta, Atlanta, Columbus, and Macon started foundries in the 1850s that survived into the 1860s. Although much smaller and less sophisticated than the comparable industry of the North, the size the southern machine-building sector should not be laid solely at the feet of slavery. Rather, the difference can be attributed, in part, to comparative advantage and the relative age of the other industrial sectors of the two regions. The small southern cotton-manufacturing industry, created to enhance the region's agricultural advantages, acted much more slowly to pull southern entrepreneurs into creating a machine-building sector to service the factories. Thus, an adolescent southern industrial sector faced robust middle-aged northern equivalent sectors. But industrial facilities throughout the South proved sufficient to convert to a war footing and support four years of modern warfare—no small feat for a reputedly immature industrial sector.[65]

In addition to industries ancillary to the textile factories, Athenians also began to invest in expanded artisan manufactures, the most important of which was a paper mill. Paper, being the medium for all business transactions and for conveying news, appeared a logical choice for the diversification of manufacturing in Athens. And Athens possessed ample supplies of the necessary clean water for paper manufacture. Albon Chase, the retired editor and master printer of Athens's *Southern Banner*, and John S. Linton, agent of the Athens Factory, built the Pioneer Paper Factory in two years, completing it in 1849. The paper mill then provided five hundred to six hundred pounds of newsprint, writing paper, or wrapping paper made from "cotton and linen rags" to its clients in northeastern Georgia each day. Originally a partnership, Linton and Chase constructed a $15,000, two-story wooden factory upon a stone basement on the site previously occupied by William Lumpkin's grist mill at the confluence of Barber and McNutt's creeks, about a half-mile beyond the Princeton Factory from Athens. In December 1851, Chase and Linton obtained insurance on their stock in the partnership, and they sold a fifth share in the paper factory for $5,000 to William P. Talmage. Like the cotton factories during the mill boom, the Pioneer Paper Company incorporated with a capitalization of $30,000 under the liberal provisions of the 1847 General Incorporation Act on February 26, 1852, while adding Alfred Grant (Dr.

Linton's cousin) to its membership. Later that year, R. G. Dun reported that Chase and Linton each invested $12,000 in the company while Talmage and Grant owned minority shares with $5,000 and $1,000 invested respectively.[66]

Although the business reportedly made large profits throughout the 1850s, it too suffered several setbacks from fire and flood. On August 27, 1852, a freshet damaged a portion of the factory, along with its dam and bridge across the creek as well as some of the materials on hand for production, with a loss estimated at $800. On April 23, 1858, with William P. Talmage as the majority shareholder owning one-quarter of the company's $40,000 stock, the main mill burned. The fire destroyed nearly everything: the building, machinery, tools, raw materials, and finished paper. "All burnt but a few reams of paper and [the] desk with the book[s]." Although insured for only $7,000 on a loss of $30,000, the company rebuilt and sent its agent, Albon Chase, north to procure new machinery. By April 1859, the factory resumed operations and in 1860 again reported full capitalization of $40,000.[67]

The final new manufacturing firm in Athens during the 1850s produced gas for lighting. Although firms could incorporate under the General Incorporation Act after 1848, many chose to seek exceptions to the law's general clauses through special incorporation acts. The Georgia legislature granted such a special incorporation to the Athens Gas Light Company on March 4, 1856, specifically naming its stockholders as Asbury Hull, Dr. Joseph Carlton, William L. Mitchell, William Morton, Ross Crane, Thomas Wray, E. L. Newton, Stevens Thomas, Thomas R. R. Cobb, Blanton M. Hill, and William Hulme, most of whom were leading businessmen and politicians in Athens, and many of whom had already invested in other industrial enterprises. Not alone in pursuing lighting technology, Augusta and Savannah incorporated their own gas companies prior to the Athens group. Although local entrepreneurs reputedly produced gas from processing the knots of "light pinewood" as early as 1851, no evidence of gas use appeared in Athens until a newspaper article of March 1857 announced that industrial investor Asbury Hull installed eighteen lighting jets in his house. By 1859, the town council contracted for eight gas lights for the streets of downtown Athens and engaged a lamplighter. However the gas company failed to find immediate success, and its stock probably changed hands several times from its incorporation until its sale to William S. Grady, Henry Grady's father, for $1,000 in October 1860.

Gas lighting probably proved too much of a luxury to gain a sufficient number of customers to become profitable before the 1860s, since it cost $150 to connect just one house to the system. Nonetheless, Grady and his family operated the gas works throughout the 1860s, the family continuing even after Grady's death in 1864. Despite manufacturing gas through an industrial process, there is no indication that the gas works supplied the town's factories or its ancillary manufacturers with increased lighting. Since the companies that insured Athens's textile factories frequently refused to allow steam engines to operate near insured structures because of the possibility of fire ignited from sparks arising from the machines' smokestacks, they would have howled with despair at the thought of a continuous open flame in a factory. However, Athenians throughout the 1850s created greater social space for integrating such manufactured products into southern society.[68]

In 1848, Athenians moved to protect their industrial (and other) investments by securing control of the Southern Mutual Insurance Company, which the legislature incorporated in 1847. Mutual insurance companies at that time embodied a special form of cooperative capitalism by paying claims out of current-year premiums and distributing anything left over back to its policyholders as a dividend. More importantly, everyone who purchased insurance owned a share of the company's stock and could vote in its annual convention. While the company originally planned to locate its headquarters at Griffin, William Morton of Athens, who had been one of the petitioners for incorporation, sold enough policies in Athens to enable his townsmen to pack the second annual convention (with Young L. G. Harris of Athens controlling the votes of 153 proxies). With a majority of the company's stock, they voted themselves the company's board of directors and subsequently moved its headquarters to Athens. The convention elected Asbury Hull, one of Athens's major industrial investors, the company's president and treasurer, and elected Charles F. McCay, professor at the University of Georgia, its actuary. A Baptist minister, John U. Parsons (a native of Maine, but then a resident of Cuthbert, Georgia), who had founded the company, temporarily remained its secretary and general agent.[69]

After moving with the company headquarters to Athens, Parsons found himself marginalized. In 1849, the company designated Albon Chase his assistant secretary, and the following year Chase became the company's secretary, taking care of the home office while Parsons remained general agent. The general agent could write policies in any territory not allotted to a specific agent, and this proved Parsons's ultimate downfall. In 1851, Southern Mutual's board of directors removed Parsons from his general agency for failing to account for all the funds he collected and for all the policies he issued. While company history refers to this affair as an embezzlement, a closer reading of the board's minutes indicates that, while they suspected him of embezzling the funds, it could not prove the charge because Parsons was such a poor bookkeeper. With Parsons removed, the board elected Albon Chase its secretary and general agent in his place, and Chase served in that capacity until his death in 1867. With the company's removal to Athens, the involvement of entrepreneurs with large industrial interests, such as Secretary Albon Chase and President Asbury Hull, shaped Southern Mutual's policy choices toward underwriting industrial ventures.[70]

Although Southern Mutual originally wrote five lines of insurance, its fire insurance proved most important. As specified in its charter, Southern Mutual could write life insurance, insurance on the lives of slaves as property, fire insurance, transportation (marine and railroad) insurance, and storage insurance (generally for recently harvested cotton or for commercial goods). By the middle of the 1850s, the company discontinued its transportation and servant policies and sold its life insurance department to a new company in South Carolina. It continued to provide storage, or "Open Policies," as a minor line. Southern Mutual primarily provided fire insurance for residential and commercial structures, but it also serviced much of Georgia's industrial sector. In Athens, Southern Mutual insured all three of the Athens cotton factories—the Princeton Factory, the Georgia Factory, and the Athens Factory—as well as the Pioneer Paper Mill and the Athens Foundry. It also insured the three cotton factories in neighboring Greene County: the Scull Shoals Factory, the Curtright Factory, and Henry Merrell's Greensboro Steam Factory. In neighboring Walton County, to the west, it insured the High Shoals Factory. A little further away, but still within the commercial reach of Athens, the company insured the Rock Mills Factory, Planters Factory, Shoals of Ogeechee Factory, Hancock Factory, Eatonton Factory; Madison Steam Factory, Newton Factory, White's Factory in Newton County, and Anthony's Shoals Factory in Elbert County. Outside Athens's direct economic sphere, but still in Georgia, Southern Mutual insured at least twenty-one other textile factories across the state's fall-line counties, between 1848 and 1865. The company also provided fire insurance to factories in Alabama, Tennessee, South Carolina, and North

Carolina (although it discontinued coverage for Alabama and Tennessee by the mid-1850s).[71]

The process for obtaining fire insurance for a cotton factory proved similar to obtaining insurance for a residence or a retail structure. A factory owner applied either to a local agent (who then referred the application to the company's board of directors) or directly to the home office. By law, the company could not insure any property for more than ten thousand dollars, but the company's by-laws further restricted the potential for losses by stipulating that it could not insure more than three-quarters of the value of any property. Typically, therefore, a cotton factory sought ten thousand dollars in insurance, and the home office then either requested a report on the factory from a local agent or it dispensed its general agent or a special committee of board members (usually those with factory experience) to evaluate the property. If approving the application, the evaluator(s) usually recommended a premium of 2 to 5 percent of the insured value, based on the type of construction of the factory, the factory's operating practices, and the type of equipment used. The report frequently recommended dividing the insurance between the factory structure, the outlying buildings, and the permanent machinery of the factory. Sometimes the evaluators advised approval with a higher premium because they felt the use of a steam engine, or the storage of unprocessed cotton in a warehouse they deemed too close to the main factory, posed a significant risk of fire. In granting a policy, the board often required the insured to hire a night watchman, to prevent arson or to sound alarm in case of accidental fire. Finally, since ten thousand dollars generally represented only 10 to 20 percent of the total value of the factory, the insured oftentimes requested permission to obtain additional insurance from other companies. Southern Mutual generally approved such requests with the proviso that the owners not over-insure their factory. When a factory burned, the company generally settled the claim quickly and, periodically, Southern Mutual sent its general agent to verify the conditions of insured properties.[72]

The existence of this insurance clarifies our understanding of antebellum industry by exposing the degree of contact between factories. Cotton factories in Georgia fit into an interlocking series of relationships. Many shared stock ownership either directly or through family ties. Factories provided work for an increasingly displaced agricultural poor and hence acted as welfare relief agencies as well as providing a financial function for investment by the elites.

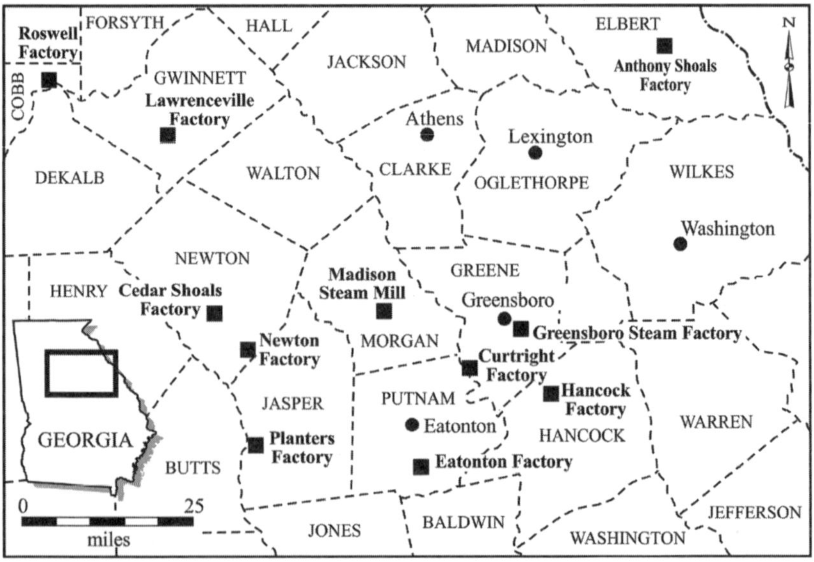

FIGURE 6. Map of factories in Athens hinterland.

Factory companies communicated with each other directly, albeit largely unsuccessfully, through their manufacturers' association at the state fair. But factories also plugged into the insurance network which systematically evaluated their risks from fire and their prospects for continued financial success. Many other insurance companies in Georgia besides Southern Mutual insured factories, and one can assume that the other companies took similar steps of evaluating and relaying this information to their boards, which included members of an emerging industrialist class. Industrialists, in antebellum Georgia, therefore did not operate in a vacuum; they were not, as Broadus Mitchell contended, visionary individuals without relation to one another, or to later developments. Instead Georgia's industrialists, by the 1850s, formed a well-knit elite whose members knew each other and kept themselves informed of the state of their industry.

At the end of the antebellum period, Athens stood poised for greater prosperity. The industrial slump which retarded southern textile profits began to fade as the nation started to recover from the Panic of 1857. The number of factories in Georgia more than doubled between 1840 and 1855, and a necessary regional ancillary industrial sector began to emerge. Financial services tailored for industrial endeavors proved useful and profitable. As an industrial town, Athens started the process of modern infrastructure building. Athens participated in every part of the industrial puzzle of the 1850s, establishing itself no longer as a model of something new and strange to the South but instead as a regional center for a well-entrenched economic sector of a continuously developing South.

Despite Athens's loss of economic ascendancy, the town's factories survived the hard times of the 1850s and left many tangible legacies. Foremost is the market penetration into Georgia's upcountry due to the development of a statewide railroad system. Without Athens's efforts at constructing the Georgia Railroad, the story of economic development in Georgia would have proceeded very differently. Atlanta would never have come into existence, and it is doubtful that the state would have systematized its railroads before the Civil War. True, while Athens never rivaled Atlanta as a transportation center, it nevertheless maintained an economic influence over northern Georgia, western Carolina, and eastern Tennessee until those areas developed railroads of their own in the 1880s. (Even after the 1880s, Athens remained the nearest destination in the upcountry for the wholesale and retail of fancy goods.) More important for Athens's future, the town's entrepreneurs serviced the needs of the textile mills within its extended reach. The coming war would cement Athens's relationship with its hinterlands.[73]

5

EPILOGUE TO ANTEBELLUM INDUSTRIALIZATION

When a Georgian . . . crosses the boundaries of Clarke, he sits down on the first log, draws a long breath, and says (in the way of internal consciousness), "*Now I'm safe.*" The people there . . . are civil, polite and well-conditioned. . . . [T]he spindle, the loom, the plough and the anvil will contest for predominance. . . . Here, in Clarke county, are all the conditions of manufacturing success accumulated.

—*Macon Telegraph* as quoted in *Southern Banner*, May 7, 1869

By the end of its second generation of industrialization, approximately 1870, Athens's experience seemed to validate arguments for southern non-agricultural economic development. For forty years, southern industrialists worked for greater economic independence from other parts of the country by claiming a need for a diversified regional economy despite the wealth amassed due to cotton cultivation. With the coming of the Civil War, industrial facilities proved essential for the war effort and, despite logistical shortcomings, these factories allowed the Confederacy to fight a truly modern war for four years against the industrial behemoth of the North. Indeed, for the factory companies in Athens, war production proved remunerative. Just as in the North, the accumulation of war profits led to efforts to find ways of safeguarding the liquidity of capital invested both productively and non-productively.

Such increases in capitalization allowed industry to emerge from "the defeat" with a greater control over the local economy than before. For the community and surrounding countryside, the very existence of local manufacturing facilities ameliorated some of the problems of wartime scarcity. But it also created social rifts over the means of distributing scarce goods. The fear of retribution for perceived profiteering prodded industrialists to contribute to patriotic and charitable causes, although ultimately relief came from the government and not from the philanthropy of manufacturers. Furthermore, the Union Army specifically targeted industrial facilities, forcing many of Georgia's cotton mills to rebuild at war's end. But direct warfare avoided Athens, and its factories remained intact. Thus, postwar Athens's textile mills shifted production to commodities needed for everyday life, and exchanged them for cash or for goods, at rates that kept pace with the conversion back to U.S. currency. With a rapid return to peace, Athens's factories and industrial ancillaries prospered as the center of manufacturing activity for most of northern Georgia. Industry provided jobs and a positive return on investment capital, despite the political vagaries of the late 1860s. By 1870, Athens already existed as the kind of New South industrial town that native son Henry Grady later held up as a model for prosperity in the aftermath of slavery. Athens came quietly full circle and, in the end, the efforts of Athens's industrialists created a widely accepted economic vision that included factory-based textile production as a central element of the South's future.

ATHENS'S INDUSTRY DURING THE CIVIL WAR

In the early 1860s, Athens's distance from the battlefront made it a small haven for war industry, permitting both the persistence of previously existing manufactures and attracting one new major industrial employer. Throughout the Civil War, Athens's three cotton factories operated as fully as their access to raw materials allowed. Likewise, textiles' ancillary industries, the bobbin mill and the foundry, found constant employment in supplying the factories. Finally, the area's distance from the battlefront attracted one new war industry, a gun manufacturer.[1]

The armory of Cook & Brother relocated from New Orleans to Athens in 1863. Ferdinand W. C. Cook and Francis L. Cook learned gun manufacture at the Enfield factory in England in the 1850s, and then settled in New Orleans. Evacuating New Orleans just one day prior to its capture by federal troops in 1862, the brothers temporarily moved the remnants of their establishment to Selma, Alabama. Since Selma already housed the national foundry of the Confederacy, Cook & Brother probably feared competition for human and other resources, and hence moved on to Athens. In July 1862, Cook & Brother contracted to manufacture thirty thousand Enfield-style rifles in their Athens armory and to deliver them to the Confederate Army between January 1863 and June 1864, at the price of $50 for a rifle with a bayonet or $43 without the blade. So, in August 1862, the brothers purchased a sixty-three-acre water-power site on Trail Creek just across the river from the town of Athens, about a half-mile above the Athens Factory. By November of that year, when the construction of their two-story factory was far enough along, the firm obtained insurance. By March 1863, the armory began a monthly production of approximately six hundred weapons—infantry rifles, artillery rifles, and musketoons, for a total wartime production of approximately four thousand weapons (falling well short of the promised thirty thousand guns). In July 1863, the Confederate government required an inventory of the new armory to secure government guarantees of a $150,000 private mortgage, and the inventory estimated the value of the land, buildings, machinery, and stock of goods at slightly more than $600,000 (Confederate dollars). Needing extra space in order to try to meet the production for which they had contracted, the company moved its business offices from the factory into town in January 1864. However, at the same time as this move, the slowness with which the Confederate government paid its bills forced Cook & Brother to promise to pay its creditors as soon as it received payment from the national government. Weapons production continued until the following July, when payment from the government ground to a complete halt, and a portion of the workers fought as state defense forces around Savannah.[2]

The armory resumed operations in January 1865, about the same time the Confederate Ordnance Bureau considered purchasing and consolidating Cook & Brothers with equipment taken from a less efficient armory in Columbia, South Carolina. While correspondence among government inspectors valued the Athens armory at over $1,000,000 in March 1865, the war ended before the government could consummate the deal. Clearly the firm prospered in Athens despite the failure of the Confederate government to pay for its goods in a timely manner. But the armory kept good company in its prosperity.[3]

Supplying war material to the Confederacy greatly enlivened the prospects of the textile industry in Athens. The cotton mills went into full production manufacturing thread and cloth for the Confederate national government and for the defense forces of the state of Georgia. The Athens Factory spun cotton yarn, sewing thread, and knitting cotton; it also wove flannel for underwear, hickory stripes, and wool jeans for uniforms, and cotton duck for tenting for the Confederate government through at least 1864. In 1864, the Athens Factory also dyed fabric for uniform pants and coats, and it sold the army an occasional cotton rope for use in a hospital's well.

Textile sales to the Confederate government proved extremely remunerative. Incomplete gross receipts demonstrate that the Confederate War Department purchased goods valued at $181,171 from the Athens Factory in 1863, and at least $351,905 worth of textiles in the first seven months of 1864. Similarly, the Princeton Factory sold the Confederate quartermasters not less than $109,080 worth of osnaburgs between January 1863 and April 1864. The Confederate Army bought at least $133,440 of osnaburgs from John White's Georgia Factory, mainly between August 1863 and April 1864.

The receipts of Clarke County's three cotton factories reflect the extreme inflation that beset the Confederacy, making estimates of total production, or of war profits, from these gross receipts problematic. The price of osnaburgs serves as a good example of the problem. In March 1862, this rough cloth retailed in Athens for $0.18 per yard. In 1863, the Confederate War Department paid $0.40 per yard for Athens-produced osnaburgs, and by 1864, the War Department paid $1.25 per yard for the same item. For textiles, this increase came from several sources. First, the Confederate government avoided direct taxation by resorting to fiat currency: simply printing money to pay its bills when the sale of war bonds failed to equal its debts. Secondly and more directly tied to manufactures, government contracts essentially drafted the productive capacity of the factories for the duration of the war. Thus increased demand by the government drove up prices while the accompanying decrease in the supply of textiles to civilians drove open market prices up even further. Clearly the factories increased their production, which can be seen in the immediate extension of hours of operation for all of Athens's factories. However, such changes entailed increased costs, both because night production required lighting and because the local insurance company altered the factories' premiums to reflect the added risk of this night work. Nonetheless, production of textiles to fulfill either state or national contracts required that the town's factories operate at full capacity for most of the war.[4]

While gross receipts fail to accurately depict profitability, dividends may better attest to the accumulated earnings on wartime industrial investment. The Athens Factory serves as a prime example of the profitable war plant. In September 1860, before the war began, the Athens Factory declared 6 percent returns on capital stock in its first dividend since rebuilding after the fire of 1857. Thereafter, with the start of the war, the factory issued dividends of not less than 25 percent every six months, while expanding its facilities at the same time. On May 3, 1862, the company declared 25 percent dividends; on October 4, 1862, the company declared another 25 percent dividend and granted its agent the authority to build an addition, to expand the dying facility, and to purchase new steam boilers. On February 19, 1863, the Athens Factory declared yet another 25 percent dividend, bringing the annual dividend to a 75 percent return on investment. Thereafter, one can see some of the effects of inflation. On October 3, 1863, the Athens Factory increased its semi-annual dividend declaration to 50 percent and then upped it again to 100 percent on January 11, 1864, and on October 1, 1864. The last of the official war dividends returned 250 percent on February 4, 1865. One can assume that Athens's other factories experienced similar returns for their production efforts from the national government on the basis of similar expansion. For example, the High Shoals Factory, at the western edge of Clarke County, doubled its capital stock from $50,000 to $100,000 as it reincorporated itself in January 1863, probably by reinvesting some of its wartime profits. Likewise, the Princeton Factory reincorporated itself in the summer of 1863, increasing its capital stock from $45,000 to $93,500.[5]

Yet despite issuing a constant stream of dividends and reinvesting what remained in the company coffers, the factories also sought means of preventing inflation from undercutting the investments of their stockholders by avoiding the national currency. Instead, the factories disbursed their dividends in kind rather than in cash. That is, they paid with manufactured goods which retained an intrinsic worth, a worth that would consistently increase its exchange value as supply grew shorter. However, the amount of stock each investor owned regulated the amount of manufactured goods each could receive. When a relative asked A. P. Dearing to intercede on his behalf to procure manufactured goods, the former Princeton Factory agent responded that he could not comply at that time because the factory company distributed goods as dividends to its investors pro rated according to their stockholdings. Since he already disposed of his last distribution, he would have to await another dividend before he gained any more that he could share with his kinsman. Thus the factory provided goods to its stockholders which they could either use themselves or sell to whomever they chose at whatever price current market conditions commanded.[6]

In-kind distributions also provided a hedge against the potential worthlessness of Confederate money, should the South lose the war. Factory stockholders worried about securing their personal investments and routinely demanded distributions so they could determine their own course of action. Thus, in June 1863, the Athens Factory Board directed the factory agent to sell the company's slaves, collect all debts owed the company, and divide all available cash among the stockholders. Transferring large amounts of capital to the stockholders gave the investors the opportunity to convert their investment returns into more tangible property, such as real estate or specie. By March 1864, the Athens Factory demonstrated continued concern about the convertibility of Confederate currency when it required stockholders to retrieve their cash dividends. The company could no longer deposit unretrieved dividends, since all the local banks had been converted into a depository for the Confederate Treasury Department; nor would it pay interest on the funds left in its hands. The lack of confidence in Confederate currency seemed widespread by 1864; at least one Athens artisan advertised his services with a preference for payment in corn over cash. When it became apparent that the war was about to end, Athens Factory stockholders met in emergency session to divide their profits in such a way that sidestepped the complications involved in changing from Confederate to U.S. currency. Without declaring an exact percentage, the company divided the goods on hand at the rate of $1.50 per yard of shirtings and $20.00 per bunch of yarn.[7]

Desiring to exert some control over their financial futures, these southern investors sought means to secure their personal fortunes without solely relying upon winning this war for southern independence. Industrialists in Athens supported the war effort by routinely investing in Confederate bonds and by making donations to support local military units. But they still hedged their bets, which in their eyes seemed wise rather than unpatriotic. The advice given by one prominent Athens merchant to his son regarding the investment potential of Confederate war bonds points to the loss of control one would experience if you did not find alternative methods to secure your fortune. Pleasant Stovall explained that he considered war bonds or any other investment that promoted the winning of the war as both lucrative and safe, if the South won the war. However, should the Confederacy lose, he anticipated the confiscation of all southern property as the penalty for treason. The industrialists, caught on the horns of this dilemma, sought and found another option: Both the Athens Factory and the Georgia Factory diverted a portion of their funds to foreign currencies. The Athens Factory purchased British currency with its extra cash, but it remains unclear if the company then sent the money abroad or stashed the currency away for the remainder of the war. Irish immigrant John White simply deposited some of the proceeds of his Georgia Factory in Irish banks and then personally retrieved the funds at war's end. Thus both factories possessed capital to insure their firms' survival (and the stockholders' investments) regardless of the outcome of the war. They fully considered themselves patriots, but patriotism precluded neither profitability nor financial security.[8]

War production by Athens's textile mills required expansion by the town's other industrial concerns. Beginning in 1862, the Athens Foundry began producing looms, which it claimed were "fully equal to Northern looms." The foundry installed some of these in the Athens Factory, while others went to factories located beyond the town's immediate economic sphere. To facilitate loom production, the town attracted George Menno, an artisan who professed to be "the only regular reed-maker in the Confederate States," to fabricate reeds, weavers' harnesses, heddles, and loom pickers. Reeds, heddles and harnesses all helped looms keep the warp ends of woven cloth evenly spaced. Meanwhile, the bobbin mill also kept busy. Throughout the early 1860s, its owner constantly advertised for the dogwood poles he needed to manufacture bobbins.[9]

War production also affected the labor supply. While general operative labor primarily utilized women, girls, and boys under the age of conscription, retaining adult white males probably proved more difficult. For instance, when advertising for a clerk for his factory in early 1864, John White required "a man not subject to military duty." Even though the Confederate government originally exempted factory workers involved in war production from conscription, the terms of the exemption required manufacturers to limit their "profits" to 75 percent in order for their male workers to qualify. While the rule never explains how to determine what constituted a profit in the face of hyperinflation, local law enforcement agencies never prosecuted any of Athens's factories under this act. Later, when the Confederate government repealed the factory workers' draft exemption, several factories in Athens organized their own militia groups as local or state defense forces in order to prevent the conscription of their workers. Although Governor Joe Brown eventually ordered some of these units into action, they never left the state and rarely withdrew from the immediate vicinity. Thus factory work provided a means of legal draft evasion for those uninterested in fighting the war. Moreover, the factories reportedly employed more male operatives than they normally needed, although the scale of operations under government contract may not have been taken into consideration by observers.[10]

Elites also found the factories a conduit for evading wartime service at the front lines. In their cases, they "served" in official capacities at various levels of government. Some filled regular elective offices. For instance, Howell C. Flournoy, a lifelong Unionist, served on the town council throughout the war and later, during Reconstruction, served as local Freedmen's Bureau agent as a reward for his political leanings. Others of Athens's elite filled appointive offices as local agents for the Confederate government. For example, John W. Nicholson (Henry Grady's uncle) specifically explained in his postwar amnesty application that he had sought just such an appointment in 1863 "in order to avoid conscription and active services in the army." While not all the elite desired to miss the war, only the few with factory connections or a factory background possessed the proper credentials to obtain such exemptions. Nicholson worked his way into the elite with his retail and factory investments in the 1850s. And others followed a similar path. For example, Enoch Steadman, who formerly operated a factory in Gwinnett County, served as a salt agent in Athens for the Confederate government. (Unlike Flournoy, Steadman's Newton County constituents later elected him a Redeemer state senator, during Reconstruction.) John Webb worked as a civilian employee of the Confederate Quartermaster Corps at the gunpowder plant in Augusta after General Sherman destroyed his factory in Newton County. Class differentiation can be seen in ways other than avoiding conscription.[11]

The scarcity of consumables elevated the importance of the cotton factories to all segments of the community. The priority of government contracts for supplying the Confederate war machine limited the supply of thread and cloth. With imported high-quality goods no longer available, even the upper crust of southern society began to seek local textile productions. The family of Howell Cobb, then a general in Georgia's defense forces, obtained thread and cloth from John White's Georgia Factory at a time when inadequate supplies of raw materials forced White to cease sales to most private citizens. White sold his wares only to Mary Ann Cobb because of the general's importance in the community. Upon making the sale, however, the factory owner instructed Mrs. Cobb that "your friends must not think because he let you have it that he must furnish them also." It must have struck Mrs. Cobb as ironic that wartime circumstances forced members of the elite, particularly the families of those who actively served in the military, to plea for materials with which they formerly would have clothed only their slaves. For once, the elite shared slightly in the deprivation suffered by the masses.[12]

Shortages of consumer goods drove up prices sharply, increasing the cost of living for all consumers but affecting the poor and less connected most severely. Toward the end of 1862, Athens experienced "thread-riots" as the town's poor clamored to be first in line during the single hour each week when the Athens Factory sold a limited amount of thread at reduced prices as a form of charity. The newspaper reported that so many people sought to purchase the scarce but necessary textile commodities "that many females fainted, and . . . the scene was occasionally enlivened by rough and tumble fights." The shortages continued, and by mid-1863, the factories turned to an exchange economy, bartering manufactured goods for raw materials. Henceforth they supplied local consumers of all classes only after obtaining raw materials with which they would fulfill their government contracts. Thus those with access to an item necessary for production could gain advantage over everyone else. Since the factories then needed wool, the upcountry sheep herder, or the merchant who purchased and transported the wool, took priority in purchasing textiles from the local factories. Advertisements thereafter always explained which items the factory wanted in exchange for its yarn and cloth. Unsurprisingly, as a result of this system, most citizens of northern Georgia came to resent the lack of access to goods manufactured in their vicinity.[13]

In light of these shortages, community opinion generally perceived wartime industrial profits as excessive. In the early days of the war, newspaper editorials warned the southern industrialists that profiteering merited legal and popular retribution. Following the rapid inflation of textile prices, in March 1862, the grand jury of neighboring Greene County indicted the owners of the Curtright Factory and the Scull Shoals Factory for "extortion," which was the current term for profiteering. Despite the county prosecutor's decision not to prosecute the cases, such anti-industrialist attitudes persisted throughout the textile region of Georgia. In October 1862, while discussing exemptions to conscription, an Athens editor expressed his contempt for industrial profiteers who claimed draft exemptions, calling them "blood-suckers" who would not avert the "hell-fire and brimstone" of their ultimate accountability. Another writer, late in 1862, expressed his concern that Georgians were waging a "rich man's war and poor man's fight" when he took local industrialists to task for failing to contribute to the war effort according to their means. Calling for accounts to be settled against the manufacturers, this writer claimed, "Here's a man reputed to be worth $50,000, who has not yet, by taxation or otherwise given $500, the one-hundredth part of his means! While next to him is a poor man, worth hardly $500, who gives not only himself, but leaves his family behind." Because this sort of view seemed endemic to the manufacturing region of Georgia from Augusta to Columbus, by the end of 1862 the Georgia legislature considered expropriating all the state's factories to prevent profiteering. While much of this reaction merely extended the anti-corporate rhetoric specifically directed at manufacturing concerns during the mill-building boom of the 1840s, Athens's industrialists responded by waging a public relations battle to prove the depth of their patriotism despite the size of their hard-earned profits.[14]

Seeking to engender a positive public opinion about the role of factories in the war effort, the industrialists immediately tried to shift the blame for high prices to retail merchants. For the remainder of the war, the factories around Athens (sometimes in concert with other factories in the state) periodically announced how they tried to regulate the price of the output they produced for private sale. In the same month that Greene County indicted its manufacturers, three of Athens's factories—the Georgia Factory, the Athens Factory, and the High Shoals Factory—jointly advertised a suggested retail schedule for the goods they manufactured. The three also advised the community that they refused to sell to "speculators" who failed to adopt their retail schedule. Additionally, they vowed to sell their goods to military families at wholesale. A week later, Princeton Factory agent Moses McWhorter published his rates, which generally coincided with the other factories, and he asked the public to understand that the extreme shortage of raw materials affected the pricing structure of the entire industry. Apparently, however, the manufacturers ignored their own schedules, and prices rose quickly. Thus by October 1862 thread retailed for $5.00 per bunch. As an act of philanthropy, for one week the Athens Factory offered its yarn for sale at $3.00 per bunch for one hour per day on a first-come first-serve basis. This "charity" resulted in the thread riots that the town's elite considered either "ludicrous" or "sad." In the same month, John White, sold his thread to soldiers' wives in adjoining counties for

$2.50 per bunch, and the local press lionized him for providing such essentials to the needy. One newspaper editor noticed White's philanthropy specifically "to place the good example before [Athens's] other two factories, that they seeing his good works, might follow in his footsteps." In January 1864, the Athens Factory sold cotton flannel, sufficient quantity for making two undershirts, to families or friends of members of all of Athens's volunteer companies at the front, at the greatly reduced rate of one dollar per yard. By April 1864, the Athens Factory's announcement that "all persons living in the town of Athens" could purchase one half-bunch of yarn or seven-and-a-half yards of cloth, indicates that mere resumption of sale of cotton goods to the general public could be considered charity, particularly since the sale excluded the rest of the countryside.[15]

Direct charity proved yet another tactic for the textile industry to distance itself from accusations of profiteering. In the same month that indictments were raised against the Greene County manufacturers for profiteering, the factory companies of Athens began investing in charity. At various times, the factories donated material needed to make tents or uniforms to the volunteer military units recruited from the area. By May 1863, manufacturers sought a joint effort to convince the state's citizenry of their philanthropic and patriotic aims. A convention of five of Georgia's yarn manufacturers—the Georgia Factory, High Shoals Factory, Troup Factory, Gwinnett Factory, and Aguadon Factory (in Newton County)—met in Atlanta and proposed donating one-eighth of their weekly production to the state's quartermaster for distribution to the destitute of every county in the state. A month later, the Athens Factory took action without waiting for compliance from the state, presenting one bunch of thread to each military family who received pay at Athens.[16]

Charity by the factories should be kept in perspective, however. Investors in factories always claimed that their enterprises served as civic entities, driven by community interest as much as by profits. Factories, they claimed, acted as agents for the generosity of the local elites in disbursing relief to the deserving poor. State officials expressed similar attitudes. State Quartermaster General Ira Foster suggested the very existence of cotton factories in southern towns constituted a resource that kept greater deprivation at bay, "that without the aid of factories, thread cannot be obtained, and the destitute poor cannot be clad." By 1864, direct donation to the needy by the factories came to an end, and their only charity remained the occasional sale of textiles to deserving townspeople. Instead, state government undertook to care for Georgia's war weary under an act which directed cash payments to indigent families of soldiers. In Clarke County, local government officials paid such families between five and twenty dollars, depending on the number of dependents. But this charity served more than one purpose. At the same time the county distributed cash to the poor, it also took a census of military-age males not yet attached to any unit to determine which families deserved philanthropy and which shirked their patriotic duties.[17]

At the immediate conclusion of the war, many in Athens feared the economic consequences of reunification. To minimize holding Confederate currency, starting in March 1865, the officers of the Southern Mutual Insurance Company voted themselves a raise and specified that all claims be paid in Confederate money. A month later, when news of Lee's surrender and Lincoln's assassination reached Athens, the insurance company suspended business and ordered its agents neither to issue nor to renew any policies, due to the "uncertain condition of the currency." At the beginning of June, Southern Mutual's directors officially declared its Confederate securities and cash a loss, and ordered "that business be generally resumed, upon the basis of the legal currency of the United States." Despite the doubts regarding the currency, the Athens Factory continued its production and, in August 1865, offered "gold, yarn and cloth" in exchange for cotton. While the exchange value of each these four items undoubtedly differed, they appeared to be the only things considered worthy of exchange in lieu of U.S. currency in immediate postwar Athens. Factory stockholders still received their dividends in manufactured goods, and so members of the textile industry seemed so exceedingly resourceful in surviving the dramatic transition back to U.S. currency that one observer in Athens paraphrased the beatitudes, "Blessed is he who is a cotton holder or a factory stockholder. Want does not seem to tarry at their thresholds." Clearly, factory goods and raw cotton served as sources of value independent of the state of the currency, thus giving industrialists an edge in determining the process of economic reconstruction in Georgia.[18]

While Sherman's scorched-earth campaign deliberately targeted many of Georgia's factories as part of the Confederacy's military delivery system, Georgia's textile industry saw the second half of the 1860s as good years. Those factories outside the Union Army's path usually found themselves in better shape than when the war started because they reinvested some of their profits in expanding their productive capacity during the war years, and they quickly managed to resume production. Despite the supposed prostration of the southern economy, many of the destroyed factories, such as those at Columbus and Roswell, rebuilt within a year of the war's end. Moreover, others with capital constructed new factories where none existed prior to the war: in Atlanta, near Newnan, and in the valley of the Chattahoochee River around the town of West Point. Economic historians of these years generally missed all of this activity because they focused on the aggregate number of cotton factories as listed in the census. Between the 1860 and 1870 censuses the number of textile factories remained static, and so historians using the census data as their primary means of evaluating southern industry erroneously claimed that the so-called industrial take-off of Georgia remained delayed until the 1880s, when the stock of manufacturing facilities finally rose above prewar numbers. This misinterprets the data because southern industrialists, in rebuilding or replacing the South's factories, substantially upgraded their technical capabilities to resume competition in the global economy for textiles that emerged in the 1870s. Like the mill-building boom of the 1840s, the expansion of facilities during the New South boom came only after investors heard reports of high profits made by southern industrialists in the era preceding the boom.[19]

Georgia's textile manufacturers again earned large profits in the immediate postwar years through speculating in cotton and through resumed production, both of which can be partially traced through federal excise tax records. Table 4 shows how industrialists in northern Georgia weathered the transition back to U.S. currency in 1865 and 1866. Many of Georgia's factories appeared to engage in as much cotton speculation as in producing manufactured goods. In nearly every case, the value of manufactured goods upon which they paid taxes equaled only about half the value of the raw cotton that each factory hoarded. While these numbers may represent an exaggeration of the value of cotton, some of the entries included the number of bales owned, as well as their value. Hence, the High Shoals Factory owned one thousand bales in the first quarter of 1866, much more than necessary for its immediate needs. However, the data also lead to an alternate reading. It may be that the High Shoals Factory purchased excess cotton as protection against a rational expectation of continued inflation, or against a similar anticipation of shortages of their raw material due to the emancipation of the slaves who normally harvested the crop. In either interpretation, that the factory owned so much

TABLE 4

Textile Production in IRS, Georgia District 4, 1865–1866

County	Factory Name	Cotton Value	Months Operated[a]	Output Value[b]	Cotton Reserve Ratio[c]
Newton	H. White's Factory	$54,000.00	9	$2,398.00	22.52
Jackson	R. White's Factory	$11,183.00	7	$2,600.70	4.30
Greene	Scull Shoals Factory	$256,450.00	12	$24,650.00	10.40
Newton	Covington Mills	$262,968.00	8	$36,902.48	7.13
Clarke	Princeton Factory	. . .	6	$45,117.89	. . .
Newton	Newton Factory	$186,615.00	10	$51,512.98	3.62
Clarke	Georgia Factory	$178,154.00	16	$61,015.50	2.92
Hancock	Montour Mfg.	$209,546.00	2	$103,702.00	2.02
Baldwin	Milledgeville Mfg.	$389,171.00	9	$105,101.19	3.70
Richmond	Richmond Factory	$63,326.00	9	$105,926.70	0.60
Greene	Curtright Factory	$262,701.00	7	$120,750.22	2.18
Clarke	Athens Factory	$209,821.00	16	$136,073.61	1.54
Walton	High Shoals Factory	$408,972.00	10	$164,372.65	2.49
Richmond	Augusta Mfg.	$2,195,069.00	11	$1,272,642.42	1.72
Total		$4,483,176.68		$2,241,588.34	

[a] Months based on dates of tax assessments. Actual time of operation probably differs.

[b] Production values calculated from taxes assessed, when actual value is missing.

[c] Cotton Reserve Ratio is Value of Output divided by Value of Cotton Held.

Source: Internal Revenue Service Assessment Lists for Georgia, 1865–1866, National Archives.

cotton demonstrates its financial capacity, which in turn would have bolstered the confidence of shareholders that the basic infrastructure still existed for cotton manufacturing to prosper. But the factories varied radically in their ratios of value of cotton holdings to value of production (which is designated as the "cotton reserve ratio" in table 4).

Clearly the three factories with cotton reserve ratios of greater than five to one (Scull Shoals Factory, Hugh White's factory on the Alcovy River, and Enoch Steadman's Covington Mills) engaged more in speculation than they did in manufacturing. Since the son of Scull Shoals Factory's owner was a cotton factor in Augusta, it is probable that the Scull Shoals Factory's seemingly excessive quantities of cotton represent storage with the intent to resell once prices increased. The two factories with ratios of less than one (Princeton Factory and Richmond Factory) indicate probable errors in accounting by federal agents which may have resulted from storing the cotton off the factory site. Five of the factories (Athens Factory, High Shoals Factory, Augusta Factory, Curtright Factory, and Montour Manufacturing) reported cotton reserve ratios between 1.5:1 and 2.5:1, which seems to establish a general benchmark of raw material reserves for such an uncertain time. The four factories (Milledgeville Factory, Newton Factory, John White's Georgia Factory, and Robert White's small hat factory in Jackson County) with a cotton reserve ratio in the ranges between roughly 3:1 and 4.5:1 either engaged in limited speculation or simply proved less efficient in determining their needs than those with a smaller ratio.[20]

These tax records also allow comparison of the factories' sizes. Overall production values seem to indicate that factories fell into one of four categories: Artisan firms produced less than $10,000 for the entire period, while smaller factories produced between $10,000 and $100,000 worth of goods. Moderate-sized factories fashioned between $100,000 and $250,000 worth of goods, while large factories manufactured more than $250,000 in overall output. Of the cohort of factories in tax district four of Georgia, only the Augusta Factory can be considered large. In Clarke County, the Athens Factory clearly qualified as a moderate-sized factory, while the Georgia and Princeton factories fit into the small range. On the periphery of Athens, High Shoals Factory proved to be a well-managed moderate-sized factory, while Scull Shoals Factory, which should have produced at about the same level as the Athens Factory, hardly operated at all.

The experience of the Athens Factory is instructive of how a well-operated southern factory could profit with the resumption of peace, despite economic and political uncertainty. Although modest in its cotton speculation, with a cotton reserve ratio of 1.5:1 (compared to the district average of 2:1), the Athens Factory consistently declared reasonably large dividends for the rest of Georgia's Reconstruction era, 1866–71. In both 1866 and 1867, the Athens Factory declared 15 percent annual dividends. In 1868 and 1869, the company granted 25 percent annual dividends to its stockholders, but it returned to a 15 percent annual dividend after increasing the company's capital stock to $125,000 in 1870. But other indications besides dividends demonstrate that high earnings also meant high profits. At the same time the company issued 15 to 20 percent return on investment to its stockholders, it also refurbished its equipment and expanded its facilities. In 1866, the Athens Factory built a new wing, to which it transferred its wool carding equipment, and so enlarged the overall facility that it increased "its capacity from 2,000 to 4,000 spindles, and 70 looms." Then, in 1869, the factory added a second shift and resumed night work, so that "the busy hum of shuttle and spindle w[ould] not cease, day or night during working days." At the same time, the Athens Factory erected a new dye house, added new equipment for spinning and weaving, and constructed new operatives' houses.[21]

The increased capitalization of the Athens Factory at the conclusion of the second generation of industrialization in Athens came from purchasing and converting the town's defunct armory into a textile mill. The Cook Armory stood vacant since the end of the war while the federal government, Francis Cook's heirs, and Cook's creditors pursued litigation over who owned the facility. One editorial commented on the long-time interest of Athens in converting the armory into a cotton factory, and it encouraged local capitalists to take on the project, noting, "There is ample idle money in Clarke county to . . . convert it into a first-class cotton factory." Not long afterwards, in 1870, the Athens Manufacturing Company purchased the armory at public auction. While the original Athens Factory already operated 5,000 spindles and more than 70 looms in consuming 2,500 bales of cotton, for an annual production valued in excess of $250,000, the company decided to introduce another line of textiles in the more than 29,000 square feet of its newest factory building. They chose to use the two-story armory building solely for weaving brown and tan gingham checks while leaving the 1859 incarnation of the Athens Factory to produce yarn for the "check factory" to weave. Yarn thus traveled by pole boats on the quarter-mile of the Oconee River between the "yarn mill" and the "check factory." Local editors expected the expanded facilities and product lines to create many more jobs in the town as well as to increase business for the firm. Reflecting business acumen usually assigned to the New South era, the Athens Manufacturing Company prepared itself for a return to an increasingly competitive environment in the 1870s, as it purchased a facility valued at $150,000 (U.S.) for only $18,000 and then filled it with 400 of the most up-to-date looms. Importantly, it did all this while only officially increasing its capitalization by $32,500.[22]

Other factory companies shared in this postwar expansion. The Princeton Manufacturing Company also improved its productive capacity in the late 1860s. After shutting down in 1866, the Princeton Factory repaired its facilities and hired a new agent, William J. Russell (grandfather of legendary Georgia Senator Richard Russell). Under Russell's management, in 1869, the Princeton Manufacturing Company upgraded by purchasing the "very best" looms from England, and by 1871 produced bed ticking and employed one hundred hands to operate its 2,700 spindles and 62 looms.[23]

John White's Georgia Factory also expanded in the late 1860s. Throughout his management of the firm, White consistently upgraded and expanded his industrial potential, having bought the defunct Charleston Factory's equipment to fill an addition to his factory in the 1850s. Thus he maintained a steady growth rate, which always evoked favorable comments from credit reporters. Turning the factory's management over to his son, James, in 1866, John White retrieved not less than $60,000 from an Irish bank to invest in organizing a new bank in Athens. Having provided 60 percent of the new bank's $100,000 capital, White became the president of the town's most important financial institution. But he did not neglect his industrial assets either as he constructed several additions to the Georgia Factory in the late 1860s. As White became more immersed in finance, he increasingly divorced himself from the daily operations of his factory and turned over the management to his sons. Certainly, one cannot fault White for this redirection of energies since credit reporters repeatedly increased their estimates of White's wealth from $300,000 in 1866 to $1,000,000 in 1880. While John White created the foundation of his wealth through years of hard work and slow accumulation in the 1840s and 1850s, he found the reward to his efforts in his war profits, just as the Civil War similarly quickened and consolidated industrial ownership in the North.[24]

The High Shoals Factory, located just across the Apalachee River from Clarke County, also "made a fortune during the war" and engaged in expansion afterward. Immediately upon cessation of hostilities, the High Shoals Factory sent some of its production north when the local market in Georgia proved insufficiently remunerative. Armed with profits from this strategy, and with its war profits, by December 1866 the High Shoals Factory also began enlarging its facilities with a 4,320-square-foot addition to its existing 100-by-50-foot main mill building. And like the other companies in Athens, High Shoals also filled the addition with the newest machines. In 1874, an insurance survey reported the mill operated 3,400 spindles and one set of woolen machinery twelve hours per day.[25]

Of all the factories of Greater Athens, only Poullain's "Fontenoy Mills" at Scull Shoals failed to undertake improvements in the late 1860s. During this time, Scull Shoals Factory proved badly managed by an absentee owner, Dr. Thomas N. Poullain, who credit reporters criticized for living like a prince. In 1866, the Scull Shoals Factory company reorganized as Fontenoy Mills, with wider Poullain family participation. Dissatisfied with the management by the family patriarch, Poullain's family forced the sale of the property in 1875, but the buyer returned the property to the Poullain family after failing to make payments on his note. So the factory reorganized again in 1875, but the mill continued to flounder under its outstanding financial burdens. In 1879, a consortium of wealthy Athenians—John White, Isaac Powell (president of the High Shoals Factory) and Ferdinand Phinizy (a merchant with ties to Augusta banking)—purchased Scull Shoals and began to refurbish the factory. Unfortunately floods destroyed the factory again in 1887, and the firm went bankrupt.[26]

Paralleling the growing prosperity of the town's factories, Athens's ancillary industries also expanded after the Civil War. During the war, the foundry changed its name to the Athens Foundry and Boiler Works, and in late 1865, it sent Reuben Nickerson north to purchase new equipment. The foundry's creditors now considered it an excellent risk with enlarged facilities, a capitalization of $20,000, and a reputation for consistent profits. After returning from his buying trip, Nickerson advertised the firm's ability to fabricate a number of industrial and agricultural implements, including "Steam Engines; circular, sash and Mulay Saw Mills; Bark Mills, Sugar Mills, Syrup Boilers, Water Wheels, Shafting, Pulleys, Mining and Mill Machinery, Iron and Brass Castings of every description." Also, through arrangements with other manufacturers, the corporation could quickly obtain any other equipment Athens's farmers and industrialists might desire. For the remainder of the decade, credit reporters commented favorably on the steady growth of the firm under Nickerson's management, estimating its annual dividend at 10 percent. By 1872, Athens Foundry won a silver medal at Augusta's agricultural fair for its production of agricultural implements, and by 1880, credit reporters estimated the company's worth at $60,000.[27]

The town's paper mill shared in similar industrial prosperity. In November 1866, R. G. Dun's agent reported that the stock of the $40,000 Pioneer Paper Factory sold at par, and he considered the facilities to be in excellent condition. In the same year, the paper mill added the use of lanterns to its insurance policy, indicating some work after dark. After the company's long-tenured agent, Albon Chase, died in 1867, new men, including Henry Grady's uncle, John W. Nicholson, took charge of the company. In 1870, they expanded its facilities and updated its equipment. Later that year, the company built a large brick addition, using the services of hydraulic engineers to improve its 104-horsepower water wheel. By 1871, the paper mill assigned its older equipment to the manufacture of wrapping paper, and its new machines produced 4,000 pounds of printing paper daily. While it sold most of its production locally, the mill also shipped paper to Macon, Charleston, and New York.[28]

The Athens Gas Works probably also expanded. In January 1865, widow Ann Grady leased the gas works to her brother Henry Gartrell as part of her administration of William S. Grady's estate. As a sign of returning community-wide prosperity, in 1868 and 1869, the town council contracted to install additional street lamps. Then, in late 1869, when Mrs. Grady sought to finish probating her husband's estate, she advertised for sale the components of her gas works and explained that most of the equipment was new and in perfect working order. This six-acre gas-production facility, which was located next to the foundry, supported ninety-eight customers and forty-five street lamps. Although federal tax collectors reported that the gas works earned only $656.24 in the last quarter of 1866, this value undoubtedly reflects the relatively small population of Athens that could afford the luxury of gas lighting. By November 1869, both Henry Grady and his uncle, Henry Gartrell, relocated to Rome, Georgia, where Gartrell had taken an interest in the gas works, and Mrs. Grady sold the firm to the estate of Howell Cobb.[29]

Athens's bobbin mill also participated in the economic resurgence of the town during the years of Radical Reconstruction by supplying bobbins of every variety to mills throughout northern Georgia as well as into neighboring regions. In filling 133 factory orders between November 1867 and February 1870, the bobbin factory sold 129,250 items valued at $4,730.85. Table 5 breaks down the sales by textile factory, showing that the bobbin mill (and Athens) serviced the general needs of Athens's economic hinterland, and special needs of more distant areas.[30]

TABLE 5
Athens Bobbin Mill Orders

Athens Relation	Factory	Orders	Items	Value	Duration
Athens	Athens Factory	17	19,726	$716.72	Jan 1868–Dec 1869
Greater Athens	High Shoals Factory	23	19,978	$716.15	March 1868–Dec 1869
Athens Ties	Cedar Shoals Factory[a]	17	15,905	$615.13	Dec 1867–Feb 1870
Athens	Georgia Factory	9	14,565	$502.68	Jan 1868–Sep 1869
Georgia Market	Trion Factory	12	10,894	$374.50	Jan 1868–May 1869
Georgia Market	Augusta Factory	4	10,024	$342.40	Sept 1868–Aug 1869
Greater Athens	Scull Shoals Factory[b]	7	8,765	$334.35	Nov 1867–June 1869
Athens	Princeton Factory	12	9,190	$311.78	Jan 1868–Feb 1870
Georgia Market	Macon Factory	3	3,400	$142.00	Aug 1868–Sept 1868
Athens Ties	Curtright Factory[c]	4	2,640	$122.85	Dec 1867–May 1868
Athens Ties	Newton Factory	4	2,550	$107.25	March 1868–Sep 1868
Georgia Market	Sargent Factory	4	2,140	$78.80	March 1868–June 1869
Unknown	Sheffield Factory	3	1,275	$52.27	Dec 1867–Nov 1868
Tennessee	Lenoir & Bro's	2	1,525	$52.00	Nov 1868–July 1869
Unknown	Potter & Son	3	1,325	$50.28	Oct 1868–April 1869
Georgia Market	Troup Factory	2	1,020	$45.90	Nov 1867–May 1868
Athens Ties	Anthony Shoals Factory	1	1,100	$41.25	Sept 1868
Athens Ties	John Thompson	3	1,245	$40.46	Nov 1867–Dec 1869
Unknown	M. S. Thomson	1	1,000	$40.00	Nov 1868
Unknown	Knox & Connog	1	200	$8.00	Dec 1868
Unknown	R. W. Saye	1	4	$0.80	March 1869
Total	21 Factories	133	128,471	$4695.57	Maximum: 2 Years

[a] Also doing business as Steadman Mills, Covington Mills, and Empire State Mills.

[b] Also doing business as Fontenoy Mills.

[c] Also doing business as Oconee Mills.

Source: Bobbin Mill Record Book 1867–1877, Hargrett Rare Book and Manuscript Library, University of Georgia.

Five of the top eight purchasers of the bobbin mill belonged to "Greater Athens" while eight of the eleven largest buyers of the bobbin mill products retained long-standing ties to the Athens economy. Put another way, "Greater Athens" consumed nearly 55 percent of the value of goods produced by the bobbin mill, and mills traditionally connected to Athens consumed a total of 72 percent of its output. However, more than a quarter of the mill's bobbins were sold to firms outside Athens's traditional economic sphere.

Athens made great bounds during the decade of the 1860s. In terms of federal census statistics, it moved up one notch from the county with the fifth most industrial capital invested in Georgia in 1860, to the fourth in 1870. But more importantly, it moved from fourth place in number of industrial workers, amount of wages paid, value of materials consumed, and value of output to second place for each of these categories in the state. Only Augusta, with its Lowell-style Augusta Factory, exceeded Athens in those four measures in 1870, and the Athens figures did not include the factories at its borders. In real terms, during the 1860s, Athens's cotton mills increased their capitalization by $135,800 (which does not include the separate figures for woolen production in 1870), increased their industrial labor force by 189 workers, and increased the value of their annual output by $288,096. In 1870, Athens's cotton mills accounted for nearly 15 percent of all cotton-mill workers in Georgia, 12 percent of wages paid to mill workers, 14 percent of materials consumed by Georgia's cotton factories, and 14 percent of the value of the state's cotton textile output. Despite claiming 12 to 14 percent in each of these previous categories, industrial investment in Athens captured only 8.5 percent of the statewide capital tied up in cotton textile production. (Augusta, the state leader in 1870, accounted for 19 percent of the state cotton textile labor force, and approximately 30 percent of its wages, materials consumed, and output produced, on 19 percent of its capitalization.) Clearly Athens proved a model of efficiency on such a return on capital. But one should also consider that these 1870 census figures do not include the conversion of the armory, which modernized and expanded Athens's industrial potential, since that event occurred after the enumeration took place. Also, in the 1860s, Athens secured its industrial financial base and labor force, as well as integrating its economic hinterland more firmly. Industry in Athens proved to be more than the visionary experiment of the 1830s, and greater than the model for emulation of the 1840s. Instead, by the 1860s, Athens emerged as a mature regional center for industrial enterprise, a status it achieved well before the arrival of the New South era.[31]

CONCLUSIONS

Exploring the forty years of Athens's industrial history from 1830 to 1870, this study raises a number of questions about our current understanding of both the Old and the New South. For the South under slavery, the presence of a class of citizens engaged in diversified investments that included industry certainly challenges the absolute primacy of slave ownership as the measure of status in southern society. Historical understanding is only now coming to appreciate that southerners who engaged in manufacturing before the New South era were not out of sync with their own times. Until recently, most historians considered these early industrialists as unsuccessful rivals to the planter class. Eugene Genovese, as is often the case, is still the best source to turn for exploring generally held implicit beliefs about southern history. In his classic *Political Economy of Slavery,* Genovese declared that antebellum southerners considered promoters of southern industrialization to be "damned fools," and that the planter class dominated the small and ineffectual manufacturing class in the South. More recent monographs on the successes of the Holt family's Alamance Factory in North Carolina, Daniel Pratt's industrial works in Alabama, and William Gregg's factory in South Carolina demonstrate the error of this particular line of thought, but they did not directly confront it. So let us now consider those two propositions in light of what we know about the process of industrialization in Athens.[32]

Was the elite status of Athens's initial manufacturers a fluke? Known antebellum manufacturers in Georgia included not only the business elite, but some of the state's premier politicians as well. Clearly a number of Athens's industrialists held prominent roles in local state and national politics. Augustin Clayton, who started industrialization in Athens, served as a judge, a congressman, a potential gubernatorial candidate, and a founder of the Whig Party in Georgia. Likewise, James Camak pursued a long political career in the state. Asbury Hull, an industrial investor who led the town's insurance company for twenty years, long served in the state legislature, which selected him their Speaker of the House of Representatives for at least one term. John White and Henry Gartrell attended the state's "Conservative" convention as the voice of white Clarke County's opposition to Radical Republican Reconstruction.

Outside Athens, other industrialists also actively participated in politics. At least two antebellum governors, William Schley and Charles McDonald (who were political opponents), actively ran cotton factories. Schley managed the one-thousand-spindle Richmond Factory, and his brother, John, operated the similarly sized Belleville Factory, just outside Augusta. In 1850, former Governor Charles J. McDonald built the $200,000 Sweetwater Factory in Campbell County, Georgia, which he operated until his death in 1860. McDonald's brother-in-law, Farish Carter, a planter of Milledgeville, invested in industries in Columbus as well as in northern Georgia. Another prominent politician-cum-industrialist, Mark Anthony Cooper, owned the Etowah Iron Works in Cass County in partnership with a relative of Athens's Baxter family. In each of these prominent cases, the political celebrity suffered no damage to his reputation for his industrial pursuits. One could hardly call these prominent politicians social pariahs or outcasts.[33]

Similarly, the families involved in manufacturing in or connected to Athens generally represented the elite of local society. Many of these elite found themselves combining their manufacturing, railroading, banking, commercial, and planting interests with the pursuit of politics. Possessing the requisite money to finance the factories, credit reports frequently spoke of them as the manufacturing towns' "leading men": They repeatedly filled town and county elective offices. They ran the local banks and merchant houses. They developed town lots and other real estate. And they represented the towns' interests in all sorts of voluntary meetings and philanthropic undertakings.

Genovese specifically explains that some leading men of Georgia invested in industrialization, but he avoids the obvious conclusion: the profits of industrialization attracted them. Instead, he suggests that such investment was a defensive rear-guard action by planters against the potential rise of a new rival class. Genovese's analysis narrowly classified the industrialists while broadly defining the planter class. In his reading of southern society, if a manufacturer engaged in any economic activity other than manufacturing, those other interests took precedence over manufacturing in defining that person's primary identity. With no room for maneuver, one took the persona of either a planter, a merchant, or a manufacturer since the categories served exclusive class interests. Thus, Genovese implies that the manufacturing class consisted of the group of northern men brought down to manage the factories, rather than the financiers who set policy for the factories. In this I think he erred, for he needed to explain the implications of multiple investment strategies by the south's business leaders.

Since the early manufacturers of Athens belonged to the town's elite, historians need better tools to define what provided access to this status. While not all the industrialists owned the requisite twenty or more slaves historians conventionally use as the standard of planter status, the majority of them did. If some planters invested in factories, we should consider whether the planter category accurately depicts the desires of everyone in the category, rather than accepting such investment as *prima facie* proof of efforts to maintain planter-class hegemony over a possibly rising industrial class. In Athens, planting provided a comfortable livelihood, but more importantly it gave one status in the community—a class identity as a person of stability and standing, much as ownership of a luxury automobile and membership in a golf club might serve as class markers today. But, as demonstrated by the economic behavior of the industrial planters of Athens, the master-slave relationship did not dominate the lives of men with multiple investment strategies. Instead, they sought financial stability by diversifying their portfolios through investments in real estate, banks, merchant businesses, railroads, factories, and, yes, plantations. But they also sold their slaves, and the slaves of the factories, when the need arose, suggesting only that the slaves be sold to someone the slaves preferred, *if possible.* Planting was simply one of many interests which returned a specific sort of value, part bankable, part not. To claim that a person with $30,000 invested in a factory, $30,000 invested in plantations and slaves, and another $30,000 invested in railroad and banking stock really thought of himself only as a planter dismisses too much of that person's activity as inessential. Being called a planter identified one as a gentleman. Neither of the two titles, planter or gentleman, limited an individual's investment activities, although they precluded certain occupations, such as manual labor or slave trading. Nor did such titles prevent southerners from envisioning an improved southern society in which market activity expanded for whites, but in which the activities of slaves continued to be carefully circumscribed.[34]

To say that being a planter precluded occupations involving manual labor did not necessarily stop southerners from acting as industrialists. Henry Merrell, the northern-born factory master at Roswell, Georgia, moaned that he could not recruit the elite young men of the South to work as apprentices within his mill because they felt it was beneath them. But one must question how many northern elite young men would have signed on for a seven-year labor-intensive apprenticeship learning both the technology and business of a factory, if his family did not already own a share in the enterprise. Elite northern boys attended college, just as they did in the South. Those who learned trades, instead, understood how those occupations limited their futures, just as Richard Dana, in *Two Years Before the Mast,* expressed concern that his time as a sailor not exceed his initial enlistment, lest he be trapped in that occupation. So Merrell sufficed with training the children of poor whites, his factory operatives, educating them in the intricacies of machinery repair and operative supervision. But Henry Merrell eventually left Roswell because he knew he would never become the factory's agent, since the same young men he could not engage as apprentices were being groomed for that post. Thus, in the South, one could become an industrialist without getting one's hands dirty. It may have been different from the North, but southerners still engaged in the business of industry. Possibly, southerners chose to maintain their cultural sensibilities about class-based occupations regardless of the opinion of their hired help, however irreplaceable the help may have been. But this sense of class allowed them to function in society as important people (that is, gentlemen) while importing new technologies that altered the way the southern economy operated.[35]

Thus we need to reconceptualize what it meant to be called a planter, when the person in question did not focus exclusively, or even primarily, upon his planting interests. In most instances, the historical actors in question identified themselves as planters, but they compartmentalized their other identities and played the role of each of these personae—planter, merchant, industrialist, railroad promoter, bank investor—to the degree to which their activities reflected their sense of commitment to each persona. Clearly one cannot determine the exact ratios of involvement in all these various activities. Tax records, despite their many flaws, provide non-quantifiable glimpses into the psychology of antebellum investment. In Athens, those with large industrial holdings usually also owned a plantation, a townhouse, slaves, banking and railroad stock, as well as an interest in a store. For some, slave ownership and land speculation took precedence over all other investment strategies, while others focused on retail as their primary business. No single trend emerged. Over time, however, slave ownership seemed to play a smaller role in the financial strategies for those investing in industry. The planter life-cycle may explain this change, as younger men who sought social status began to use industrial investments as a means to their goal, in lieu of additional purchases of slaves and land. Ultimately, in Athens, the longevity and the depth of financial commitment of townsmen toward industrialization, rather than any specific investment ratio, increasingly reveal that the way Lacy Ford, Mills Thornton, Dan Dupre, Bess Beatty, Tom Downey, and others depict antebellum southern entrepreneurship is more realistic than the largely discredited analysis by Genovese from the 1960s. It may be that further exploration into the compartmentalization of planter personae will reconcile our understanding of the planter's belief in a pre-capitalist relationship between himself and certain slaves, while simultaneously and unemotionally selling other slaves as a routine matter.

Further, historians need to consider how the adaptation of technology and business systems fit local culture. Southern industrialists understood the general process of industrialization in the North and in England. They worried that industrialization inevitably resulted in urbanization, which would increase class conflict. They took particular glee in pointing out the gender disruptions as women struck for better wages in New England, while they also began to hone their wage-slave critique of northern wage labor. They nonetheless cautiously adopted technologies and business systems associated with those disruptions. Yet, despite their claims of desiring to use slave labor in the mills, they primarily utilized free-white labor in their factories from the very start. Although all successful entrepreneurs can be considered opportunists of sorts, one should not think these men hypocrites. Nor did their contemporaries see them as such. The industrialists honestly believed they could create a unique southern path to increased industrial activity, different from those developed in the industrial economies of the North and of England. They believed the key to their success lay not in the institutions of liberal capitalism that they shared with the North and England, but in the cultural differences that manifested themselves in the southern economy.

Slavery made a difference even if costs prohibited the use of slaves in the factories. First, southerners understood the importance of the race card in maintaining a docile labor force. Enslaved African Americans served as an untapped reserve of unskilled labor should white workers make excessive demands on capital. Second, the latent effect of slavery to discourage immigration effectively maintained a low population density in the South that guaranteed a degree of control over urbanization unobtainable in the North. More to the point, however, the price of renting surplus slaves determined the cost of free labor. All things being equal, if the labor of a slave cost less, southern capital chose slave labor over free labor. By the time William Gregg espoused saving factory work for whites in order to bind the poor whites to the elite classes, economic trends already ruled out the use of slave labor in his mill and elsewhere. In the 1850s, cotton cultivation proved simply too profitable to take slaves from the fields to staff a factory. Therefore, factory work became the domain of poor whites by default. However, should conditions change, slave labor could be reintroduced. So the industrialists remained clear that they considered factory work a form of charity that they generously provided to poor whites, a charity that could disappear if the poor disappointed their employers.

Southern industrialization in the 1850s also challenges the notion of new men emerging as the South's business leaders only after emancipation destroyed the power of the planter class. The "new men" C. Vann Woodward found typifying the leadership in New South industrialization came to the fore in Athens starting in the 1850s. William Grady provides an accurate depiction of this category. He refused to play by conservative business or social rules. Yet he found respectability as an industrial gas producer. The New Jersey blacksmith William P. Talmage also fit the pattern with his many varied economic investments, and his marriage to the daughter of a fellow tradesmen. The New Hampshire–born printer Albon Chase made the transition to polite society as the staid Methodist general agent of the most prominent insurance company in the area, but he too experimented with many money-making schemes, including a journal aimed at silk production. Like Grady and Talmage, he never considered his social origins to have been shameful. By the 1860s, these industrialists all belonged to the town's elite, even if the planters sometimes chafed at admitting them to their club. By the end of the war, the social acceptance of manufacturing in Athens became even more apparent: textile man John White and gas manufacturer Henry Gartell represented Athens, as conservatives, in the convention at Macon that intended to rewrite the state constitution in December 1867. Third-generation industrialists John W. Nicholson and R. L. Bloomfield also came from this mold.[36]

John W. Nicholson began clerking in Athens in the 1840s and worked his way up to partner in a successful retail business during the antebellum period. By the late 1850s, Nicholson took to industrial investment by purchasing ten shares of the High Shoals Factory in conjunction with his partner, William S. Grady. While John W. Nicholson served as a municipal official and as a civilian agent of the Confederate Quartermaster during the Civil War, he continued to operate his store in Athens when others went off to fight. By the late 1860s and early 1870s, Nicholson re-emphasized his industrial interests when he bought a controlling share of the paper mill and then purchased Henry Grady's inheritance of William Grady's estate, including the gas works. By the early 1890s, Nicholson headed the promotion of the Northeastern Railroad, which finally freed Athens from continued subjugation by Augusta's Georgia Railroad. Thus Nicholson became a minor industrial investor during the second generation but made his mark more appropriately in the third generation.[37]

Robert Lee Bloomfield's history demonstrates a similar pattern. Twenty-year-old Bloomfield, whose business activity eventually led a journalist to refer to him as "a steam engine encased in breeches," moved from New Jersey to Athens in 1849. Originally selling ready-made clothing in Athens for a Newark firm, by the mid-1850s he obtained sufficient patronage to routinely keep people's measurements on hand so he could special-order clothes rather than just selling items off the rack. Credit reporters estimated that, within six months of his arrival in Athens, Bloomfield's real estate holdings came to $3,000. During the Civil War, Bloomfield remained in Athens, claiming to have changed from northern suppliers to European ones. In 1862, Bloomfield moved his stock of clothing to Atlanta while speculating in commodities necessary to life in Athens. In June 1863, he and a minor partner from Atlanta purchased controlling stock in the Athens Factory, with Bloomfield becoming its agent. By the end of the Civil War, he paid taxes on $24,000 in real estate, which steadily increased to more than $40,000 in the early 1870s. While his vision kept the Athens Manufacturing Company expanding its facilities in the 1860s and 1870s, it forced the company into bankruptcy by the 1890s when Bloomfield financed an unsuccessful electrification scheme using company assets. While calling his "financiering" faulty, a contemporary claimed Bloomfield simply got ahead of his time since another company ultimately completed what Bloomfield attempted twenty years previously. The same commentator placed Bloomfield and Nicholson among an elite corps of boosters that developed the Athens economy after 1870, writing, "No enterprise was ever inaugurated to promote the interests of the city which did not receive their support and financial aid." This statement would have been equally true of all three generations of Athens's town boosters.[38]

While Nicholson and Bloomfield represented the continuation of the "new men" in Athens's development, one can see the change from being labeled a "new man" at an early stage to being categorized as "old money" at a later time. Nonetheless, such "new" "old money" controlled the local economy by 1900. By 1896, descendants of John White controlled two of Athens's textile mills as well as one of its banks. The Thomas family, whose roots in Athens dated to the last decade of the eighteenth century, dominated the local insurance company from the death of Albon Chase in 1867 to the death of W. W. Thomas in 1904. Other new men came forward, such as Lon Dudley rising from child factory operative to owner of several textile mills in Athens in the early twentieth century—including the Athens Manufacturing Company, as a wholly owned subsidiary of Climax Hosiery Mill—from the 1920s to 1947. But, once arrived, the families of the "new men" became the "old money." Thus the second generation of industrialization, beginning in 1850, set the pattern for late-nineteenth- and early twentieth-century industrial ownership in Athens. The "new men" of the third generation individually may have been new to the town, but as a class of entrepreneurs in Athens, they fit within an established archetype.[39]

Thus, in a forty-year period, Athens, Georgia, transformed its small industrial base from an experiment in political economy to the prototype of the typical New South mill town. Although founded for the political purpose of proving a form of taxation unnecessary, and initially nurtured on pro-slavery ideology, textile production ultimately took hold in the South because of southern desires for its profit potential. But, to secure their investments, manufacturers necessarily developed transportation and communication networks, primarily by leading the way in building railroads and in organizing the commercial conventions. It is not coincidental that Georgia, as the most industrialized state in the antebellum Deep South, contained the most railroad mileage as well. Textile production required markets, and markets demanded relatively inexpensive and reliable transportation. In the process of building factories, these early southern industrialists began the transformation of the southern economy from a relatively isolated agrarian economy, supporting both export-based plantation capitalism and safety-first yeoman surplus production, to an economy containing industrial sectors relatively well integrated into national and international markets. Despite cyclic periods of contraction, primarily when the price of labor and raw materials dramatically increased, and of expansion, when the reverse encouraged mill construction, the textile industry in Georgia both survived and matured. During the part of the business cycle when textiles proved relatively unprofitable, Athens developed ancillary industries that enabled it to become a regional center for supplying the needs of mills within the town's economic hinterland, and to tie them more closely to Athens's interests.

Like the industrial contraction of the 1850s, the Civil War proved a calamity only to those mills with insufficient capital or foresight to take advantage of war production. The aura of patriotic service developed by an industry seeking to avoid charges of profiteering became part of the catechism of New South boosterism. By 1870, Athens possessed a self-replicating working class that rarely, if ever, challenged the social structure of the town, a social structure reinforced by an economic system that allowed an ambitious few the opportunity to advance beyond unskilled or semi-skilled industrial labor. Finally, it is not coincidental that, as Athens's industry matured, a person such as Henry Grady, the son of an industrial entrepreneur, could envision an economic future that reflected his life experiences. Grady's plan for a New South projected the reality of industrial development in Athens onto the rest of the region, for better or for worse. For some localities, this vision proved as revolutionary in its expression as the New South boosters of the 1880s claimed, but for Athens, and for Georgia, it was old hat. Thus early twentieth-century Georgia historian Lucian Lamar Knight would remark as a corrective to those boosters, that "Georgia, since the early [18]30s . . . has been styled the "Empire State of the South. But she did not receive this title on account of area or population. Virginia at that time excelled Georgia in both these particulars. . . . Although Georgia was recognized as an agricultural state, . . . commerce and manufactures were receiving much attention."[40]

Abbreviations

Chicopee Minute Books	Athens Factory Directors' Minute Books, Chicopee Manufacturing Company, Hargrett Rare Book and Manuscript Library, University of Georgia.
Deed Book	Deed Book, Real Estate Office, Clerk of the Superior Court, Clarke County Court House, Athens, Ga.
Georgia Archives	Georgia Archives, Morrow, Ga.
Hargrett Library	Hargrett Rare Book and Manuscript Library, University of Georgia.
Perkins Library	Perkins Library Special Collections, Duke University.
R. G. Dun	Dun & Co. Collection, Baker Library Historical Collections, Harvard Business School.
Report of Scull Shoals	Caroline C. Hunt, "The Settlement, Development, and Decline of the Scull Shoals Community in Green and Oconee Counties, 1784–1920," Historical Survey Report of Scull Shoals community, Greene County, Ga., performed for the United States Department of Agriculture Forest Service Contract 38-3231. May 1980.
SMIC	Southern Mutual Insurance Company, Athens, Ga.
Southern Mutual Minute Book	Board of Directors Minute Book, Southern Mutual Insurance Company, Athens, Ga.

Notes

INTRODUCTION

1. Fred Bateman and Thomas Weiss, *A Deplorable Scarcity: The Failure of Industrialization in the Slave Economy* (Chapel Hill: University of North Carolina Press, 1981), 26; Robert W. Fogel and Stanley L. Engerman, *Time on the Cross: The Economics of American Negro Slavery* (Boston: Little, Brown and Co., 1974), 6, 255.

2. Allen Heath Stokes, "Black and White Labor and the Development of the Southern Textile Industry, 1800–1920," Ph.D. diss., University of South Carolina, 1977; John Richard de Treville, "The Little New South: Origins of Industry in Georgia's Fall-Line Cities, 1840–1865," Ph.D. diss., University of North Carolina–Chapel Hill, 1986; Randall M. Miller, *The Cotton Mill Movement in Antebellum Alabama* (New York: Arno Press, 1978); Broadus Mitchell, *The Rise of Cotton Mills in the South* (Gloucester, Mass.: Peter Smith, 1921), 9.

3. Eugene D. Genovese, *The Political Economy of Slavery: Studies in the Economy and Society of the Slave South* (New York: Random House, 1965), 180–220; Bateman and Weiss, *A Deplorable Scarcity*, 47–48; Gavin Wright, "Cheap Labor and Southern Textiles before 1880," *Journal of Economic History* 39 (1979): 565; James C. Cobb, "Beyond Planters and Industrialists: A New Perspective on the New South," *Journal of Southern History* 54 (February 1988): 45–51; David L. Carlton, "The Revolution from Above: The National Market and the Beginnings of Industrialization in North Carolina," *Journal of American History* 77 (1990): 446–48; J. Mills Thornton III, *Politics and Power in a Slave Society: Alabama, 1800–1860* (Baton Rouge: Louisiana State University Press, 1978); Daniel Dupre, "Ambivalent Capitalists on the Cotton Frontier: Settlement and Development in the Tennessee Valley of Alabama." *Journal of Southern History* 106 (May 1990): 215–40.

4. Bess Beatty, *Alamance: The Holt Family and Industrialization in a North Carolina County, 1837–1900* (Baton Rouge: Louisiana State University Press, 1999); Curtis J. Evans, *The Conquest of Labor: Daniel Pratt and Southern Industrialization* (Baton Rouge: Louisiana State University Press, 2001); Harold S. Wilson, *Confederate Industry: Manufacturers and Quartermasters in the Civil War* (Jackson: University Press of Mississippi, 2002); and Tom Downey, *Planting a Capitalist South; Masters, Merchants, and Manufacturers in the Southern Interior, 1790–1860* (Baton Rouge: Louisiana State University Press, 2009).

5. Alice C. Galenson, "The Migration of the Cotton Textile Industry from New England to the South: 1880–1930," Ph.D. diss., Cornell University, 1975, 2, "Table I.1: Number of Active Spindles, by State, New England and South, 1859 to 1929." *Report on Manufacturing Industries in the United States at the Eleventh Census: 1890*, Part 3, Selected Industries (1895; rpt. New York: Norman Ross Publishing Inc., 1993), 188–91. Jonathan Prude, *The Coming of Industrial Order:*

Town and Factory Life in Rural Massachusetts, 1810–1860 (New York: Cambridge University Press, 1983); Anthony F. C. Wallace, *Rockdale: The Growth of an American Village in the Early Industrial Revolution* (New York: Alfred A. Knopf, 1978); Philip Scranton, *Proprietary Capitalism: The Textile Manufacture at Philadelphia, 1800–1885* (New York: Cambridge University Press, 1983).

6. Richard W. Griffin, "Origins of Southern Cotton Manufactures, 1807–1816," *Cotton History Review* 1 (January 1960): 8–9; Garnett Andrews, "History of the Cotton Gin in Georgia," *De Bow's Review* 14 (May 1853): 511 (as cited in Richard W. Griffin, "The Ante-Bellum Southern Factory as seen by Contemporaries, 1775–1865," in file 59, Richard Worden Griffin Papers, Z. Smith Reynolds Library Special Collections, Wake Forest University); *Southern Banner* (Athens, Georgia), "TO MANUFACTURERS A GREAT BARGAIN," September 28, 1833; Richard W. Griffin, "A Documentary History of the Georgia Ante-Bellum Cotton Textile Industry, 1808–1865," in box 1, file 75, Griffin Papers; Broadus Mitchell, *William Gregg; Factory Master of the Old South* (1928; rpt. New York: Octagon Books, 1966), 4; Richard W. Griffin and Harold S. Wilson, "The Ante-Bellum Textile Industry of Georgia, 1798–1865," unpublished manuscript in possession of Tom Terrill, Columbia, S.C., 78–80. Stephen J. Goldfarb in "A Note on the Limits to the Growth of the Cotton-Textile Industry in the Old South," *Journal of Southern History* 48 (November 1982): 545–58.

7. E. Merton Coulter, "The Birth of a University, a Town, and a County," *Georgia Historical Quarterly* 46 (1962): 113–50. Sylvanus Morris, *History of Athens and Clarke County* (Athens, Ga.: H. J. Rowe, 1923), 4. Shaler G. Hillyer, *Reminiscences of Georgia Baptists* (Atlanta: Foote and Davies, 1902). *Southern Banner,* July 27, 1832, "Commencement."

8. Adiel Sherwood, *A Gazetteer of the State of Georgia* (1827; rpt. Athens: University of Georgia Press, 1939), 26. *Athenian,* May 27, 1828; April 21, 1829.

9. Jimmy Paul Hunke, "Fluvial Morphometry as a Tool in Rediscovering Historical Waterpowers: A Case Study on the Georgia Piedmont," master's thesis, University of Georgia, 1983, 163.

10. Gary Kulik, "Dams, Fish, and Farmers: Defense of Public Rights in Eighteenth-Century Rhode Island," in *The Countryside in the Age of Capitalist Transformation: Essays in the Social History of Rural America,* ed. Steven Hahn and Jonathan Prude (Chapel Hill: University of North Carolina Press, 1985); Morton J. Horwitz, *The Transformation of American Law 1780–1860* (Cambridge, Mass.: Harvard University Press, 1977); Tom Downey, "Riparian Rights and Manufacturing in Antebellum South Carolina: William Gregg and the Origins of the 'Industrial Mind,'" *Journal of Southern History* 65 (February 1999): 77–108.

11. H. J. Habakkuk, *American and British Technology in the Nineteenth Century* (Cambridge, U.K.: Cambridge University Press, 1962).

12. *Georgia Journal* as quoted in *Athenian,* August 19, 1828; *Athenian,* August 26, 1828, "Value of Cotton." Both articles suggest this connection. All cotton prices quoted are average prices paid in New York for middling upland cotton. See James L. Watkins, *King Cotton: A Historical and Statistical Review 1790–1908* (1908; rpt. New York: Negro Universities Press, 1969), 29–31. These numbers do not reflect the factories enumerated in the 1850 census. Several mills constructed as part of the 1847–53 mill-building boom were not enumerated because they had not yet begun operations at the time of the census.

CHAPTER ONE

1. *Athenian,* March 10, 24, 1829; April 28, 1829, "Severe Cold"; June 2, 1829, "Snow."

2. Habakkuk, *American and British Technology in the Nineteenth Century*, 42–3, 82, and 98.

3. Richard E. Ellis, *The Union At Risk: Jacksonian Democracy, States' Rights, and the Nullification Crisis* (New York: Oxford University Press, 1987); Anthony G. Carey, "Parties and Politics in Antebellum Georgia," Ph.D. diss., Emory University, 1992; U. B. Phillips, *Georgia and State Rights* (n.p.: Antioch Press, 1968); E. Merton Coulter, "Nullification Crisis in Georgia," *Georgia Historical Quarterly* 5 (1921): 5–39.

4. Ernest M. Lander Jr., *The Textile Industry in Antebellum South Carolina* (Baton Rouge: Louisiana State University Press, 1969).

5. *Athenian*, January 25, 1828, emphasis in the original.

6. *Athenian*, January 26, 1827, "Foreign News"; January 26, 1827, "England and the United States." *Free Trade Advocate* as quoted in *Athenian*, June 30, 1829, "Extract." *Athenian*, January 25, 1828, and December 8, 1829.

7. *Athenian*, April 6, 1830, "Manufacturing."

8. *Alabama Journal* as quoted in *Athenian*, March 16, 1830.

9. Bernard Bailyn, *The Ideological Origins of the American Revolution* (Cambridge, Mass.: Belknap Press, 1967); Daniel T. Rodgers, "Republicanism: Career of a Concept," *Journal of American History* 79 (1992): 11–38. *Athenian*, January 26, 1827, "England & the United States"; July 20, 1827, "Anti-Tariff Meeting"; September 21, 1827, "Meeting in Elberton"; October 3, 1827, "Returns of the Election"; January 25, 1828; February 22, 1828, "Extracts from the REPORT of the Committee on Manufactures"; April 18, 1828, "The Tariff"; April 25, 1828, "Congressional Summary"; May 9, 1828; May 9, 1828, "The Tariff"; May 27, 1828; June 24, 1828, "Anti-Tariff Meeting." *Athenian*, January 25, 1828, and December 8, 1829.

10. *Athenian*, July 20, 1827, "Anti-Tariff Meeting"; September 21, 1827, "Meeting in Elberton"; June 24, 1828, "Anti-Tariff Meeting"; July 15, 1828, "Milledgeville Anti-Tariff Meeting"; August 5, 1828, "The Tariff and Taxes on Sales at Auction." *Athenian*, December 9, 1828, "Extract from the minutes of the Trustees of the University of Georgia, at its session in Milledgeville, in November, last." *Southern Banner*, August 3, 1832, "Public Meeting." *Athenian*, December 9, 1828, "Extract from the minutes of the Trustees of the University of Georgia, at its session in Milledgeville, in November, last." *Southern Banner*, August 3, 1832, "Public Meeting." *Athenian*, August 5, 1828, "The Tariff, and Taxes on Sales at Auction." *Southern Banner*, September 12, 1844, "Oglethorpe Meeting of 1832 to Resist the Tariff."

11. *Athenian*, July 15, 1828, "Communication"; July 22, 1828, "Communications"; August 5, 1828, "A Question"; August 5, 1828, "Resolutions unanimously adopted at the great Anti-Tariff meeting held at Edgefield Court House, on the 26th July, 1828"; August 19, 1828.

12. *Athenian*, August 12, 1828, "Athens Anti-Tariff Meeting"; Coulter, "Nullification Crisis," 8.

13. *Athenian*, July 22, 1828, "Mr. Shaw" Toasts 11 and 12 of a series of Fourth of July Toasts offered by "Senex" and "The Fourth of July at Danielsville"; July 14, 1829, 12th toast. *Athenian*, July 22, 1828, "Communications"; July 20, 1827, "Anti-Tariff Meeting"; September 21, 1827, "Meeting in Elberton"; June 24, 1828, "Anti-Tariff Meeting"; July 15, 1828, "Milledgeville Anti-Tariff Meeting"; August 5, 1828, "The Tariff and Taxes on Sales at Auction."

14. *Athenian*, July 22, 1828, "Report" December 9, 1828, "Extract of the minutes of the Trustees of the University of Georgia, at its session in Milledgeville, in November, last." *The Southron* as quoted in *Athenian*, January 6, 1829, "Captions and Provisions of the Acts passed in November and December, 1828." *Athenian*, March 3, 1829, "Beer."

15. *Athenian*, August 26, 1828, "Value of Cotton."

16. *American Farmer,* September 28, 1827, "Cotton Bagging"; October 5, 1827, "Manufacture of Cotton in the Southern States . . . No. II"; October 12, 1827, "No. III"; October 19, 1827, "No. IV"; October 26, 1827, "No. V"; November 2, 1827, "No. VI"; November 16, 1827, "No. VII"; November 30, 1827, "No. XI"; December 7, 1827, "No. X"; December 14, 1827, "No. XI"; December 21, 1827, "No. XII"; January 4, 1828, "No. XIII"; January 18, 1828, "No. XIV"; January 25, 1828, "No. XV"; February 29, 1828, "No. XVI"; March 14, 1828, "No. XVII"; April 4, 1828, "No. XX"; and April 25, 1828, "No. XXI." Nos. XIV (January 18, 1828) and XV (January 25, 1828) comprise the Fisher Report.

17. *American Farmer* 9 (January 18, 1828), "A Report on the establishment of Cotton and Woollen Manufactures, and on the growing of Wool; made to the House of Commons of North Carolina by Mr. Fisher, from Rowan, on Tuesday, January 1, 1828," concluded on January 25, 1828. The quotation is from page 354. *Athenian,* December 2, 1828, "A Report made before the Legislature of North Carolina, on the Establishment of Manufactories in that State." Richard Griffin and Diffee Standard, "The Cotton Textile Industry in Ante-Bellum North Carolina, Part 1: Origin and Growth to 1830," *North Carolina Historical Review* 34 (1957): 29–34.

18. *Athenian,* January 4, 1828.

19. Savannah *Statesman & Patriot;* August 26, 1828, "Value of Cotton," as quoted in *Athenian,* August 26, 1828, "Cotton Bagging." *Athenian,* November 25, 1828.

20. *Charleston Courier* as quoted in the *Athenian,* February 17, 1829, "South Carolina Manufactures." Lander, *The Textile Industry in Antebellum South Carolina,* 10, 72. *Athenian,* March 3, 1829, "Beer"; March 24, 1829. Augusta *Constitutionalist* as quoted in *Athenian,* July 22, 1828.

21. *Georgia Journal* as quoted in the *Athenian,* August 19, 1828. Charleston *Mercury* as quoted by *National Intelligencer,* April 18, 1829, as cited in Richard W. Griffin, "The Origins of the Industrial Revolution in Georgia: Cotton Textiles, 1810–1865," *Georgia Historical Quarterly* 42 (December 1958): 359–60.

22. *Athenian,* January 26, 1827, "Foreign News"; March 9, 1827, "English Manufactures."

23. *Athenian,* January 27, 1828, "Grand turn out among Females."

24. *Athenian,* March 9, 1827, "English Manufactures."

25. *Gales & Seaton's Register of Debates in Congress,* 22nd Congress, 1st sess., vol. 8, pt. 3: 1832, 3555.

26. *American Farmer* as quoted in *Athenian,* November 2, 1827. *American Farmer,* January 18, 1828; January 25, 1828. *Mississippian* as quoted in *Athenian,* May 9, 1828, emphasis in the original. Enoch Steadman, "A Brief Treatise on Manufacturing in the South" (rpt. from pamphlet printed in Clarksville, Tenn., in 1851), *Cotton History Review* 2 (April 1961): 111.

27. *Georgia Journal* as quoted in *Athenian,* August 19, 1828.

28. *Georgia Journal* as quoted in *Athenian,* April 6, 1830, "Manufacturing."

29. *Athenian,* January 4, 1828. Schley's brother, William, was connected to the Clarke Party, which was then out of power. Thus, not only the nature of the request, but who was making the request is important. *Athenian,* December 7, 1827, "Bills Passed"; January 4, 1828. *Georgia Courier* as quoted in *Athenian,* July 15 and 29, 1828. *Athenian,* December 2, 1828, "Bills Passed." Lander, *The Textile Industry in Antebellum South Carolina,* 35. *Athenian,* November 25, 1828, "Bills Passed."

30. *Athenian,* March 31, 1829.

31. Deed Book "O," 147–48.

32. *Athenian*, March 31, 1829; David Jeremy, *Transatlantic Industrial Revolution: The Diffusion of Textile Technologies Between Britain and America, 1790–1830s* (Cambridge: MIT Press, 1981), 98.

33. Deed of Carr to Dearing, Nisbet, Clayton & Walker, May, 28, 1832, Deed Book "P," 60–61. Quit-claim of Augustin S. Clayton for his quarter share of the factory for $12,000 in Deed Book "P," 189–90. Quit-claim of Augustin S. Clayton, Chicopee Manufacturing Company, Legal Papers—1833 (Henceforth Chicopee Legal Papers), Hargrett Library. *Southern Banner*, September 20, 1834, put the loss at $40,000, which would have been the cost of buildings, equipment, and materials without the value of the land.

34. Deed of Noah Prince and Noah F. Prince to James Camak, Asbury Hull, William Lumpkin, Daniel Grant, E. L. Newton, E. R. Ware, Thomas Grant, Thomas Mitchell, all of Clarke County, R. W. Orme, of Baldwin County, and Sharp & Company, of Monroe County, Deed Book "P," 296–97. *Southern Banner* June 29, 1833, "Rail Road Meeting"; May 17, 1834, "The Rail Road"; May 31, 1834, "The Georgia Rail Road." Joseph B. Cummings, *A History of the Georgia Railroad Company and Banking Company and its Corporate Affiliates 1833–1958* (Augusta: Georgia Railroad and Banking Company, 1958) 21–22. Mary G. Cummings, *Georgia Railroad & Banking Company 1833–1945* (Augusta: n.p., 1945). Deed Book "Q," 51–63. Williams began purchasing the shares in the factory in November 1834 and completely owned the factory by September 1836.

35. Deed Book "Q," 58–60.

36. Southern Mutual Minute Books 1848–68, July 30, 1853; February 24, 1854; May 19, 1854; July 12, 1855; July 25, 1856; March 1, 1862; June 17, 1864; and January 3, 1868. *Athenian*, August 9, 1831, "Edgefield Factory Burnt." *Southern Banner*, September 20, 1834, "Great Calamity"; March 27, 1840, "Eatonton Factory Destroyed by Fire!"; September 3, 1841, "Fires"; November 11, 1845, "Skull Shoal Factory Burnt"; November 12, 1857, "Fire." Josiah Daniel Almanac Diary and Deaths in Clarke County 1834–1877 (MS 462), August 11, 1850 entry, Hargrett Rare Book and Manuscript Library, University of Georgia. *Southern Banner*, May 29, 1840, "Great and Disastrous Freshet"; William Price Talmage Diary, 1847–1877 (MS 603), Hargrett Library, 6, and 28–29; A. P. Dearing to John J. Dearing, April 5, 1854, John J. Dearing (Covington, Ga.) Papers, 1820–56, Perkins Library.

37. *Southern Banner*, February 22, 1834, "Died." First sale date of first Tuesday in January 1835 first advertised in *Southern Banner*, November 8, 1834, "Valuable Property." The advertisement stopped running in late December and then reappeared in the *Southern Banner*, February 12, 1835, "Valuable Property in Market," with a new sale date of March 16, 1835. Chicopee Legal Papers, March 18 and 19, 1835. Chicopee Minute Books, March 23, 1835, and June 16, 1836. Chicopee Minute Books, February 24 and August 24, 1844. *Southern Banner*, December 28, 1839, "The Legislature"; August 17, 1848, "Georgia, Clark County." De Treville, "The Little New South." R. G. Dun, Georgia, vol. 6: 90.

Georgia Factory—Deed of William Dearing to Thomas Moore, August 18, 1835, Deed Book "T," 380–81; deed of Walker Estate to William Carr, dated August 7, 1838, Deed Book "Q," 305; deed of Thomas Moore to John White, July 22, 1839, Deed Book "Q," 409; deed of Thomas Moore to John White, February 6, 1842, Deed Book "R," 215; deed of Thomas Moore to John White, March 18, 1842, Deed Book "R," 224–25; deed of estate of Augustin S. Clayton to John White, January 14, 1844, Deed Book "S," 290; deeds of John Nisbet estate and Thomas Morrow to John

White, November 4 and 5, 1844, Deed Book "S," 131–32; deed of William A. Carr to John White, January 8, 1846, Deed Book "S," 291.

Athens Factory—deed of William Dearing of Charleston, to John S. Linton as agent of Athens Factory, April 22, 1848, Deed Book "T," 138–39; Chicopee Minute Books, July 28, 1849.

Princeton Factory—Deed Book "Q," 51–63; Deed Book "S," 216–20, 392–98. R. G. Dun, Georgia, vol. 6: 91.

38. Robert Dalzell, *Enterprising Elite: The Boston Associates and the World They Made* (Cambridge, Mass.: Harvard University Press, 1987); *Southern Banner,* May 12, 1836, "Railroad Convention."

39. *Southern Banner,* August 18, 1846, "Atlanta Enterprise."

40. Chicopee Minute Books, June 16, 1836; April 3, 1837; and May 1, 1839. *Southern Banner,* May 29, 1840, "Great and Disastrous Freshet"; September 25, 1840, "Negro Clothing." Chicopee Minute Books, October 13, 1841.

41. *Gales & Seaton's Register of Debates in Congress,* 22nd Congress, 1st sess., vol. 18, pt. 3: 1832, 3549–50; "The Tariff—June 23, 1832," 3727–28. New York *Journal of Commerce* as quoted in *Athenian,* May 5, 1829, "Manufactures in Georgia." *Athenian,* July 26, 1831, "Athens Factory."

42. Chicopee Minute Books, April 3, 1837; Deed Book "S," 216–20, 392–98.

43. Chicopee Minute Books, February 24, August 24, 1844. Between these two dividends, the company declared a 30 percent dividend returned to shareholders in that year alone. U.S. Congress, "Report of the Secretary of the Treasury," House Executive Document #6, 29th Congress, 1st sess., 1845, vol. 2, doc. 6M, 625–27. Rpt. in "Walker Tariff Report 1846 . . . Circulars of the Secretary of the Treasury & abstract of Replies to them in regard to the Tariff," 62nd Congress, 1st sess., Senate Document 72, pt. 3, vol. 10, ser. 6088: 1872–73.

44. *Athenian,* March 15, 1831, "Athens Factory." *Southern Banner,* July 26, 1831, "To the Public." *Athenian,* February 2, 1830, "Athens Factory." *Southern Banner,* January 14, 1836, "For Sale."

45. *Athenian,* February 2, 1830, "Athens Factory," lists prices for yarn qualities five through eight, with an increase in price corresponding to an increase in number, which should also correspond to an increase in output quality. Jeremy, *Transatlantic Textile Revolution,* 286, 294. *Southern Banner,* March 3, 1838, "Merchants & Planters." Scranton, *Proprietary Capitalism.*

46. Chicopee Minute Books, October 3, 1836. Jeremy, *Transatlantic Textile Revolution,* 289. *Southern Banner,* December 24, 1835, "Princeton Factory." *Southern Banner,* October 20, 1838, "New Goods!!"

47. *Athenian,* October 13, 1829, "Wool Carding"; April 13, 1830, "Wool Carding." *Southern Banner,* September 21, 1833; January 14, 1836, "For Sale." Bobbin Mill Record Book 1867–1877 (MS 108, henceforth Bobbin Mill Record), January 16, 1875, Hargrett Library.

48. While Georgia Railroad histories claim the Georgia Railroad got its start when muddy roads prevented delivery of textile machinery for several months, the reports are unlikely since the initial meetings of the incorporators of the Georgia Railroad and of the incorporators of the Camak Factory (both headed by James Camak) took place within two months of each other. *Southern Banner,* May 11, 1833, "Manufactures"; July 6, 1833, "Rail Road Meeting."

Very little is known about the textile-machinery building aspect of the Rogers works in Paterson. "Documents relative to The Manufactures in the United States collected and transmitted To the House of Representatives in compliance with a resolution of Jan. 19, 1832 by the Secretary of the Treasury," otherwise known as the "McLane Report," vols. 3 and 4 (rpt. New York: Burt Franklin, 1976), 156–57, document 11, no. 16, for reply of Rogers, Ketchum & Grosvenor of Paterson, N.J. "The Rogers Locomotive 'Sandusky,'" in *Bulletin* 44 of the Railway and Locomotive Historical Society (October 1937): 42–45. *The Rogers Locomotive Catalog, 1876* (Newark: New Jersey Historical Society, 1983). "Thomas Rogers," *Dictionary of American Biography* 16: 112–13.

Chicopee Minute Books, April 3, 1837. Jeremy, *Transatlantic Textile Revolution,* "Glossary," 284–94.

49. *Southern Banner,* July 26, 1831, "To the Public"; March 3, 1838, "Merchants & Planters." A nankeen is a buff-colored durable cotton cloth, originally from China, used for making trousers. *Webster's New Twentieth Century Dictionary* (2nd ed., New York: Simon & Schuster, 1979), 1193. George White, *Statistics of the State of Georgia* (Savannah, Ga.: W. Thorne Williams, 1849), 182–83.

50. James C. Cobb, "Beyond Planters and Industrialists: A New Perspective on the New South," *Journal of Southern History* 54 (February 1988): 45–56; John McCardell, *The Idea of a Southern Nation: Southern Nationalists and Southern Nationalism, 1830–1860* (New York: W. W. Norton, 1978).

51. Steven Hahn, *Roots of Southern Populism: Yeoman Farmers and the Transformation of the Georgia Upcountry, 1850–1890* (New York: Oxford University Press, 1983); Michael Merrill, "Cash Is Good to Eat: Self-Sufficiency and Exchange in the Rural Economy of the United States," *Radical History Review* 4 (Winter 1977): 42–71; James Henretta, "Families and Farms: Mentalité in Preindustrial America," *William and Mary Quarterly,* 3rd ser., vol. 35 (January 1978): 3–32; and Christopher Clark, "Household Economy, Market Exchange and the Rise of Capitalism in the Connecticut Valley, 1800–1860," *Journal of Social History* 13 (Winter 1979): 19–89. Jackson County, Georgia, one of the two counties researched by Hahn, is immediately adjacent to industrializing Clarke County, where four cotton factories were located. And Jackson County itself briefly housed two small factories, probably artisanal, in the 1840s. *Southern Banner,* September 3, 1841, "Wool Factory." This "factory" was, in fact, a water-powered wool-carding operation and not a complete factory as we would understand it. Hugh White's cotton factory, located in the community of Mulberry, was valued at $4,500 to $6,000; R. G. Dun, Georgia, vol. 18: 49, and *Southern Banner,* April 24, 1845, "The Cedar Creek Cotton and Wool Factory." Robert White obituary clipping, 1897, in possession of John White descendent Marguerite Hodgson, of Athens, Georgia (henceforth called Hodgson Collection).

52. *Southern Banner,* July 27, 1843, "For the Banner." White, *Statistics of the State of Georgia,* 182–83.

53. James Silk Buckingham, *The Slaves States of America* (London: Fisher, Son & Co., 1843), vol. 2: 112. *Southern Banner,* June 28, 1839, "Mr. Buckingham's Lectures" and "Bible Society Meeting"; July 5, 1839, "Mr. Buckingham's Lectures."

54. See de Treville, "The Little New South," for development of machine shops in Augusta, Macon, and Columbus, Georgia, in the 1850s; James Michael Russell, *Atlanta, 1847–1890: City Building in the Old South and the New* (Baton Rouge: Louisiana State University Press, 1988), for development of extensive machine shops for Atlanta's railroad yards in the 1850s. Athens developed a machine shop in 1850; *Southern Banner,* October 17, 1850, "Georgia, Clark County" and R. G. Dun, Georgia, vol. 6: 99, 134.

55. White, *Statistics of the State of Georgia,* 182. *Southern Banner,* February 16, 1833, "For the Southern Banner." Chicopee Minute Books, March 3, 1837. Also see *Niles' National Register,*

June 20, 1840, "Georgia." John S. Linton to Annie Linton, July 10, 1853, and February 11, 1858 (typescript copies), Linton Gift, Hargrett Library.

56. James L. Skinner, ed., *The Autobiography of Henry Merrell: Industrial Missionary to the South* (Athens: University of Georgia Press, 1991), 135 and 455–56n.

57. *Gales and Seaton's Register of Debates in Congress,* 22nd Congress, 1st sess., vol. 18, pt. 3: 1833, 3554. *Athenian,* January 17, 1832, "Athens Factory." Stephen F. Miller, *Bench and Bar of Georgia* (Philadelphia: J. B. Lippincott & Co., 1858), vol. 1: 151–52 (quoting letter of A. S. Clayton to the editor of the *Globe*) shows that Johnson went to arbitration to get all he thought was due him, that Johnson had invested $4,000 in the concern, and that he obtained an additional $4,182.78 as settlement for his stock in the company. John A. Caramia Jr., "Teaching about the Local Community: Focus, Techniques and Resources," *Georgia Social Science Journal* 12 (Spring 1981): 8–9; Southern Historical Association, *Memoirs of Georgia* (Atlanta: Southern Historical Association, 1895), vol. 1: 488. Chicopee Minute Books, June 16, 1836. The timing of Robert White's purchase of a minor partnership in the Athens Factory coincides with John White's employment at the nearby Georgia factory in 1836.

58. Chicopee Minute Books, November 1, 1843; Steadman, "A Brief Treatise on Manufacturing in the South," 107–8.

59. Steadman, "A Brief Treatise on Manufacturing in the South," 107–8.

CHAPTER TWO

1. *Athenian,* May 27, 1828; April 21, 1829. Augustus Longstreet Hull, *Annals of Athens, Georgia 1801–1901* (Athens, Ga.: Banner Job Office, 1906), 391–92.

2. *Athenian,* February 2, 1830. Habakkuk, *American & British Technology in the Nineteenth Century*; Thomas Dublin, *Women at Work: The Transformation of Work and Community in Lowell, Massachusetts, 1826–1860* (New York, Columbia University Press, 1979), 86–131; Jonathan Prude, *The Coming of Industrial Order: Town and Factory Life in Rural Massachusetts, 1810–1860* (New York, Cambridge University Press, 1983), 133–58; Wallace, *Rockdale,* 63–65; Louis De Vorsey Jr., "Early Water-powered Industries in Athens and Clarke County," *Papers of the Athens Historical Society* 2 (1979): 50n.

3. Robert S. Starobin, *Industrial Slavery in the Old South* (New York: Oxford University Press, 1970); S. Sydney Bradford, "The Negro Ironworker in Ante Bellum Virginia" *Journal of Southern History* 25 (1959): 194–206; Charles B. Dew, "Disciplining Slave Ironworkers in the Antebellum South: Coercion, Conciliation, and Accommodation," *American Historical Review* (1974): 393–418; Charles B. Dew, "David Ross and the Oxford Iron Works: A Study of Industrial Slavery in the Early Nineteenth-Century South," *William and Mary Quarterly,* 3rd ser., vol. 31 (1974): 189–224; Ronald L. Lewis, *Coal, Iron, and Slaves: Industrial Slavery in Maryland and Virginia, 1715–1865* (Westport, Conn.: Greenwood Press, 1979); Charles B. Dew, "Sam Williams, Forgeman: The Life of an Industrial Slave in the Old South", in J. Morgan Kousser and James M. McPherson, eds., *Region, Race, and Reconstruction: Essays in Honor of C. Vann Woodward* (New York: Oxford University Press, 1982), 199–239; Charles B. Dew, "Slavery and Technology in the Antebellum Southern Iron Industry: The Case of Buffalo Forge," in Ronald L. Numbers and Todd L. Savitt, eds., *Science and Medicine in the Old South* (Baton Rouge: Louisiana State University Press, 1989), 107–26;

Charles B. Dew, *Bond of Iron: Master and Slave at Buffalo Forge* (New York: W. W. Norton, 1994); T. Stephen Whitman, "Industrial Slavery at the Margin: The Maryland Chemical Works," *Journal of Southern History* 109 (February 1993): 31–62; Ernest M. Lander, "Slave Labor in South Carolina Cotton Mills," *Journal of Negro History* 38 (1953): 161–73; Norris W. Preyer, "The Historian, the Slave, and the Ante-Bellum Textile Industry" *Journal of Negro History* 46 (April 1961): 67–82; and Stokes, "Black and White Labor." *Southern Whig*, July 12, 1849, "Employment of Slave Labor in Factories"; *South Carolinian* as quoted in *Southern Banner*, June 28, 1849, "Manufacturing at the South," and July 12, 1849, "Industrial Pursuits—Slave Labor." *Southern Banner*, October 4, 1834, as cited in De Vorsey, "Early Water-powered Industries," 45. Chicopee Minute Books, February 2, 1843. "One of the Oldest Negroes." *The Atlanta Constitution (1881–1945)*, October 17, 1898, 3, http://search.proquest.com/docview/495489008.

4. Chicopee Minute Books, June 6, 1863. James D. B. De Bow, *The Industrial Resources, etc., of the Southern and Western States* (New Orleans: De Bow's Review, 1853), vol. 2, "Manufactures—Inducements for in the South and West," 112. Stokes, "Black and White Labor."

5. Chicopee Minute Books, October 3, 1836. Buckingham, *The Slave States of America* 2: 112–13.

6. *Southern Banner*, September 6, 1834; June 2, 1838, "Public Meeting"; February 15, 1844, "Augusta Home Industry Society." Charles E. Rosenberg, *The Care of Strangers: The Rise of America's Hospital System* (New York: Basic Books, 1987); David J. Rothman, *The Discovery of the Asylum: Social Order and Disorder in the New Republic* (Boston: Little Brown & Co, 1971); Neil L. York, *Mechanical Metamorphosis: Technological Change in Revolutionary America*, Contributions in American Studies, no. 78 (Westport, Conn., Greenwood Press, 1985); *Georgia Journal* as quoted in *Southern Banner*, March 27, 1840, "Eatonton Factory Destroyed by Fire!"; Buckingham, *The Slave States of America* 2: 112–13.

7. Stephanie McCurry, *Masters of Small Worlds: Yeoman Households, Gender Relations, and the Political Culture of the Antebellum South Carolina Low Country* (New York: Oxford University Press, 1995), 50.

8. Jacquelyn Dowd Hall et al., *Like A Family: The Making of a Southern Mill World* (Chapel Hill: University of North Carolina Press, 1987). Richard W. Griffin, "Poor White Laborers in Southern Cotton Factories 1789–1865," *South Carolina Historical Magazine* 61 (1960): 26–40; Tom Terrill, "Eager Hands: Labor for Southern Textiles, 1850–1860," *Journal of Economic History* 36 (1976): 84–101; Gavin Wright, "Cheap Labor and Southern Textiles before 1880," *Journal of Economic History* 39 (September 1979): 655–80; Stokes, "Black and White Labor."

9. Skinner, ed., *The Autobiography of Henry Merrell*, 197; Frederick Law Olmstead, *Journey through the Seaboard Slave States*, 544, as cited in Ulrich Bonnell Phillips, ed., *Plantation and Frontier Documents: 1649–1863, Illustrative of Industrial History in the Colonial & Ante-bellum South* (Cleveland: A. H. Clark Co., 1909), 341; *Southern Banner*, May 18, 1854, "Factory Hands Wanted."

10. I am not attempting a true statistical analysis of the data since the sample is so small and the errors made by the census marshals were so egregious. Also, others have attempted a much fuller dissection of Athens's social structure, with little more success than I get from this simple data manipulation. See Frank Jackson Huffman, "Old South, New South: Continuity and Change in a Georgia County, 1850–1880," Ph.D. diss., Yale University, 1974. My methodology is very simple. Since I am primarily interested in exploring how workers fit within the factory environ-

ment, I collected only data on families who reported at least one person working in the factory in some capacity. By focusing on the family as the agent of persistence, I can look for connections even while individuals do not persist within the industrial workforce. One major drawback to this approach is that I cannot explore what happens to individuals whose families leave the industrial workforce altogether. I cannot tell if they left Athens or if they remained and worked at other occupations. Nor can I compare the industrial workforce to the entire community. However, given my focus on process rather than individuals, I feel satisfied with this approach. To simplify further, I attempt to analyze data only when collection by census marshals appeared reasonably consistent over time. One can usefully explore the nature of the industrial workforce through its sex, age, nativity, householder status, and number of dependents. One exception to this rule is my analysis of property as reported by the census. The 1850 census reported only real estate, while later censuses delineated both real and personal property. However, only the 1860 census consistently reported property holdings under $100. Since I acknowledge the problems with the data set, I consider the analysis on par with other forms of anecdotal evidence of less than perfect reliability. My analysis is instructive rather than "true."

11. 1850, 1860, and 1870 Population Schedules for Clarke County, Georgia, Manuscript Census, National Archives; 1850 Manuscript Census kept by Clarke County (Incomplete), Schedule 5, Products of Industry, Georgia Archives; *Manufactures of the United States in 1860; Compiled from the original returns of the Eight Census* (Washington, D.C.: Government Printing Office, 1865; rpt. New York: Norman Ross Publishing Inc., 1990), 64; and Francis A. Walker, *The Statistics of the Wealth and Industry of the United States . . . compiled from the original returns of the Ninth census* (1872; rpt. New York: Norman Ross Publishing Inc., 1990), 506 and 646.

12. For women in mills elsewhere, see Cynthia J. Shelton, *The Mills of Manayunk: Industrialization and Social Conflict in the Philadelphia Region, 1787–1837* (Baltimore: Johns Hopkins University Press, 1986), 28, 33, 49–50, 61–64, 70, 74–75, 97, and 171; Dublin, *Women at Work;* and Wallace, *Rockdale,* 36–37.

13. For the 1870 male operatives, I had to massage the data in order to generate comparative information. In 1870, since census marshals generally did not differentiate between different levels of factory work, I used property holdings of $100 as the determinative factor as to who belonged to the managerial cohort and who was strictly working class. I defined operatives as anyone owning less than $100 because in 1870 this was the level at which property generally began to be reported. This was not a perfect solution because at least one "manager," carding-room overseer Henry Lovern, reported no property, and was therefore included with the operatives. However, it proved somewhat elegant since it generated a curve much like those for previous censuses.

14. Southern factories were not alone in seeking this middle level of factory management. *Southern Banner,* April 28, 1846, "Cotton Manufactures in Brazil," explains the export of factory operatives from Rhode Island to run a new cotton factory in Brazil, and specifically states that the men sent would include an overseer for each department. Chicopee Minute Books, October 3, 1836.

15. *Southern Banner,* July 12, 1839, "Married." For an example of northern-born artisan journeymen traveling southward, see Talmage Diary; also Michele Gillespie, "Artisan Accommodation to the Slave South: The Case of William Talmage, A Blacksmith, 1834–1847," *Georgia Historical Quarterly* 81 (1997): 265–86.

16. *Southern Banner,* May 9, 1844, "Married"; for Center and Reeves, see R. G. Dun, Georgia, vol. 6: 112.

17. For Lovern, see 1850 Clarke County Manuscript Census (Household number 24); 170 Clarke County Manuscript Census (Household number 278); and Fulton County Superior Court Records (Atlanta). Alexander S. Atkinson and others, Executors of Charles M. McDonald v. A. V. Brumby and William J. Russell, "Interrogatories of Henry Lovern," dated December 11, 1867 (photocopy obtained from Monroe King of Douglasville, Ga.).

18. Skinner, ed., *The Autobiography of Henry Merrell,* 70–83.

19. *Southern Banner,* October 22, 1862, "Wanted." Francis Bazley Lee, ed., *Genealogical Memorial History of the State of New Jersey* (New York: Lewis Historical Publishing Co., 1910), vol. 2: 786. *Southern Banner,* December 16, 1858, "Athens Factory"; and June 30, 1871, "Athens Factory."

20. While census data is a less than perfectly reliable source for enumerating property, one can use it to report the community's expectations of the enumerated person. Miller, *Bench and Bar of Georgia* 1: 152.

21. Sergeant Newton Chapter of Daughters of the American Revolution, "Wills and Family Records," vol. 190 (1971): 62. Transcribed notes of Rosena Bradshaw (daughter of John White) entitled "John White (1799–1881)." The Larne Saving Bank document was inserted in the White family bible, which was in possession of Julia Aiken of Covington, Georgia, in the 1970s; transcribed copy of the bank document and the Bradshaw document were taken from Agnes White Milner notes in possession of Marguerite Hodgson of Athens, Georgia; "Hugh White Celebrates His Ninetieth Birthday," from the *Enterprise* (Covington, Ga.), March 1906; all notes obtained from Ms. Hodgson will henceforth be called Hodgson Collection. Ernest M. Lander, "The Development of Textiles in the South Carolina Piedmont Before 1860," *Cotton History Review* 1 (July 1960): 93–94. *South Carolina Magazine of Ancestral Research* 14, no. 1 (Winter 1986): 24. *Southern Banner,* January 8, 1835, "A List of Letters"; Rosena Bradshaw note and Hugh White article, in Hodgson Collection, place the White family in Athens by 1833. Chicopee Minute Books, August 19, 1836. Clarke County Tax Digests, 1840–45, Georgia Archives. *Southern Banner,* May 6, 1842, "Valuable Property for Sale." White invested briefly in an Elbert County, Georgia, factory. Deed of Robert White of Elbert County, Ga., August 10, Anderson County, South Carolina, Deed Book "Y," 304, Hodgson Collection; 1906 *Enterprise;* also summary chart composed by Louise Cole Roth and Marguerite T. Hodgson. Newton County Historical Society, *History of Newton County Georgia* (Covington, Ga.: Newton County Historical Society, 1988), 218, 225–26. J. Adger Stewart, *The Webb and Allied Families consisting of the Manuscript of John Webb* (Louisville, Ky.: J. Adger Stewart, 1921) 20.

22. John A. Caramia Jr., "Teaching about the Local Community: Focus, Techniques, and Resources," *Georgia Social Science Journal* 12 (Spring 1981): 7–8; Hodgson Collection, Rosena White Bradshaw Papers, "John White (1799–1881)," and "Hugh White Celebrates His Ninetieth Birthday" (transcribed from the *Enterprise,* March 1906); also Hodgson Collection, Katherine Richards Morton Thomas Papers, "Mama Katie's Notes" (dated April 2, 1947). James White Jr., "Jim White's Story" (probably written in the 1960s) in possession of Gilbert Milner of Athens (copy provided by Dr. Goodloe Erwin Jr. of Athens). Deed of Thomas Moore to John White, Deed Book "Q," 409; Thomas Moore to John White, Deed Book "R," 215; Deed Book "R," 224–25;

Estate of Augustin Clayton to John White, Deed Book "S," 290; Thomas Morrow (of Hall County, Ga.) to John White, Deed Book "S," 132; Estate of John Nisbet to John White, Deed Book "S," 131; William A. Carr (of Florida) to John White, Deed Book "S," 291. Deed of R. H. Moore to Trustees of Janet White, Deed Book "T," 248. Janet (also known as Jane) White received a $2,000 estate from the will of her uncle in Alexandria, which was used to purchase a 414-acre tract adjacent to her husband's property. *Acts of the General Assembly of the State of Georgia Passed in November and December, 1839*, 112–13, "An Act to incorporate the Georgia Manufacturing Company of the county of Clark."

23. *Southern Banner*, June 14, 1849, "For Sale." R. G. Dun, Georgia, vol. 6: 93, 107, and 114; *Southern Watchman*, April 28, 1869, "Our Cotton Factories"; *Southern Banner*, September 10, 1869, "Progressive"; Robert S. Gamble, "Athens: The Study of a Georgia Town during Reconstruction 1865–1872, master's thesis, University of Georgia, 1967, 49; Huffman, "Old South, New South," 13, 143–44.

24. Skinner, ed., *The Autobiography of Henry Merrell*, 165, 167–68, 207–8, 202–4, 414; de Treville, "The Little New South," 168–69; Enoch Steadman, *The Southern Manufacturer* (Gallatin, Tenn.: Gray & Boyer, 1858), 49–51.

25. Skinner, ed., *The Autobiography of Henry Merrell*, 167–68.

26. Paul Johnson, *A Shopkeeper's Millennium: Society and Revivals in Rochester, New York, 1815–1837* (New York: Hill and Wang, 1978); Mary Ryan, *Cradle of the Middle Class: the Family in Oneida County, New York, 1790–1865* (New York: Cambridge University Press, 1981); Sean Wilentz, *Chants Democratic: New York City and the Rise of the American Working Class, 1788–1850* (New York: Oxford University Press, 1984); Lawrence Levine, *Highbrow/Lowbrow: the Emergence of Cultural Hierarchy in America* (Cambridge, Mass.: Harvard University Press, 1988); and Elliott J. Gorn, *The Manly Art: Bare-knuckle Prize Fighting in America* (Ithaca, N.Y.: Cornell University Press, 1986).

27. John William Nicholson Manuscript 1824–86 biographical info, Ms 2184(m), Hargrett Library. Applications for Presidential Pardons, Microcopy 1003, roll 21, frames 1223–32 (particularly frames 1226–27), National Archives. R. G. Dun, Georgia, vol. 6: 97, 155, 112, 166A, 166L, 168, and 180; Report of Scull Shoals, 200–201, 289, and 296; Will of John W. Nicholson, Will Record Book "F," 20–25 (particularly item 13, regarding sale of paper-mill property, and item 17 regarding Powell's Mills at Scull Shoals), Clarke County Probate Court, Clarke County Court House, Athens, Ga., and repeated in Will Record Book "E," 28–33; Deed of Henry Grady to John W. Nicholson, October 9, 1871, Deed Book "Z," 236–237. Henceforth all Will Record Books will be assumed to originate in Clarke County Probate Court.

28. *Southern Banner*, October 21, 1847, "Wanted." Skinner, ed., *The Autobiography of Henry Merrell*, 167–68.

29. *Southern Banner*, November 11, 1845, "Dissolution"; Clarke County Tax Digests, Georgia Archives; R. G. Dun, Georgia, vol. 6: 91; 1850–70 Population Schedules for Clarke County, Ga., National Archives; A. P. Dearing to John J. Dearing, December 10, 1857, John J. Dearing (Covington, Ga.) Papers, 1864–99 (henceforth Dearing Papers), Perkins Library; *Southern Watchman*, July 15, 1863, "List of Stockholders."

30. "Bills & Receipts" folders for 1849–55, box 6, Dubose Family Papers, Hargrett Library; R. G. Dun, Georgia, vol. 6: 108 and 162; 1850–70 Population Schedules for Clarke County, Ga., Nation-

al Archives; Policy # 25, 225, September 26, 1868, vol. 1: 4, Athens Agency Fire Register, SMIC.

31. James Oakes, *Slavery and Freedom: an Interpretation of the Old South* (New York: Knopf, 1990).

32. Letter of William W. Clayton and letter of George R. Clayton, in Miller, *Bench and Bar of Georgia* 1: 183, 188.

33. Clarke County Tax Digests, 1822, Georgia Archives. Atticus, "A Vindication of the Recent and Prevailing Policy of the State of Georgia, Both in Reference to Its Internal Affairs, and Its Relations with the General Government" (Athens: O. P. Shaw, 1827), was originally published as a series of letters in the *Columbian Centinel* in 1825, discussing the cessation of lands from the Creek Nation. Theda Perdue and Michael D. Green, eds., *The Cherokee Removal: A Brief History with Documents* (Boston: St. Martin's Press, 1995), 58–62. *Athenian*, December 15, 1829, "To the Editor of the Cherokee Phoenix"; March 23, 1830, "Judge Clayton's Opinion"; August 17, 1830 (rpt. in *Niles Register*, October 2, 1830, "Georgia and the Judiciary"); August 17, 1830, "Presentments of the Grand Jury of Clark County at August Term, 1830"; November 30, 1830, "Decision of the Convention of Judges, on the right of the jurisdiction of the State over the Indians. Question arising in the case of the State vs. George Tassels"; December 21, 1830, "George Tassels"; March 2, 1831, "Superior Court—Western Circuit"; April 5, 1831, "Worcester Case"; September 27, 1831, "The Missionaries"; November 29, 1831, "Judge Clayton" and "Remarks"; October 11, 1831, "Judge Clayton's Opinion"; October 18, 1831, "Judge Clayton's Opinion (concluded)." Letter of Gilmer to Sanford, *Athenian*, September 27, 1831. *Cherokee Phoenix*, January 8, 1831, as transcribed in Perdue and Green, eds., *The Cherokee Removal*, 133. *Niles Register*, December 3, 1831, "Judge Clayton of Georgia." *Philadelphia Enquirer*, April 13, 1832, as qtd. in *Southern Banner*, May 8, 1832.

For Augustin Clayton and the Second Bank of the United States, *Southern Banner*, April 3, 1832, "United States Bank, John Q. Adams, etc."; May 15, 1832; May 15, 1832, "The Bank Report"; May 29, 1832, "Bank of the United States" (quoting letter of Clayton, dated May 15, 1832, and published in the *National Intelligencer*). For Augustin Clayton's opposition to Andrew Jackson, and his new affiliation with the Whig Party, *Southern Banner*, April 19, 1834, "The Question Settled"; July 19, 1834, "Franklin County Fourth of July Toasts"; July 20, 1832, "Regular Toasts"; September 20, 1834, "Sound Logic"; October 4, 1834, "Peter Forces' Epistle"; January 22, 1835, "Mr. Clayton's Doctrine"; January 29, 1835, "The Editor of the Southern Whig"; March 26, 1835, "Hon. A. S. Clayton." Augustin Clayton, "Speech of Mr. Clayton of Georgia on the question of the removal of the deposites; delivered in the House of Representatives, March 11, 1834" (Washington: Gales & Seaton, 1834), esp. 3–4.

Paul Murray, *The Whig Party in Georgia 1825–1853* (Chapel Hill: University of North Carolina Press, 1948), 63. Clarke County Tax Digests, 1839, Georgia Archives. Whitefoord Smith, "A Discourse on the Occasion of the Death of the Hon. Augustin S. Clayton, delivered in the College Chapel, Athens, Ga., on the 23d June, 1839" (Athens, Ga.: n.p., 1839).

34. *History of Newton County*, 645. Application of Alice E. Dearing to DAR, Dearing Papers. Wilkes County Tax Digests, 1809, Georgia Archives. Note from Mary Bondurant Warren indicating that, at the Georgia Archives, among the loose paper from Wilkes County, Original Marriage Licenses, is that of William Dearing to Eliza Pasteur, dated April 24, 1813, folder 1:4, Dearing Collection (MS 742), Hargrett Library. Stewart, *Manuscript of John Webb*, 20. E. Merton Coulter, *Georgia Waters* (Athens: Georgia Historical Quarterly, 1965), 58–60.

35. Michael Tadman, *Speculators and Slaves: Masters, Traders, and Slaves in the Old South* (Madison: University of Wisconsin Press, 1989).

36. *Southern Banner*, July 29, 1837, "Circular"; October 27, 1838, "Commercial Convention."

37. *Southern Banner*, July 30, 1841, "Notice." Stock certificate dated November 11, 1843, first folder labeled "Stock Certificates," box 18; "Papers—1848," box 11, Chicopee Manufacturing Company, Hargrett Library. *Southern Banner*, June 9, 1853, "Death of an Old Citizen."

38. Charlotte Thomas Marshall, ed., *Oconee Hill Cemetery; Tombstone Inscriptions for that Part of Cemetery West of Oconee River and Index to Records of Interments* (Athens, Ga.: Athens Historical Society, 1971), 55. *Southern Banner*, June 22, 1847. *Southern Whig*, June 24, 1847, as transcribed in "Obituaries," folder 11, box 95, Coulter Collections (MS 1750), Hargrett Library. Murray, *Whig Party in Georgia*, 14. Susan B. Tate, "James Camak," in Kenneth Coleman and Stephen Gurr, eds., *Dictionary of Georgia Biography* (Athens: University of Georgia Press, 1983) 154–55; E. Merton Coulter, *College Life in the Old South* (Athens: University of Georgia Press, 1951), 39; *Athenian*, January 13, 1829, "Appointments by the Governor"; June 9, 1829, "The Penitentiary"; November 17, 1829, "From Milledgeville"; December 1, 1829, "Letter from Governor Troup"; July 12, 1831, "From the Southern Recorder"; October 4, 1831, "Executive Clemency." *Southern Banner*, June 22, 1847, "Obituary." *The Argus*, May 9, 1829, qtd. in Murray, *Whig Party in Georgia*, 14. Larry Schweikart, *Banking in the American South from the Age of Jackson to Reconstruction* (Baton Rouge: Louisiana State University Press, 1987), 116. *Southern Banner*, January 4, 1834, "List of Acts Passed by the Legislature"; February 1, 1834; Deed Book "P," 296–97, and Deed Book "Q," 51–63. Charlotte Thomas Marshall, *Historic Houses of Athens* (Athens, Ga.: Athens Historical Society, 1987), 6. *Southern Banner*, February 15, 1834, "To the Stockholders of the Georgia Rail Road Company"; May 13, 1842, "Rail Road Convention." Directors Minutes, vol. 1, March 10, 1834 entry, Georgia Railroad and Banking Company Collection, Augusta College and State University Library. *Southern Banner*, July, 17, 1845, "Agricultural Meeting"; December 19, 1844, "Prospectus of the Southern Cultivator"; June 22, 1847, "Obituary."

39. Receipt for slaves dated January 3, 1818, folder 3, box 1, location 52-G-4, Varner Family Papers (Collection # 1256), Georgia Historical Society, Savannah. *Index to United States Census of Georgia for 1820* (Savannah: Georgia Historical Quarterly, 1963), 161. *Index to the 1830 Census of Georgia* (Baltimore: Genealogical Publishing Co., 1982), 502. *History of the Baptist Denomination in Georgia: with Biographical Compendium and portrait Gallery of Baptist Ministers and other Georgia Baptists*, compiled for the Christian Index (1881; rpt. Easley, S.C.: Southern Historical Press, n.d.), 587–88. *Southern Banner*, September 27, 1831, "Strayed." Hillyer, *Reminiscences of Georgia Baptists*, 266; Charlotte Marshall of Athens also provided genealogical materials on Williams, which she obtained from "Mrs. Ames," which refer to Williams as "Money" Williams. *Southern Banner*, June 22, 1833, "Items"; June 29, 1833, "Rail Road Meeting"; July 6, 1833, "Rail Road Meeting"; November 9, 1833, "Rail Road," and "Money to Lend"; February 15, 1834, "Rail Road Charter Secured!"; and March 15, 1834, "The Railroad." Schweikart, *Banking in the American South*, 51, 170–71. *Southern Banner*, March 16, 1839, "Free Banking." *History of the Baptist Denomination*, 587–88 of the Biographical Compendium. R. G. Dun, Georgia, vol. 15: 87.

40. Third page of genealogical information attached to manuscript inventory of John Nisbet Collection (MS 943), Southern Historical Collection, Wilson Library, University of North Carolina.

41. *Athenian*, November 11, 1828, "For Sale or Rent"; December 8, 1829; December 20, 1831; and April 24, 1832. *Southern Banner*, November 2, 1833; January 4, 1834; September 6, 1834; July 23, 1835; November 19, 1836; December 17, 1836; January 28, 1837; October 28, 1837; December 30, 1837; January 13, 1838; February 17, 1838; September 22, 1838; November 24, 1838; April 20, 1839; September 13, 1839; October 19, 1839; and December 11, 1840. *Southern Banner*, August 3, 1833, "Clark Sheriff's Sale"; May 29, 1832; October 18, 1834; March 5, 1835; May 8, 1845; and May 4, 1847. *Southern Banner*, October 19, 1839, "For Sale," offers Benton County, Alabama, property for sale.

42. *Southern Banner*, October 4, 1834, "For Sale." Clarke County Tax Digests, Georgia Archives. *Athenian*, December 20, 1831, "For Sale or Rent."

43. *Southern Banner*, June 29, 1833 "Rail Road Meeting"; July 6, 1833, "Rail Road Meeting"; March 15, 1834, "The Rail Road"; January 29, 1835, "By-Laws of the Ga. Railroad Company"; May 13, 1835, "The Rail Road"; May 20, 1835, "Extracts from the Minutes of a Convention of the Stockholders of the Georgia Rail Road Company"; May 21, 1836, "Rail Road Convention"; May 26, 1836, "Georgia Rail Road and Banking Company"; May 20, 1837, "Georgia Rail Road"; June 3, 1837, "Bank Report"; May 19, 1838, "Rail Road Convention"; May 17, 1839, " Convention"; May 14, 1840; June 5, 1840, "Bank Reports." *Southern Banner*, February 1, 1834; June 3, 1835, "Bank of the State of Georgia"; June 18, 1835, "Bank Reports." Entries for John Nisbet as a note shaver, Clarke County Tax Digests 1834 and 1841, Georgia Archives. March 28, 1835 entry, Edward Harden Diary, Edward Harden Collection, Perkins Library. *Southern Banner*, November 26, 1841, "Obituary."

44. John S. Linton to I. A. A. Wray (of Shelby, N.C.), June 5, 1894, folder 5, box 18, Linton Family Papers (MS 2012), Hargrett Library. *Athenian*, August 18, 1829, "Obituary"; June 8, 1830. *Southern Banner*, April 27, 1833, "Linton & Bacon"; April 12, 1834, "Doctors Linton and Palmer"; October 25, 1834, "Medical"; and January 15, 1835, "Dissolution." Lucy Linton, "Random Recollections or Leaves from the Linton Branch of the Hull Family Tree by the Last Leaf," *Papers of the Athens Historical Society* 1 (1964): 53–54. Clarke County Tax Digests, 1832–40, Georgia Archives. *Southern Banner*, November 10, 1832, "Gold Lottery"; December 8, 1838, "Died."

45. *Index to the 1830 Census of Georgia*, 29. *Southern Banner*, September 28, 1832; "To The Public"; February 5, 1835, "The Vacancies." Chicopee Minute Books, June 16, 1836. *Southern Banner*, February 29, 1840, "Augusta & Waynesboro' Railroad"; November 19, 1841, "Notice." Clarke County Tax Digests, 1837–44, Georgia Archives, for the taxes Baxter paid on slaves. Will Record Book "C," 40–46, for Thomas W. Baxter, and Will Record Book "D," 238–39, for Mary Wiley Baxter. Chicopee Minute Books, 1844. Also see the frequent listing of letters left for Baxter to retrieve from Athens post office as an indication of his travels taking him away from town: *Southern Banner*, July 9, 1836, "A list of letters"; February 17, 1838, "List of letters"; March 3, 1838, "List of letters"; April 7, 1838, "List of letters"; June 2, 1838, "List of letters"; June 7, 1839, "List of letters"; November 2, 1839, "List of letters"; March 7, 1840, "List of letters"; and March 5, 1841, "List of letters." *Southern Banner*, August 22, 1844, "Died"; September 12, 1844, "Lines suggested by the recent death of Mr. Baxter."

46. James Camak to Maribeau B. Lamar, June 24, 1839, Maribeau B. Lamar Papers, Texas State Archives, Austin.

47. Evans, *The Conquest of Labor*.

48. R. G. Dun, Georgia, vol. 6: 91 and 166G; J. U. Parsons to A. P. Dearing, August 10, 1850, Letter Book 3, p. 70, SMIC; Southern Mutual Minute Books, June 19, 1867; Mary E. G. Harden Diary, 1853–83, June 12, 1856, Edward Harden Collection; A. P. Dearing to John J. Dearing, December 16, 1857, John J. Dearing (Covington, Ga.) Papers, 1857–63, Perkins Library; James S. Hamilton to Benjamin Yancey in Buenos Aires, February 27, 1859, Benjamin C. Yancey Papers, 1846–82, Perkins Library.

49. Chicopee Minute Books, August 26, 1844. Clarke County Tax Digests, 1839–45, Georgia Archives. *Southern Banner,* February 9, 1839, "Executor's Sale"; February 16, 1839, "Notice"; August 30, 1839, "Executor's Sale"; September 27, 1839, "Executor's Sale"; March 27, 1840, "Executor's Sale"; November 6, 1840, "Executor's Sale"; October 24, 1844, "Wanted"; August 17, 1848, "Georgia, Clark County"; December 13, 1849, "A Train of Cars at Chattanooga!"; January 10, 1850, "Pioneer Paper Mill"; October 17, 1850, "Georgia, Clark County"; April 18, 1852, "Georgia, Clarke County"; December 9, 1858, "The Athens Factory"; December 16, 1858, "The Athens Factory"; December 23, 1858, "The Athens Manufacturing Company"; February 25, 1863, "Liberal Donation"; December 16, 1858, "The Athens Factory." *Southern Watchman,* June 3, 1863, "Cotton Mill Stock." Southern Mutual Minute Book 1848–68, December 25, 1851, January 20, 1854, February 24, 1854, October 24, 1856, August 13, 1858, January 25, 1861, January 24, 1862, and January 23, 1863; First folder labeled "Stock Certificates," box 18, Chicopee Manufacturing Company (MS 1664), Hargrett Library; William Letcher Mitchell to Sarah Mitchell, June 5, 1850, folder 2 (1848–1850), William Letcher Mitchell Papers (MS 2983), Southern Historical Collections, Manuscript Department, Williams Library Special Collections, University of North Carolina–Chapel Hill; R. G. Dun, Georgia, vol. 6: 94, 90; "Confederate Treasury Department, Field Offices—Entry 135, Athens, Georgia, Incomplete Name Index to (Box 14) Entry 136—Athens Bonds issued," Record Group 365, National Archives; "Message from the President of the United States in Answer to a Resolution of the House of the 5th of March last, Relative to Pardons and Property Seized as Enemies' Property, and Returned to Those Who Claimed to be the Original Owners," U.S. Congress, Microprint Series 1236, House Executive Document 99, 39th Congress, 1st sess., 1866, p. 32; Mary Bondurant Warren, *The Hills of Wilkes County, Georgia and Allied Families* (Danielsville, Ga.: Heritage Papers, 1987), vol. 2: 629–30; Hull, *Annals of Athens,* 394–95; Linton, "Random Recollections," 53–68.

50. *Athenian,* July 12, 1831, "Volunteer Toasts"; January 3, 1832. *Southern Banner,* March 20, 1832; June 12, 1832, "Congress, the Tariff, Nullification, &c"; October 12, 1833, "Married"; March 24, 1836, "To the Patrons of the Southern Banner"; June 25, 1836, "Mechanics' Association"; July 22, 1837, "From the Southern Recorder"; January 12, 1839, "Town Election"; June 21, 1839, "Prospectus of the Southern Silk Grower And Agricultural Register"; November 23, 1839, "Southern Silk Grower"; January 25, 1840, "Co-Partnership"; March 7, 1840, "Died"; May 8, 1840, "Co-Partnership"; July 31, 1840, "Wanted"; August 28, 1840, "Something New and Very Useful"; January 8, 1841, "Dissolution" and "New Arrangement"; November 19, 1841, "New Book Bindery"; January 14, 1842, "Dissolution" and "Georgia, Clarke County"; February 4, 1842, "Wholesale Domestic Store"; March 25, 1842, "Georgia Nankeens"; May 13, 1842, "Notice—Look Sharp!"; July 29, 1842, "Agricultural Meeting"; January 6, 1843, "Book-Store"; January 11, 1844, "Dissolu-

tion"; January 11, 1844, "Municipal Elections"; August 1, 1844, "To Those Candid Men"; January 2, 1845, "Communicated"; March 3, 1846, "Book Bindery"; September 8, 1846, "Notice" and "To the Patrons of the Southern Banner"; October 27, 1846, "Brandreth's Pills"; February 23, 1847, "Paper Factory"; January 10, 1850, "New Arrangement" and "Pioneer Paper Mill"; April 18, 1852, "Georgia, Clarke County"; May 31, 1855, "A. A. & N. Telegraph Co."; March 27, 1863, "Rags Wanted." *Southern Whig*, June 14, 1849, "Newspaper Files"; September 20, 1849, "The Agricultural Fair at the Stone Mountain." *Southern Watchman*, April 29, 1858, "Burning of the Pioneer Paper Mill"; July 17, 1867, "Another Old Citizen Gone!" Southern Mutual Minute Book, 1848–68, February 2, 1849; October 16, 1851; April 2, 1858; May 7, 1858; April 25, 1862; and July 19, 1867. R. G. Dun, Georgia, vol. 6: 92, entries of Albon Chase and of Edward R. Hodgson and Brothers; 94, entries of Chase and Linton and of Pioneer Paper Company; 154, entry for Southern Mutual Insurance Company. White, *Statistics of the State of Georgia*, 183; Ernest C. Hynds, *Antebellum Athens and Clarke County Georgia* (Athens: University of Georgia Press, 1974), 94–95, 163–65, 176–77, 182.

51. *Southern Banner*, November 5, 1841, "Blacksmithing"; March 25, 1842, "Married." *Southern Watchman*, January 15, 1862, "People's Mill Sold"; Gillespie, "William Talmage," 265–86; Marshall, *Oconee Hill Cemetery*, 39; Maude Talmage Wood, *Once Apunce A Time* (Athens, Ga.: Classic Press, 1977) ii–iii; R. G. Dun, Georgia, vol. 6: 94, entries of Chase and Linton and of Pioneer Paper Company; 134, entry for Athens Foundry and Machine Works; Talmage Diary; Ledgers for 1866–69, 1871–73, and 1875, box 2, section: B Tax Digests, Athens, Ga., City Records (MS 1633), Hargrett Library.

52. Deed of R. D. Moore to William S. Grady, October 18, 1860, Deed Book "X," 178. R. G. Dun, Georgia, vol. 6: 92, 97, 112, 117, 119, 155, 159, 163, 165, 166J, and 180; vol. 16: 166; and vol. 19: 252. *Southern Banner*, July 4, 1844, "List of Letters"; October 18, 1846, "French Fancy Goods"; July 16, 1857, "Local Improvements"; July 9, 1864, "To Gas Consumers"; October 1, 1869, "Valuable Property"; November 12, 1869, "The Rome Fair." *Southern Whig*, June 14, 1849, "New Clothing Store." *Southern Watchman*, January 25, 1865, "To Rent"; December 11, 1867, "Delegates to the Conservative Convention." Henry Grady to Julia King, Summer 1868, folder 1, box 1, Henry Grady Papers, Emory University; Tribute of Respect from Fireman's Hall, June 24, 1865, folder 7, box 1, Henry Grady Papers. Biographical Info, John William Nicholson manuscript 1824–86 (MS 2184m), Hargrett Library; Ledger for 1866–69, Section: B Tax Digests, box 2, Athens, Ga., City Records (MS 1633), Hargrett Library; map of a tract of land belonging to the estate of William S. Grady, deceased, Clarke County Maps to 1900 (map collection 1916 03), Hargrett Library; AHS Newsletters, November 1963, folder 3:1a, Athens Historical Society (MS 2306), Hargrett Library. Hynds, *Antebellum Athens*, 47 and 143n, but citation of *Southern Banner*, May 11, 1854, does not support the allegation that the gas manufacturing process in Athens originated from firm of Grady & Nicholson; James H. Tate, *Keeper of the Flame: The Story of Atlanta Gas Light Company 1856–1985* (Atlanta: Atlanta Gas Light Co., 1985), 158, also claims the gas works in Athens were built in 1852 by Nicholson & Grady. Report of Scull Shoals 200–201, 289. John F. Stegeman, *These Men She Gave: Civil War Diary of Athens, Georgia* (Athens: University of Georgia Press, 1964), 28. Kenneth Coleman, *Confederate Athens* (Athens: University of Georgia Press, 1967), 38. Gamble, "Athens: The Study of a Georgia Town," 87.

For Cobb and Newton ownership and administration of Athens Gas Works in 1870s, see

Deed Book "Z," 48 (May 6, 1870) and 302 (August 1871). Receipt of Messrs Lampkin & Crane, Business Papers 1860–69, folder 21:9; mortgage of gas works between Cobb and Grady, Business Papers 1870, folder 21:10; gas works promissory note, Business Papers 1872, folder 21:12; and receipt of R. D. Moore, Business Papers 1874, folder 21:14; box 21, Cobb Erwin Lamar Collection (MS 86), Hargrett Library.

For tax records of Athens Gas Works: 1871 Ledger, 1872 Ledger, 1873 Ledger (see taxes of Cobb Erwin & Cobb), 1875 Ledger, Section: B Tax Digests, box 3, Athens, Ga., City Records (MS 1633), Hargrett Library.

For gas maps: "Portion of Athens Ga—Copied from Authoritative Map of 1874 by W. W. Thomas, C.E.," Clarke County Maps to 1900 (map 1874 T5), Hargrett Library. "Contract between Athens and Athens Gas Light Co 1884," Athens, Ga., City Records (MS 1633), located in oversize MSS drawer (map neg #3710), Hargrett Library.

53. Clarke County Tax Digests, 1823–31, Georgia Archives; *Athenian*, July, 6, 1827; February 1, 1831, untitled editor comments on page 2 on recent meeting of Board of Trustees of University of Georgia; January 24, 1832, "To the Public"; February 14, 1832, "To The Public." *Southern Banner*, April 17, 1832, "Auction"; April 24, 1832, "Notice"; December 7, 1833, "House of Representatives"; February 22, 1834, "Died"; March 26, 1835, "The Athens Factory." Bill for Injunction Relief, Papers 1835 folder, box 11, Chicopee Manufacturing Company, Hargrett Library; Chicopee Minute Books, March 23, 1835 entry. Deed Book "Q," 305.

54. For Daniel Grant: Clarke County Tax Digests, Georgia Archives. *Southern Banner*, January 4, 1834, "Elected Officials"; December 28, 1839, "Mr. Chase." Inferior Court Minutes 1815–36, Bridges, etc. (Henceforth Inferior Court Minutes), June 13, 1834 entry, Probate Court Office Clarke County Court House, Athens, Ga. De Vorsey, "Early Water-powered Industries," 46. Also genealogical chart of Daniel Grant of Greene County, provided by Charlotte Thomas Marshall of Athens.

For William Lumpkin: Clarke County Tax Digests, Georgia Archives. Warren, *Hills of Wilkes County*, 622–23. Hynds, *Antebellum Athens*, 174–75. *Athenian*, November 4, 1828, "Boarding"; June 1, 1830, "American Bible Society." *Southern Banner*, July 6, 1833, "Rail Road Meeting"; March 13, 1834, "The Rail Road"; January 29, 1834, "By-Laws of the Ga. Rail road Company"; July 30, 1835, "For Sale"; March 17, 1836, "General Pope's Departure"; November 26, 1836, "Notice"; July 29, 1837, "For Sale"; November 3, 1838, "Married"; February 12, 1841, "Obituary." Hodding Carter, "A Proud Struggle for Grace: Holly Springs, Mississippi," in Thomas C. Wheeler, ed., *A Vanishing America: The Life and Times of the Small Town* (New York: Holt, Rinehart and Winston, 1964), 57–58.

For Asbury Hull:, Clarke County Tax Digests, Georgia Archives. Will Record Book "D," 184–86; *Georgia Alumni Record*, February 1939, 120–21; Genealogical chart of descendants of Hopewell Hull, provided by Charlotte Thomas Marshall of Athens, Ga.; Augustus Longstreet Hull, *The Hulls of Georgia* (Athens: n.p., 1904), 4, 6–7; Hynds, *Antebellum Athens*, 161–65. Herbert Wender, *Southern Commercial Conventions, 1837–1859* (Baltimore: Johns Hopkins University Press, 1930), 30–31. *Athenian*, July 20, 1827, "October Election"; May 2, 1828, "Mr. Mulkey's Analytical Spelling Book"; September 23, 1828, "To the Republicans of Clarke County"; October 7, 1828, "State of the Poll"; December 2, 1828, "Anti-Duelling Society"; December 9, 1828, "Extract from the Minutes of the Trustees of the University of Georgia"; December 8, 1829, "Proceedings of the

Legislature"; November 2, 1830, "Georgia Legislature"; December 7, 1830, "House of Representatives"; November 1, 1831, "Public Meeting"; November 15, 1831, "Georgia Legislature." *Southern Banner,* August 3, 1832, "Public Meeting"; November 10, 1832, "Georgia Legislature"; February 23, 1833, "Public Meeting in Watkinsville"; June 29, 1833, "Rail Road Meeting"; July 6, 1833, "Rail Road Meeting"; May 10, 1834, "Bank of the State of Georgia"; August 2, 1834, "For the Southern Banner"; November 22, 1834, "Office Discount and Deposite"; May 20, 1835, "Extract from the Minutes"; December 3, 1836, "Georgia Legislature"; June 3, 1837, "Bank Statement"; July 29, 1837, "Circular"; June 2, 1838, "Bank Conventions"; November 3, 1838, "For the Southern Banner"; April 27, 1839, "Commercial Convention"; May 15, 1840, "Bank Reports"; June 5, 1840, "Bank Reports"; January 14, 1842, "Georgia, Clarke County"; July 29, 1842, "Agricultural Meeting"; July 4, 1844, "Methodist Church"; August 17, 1848, "Georgia, Clark County"; July 3, 1856, "Letter from Hon Asbury Hull." *Southern Watchman,* January 31, 1866, "Death of Hon. Asbury Hull"; February 5, 1866, "Tribute of Respect." First folder labeled "Stock Certificates," box 18, Chicopee Manufacturing Company, Hargrett Library. R. G. Dun, Georgia, vol. 6: 90, entry for Athens Factory; 91, entry for Princeton Factory; 154, entry for Southern Mutual Insurance Company. Southern Mutual Minute Book 1848–68, October 16, 1851; January 27, 1866; February 2, 1866. 1866 Ledger, Section: B Tax Digests, box 2, Athens, Ga., City Records, Hargrett Library.

For Ware's background: Hynds, *Antebellum Athens,* 161–65, 168, 178–79, 183–84. Marshall, *Oconee Hill Cemetery,* 53–54. *Athenian,* April 20, 1830, "Married." *Southern Banner,* July 29, 1842, "Agricultural Meeting"; May 25, 1847; May 29, 1856, "Branch Bank of the State of Georgia at Athens"; November 27, 1856, "Banks in Athens"; Southern Mutual Minute Book 1848–68, February 2, 1849; January 1, 1851; October 16, 1851. Southern Mutual Minute Book 1868–79, June 13, 1873, and July 4, 1873.

For E. L. Newton: *Athenian,* July 15, 1828, "We the undersigned"; February 7, 1832, "Ordinance." *Southern Banner,* June 12, 1832, "Casualties"; January 4, 1834, "The Co-partnership"; March 15, 1834, "The Rail Road"; April 12, 1834, "New Goods"; August 2, 1834, "For the Southern Banner"; January 29, 1835, "By-Laws of the Ga. Rail Road Company"; March 5, 1835, "Geo A. Connally & Co."; May 13, 1835, "The Rail Road"; May 20, 1835, "Extracts from the Minutes of a Convention of the Stockholders of the Georgia Rail Road Company"; December 24, 1836, "100 Negroes Wanted"; June 3, 1837, "Bank Report"; May 27, 1842, October 2, 1845, "New Fall and Winter Goods." Southern Mutual Minute Book 1848–68, January 1, 1851. Elizur L. Newton File, Biography Vertical Files, Hargrett Library. Elizur L. Newton Bible Transcript, Hargrett Library. 1867 Ledger, Section: B Tax Digests, box 2, Athens, Georgia City Records, Hargrett Library. "List of Life Members & Amts Paid," Clarke County Grange Records, Hargrett Library. Will Record Book "D," 417–19. Hynds, *Antebellum Athens,* 18, 163–65, 179–80. Warren, *Hills of Wilkes County,* 615.

55. For the extended Baxter family: *Southern Banner,* June 2, 1843, "Married"; February 3, 1846, "Married"; August 17, 1848, "Georgia, Clark County." James T. Davis as agent for widow of Edwin G. Baxter Sr. to R. L Bloomfield, "Papers 1868" folder; Note of Richard B. Baxter of Sparta giving R. L. Bloomfield power of attorney over his thirteen shares of Athens Factory stock, "Papers 1871" folder, box 11; Sale of forty shares of Athens Mfg Co. stock by Sara C. J. Bird (a Baxter descendent) to her cousin John S. Baxter, of Macon, "Papers 1878" folder, box 11, Chicopee Manufacturing Company, Hargrett Library. De Treville, "The Little New South," 121, 161. Hull, *Annals*

of Athens, 443. John Rozier, ed., *The Granite Farm Letters: The Civil War Correspondence of Edgeworth and Sallie Bird* (Athens: University of Georgia Press, 1988), 34, 35n, 166, 168n, 193, 198, 202.

For the Nisbet connection: George R. Gilmer, *Sketches of Some of the First Settlers of Upper Georgia, of the Cherokees and the Author* (1855; rpt. Baltimore: Genealogical Pub. Co., 1965). Clarke County Tax Digests, 1837–44, Georgia Archives. *Southern Banner*, December 6, 1849, "Earle's Iron Works"; and December 13, 1849, "House of Representatives . . . November 30, 1849"; White, *Statistics of the State of Georgia*, 152–53. Warren, *Hills of Wilkes County*, 541, 547. Hull, *Annals of Athens*, 470.

56. Warren, *Hills of Wilkes County*, 629–30. Hull, *Annals of Athens*, 460–61, 474. Hull, *The Hulls of Georgia*, 5, 7. Marshall, *Oconee Hill Cemetery*, 53–54. *Southern Banner*, October 17, 1844, "Married"; August 17, 1848, "Georgia, Clark County." *Southern Whig*, November 26, 1846, "Married." R. G. Dun, Georgia, vol. 6: 90. Genealogical chart of the descendants of Hopewell Hull (which included Asbury Hull and Dr. Henry Hull) provided by Charlotte Thomas Marshall, of Athens.

Baxter-Nisbet-Linton-Hull-Thomas Family members as stockholders of the Athens Factory: There were four Baxters: Mary Baxter, executrix, and Andrew Baxter and Eli H. Baxter, acting for the estate of Thomas W. Baxter; and Andrew and Thomas W. Baxter acting as trustees for Sarah C. J. Baxter. Two were part of the Linton family: John S. Linton and Linton's brother-in-law, Thomas Sparks (husband of Linton's sister, Ann). The Nisbets accounted for eight stockholders: Harriet C. Nisbet; Thomas C. Nisbet; Dr. Henry Hull, acting as trustee of his wife, Mary A. (Nisbet) Hull; Thomas C. Nisbet and Lewis LeConte, acting as trustees of Sarah E. (Nisbet) Smith; John LeConte and Thomas C. Nisbet, acting as trustees of Hariet (Nisbet) LeConte; and Thomas C. Nisbet, acting as guardian of Margaret J. Nisbet. Only Asbury Hull represented the Hull family directly. And the Thomas family manifested itself in Peninah Thomas and Leonidas Franklin, acting as trustee for Corrina (Thomas) Franklin (daughter of Peninah Thomas's brother-in-law, Jett Thomas).

57. Thornton, *Politics and Power*, esp. 267–321; Dupre, "Ambivalent Capitalists," 215–40; Lacy K. Ford Jr., *Origins of Southern Radicalism: The South Carolina Upcountry, 1800–1860* (New York: Oxford University Press, 1988), esp. 267; and Susanna Delfino, "Antebellum East Tennessee Elites and Industrialization: The Examples of the Iron Industry and Internal Improvements," East Tennessee Historical Society *Publications* 56 and 57 (1984–85): 102–19.

58. Oscar Handlin and Mary Flug Handlin, *Commonwealth: A Study of the Role of Government in the American Economy: Massachusetts, 1774–1861* (rev. ed., Cambridge, Mass.: Harvard University Press, 1969). Alfred D. Chandler Jr., *The Visible Hand: The Managerial Revolution in American Business* (Cambridge, Mass.: Harvard University Press, 1977).

CHAPTER THREE

1. For example, see the American history college survey textbook by James West Davidson et al., *Nation of Nations: a Narrative History of the American Republic* (New York: McGraw-Hill Inc, 1994), vol. 1: 433, "The temperance movement . . . was the only reform movement with significant support in the South."

2. *Southern Banner*, December 10, 1835, "The Bubble Burst"; November 26, 1836, "Governor Schley's Message"; August 12, 1837, "To the Citizens of Athens"; August 19, 1837, "A Card";

December 1, 1838, "Correspondence"; March 23, 1839, "Industry & Genius"; January 14, 1842, "State Bonds"; May 16, 1844, "Errors of Merchants"; May 30, 1844, "Communicated"; August 8, 1844, "The Bankrupt Law"; August 22, 1844, "Died"; May 29, 1845, "Communicated"; March 7, 1850, "Absconded"; May 16, 1850. R. G. Dun, Georgia, vol. 6: 93, William Sage entry.

3. Eugene D. Genovese, *The Slaveholders' Dilemma: Freedom and Progress in Southern Conservative Thought, 1820–1860* (Columbia: University of South Carolina Press, 1992).

4. *Athenian,* December 15, 1829, "Speech of Judge Clayton."

5. *Southern Banner,* December 10, 1836, "Report of the Committee on Finance"; July 9, 1835, "Georgia Internal Improvement—Central Rail Road."

6. Huffman, "Old South New South," 32. 1829 diary of Martha Redd Jones as quoted in Charlotte Thomas Marshall, "Glimpses into the Antebellum History of the First Baptist Church, Athens, Georgia, with Appendix," lectures presented at First Baptist Church (Athens) in 1981, 15, 17. *Southern Banner,* June 26, 1832, "Notice." Buckingham, *The Slave States of America* 2: 72, 74.

7. Thomas G. Dyer, *The University of Georgia: A Bicentennial History, 1785–1985* (Athens: University of Georgia Press, 1985), 18; *Athenian,* July 15, 1828; October 27, 1828, "Just Published"; February 1, 1831, "To Mechanics." Hull, *Annals of Athens,* 54–55.

8. *Southern Banner,* June 22, 1847, "Obituary." *Athenian,* February 1, 1831, "To Mechanics"; August 9, 1831, "Georgia University." *Southern Banner,* August 9, 1834, "Franklin College"; July 1, 1837, "Franklin College"; June 30, 1838, "Board of Visitors"; June 19, 1843, "Franklin College"; October 19, 1833, "Notice"; March 10, 1836, "Catalogue of the Officers and Students of Franklin College." Henry Cleveland, *Alexander H. Stephens in Public and Private* (Atlanta: National Printing Co., 1866). Letter in possession of Lin Dearing, Clemson, S.C.

9. *Athenian,* March 16, 1830, "To the Citizens of Athens & Vicinity"; *Southern Banner,* January 19, 1847, "Improvement of the College Grounds."

10. Junius Hillyer, *The Life and Times of Judge Junius Hillyer (From His Memoirs)* (Tignall, Ga.: Boyd Publishing Co., 1989), 88–89. *Athenian,* August 24, 1830, untitled editorial suggesting a plan of public service in exchange for funding a college education; December 28, 1839, "The Parley Place Primary School." *Compendium of the Enumeration of the Inhabitants and statistics of the United States as obtained at the Department of State, from the returns of the 6th Census* (1841; rpt. New York: Norman Ross Publishing Inc., 1990), 51; J. D. B. De Bow, *The Seventh Census of the United States: 1850* (1853; rpt. New York: Norman Ross Publishing, Inc.), vol. 12 (1990): 369–73.

11. Coulter, *College Life in the Old South,* 36–37. *Athenian,* December 15, 1829, "Grammar School at Athens"; January 19, 1830, "Private School"; November 1, 1831, "Public Meeting"; December 27, 1831, "Wanted." *Southern Banner,* December 14, 1833, "Athens Grammar School"; January 18, 1834, "Athens Male Academy." Hynds, *Antebellum Athens,* 82. Hillyer, *Reminiscences of Georgia Baptists,* 267.

12. Hynds, *Antebellum Athens,* 85–86; *Athenian,* November 15, 1828, "Athens Female Academy"; *Southern Banner,* December 7, 1833, "Athens Female Academy." *Athenian,* June 9, 1829, "Communicated"; December 1, 1829, "Communicated"; November 9, 1830, "Athens Female Academy"; November 8, 1831, "Athens Female Seminary." *Southern Banner,* January 14, 1836; January 14, 1836, "Athens Female Academy." Hynds, *Antebellum Athens,* 84–85; *Southern Banner,* October 21, 1842, "Private High School for Young Ladies."

13. *Athenian*, June 22, 1830, "Communicated"; November 9, 1830, "Athens Female Academy."

14. *Athenian*, January 11, 1828, "Dr. Barber's Report on County Academics"; January 6, 1829, "Captions and Provisions of the Acts passed in November and December, 1828"; October 20, 1829, "Executive Department, Georgia"; May 14, 1830, "Poor School Fund." *Southern Banner*, November 17, 1832, "Governor's Message"; January 6, 1843, "List of Acts"; February 20, 1845, "Georgia, Clark County." James Allison Jones, "History of the First Presbyterian Church of Athens, Georgia," master's thesis, University of Georgia, 1949, 54.

15. First Presbyterian Church of Athens, Georgia, "Report of Committee of W. H. Presbytery on Instruction of Col'd People" (ca. 1832), transcribed in updated typescript "History of First Presbyterian Church, Vol. I , 1820–1949," in possession of First Presbyterian Church, Athens. Opposition in Athens did not reach the same level of animosity found by University of Georgia President Moses Waddel when he gave religious instruction to slaves in South Carolina in the 1810s. See Jeremiah Evarts Diary (Collection # 240), 37–40, April 26, 1822 entry, Georgia Historical Society. For opposition in Athens, *Southern Banner*, August 29, 1844, "Notice." *Southern Banner*, October 4, 1839, "List of Letters," is an extreme example of slave participation in literacy, with public notice of at least four letters remaining in the post office for slaves. Perhaps a dozen such letters usually appeared in the published lists each year. *Southern Banner*, June 27, 1844, "Fourth of July"; July 11, 1844, "Fourth of July."

16. George P. Rawick, ed., *The American Slave: A Composite Autobiography* 12: *Georgia Narratives*, Parts 1 and 2 (WPA Federal Writers' Project report, 1941; rpt. Westport, Conn.: Greenwood Press, 1972), 177–83; John Brother Cade, *Holsey—The Incomparable* (New York: Pageant Press, 1963), 4–5; Michael Thurmond, *A Story Untold: Black Men and Women in Athens History* (Athens, Ga.: Clarke County School District, 1978), 123.

17. *Southern Banner*, October 26, 1832, "Address of the Convention assembled at Athens on the 19th and 20th of October 1832 for the purpose of establishing a Manual Labour School"; December 8, 1832, "Manual Labor School"; October 3, 1833, "Letter on Manual Labor Schools"; December 14, 1833, "Manual Labor School"; August 30, 1834, "For Sale"; October 8, 1834, "Notice"; November 29, 1834, "Notice."

18. Hynds, *Antebellum Athens*, 83. *Southern Banner*, December 13, 1834, "To the Public"; December 29, 1834, "The Gwinnett Institute."

19. *Southern Banner*, June 2, 1838, "Constitution of the Athens Mechanics' Mutual Aid Association"; October 2, 1842, "Mechanics' Association"; January 6, 1848, "Male School"; January 10, 1850, "English School"; February 14, 1850, "A Good Teacher." Deed of Shubael Tenney to Athens Mechanics Mutual Aid Association, September 8, 1840, Deed Book "R," 36, Real Estate Section, Office of the Clerk of the Superior Court, Clarke County Court House, and deed of Athens Mechanics Mutual Aid Association (E. R. Hodgson, President) to John S. Riden, December 1, 1848, Deed Book "T," 175.

20. Biographical information, John William Nicholson manuscript 1824–86 (MS 2184m), Hargrett Library. Receipt for Athens Manufacturing Co., "Bills & Receipts, 1849" folder, box 6, Dubose Family Papers (MS 1738), Hargrett Library. R. G. Dun, Georgia, vol. 6: 91, Moses E. McWhorter entry; 162, E. Palmer entry.

21. *Athenian*, October 7, 1828, "The Mechanic"; May 12, 1829, "The Mechanic." *Southern*

Banner, February 19, 1835, "The Discharged Workman"; June 25, 1835, "Mechanics"; May 26, 1838, "Support Your Mechanics"; May 26, 1838, "Independence"; April 10, 1840, "The Widow—a Picture of Life"; April 2, 1841, "The Lesson"; April 15, 1842, "The First Offer"; January 2, 1845, "Old Fudge of an Uncle"; June 26, 1845, "The Factory Girl."

22. *Athenian*, September 14, 1830, "To A Friend of Politeness."

23. "Application of John W. Nicholson" manuscript, August 14, 1865, starting at frame 1223, Roll 21, Applications for Presidential Amnesty (m1003), National Archives. For postbellum continuations, see Huffman, "Old South New South," 31. *Athenian*, July 5, 1831, "The Way They Do Things in Athens."

24. *Southern Banner*, October 15, 1836, "Notice of Athens, GA., in 1836"; February 28, 1840, "For the Southern Banner"; January 15, 1841, "For the Southern Banner"; February 4, 1842, "For the Southern Banner."

25. *Southern Banner*, March 24, 1838, "Contractor's Notice"; May 26, 1838, untitled notice of desire to start a society for administering charity to the poor of Athens after raising funds for Charleston fire victims; June 2, 1838, "Public Meeting"; June 9, 1838, "For the Southern Banner"; June 23, 1843, "Public Meeting"; February 15, 1844, "Augusta Home Industry Society"; February 27, 1845, "Young Ladies Fair"; June 12, 1845, "Athens Benevolent Society"; December 23, 1845, "Remember the Poor." Athens Benevolent Society ledger, dated 1825–55, Seaborn J. Mays Papers (MS 803), Hargrett Library.

26. *Southern Banner*, June 3, 1837, "Mechanics"; *Athenian*, September 14, 1830, "To A Friend of Politeness."

27. *Southern Banner*, November 2, 1839, "For the Southern Banner" letter of Senex. Johnson, *A Shopkeeper's Millennium*; Ryan, *Cradle of the Middle Class*; Wilentz, *Chants Democratic*. R. G. Dun, Georgia, vol. 6: 92.

28. *Athenian*, January 31, 1832, "Notice." *Southern Banner*, May 12, 1836, "For the Southern Banner."

29. *Southern Banner*, March 7, 1840, "Died"; February 26, 1841, "Died"; June 25, 1836, "Mechanics' Association"; October 15, 1836, "Mechanics' Association"; November 12, 1836, "Mechanics' Association"; February 25, 1837, "Mechanics' Association"; June 2, 1838, "Constitution of the Athens Mechanics' Mutual Aid Association"; March 30, 1839, "Mechanics' Association"; October 4, 1839, "Mechanics' Association"; March 27, 1840, "Mechanics' Association"; January 1, 1841, "Mechanics' Association"; March 26, 1841, "Mechanics' Association"; March 25, 1842, "Mechanics' Association"; March 24, 1843, "Athens Mechanics' Mutual Aid Association"; March 30, 1847, untitled notice of tenth anniversary oration and elections; March 30, 1848, "Anniversary Meeting"; and March 22, 1849, "Athens Mechanics' Mutual Aid Association"; December 3, 1836, "For the Southern Banner"; June 2, 1838, "Constitution of the Athens Mechanics' Mutual Aid Association"; March 14, 1844, "Mechanics' Reading Room." The mechanics library was probably the public library enumerated in the 1850 census. De Bow, *The Seventh Census of the United States: 1850* 12 (1990): 384–85. *Southern Banner*, June 2, 1838, "Constitution of the Athens Mechanics' Mutual Aid Association"; October 2, 1842, "Mechanics' Association"; January 6, 1848, "Male School"; January 10, 1850, "English School"; February 14, 1850, "A Good Teacher."

30. *Southern Banner*, July 20, 1832, "Oratorio"; April 23, 1835, "Concert"; July 29, 1837, "Concert"; October 21, 1837, "Concert"; May 3, 1839, "May Party"; March 20, 1840, "Concert!"; July 31, 1840, "Grand Vocal and Instrumental Concert"; June 18, 1841, "Lectures on Ventriloquism, with Illustrative Exercises"; February 25, 1842, "Concert"; August 5, 1842, "Commencement Week"; March 3, 1843, "Miss Guttenberger's Concert"; July 13, 1843, "Temperance Festival"; June 27, 1844, "Fourth of July"; July 11, 1844, "Fourth of July"; November 14, 1844, "Democratic Jubilee"; November 21, 1844, "The Democratic Jubilee"; April 10, 1845, "The Hughes Family"; June 26, 1845, "Order of the Procession to be observed on the 4th of July, at the Funeral services, in honor of Gen. Andrew Jackson"; February 10, 1846, "The Orphean Family"; April 13, 1847, untitled notice of two separate musical troupes visiting Athens; April 27, 1848, "Odd Fellow's Celebration"; February 8, 1849, "The Steyermark Company"; February 22, 1849, "The Aeolian Minstrels"; May 24, 1849, "The Sable Melodists"; August 3, 1833, "The Theatre"; July 26, 1839, "Theatre"; January 13, 1843, "Novel Performance"; June 30, 1843, "Theatre—The Stranger—Mrs. Phillips"; February 10, 1846, "Grand Soiree"; March 2, 1848, untitled notice of Pedee Ethiopian Opera Troupe. *Athenian*, August 5, 1828, "Circus." *Southern Banner*, March 28, 1838, "Menagerie and Circus United"; April 13, 1839, "Siamese Twins"; April 20, 1839, "Siamese Twins"; December 10, 1839, "Combined Attraction"; October 3, 1844, "National Circus"; October 24, 1844, "New York Circus"; May 25, 1847, "Great Western Circus"; October 21, 1847, "Robertson & Eldred's"; August 9, 1849, "Stickney's Great New Orleans Circus."

31. *Southern Banner*, July 20, 1832, "Oratorio"; July 2, 1836, "Phrenology"; May 15, 1840, "Lectures on the Natural Sciences"; May 22, 1840, "Scientific Recreation"; June 5, 1840, "Mr. Richard's Lectures"; February 26, 1841, "Athens Female Academy"; June 18, 1841, "Lectures on Ventriloquism, with Illustrative Exercises"; April 28, 1843, "Lectures on Natural Sciences"; April 4, 1844, "Dr. Lardner's Lectures"; October 9, 1845, "Mr. Richard's Lectures"; October 9, 1845, "Grand Philosophical Entertainments"; May 12, 1846, "Animal Magnetism"; May 19, 1846, "Animal Magnetism"; March 9, 1847, "Lecture on Phreno-Mnenotechy"; and May 11, 1847, "Dr. Boynton"; June 28, 1839, "Mr. Buckingham's Lectures"; July 5, 1839, "Mr. Buckingham's Lectures"; October 1, 1841, "Lectures on the Poetry of the Bible"; March 11, 1842, "Lectures on Jerusalem"; July 12, 1834, "Notice"; July 29, 1842, "Agricultural Improvement"; August 5, 1842, "Commencement Week"; February 24, 1843, untitled notice of lecture on primary education; February 1, 1844, "Temperance—Mr. Hawkins"; February 26, 1841, "A Lecture"; May 29, 1845, untitled notice of two lectures defending botanic "Thomsonian" medicine; May 27, 1842, "An Ordinance."

32. Edward Harden Diary and Account Book 1834, entries for January 28 and 30, 1834, Edward Harden Collection, Perkins Library. *Southern Banner*, February 1, 1834; and February 8, 1834; March 29, 1834, "The Lyceum"; April 5, 1834, "Athens Lyceum"; April 12, 1834, "Address Delivered by Wm. L Mitchell"; July 5, 1834, untitled report of Augustin Clayton as Franklin College's delegate to American Lyceum in New York; April 29, 1837, "For the Southern Banner"; July 4, 1844, "Athens Independent Lyceum"; July 44, 1844, "Fourth of July"; January 9, 1845, "Athens Independent Lyceum"; June 26, 1845, "Order of the Procession to be observed on the 4th of July, at the Funeral Services, in honor of Gen. Andrew Jackson"; June 30, 1846, "Anniversary Oration"; July 6, 1847, "Celebration of Independence"; August 17, 1848, untitled notice of Athens

Independent Lyceum meeting; June 28, 1849, "Notice"; February 14, 1850, "Lyceum Hall, Feb 7th, 1850."

33. Buckingham, *The Slave States of America* 2: 70–71.

34. *Southern Banner,* July 26, 1834, "Communications"; September 6, 1834, "Notice"; October 18, 1834, "Early History of Georgia"; July 2, 1835, "An Oration will be delivered"; September 24, 1835, "A Meeting of the Citizens Polemic Club." *Athenian,* December 27, 1831, "Law Notice." *Southern Banner,* May 4, 1833, "Law Notice"; March 12, 1841, "Democratic Meeting"; March 26, 1841, "The Meeting at Athens"; May 27, 1842, "Democratic Meeting in Clark County"; June 17, 1842, untitled notice that Harden would substitute as a delegate to the State Democratic Convention; March 17, 1843, "U.S. Marshal for Georgia"; June 27, 1844, "Collectorship of Savannah"; April 17, 1845, "Collector at Savannah"; March 8, 1849, "Death of General Harden." Edward Harden Collection, Edward Harden Diary and Account Book 1835–36, entries for December 11, 1835, December 16, 1835, and February 27, 1836, and in his 1839 Diary, the entries for April 13, 1839, April 15, 1839, April 17, 1839, and June 23, 1839, Perkins Library. Anthony Gene Carey, *Parties, Slavery, and the Union in Antebellum Georgia* (Athens: University of Georgia Press, 1997), 26–29. Buckingham, *The Slave States of America* 2: 88–91.

35. *Athenian,* June 29, 1830, "The Athens Vocal Music School." *Southern Banner,* October 22, 1835, "Musical Academy & Depository"; January 14, 1837, "John F. Goneke"; July 29, 1837, "Concert"; August 5, 1837, "To the Citizens of Athens"; August 12, 1837, "To the Citizens of Athens"; August 19, 1837, "A Card"; October 21, 1837, "Concert"; July 28, 1838, "Theatre"; July 26, 1839, "Theatre"; June 25, 1841, "New Music School"; March 11, 1842, "Valuable Property for Sale"; June 2, 1846, "Vocal Music."

36. Jack Larkin, *The Reshaping of Everyday Life: 1790–1840* (New York: Harper & Row, 1988). Hynds, *Antebellum Athens,* 88. *Southern Banner,* July 1, 1837, "Fencing Exhibit"; July 1, 1837, "Mr. Bauge's Fencing Exhibition"; August 5, 1837, "Fencing School"; August 25, 1838, "Mr. Bauge."

37. *Southern Banner,* October 22, 1835, "Writing School"; April 28, 1838, "Book-Keeping"; May 29, 1845, "Beware the Imposter."

38. Hynds, *Antebellum Athens,* 19; Hillyer, *Reminiscences of Georgia Baptists,* 27–28, 76–81; Marshall, "Glimpses into the Antebellum History of the First Baptist Church," 8, 14. *Athenian,* February 2, 1827, untitled notice of meeting of subscribers to the African Church; February 1, 1828, untitled notice of the three church buildings in Athens. Marshall, "Glimpses into the Antebellum History of the First Baptist Church," 39–40, indicates the Baptist church built a separate meeting house for blacks in 1849, so the first church for people of color must have been Presbyterian, Methodist, or non-denominational.

39. Wallace, *Rockdale,* particularly chapters 6 and 7: 243–349.

40. *Athenian,* June 1, 1830, "American Bible Society"; June 15, 1830, "To the Editor of the Athenian"; May 31, 1831, "Revival of Religion." *Southern Banner,* July 1, 1837, "Methodist Appointments"; September 1, 1838, "Religious Revival"; April 24, 1840, "Religious Revival"; January 9, 1845, untitled notice of upcoming Baptist revival; March 30, 1848, "Obituary" notices, Presbyterian revival two years earlier; and August 31, 1848, "Religious Revival." Junius Hillyer, *Life and Times,* 99–101. Buckingham, *The Slave States of America* 2: 134–39. Cade, *Holsey,* 14. Hynds, *Antebellum Athens,* 109–10. Edward Harden Diary, entry of May 22, 1835, and Mary E. G. Harden

Diary, 1853–83, entry for September 30, 1853; Letter of Mother Sarah B. Hamilton to Sarah Yancey, April 18, 1858, Benjamin C. Yancey Papers, 1846–82, Perkins Library. Talmage Diary, 34, entry of April 25, 1857. Smith, "A Discourse, on the Occasion of the Death of the Hon. Augustin S. Clayton," esp. 8–11 and 15–16. Miller, *Bench and Bar of Georgia* 1: 176–78. A. S. Clayton to George Clayton, August 21, 1838, transcribed in Miller, *Bench and Bar of Georgia* 1: 189–90. Buckingham, *The Slave States of America* 2: 60–64.

41. *Athenian,* October 6, 1829, untitled list of religious affiliations of past and present professors at the University of Georgia; December 1, 1829, "Letter from Governor Troup." First Presbyterian Church Session Minutes (in possession of First Presbyterian Church, Athens, Ga.), vol. 1, 1830–61: 306, for entry of Helen Camak as church member.

42. "Manual Presbyterian Church in Athens," 2; typescript, "History of First Presbyterian Church, Vol. I, 1820–1949," First Presbyterian Church (Athens, Ga.), lists the dates of election of ruling elders 1829–66. Notes of Rosena White Bradshaw, transcribed by Agnes White Milner, photocopy in possession of Marguerite Hodgson of Athens. *Southern Banner,* August 20, 1835, "For the Southern Banner"; *Christian Index,* May 5, 1843, 287; Marshall, "Glimpses into the Antebellum History of the First Baptist Church," 75. Marshall hypothesizes that the first volume of the church's minutes was misplaced when Williams died because he kept them at his factory and they probably were destroyed when his estate sold the Princeton Factory. Conversation with Charlotte Thomas Marshall, February, 1994. White, *Statistics of the State of Georgia,* 182.

43. Jones, "History of the First Presbyterian Church," 11; *Athenian,* October 20, 1829, untitled notice of anniversary meeting of Clarke County Bible Society; June 1, 1830, "American Bible Society." *Southern Banner,* June 28, 1839, "Bible Society Meeting." Buckingham, *The Slave States of America* 2: 64–67. Barbara L. Bellows, *Benevolence Among Slaveholders: Assisting the Poor in Charleston, 1670–1860* (Baton Rouge: Louisiana State University Press, 1993). John W. Quist, *Restless Visionaries: The Social Roots of Antebellum Reform in Alabama and Michigan* (Baton Rouge: Louisiana State University Press, 1998). *Southern Banner,* June 10, 1842, "To the Friends of the Bible Cause."

44. *Athenian,* December 1, 1829, "Proceedings of the Legislature"; June 28, 1831, "Cheap Beverage"; August 16, 1831, "Presentments of the Grand Jury of Clark County, August Term." *Southern Banner,* February 26, 1835, "An Appeal"; April 16, 1835, "Drunkards in the United States"; August 23, 1839, "The Retail Question"; September 2, 1842, "Electricity as a Temperance Agent"; November 3, 1843, "Fire on the Central Rail Road"; April 4, 1844, "Georgia, Hall County." W. J. Rorabaugh, *The Alcoholic Republic, an American Tradition* (New York: Oxford University Press, 1979); and Steven Mintz, *Moralists and Modernizers: America's Pre-Civil War Reformers* (Baltimore: Johns Hopkins University Press, 1995), 72–78.

45. *Athenian,* June 23, 1829, "Communicated, Franklin College"; July 6, 1830, "Address at the Anniversary Meeting of the Temperance Society of Franklin College"; June 22, 1830, "Communicated." First Presbyterian Church (Athens, Ga.) Session Minutes, vol. 1: 25, 27. *Athenian,* June 22, 1830, "Communicated"; June 4, 1831, "Notice"; January 10, 1832, "Notice." *Southern Banner,* March 8, 1834, "For the Southern Banner"; October 5, 1848, "Temperance Address"; May 17, 1849, "Father Matthew Division." Sons of Temperance Certificate, folder 2 (1848–50), William Letcher Mitchell Papers (MS 2983), Southern Historical Collections, Manuscript Department, Williams Library Special Collections, University of North Carolina–Chapel Hill. *Athenian,*

August 31, 1830, "Appointments." *Southern Banner,* November 2, 1833, "Temperance Society"; July 26, 1834, "Commencement Week"; August 16, 1834, "Communicated"; August 20, 1835, "For the Southern Banner"; July 23, 1836, "Notice"; August 9, 1839, "Temperance Meeting"; May 27, 1842, untitled notice of Washington Temperance Society meeting; June 24, 1842, "A meeting of the Athens Washington Temperance"; July 29, 1842, "A meeting of the Washington Total Abstinence"; September 9, 1842, "Temperance Meeting"; October 28, 1842, "Temperance Meeting"; November 4, 1842, "Washington Temperance Society"; May 19, 1843, untitled notice of Washington Temperance Society meeting; June 30, 1843, "Free Temperance Barbeque"; July 13, 1843, "Temperance Festival"; February 1, 1844, "Temperance—Mr. Hawkins." Josiah Daniel Almanac Diary and Deaths in Clarke County 1834–77, entries for 1834 and October 2, 1850, Hargrett Library. *Southern Banner,* June 30, 1843, "Free Temperance Barbeque"; July 13, 1843, "Fourth of July at Watkinsville"; July 13, 1843, "Temperance Festival." Hynds, *Antebellum Athens,* 183; *Southern Banner,* December 30, 1842, "Temperance Coffee House"; April 28, 1844, "Bath House"; January 12, 1847, "Temperance Coffee House"; November 4, 1842, "Washington Temperance Society."

46. *Southern Banner,* March 8, 1834, "For the Southern Banner"; August 16, 1834, "Communicated"; August 20, 1835, "For the Southern Banner."

47. *Athenian,* January 18, 1831, "Preamble and Resolutions of the Anti-Semi-Temperance Society."

48. *Southern Banner,* July 26, 1839, "Temperance Petitions"; August 9, 1839, "Temperance Meeting"; August 16, 1839, "Temperance Petitions"; August 23, 1839, "The Retail Question."

49. *Southern Banner,* February 1, 1844, "Temperance—Mr. Hawkins"; February 8, 1844, "Remarks."

50. Ian R. Tyrrell, "Drink and Temperance in the Antebellum South: An Overview and Interpretation," *Journal of Southern History* 48 (1982), 488–89, 502–8. Quist, *Restless Visionaries.* John F. Quinn, *Father Mathew's Crusade: Temperance in Nineteenth Century Ireland and Irish America* (Amherst: University of Massachusetts Press, 2002). *Southern Banner,* October 5, 1848, "Temperance Address"; May 17, 1849, "Father Mathew Division." Sons of Temperance Certificate, William Letcher Mitchell Papers.

51. Jeremiah Evarts Diary, 39–40. *Southern Banner,* July 13, 1833; February 18, 1836, "The Abolition Memorials"; September 3, 1835, "Public Meeting"; February 18, 1836, "Judge Clayton's Letter." Hynds, *Antebellum Athens,* 95

52. E. Merton Coulter, *John Jacobus Flournoy: Champion of the Common Man in the Antebellum South* (Savannah: Georgia Historical Society, 1942). *Southern Banner,* August 27, 1835, "To the Public"; March 31, 1836, "To all the World"; September 24, 1836, "To the Sub-Editor of the Whig." Buckingham, *The Slave States of America* 2: 83–87. *Southern Banner,* September 2, 1837, speech of R. R. Gurley; September 23, 1837; June 30, 1838, "Public Notice." Vivien Elizabeth Sandlund, "To Arouse and Awaken the American People: the Ideas and Strategies of the Gradual Emancipationists, 1800–1850," Ph.D. diss., Emory University, 1995.

53. *Southern Banner,* August 24, 1833, "The Farmer"; September 17, 1835, "The Farmer." James C. Bonner, *A History of Georgia Agriculture 1732–1860* (Athens: University of Georgia Press, 1964), 169, 194–95. *Southern Banner,* September 20, 1839, "Alvarado Cotton"; May 12, 1838, "Mammoth Strawberry."

54. Bonner, *A History of Georgia Agriculture,* 119–20; *Southern Banner,* July 29, 1842, "Proposals for Publishing an Agricultural Paper, to be entitled the SOUTHERN CULTIVATOR"; December 19, 1844, "Southern Cultivator"; February, 27, 1845; May 15, 1845. Bonner, *A History of Georgia Agriculture,* 150, 160.

55. *Southern Banner,* June 21, 1839, "Prospectus of the Southern Silk Grower and Agricultural Register"; November 23, 1839, "Southern Silk Grower"; November 23, 1839, "Public Meeting"; May 27, 1842, notice of cocoonery of E. L. Newton. Schedules of Mines, Agriculture, Commerce, Manufactures, etc. (1840)—Georgia, vol. 16: Clarke County, Records of Census Bureau, Record Group 29, National Archives.

56. *Southern Banner,* July 19, 1834, "Cattle Show"; July 29, 1842, "Agricultural Meeting," and "Agricultural Improvement"; February 20, 1845, "To the People of Georgia"; April 17, 1845, "Farmers Convention"; June 26, 1845, "Agricultural Meeting"; July, 17, 1845, "Agricultural Meeting"; September 4, 1845, notice of Clarke County Agricultural Society; March 31, 1846, "Agricultural Meeting"; June 27, 1847, "Obituary"; May 25, 1848, "Clarke County Agricultural Society." Bonner, *A History of Georgia Agriculture,* 112–13. *Southern Banner,* March 31, 1846, "Agricultural Fair"; August 25, 1846, "Agricultural Meeting"; August 5, 1847, notice of state fair at Stone Mountain; August 3, 1848, "Democratic Mass Meeting at Stone Mountain—Agricultural Fair"; July 12, 1849, "Southern Central Agricultural Association." *Southern Whig,* June 28, 1849, "The Central Agricultural Association"; July 19, 1849, "Manufacturers' Convention"; September 20, 1849, "The Agricultural Fair at the Stone Mountain." Talmage Diary, August 14, 1848.

57. James David Miller, *South by Southwest: Planter Emigration and Identity in the Slave South* (Charlottesville: University Press of Virginia, 2002). *Southern Whig,* June 28, 1849, "The Central Agricultural Association"; July 19, 1849, "Manufacturers' Convention"; September 20, 1849, "The Agricultural Fair at the Stone Mountain." *Southern Banner,* December 6, 1849, "The Charleston Fair"; May 20, 1863, "Cotton Spinner's Convention." *Central Georgian* (Sandersville and Sparta), November 5, 1857. Chicopee Minute Books, August 24, 1855. Richard W. Griffin, "The Textile Industry in Greene County, Georgia, Before 1860," *Georgia Historical Quarterly* 48 (1964): 83.

58. *Athenian,* July 6, 1827, notice of Fourth of July celebrations; October 13, 1829, "Athenian Fair"; March 9, 1830, notice of upcoming charitable fair by Athens's ladies; *Southern Banner,* May 3, 1839, "May Party"; July 29, 1842, "Young Ladies' Fair"; August 5, 1842, "Commencement Week"; February 27, 1845, "Young Ladies' Fair"; July 26, 1849, "The Fair."

59. Buckingham, *The Slave States of America* 2: 92–93, 124–26, 139.

60. *Athenian,* January 6, 1829, "Captions and Provisions of the Acts passed in November and December, 1828"; October 20, 1829, "Executive Department, Georgia"; May 14, 1830, "Poor School Fund"; *Southern Banner,* November 17, 1832, "Governor's Message"; January 6, 1843, "List of Acts" (#6); February 20, 1845, "Georgia, Clark County"; February 8, 1849, "Watkinsville, Georgia."

G. S. Eberhart, Superintendent of Education for Georgia, to Maj. John J. Knox, April 1, 1867, Letters Received (registered in vol. 165), January–October 1867, box 5, entry 720, Georgia—Athens, Sub-Assistant Commissioner; Maj. John J. Knox to E. A. Ware, State Supt. of Education, October 29, 1868, Letters Received (Unregistered), March 1867 to November 1868. John J. Knox to G. L. Eberhart, March 27, 1867; John J. Knox to Capt. Eugene Pickett, April 14, 1867, and May

17, 1867; W. Tilley (Clerk) for John J. Knox to Eugene Pickett, July 10, 1867; John J. Knox to Maj. J. A. Lewis, States Supt. of Education, August 18, 1867; John J. Knox to E. A. Ware, August 27, 1867; John J. Knox to Ed P. Smith, General Field Agent, American Missionary Association, New York, September 16, 1867, Athens Sub-Assistant Commissioner, Letters Sent, vol. 169, part 1. Howell C. Flournoy to E. A. Ware, September 21, 1868, Athens Agent Letters Sent, vol. 172, part 2: 148–49. Sub Assistant Commissioner for Athens Subdistrict Register of Complaints, vol. 174: 3, February 15, 1867, entry, Bureau of Refugees, Freedmen, and Abandoned Lands (henceforth Freedmen's Bureau Collection), Record Group 105, National Archives. Eric Foner, *Reconstruction: America's Unfinished Revolution, 1863–1877* (New York: Harper & Row, 1988). Southern Mutual Minute Book 1848–68, 527, February 8, 1867.

61. *Southern Banner*, September 18, 1840, "Died."

CHAPTER FOUR

1. Schedules of Mines, Agriculture, Commerce, Manufactures, etc. (1840)—Georgia vols. 16 and 17, entry 322, Records of Census Bureau, Record Group 29, National Archives.

2. Partnership papers, September 27, 1832, "Scull Shoals Mfg Company Papers" folder, box 14, Dubose Family Papers (MS 1738), Hargrett Library. Report of Scull Shoals, 44–45. Scull Shoals partnership papers 1846, Dubose Family Papers.

3. *Athenian*, October 6, 1829. *Southern Banner*, March 16, 1839, "Wholesale and Retail Grocery Store"; May 27, 1842, "Democratic Meeting in Clark county"; June 19, 1843, "Franklin College"; August 31, 1843, "Georgia, Clark County, Superior Court"; June 12, 1845, March 30, 1847, "War Meeting"; April 27, 1847, "Democratic Meeting in Clark"; June 14, 1849, "Democratic Meeting"; and January 24, 1850, "Georgia, Morgan County." Report of Scull Shoals, 192–94. R. G. Dun, Georgia, vol. 6: 93, E. S. Hopping and Company entry.

4. *Southern Banner*, September 3, 1841, "Wool Factory"; January 5, 1847, "Married"; May 15, 1856, "Wool Hat Manufactory." R. G. Dun, Georgia, vol. 18: 49. 1906 clipping from the *Enterprise*, in possession of Marguerite T. Hodgson of Athens. *History of Newton County*, 218, 225–26. Stewart, *Manuscript of John Webb*, 20. Southern Mutual Minute Book, vol. 1, December 19, 1856; December 25, 1857; December 24, 1858; and December 30, 1859. R. G. Dun, Georgia, vol. 25: 54.

5. I've added the number of spindles reported in the 1840 census for Scull Shoals Factory (27,000 corrected to 2,700) and for Cedar Shoals Factory (396 spindles) to the Clarke County enumerated total of 5,630 to arrive at 8,726 spindles for enumerated Clarke and affiliated factories. This number would grow if we knew the number of spindles missed by the census for the Mars Hill Factory, in Clarke County, and White's Factory in Jackson County. Both factories were mentioned in anecdotal evidence as being small, so one should assume that each probably contained less than 500 spindles.

6. John Lauritz Larson, *Internal Improvement: National Public Works and the Promise of Popular Government in the Early United States* (Chapel Hill: University of North Carolina Press, 2001. George Rogers Taylor, *The Transportation Revolution, 1815–1865* (New York: Rinehart and Co., 1951). Ulrich B. Phillips, *A History of Transportation in the Eastern Cotton Belt to 1860* (1908; rpt. New York: Octagon Books, 1968). Milton Sydney Heath, *Constructive Liberalism: The Role of the State in Economic Development in Georgia to 1860* (Cambridge, Mass.: Harvard University Press,

1954), esp. chap. 11. Frederick Beck Gates, "An Imitative Enterprise: Canal Construction in Georgia, 1820–1860," master's thesis, University of North Carolina at Charlotte, 1995, esp. chap. 2, "Georgia's Transport Canals: The Failure of Imitation." Judson C. Ward, "Internal Improvements in Georgia, 1817–1843," master's thesis, Emory University, 1934. Phillips, *A History of Transportation*, 17, 117–18, 139. Heath, *Constructive Liberalism*, 254. Carter Goodrich, *Government Promotion of American Canals and Railroads 1800–1890* (New York: Columbia University Press, 1960), 103. Albert Fishlow, *American Railroads and the Transformation of the Ante-Bellum Economy* (Cambridge, Mass.: Harvard University Press, 1965), 86n. Frederick A. Cleveland and Fred Wilbur Powell, *Railroad Promotion and Capitalization in the United States* (New York: Longmans, Green and Co., 1909), 62. John F. Stover, *Iron Road to the West: American Railroads in the 1850s* (New York: Columbia University Press, 1978), 69–71.

7. *Athenian*, October 20, 1829, "At Walton Superior Court"; November 22, 1829, "Proceedings of the Legislature."

8. *Athenian*, December 29, 1829; January 12, 1830; February 2, 1830; April 6, 1830; February 21, 1832, "Presentments of the Grand Jury of Clark County."

9. Phillips, *A History of Transportation*, 225–26. Heath, *Constructive Liberalism*, 255–58.

10. *Southern Banner*, July 3, 1833, "Railroad Meeting."

11. *Washington News* (Washington, Ga.) as quoted in *Southern Banner*, June 29, 1833.

12. *Southern Banner*, June 29, 1833, "Railroad Meeting."

13. Mary G. Cumming, *Georgia Railroad & Banking Company: 1833–1945* (Augusta, Ga.: n.p., 1945), 10. Transcript of material sent to T. B. Rice by Mrs. Harold Lamb, of Union Point, who received it from James W. Camak sometime before 1934, entitled "By 'Brockett,'" 1–2, T. B. Rice Collection, Georgia Archives.

14. Walker, *The Statistics of the Population of the United States*, 20–22, table II: "Population by counties 1790–1870." *Southern Banner*, July 6, 1833, "Rail Road Meeting"; January 8, 1835, "To James Camak."

15. *Southern Banner*, March 3, 1838, "Merchants and Planters"; July 13, 1843, "Georgia Cotton Bagging"; July 27, 1843, "For the Banner."

16. Elizabeth Fox-Genovese and Eugene D. Genovese, *Fruits of Merchant Capital: Slavery and Bourgeois Property in the Rise and Expansion of Capitalism* (New York: Oxford University Press, 1983).

17. Allan Kulikoff, "The Transition to Capitalism in Rural America" *William and Mary Quarterly*, 3rd ser., vol. 46, no. 1 (January 1989): 141; Allan Kulikoff, "Households and Markets: Toward a New Synthesis of American Agrarian History" *William and Mary Quarterly*, 3rd ser., vol. 50, no. 2 (April 1993): 344 and 352.

For peddlers: *Athenian*, May 17, 1831, "In Senate, 19th December 1825"; October 4, 1831, "In Senate, 19th December 1825"; February 7, 1832, "In Senate, 19th December 1825." *Southern Banner*, May 29, 1840, "Descriptions of Pedlers Licensed"; June 4, 1841, "Descriptions of Pedlers Licensed"; September 3, 1841, "Descriptions of Pedlers Licensed"; January 28, 1842, "Descriptions of Pedlers Licensed"; May 27, 1842, "Licensed Pedlers"; September 2, 1842, "Licensed Pedlers"; January 20, 1843, "Licensed Pedlers"; July 27, 1843, "Licensed Pedlers"; August 3, 1843, "Licensed Pedlers"; and November 9, 1843, "Licensed Pedlers."

Reports of trade with the upcountry: *Athenian*, July 22, 1828, "Communications"; June 22, 1829, "Notice"; June 22, 1830, "Bacon." *Southern Banner*, July 12, 1833, "Crops"; August 12, 1837, "Wheat."

18. *Southern Banner*, August 14, 1845, "For the Southern Banner IV." White, *Statistics of the State of Georgia*, 182.

19. *Southern Banner*, July 6, 1833, "Rail Road."

20. Augusta *Constitutionalist* as quoted in *Southern Banner*, August 10, 1833, "Putnam County Rail Road Meeting."

21. Augusta *Constitutionalist*, June 28, 1833, as quoted in *Southern Banner*, July 6, 1833.

22. *Southern Banner*, July 27, 1833, "Rail Road Meeting"; August 17, 1833, "Rail Road Meeting"; and September 14, 1833, "Internal Improvement," "From the Washington News," and "Railroad Intelligence." *Washington News* as quoted in *Southern Banner*, August 31, 1833, "The Railroad."

23. *Southern Banner*, September 14, 1833, "Internal Improvement."

24. *Southern Banner*, October 26, 1833, "Rail Road Conference"; and November 9, 1833, "Rail Road."

25. *Southern Banner*, January 11, 1834, "Georgia Rail Road."

26. *Southern Banner*, June 15, 1833, "Railroad"; July 27, 1833, "Augusta Rail Road Meeting"; August 17, 1833, "The Augusta Chronicle"; August 24, 1833, "The Chronicle and Rail Roads"; August 31, 1833; September 7, 1833; and October 26, 1833, "Rail Road Report."

27. Cummings, *Georgia Railroad*, 20–21. J. Clyde Mixon, president-general manager of the Atlanta & West Point Railroad Company, address to the Athens Historical Society, May 31, 1963, "History of the Georgia Railroad," 9, folder 1:6 "Misc Georgia History," Coulter Papers, Hargrett Library. *Southern Banner*, February 15, 1834, "Rail Road Charter Secured." Hillyer, *Reminiscences of Georgia Baptists*, 266.

28. John Majewski, *A House Dividing: Economic Development in Pennsylvania and Virginia before the Civil War* (New York: Cambridge University Press, 2000).

29. *Southern Banner*, May 17, 1834, "Georgia Rail Road"; and May 25, 1834.

30. *Southern Banner*, September 14, 1833, "Internal Improvement." *Macon Messenger* as quoted in *Southern Banner*, September 14, 1833, "From the Macon Messenger." *Georgia Journal* as quoted in *Southern Banner*, July 27, 1833, "For the Southern Banner"; August 17, 1833, "From the Georgia Journal"; October 19, 1833, "Internal Improvement"; and November 30, 1833, "From the Georgia Journal." *Southern Banner*, January 18, 1834, "City Council."

31. *Southern Banner*, March 27, 1840, "Eatonton Factory Destroyed by Fire!"; August 10, 1833, "Putnam County Rail Road Meeting"; November 9, 1833, "Rail Road"; and January 4, 1834, "Georgia Rail Road."

32. Goodrich, *Government Promotion;* 10. Majewski, *A House Dividing*, esp. chap. 2.

33. *Southern Banner*, July 6, 1833, "Rail Road," second resolution at the end of the article.

34. Captain Benjamin Sherrod, of Courtland, Alabama, to William Dearing, December 13, 1833, *Southern Banner*, January 18, 1834, "Communications." *American Railroad Journal and Advocate of Internal Improvements*, March 29, 1834, folder 1, box 17, Camak Collection (MS 53) Hargrett Library. W. K. Wood, "The Georgia Railroad and Banking Company," *Georgia Historical Quarterly* 57 (Winter 1973): 547. Phillips, *A History of Transportation*, 304–6; Richard G. Wood, *Stephen Harriman Long 1784–1864: Army Engineer, Explorer, Inventor* (Glendale, Calif.: Arthur H.

Clark Co., 1966), 164–65. *Southern Banner,* January 18, 1834, "Communications" and "Rail Roads"; May 31, 1834, "Georgia Rail Road"; June 28, 1834; July 19, 1834, "Internal Improvements"; August 16, 1834, "Rail Road Intelligence"; August 30, 1834, "Rail Road Intelligence"; and October 11, 1834, "Internal Improvement."

35. Phillips, *A History of Transportation,* 182–84. Heath, *Constructive Liberalism,* 266–67. *Southern Banner,* July 30, 1836, "Knoxville Convention . . . *Report of J. Edgar Thompson, Engineer, as to the practicability of running a rail road thro' the Rabun Gap, and also by McNair's in Murray county or Walker*"; November 19, 1836, "Governor's Message"; December 3, 1836, "Georgia Legislature." *Macon Messenger,* July 28, 1836, "Extract of a report made by a Committee of the Georgia Delegation to that body on the advantages and facilities possessed by Georgia, for rail road communications with the Western States—adopted by the Delegation and ordered to be laid before the General Convention."

36. Ward, "Internal Improvements in Georgia," 31–69; Gates, "An Imitative Enterprise," 60–72. Carol Sheriff, *The Artificial River: The Erie Canal and the Paradox of Progress, 1817–1862* (New York: Hill & Wang, 1996). "Report of Lt. Col. S. H. Long, on a reconnaissance for railroads from Augusta, Georgia, to Memphis, Tennessee, in February, 1835," 23rd Congress, 2nd session, House doc. no. 177, appendix B, 81–88. Directors Minute Book, vol. 1, June 28, 1834 entry, Georgia Railroad and Banking Company Collection, Reese Library Special Collections, Augusta State University (henceforth Georgia Railroad Minute Book).

37. Chandler, *The Visible Hand.* Georgia Railroad Minute Book 1, October 24, 1835, and September 20, 1836. *Macon Messenger,* July 28, 1836, "Another Railroad Convention."

38. *Macon Messenger,* July 21, 1836.

39. *Macon Messenger,* July 14, 1836.

40. "Report of J. Edgar Thomson," *Southern Banner,* July 30, 1836, "Knoxville Convention." *Southern Banner,* August 6, 1836, "Report, On a reconnaissance of the country between Knoxville and Athens, Georgia, to ascertain the practicability of constructing a Rail Road around the Blue Ridge." The McNair's Gap route was more expensive primarily because of the rough terrain between the Chattahoochee River Valley and the Etowah River Valley.

41. Cummings, *Georgia Railroad,* 13. *Southern Banner,* July 27, 1833, "Augusta Rail Road Meeting"; August 8, 1833, "The Augusta Chronicle"; July 27, 1833 (second letter of Marcellus responding to letter of Epimondias in *Savannah Georgian,* July 7, 1833); November 9, 1833, "Internal Improvement"; August 17, 1833, "From the Georgia Journal."

42. *Southern Banner,* December 10, 1841, "Georgia Rail Road"; December 17, 1841, "Business"; March 25, 1842, "Market Roads."

43. Augusta *Constitutionalist* as quoted in *Southern Banner,* March 24, 1836, "Improvement of Augusta." *Southern Banner,* May 26, 1836, "Georgia Railroad and Banking Company"; May 24, 1839, "For Sale"; May 31, 1839, "250 shares of Rail Road Stock For Sale"; May 31, 1839, "For Sale"; September 27, 1839, "Executor's Sale"; March 27, 1840, "Executor's Sale"; and November 6, 1840, "Executor's Sale"; June 25, 1841, "A Few Reflections on the policy and effects of the Western and Atlantic Rail Road"; May 13, 1842, "Rail Road Convention."

44. Georgia Railroad Minute Book 1. *Southern Banner,* May 14, 1841, "Convention of Stockholders"; May 13, 1842, "Railroad Convention." *150 Years: Railroad & Banking Company of Georgia, 1833–1983* (Augusta: Georgia Railroad & Banking Company of Georgia, 1983), 13, 19.

45. Peter S. McGuire, "Athens and the Railroads: The Georgia and the Northeastern," Part 1, *Georgia Historical Quarterly* 16 (March 1934): 7. *Southern Banner*, April 1, 1842, "Georgia Railroad"; August 6, 1842, "Georgia Railroad"; December 9, 1842, "Georgia Railroad"; July 13, 1843 "Georgia Rail Road"; November 14, 1844, "Georgia Railroad"; December 30, 1845, "Georgia Rail Road"; June 9, 1846, "Georgia Railroad"; November 25, 1847, "Notice!"; January 6, 1848, "Notice"; February 17, 1848, "Communicated"; September 7, 1848, "The Democratic Mass Meeting at Stone Mountain—State Agricultural Fair."

46. Augusta *Constitutionalist*, as quoted in the *Southern Banner*, October 27, 1838. *Southern Banner*, July 29, 1837, "Circular"; August 5, 1837, "For the Southern Banner"; October 28, 1837, "Convention"; April 14, 1838, "Merchants' Convention"; September 8, 1838, "Public Meeting"; September 15, 1838, "For the Southern Banner"; October 27, 1838, "Commercial Convention." William Watson Davis, "Ante-Bellum Southern Commercial Conventions," *Transactions of the Alabama Historical Society* 5 (1904): 156, 164–65. Wender, *Southern Commercial Conventions*, 10–12, 22. McCardell, *The Idea of a Southern Nation*, 92–93. Vicki Vaughn Johnson, *The Men and the Vision of the Southern Commercial Conventions, 1845–1871* (Columbia: University of Missouri Press, 1992), 16. *Southern Banner*, March 13, 1840; December 23, 1842, "Important Movement"; July 14, 1843, "New Facilities for Transporting Goods"; August 24, 1843, "A Dialogue"; and December 23, 1845, "Summary." *Augusta Chronicle and Sentinel*, February 3, 1841, as quoted in *Southern Banner*, "The Georgia Rail-Road—Its Prospects." *Southern Banner*, July 8, 1837, "Married." Augusta *Constitutionalist*, as quoted in the *Southern Banner*, December 13, 1849, "A Train of Cars at Chattanooga." Cummings, *A History of the Georgia Railroad Company*, 22.

47. Goldfarb, "A Note on Limits to the Growth of the Cotton-Textile Industry," 545–58. Russell, *Atlanta: 1847–1890*.

48. John W. Sprague in Charleston, S.C., to his mother, Mrs. P. Sprague Charlton, at Saratoga, N.Y., August 3, 1847, John Sprague Papers (Collection # 751), Georgia Historical Society.

49. One cannot directly compare the aggregated state data cited in Joseph C. G. Kennedy, *Abstract of the Statistics of Manufactures according to the returns of the Seventh Census* (1859; rpt. New York: Norman Ross Publishing Inc.), vol. 13 (1990): 43, to the county-level data for Clarke County on 206–11, as that local data includes all manufacturing in Athens, not just textiles. Instead one must aggregate the textile data from the 1850 Manuscript Census kept by Clarke County (Incomplete), Schedule 5, Products of Industry, Georgia Archives.

50. U.S. Congress, "Report of the Secretary of the Treasury," 1872–73.

51. New York *Journal of Commerce*, September 6, 1855, as transcribed in Skinner, ed., *The Autobiography of Henry Merrell*, 214.

52. De Treville, "The Little New South," and Heath, *Constructive Liberalism*, 312, 346. *Southern Banner*, March 30, 1848, "The Liberal Charter Policy"; May 4, 1848, "Additional Employment to Women and Children."

53. *Southern Banner*, August 14, 1845, "For the Southern Banner IV"; April 13, 1847, "Manufacturing in Sober Earnest, No. II" as transcribed in Skinner, ed., *The Autobiography of Henry Merrell*, 407. Also see White, *Statistics of the State of Georgia*, 134, 182–83, 189, 446, and 550 for lists of the destinations of the manufactured goods of Georgia.

54. New York *Journal of Commerce*, September 8, 1855, "Cotton Manufacturing in Georgia, No. 3" as transcribed in Skinner, ed., *The Autobiography of Henry Merrell*, 417.

55. Robert Royal Russel, *Economic Aspects of Southern Sectionalism, 1840–1861, University of Illinois Studies in the Social Sciences* 11, no. 1 and 2 (March–June 1923) (Urbana: University of Illinois, 1924), 60–61. Skinner, ed., *The Autobiography of Henry Merrell*, 420. Russel, *Economic Aspects*, 62, citing *De Bow's Review* 39: 627.

56. Chicopee Minute Books, June 7, 1853, and December 23, 1857. Typescript cards, John S. Linton to Ann Linton, July 10, 1853, and February 11, 1858, Linton Gift (MS 585), Hargrett Library. John S. Linton to Ann Linton, July 19, 1853, *Cotton History Review* 1, no. 2 (April 1960): 76–77.

57. *Southern Banner*, June 14, 1849, "For Sale." R. G. Dun, Georgia, vol. 6: 93. *Southern Watchman*, April 28, 1869, "Our Cotton Factories." Talmage Diary, 28–29, entries relating to freshet of August 27, 1852. A. P. Dearing to John J. Dearing, April 5, 1854, John J. Dearing (Covington, Ga.) Papers, 1820–56, Perkins Library. Skinner, ed., *The Autobiography of Henry Merrell*, 198–99.

58. Here I am using "industry" differently from previous uses. None of these new "industries" belong in the same category as a textile factory. I argue that they improved and enhanced the ability of the factories.

59. *Southern Banner*, February 3, 1853, "Telegraph to Athens."

60. 1850 Clarke County, Products of Industry, 1st page in series; Household #893 (McCall), Athens District, Clarke County, Georgia, 1860 Population Schedules, Bureau of the Census, National Archives.

61. *Southern Banner*, March 8, 1849, "Manufacturer's Supply Store"; May 11, 1854, "Notice." *Southern Watchman*, May 6, 1858, "Home Manufactures." *Southern Business Directory* (Charleston: Walker & James, 1854), vol. 1: 234. R. G. Dun, Georgia, vol. 6: 112, Summey & Newton entry. *Southern Banner*, July 18, 1844, "Notice." Household #25 (Richard S. Schevenell) and Household #26 (Peter A. Summey), Athens District, Clarke County, 1850 Population Schedules, Bureau of the Census, National Archives. Deed of Harmon Schevenell to Edward McCall, May 23, 1858, Deed Book "V," 414–15.

62. *Columbus Times* as quoted in *Southern Banner*, November 9, 1848, "Result of the 'Liberal Charter' Policy." *Muscogee Democrat* as quoted in *Southern Whig*, June 21, 1849, "Manufacturing in Columbus and Vicinity." Southern Mutual Minute Book, April 15, 1852; August 20, 1858; September 3, 1858; and April 20, 1860. De Treville, "The Little New South," 113–14, 146, 150. Southern Mutual Minute Book, June 18, 1853, January 11, 1855; September 26, 1856; February 11, 1859; and May 4, 1860.

63. Deed of estate of William Dearing, February 5, 1856, Deed Book "V," 134–35; "July 25, 1850, Incorporation Agreement," Deed Book "T," 364. 1850 Clarke County, Products of Industry, second partial page of series. *Southern Banner*, October 17, 1850, "Georgia, Clark County"; January 16, 1851, "A Card." Talmage Diary, 26, February 8 and September 20, 1851.

64. *Southern Banner*, March 18, 1852, "The Athens Steam Company," and May 6, 1852, "The Athens Steam Company," are the same advertisement, with its original date of publication the previous November identified; March 3, 1853, "Athens Foundry Burnt!" William P. Talmage Diary, 29–30, February 23, 1853. *Georgia Laws 1853–1854*, 383–84, sections 3 and 4 of "An Act . . . to Incorporate the Athens Steam Company," as transcribed in notes made by R. N. Fickett III, November 10, 1960, "Athens: Athens Steam Company" vertical file, Hargrett Library. *Southern Banner*, March 16, 1854, "An Athens-Made Engine"; June 15, 1854, "Iron Brass & Foundry";

January 18, 1855, "Iron Brass & Foundry"; May 14, 1857, "Athens Steam Company"; July 16, 1857, "Local Matters"; May 26, 1859, "Foundry." *Southern Watchman*, February 3, 1856, "Athens Foundry"; December 25, 1856, "The Athens Cemetery." Minutes of the Intendant and Wardens of the Town of Athens (microfilm in Hargrett Library, also at Georgia Archives), July 8, 1858. R. G. Dun, Georgia, vol. 6: 99, Athens Steam Company entries.

65. John S. Linton to Ann Linton, July 10, 1853, July 19, 1853, and February 11, 1858, Linton Gift. *Cotton History Review* 1 (April 1960): 76–77. Steadman, *The Southern Manufacturer*, 74–75. Augusta: de Treville, "The Little New South," 162–63, 210; *Southern Banner*, January 10, 1850, "House of Representatives." Southern Mutual Minute Book, July 26, 1851; April 20, 1852; August 14, 1852; August 27, 1853. Columbus: de Treville, "The Little New South," 150–51, 205, 207; *Muscogee Democrat* as quoted in *Southern Whig*, June 21, 1849, "Manufacturing in Columbus and Vicinity." Southern Mutual Minute Book, June 13, 1856; August 25, 1865; September 15, 1865. Macon: de Treville, "The Little New South," 169–71, 203. *Southern Whig*, August 9, 1849, "Macon Foundries." *Macon Journal & Messenger* as quoted in *Southern Whig*, September 20, 1849, "Georgia Power Loom Manufactory." Southern Mutual Minute Book, December 19, 1851; February 12, 1852; April 27, 1852; August 30, 1861. Atlanta: Southern Mutual Minute Book, May 19, 1851; June 16, 1851; May 13, 1861. De Treville, "The Little New South," 214–22. Robert S. Davis, *Cotton, Fire, & Dreams: The Robert Findlay Iron Works and Heavy Industry in Macon, Georgia 1839–1912* (Macon, Ga.: Mercer University Press, 1998).

66. Judith McGaw, *Most Wonderful Machine: Mechanization and Social Change in Berkshire Paper Making, 1801–1885* (Princeton, N.J.: Princeton University Press, 1987). Deed of John Felton to Albon Chase & John S. Linton, January 13, 1847, Deed Book "T," 10–11. *Southern Banner*, July 30, 1836, "Very Valuable Lots and Lands for Sale"; February 23, 1847, "Paper Factory"; January 10, 1850, "Pioneer Paper Mill." White, *Statistics of the State of Georgia*, 183. Southern Mutual Minute Book, December 25, 1851. Talmage Diary, 27, January 1, 1852. *Southern Banner*, April 18, 1852, "Georgia, Clarke County." R. G. Dun, Georgia, vol. 6: 94, June 29, 1852, entry for Chase & Linton, Papermakers.

67. Talmage Diary, 28–29, 35; Southern Mutual Minute Book, April 30, 1858.

68. "Story of Athens Gas Company," folder 11, box 6, C. D. Flanigen Collection, Hargrett Library. "An Act to incorporate the Athens Gas Light Company," *Georgia Laws 1855–1856*, 422–25. Hynds, *Antebellum Athens*, 47, 143. *Southern Banner*, May 11, 1854. Tate, *Keeper of the Flame*, 158. *Southern Banner*, December 13, 1849, "Senate"; March 26, 1857, "Gas in Athens." Hynds, *Antebellum Athens*, 47, 160, 180. Deed of R. D. Moore to William S. Grady, October 18, 1860, Deed Book "X," 178; R. G. Dun, Georgia, vol. 6: 119. "Bill & Receipt 1861," Grady, W. S. (MS 633), Hargrett Library.

69. A. E. Griffith, *History of the Southern Mutual Insurance Company: Athens, Georgia, 1848–1923* (Rev. ed., Athens: McGregor Co., 1931), 11; Convention Minutes Ledger (henceforth called Southern Mutual Convention Minutes), December 6, 1848, SMIC. Household #521 (J. U. Parsons), Athens District, 1850 Clarke County Manuscript Census.

70. Griffith, *History of the Southern Mutual*, 24–25; Hynds, *Antebellum Athens*, 53. Southern Mutual Minute Book, February 18, 1851; March 1, 1851; April 26, 1851; April 30, 1851; May 5, 1851; May 7 1851; May 10, 1851; May 19, 1851; June 2, 1851; July 26, 1851; August 27, 1851; September 3, 1851; September 30, 1851; October 6, 1851; October 8, 1851; October 31, 1851;

and November 1, 1851. A look at Parsons's accounting is enlightening. Unlike later entries, his accounting is impossible to follow, and his summaries are both incomplete and opaque.

71. Griffith, *History of the Southern Mutual,* 12 and 16. Announcement of sale of life department, January 18, 1855, Southern Mutual Insurance Company Vertical File, Hargrett Library.

Factories in Athens: Athens Factory: Southern Mutual Minute Book, September 23, 1853; January 20, 1854; February 24, 1854; November 16, 1854; November 23, 1854; August 13, 1858; January 21, 1859; February 18, 1859; January 25, 1861; September 27, 1861; December 6, 1861; January 24, 1862; January 22, 1864; December 27, 1867; January 3, 1868; January 20, 1871; January 30, 1880. Princeton Factory, Southern Mutual Minute Book, March 20, 1849; July 21, 1854; September 22, 1854; September 27, 1861; December 13, 1861; October 3, 1862; October 31, 1862; February 27, 1863; October 23, 1863; October 28, 1864, October 11, 1867; December 27, 1867; April 25, 1879; August 1, 1879. Itemized descriptions of insured Princeton Factory property, Athens Agency Fire Policy Register (henceforth Athens Fire Register), vols. 1, 5, and 7, SMIC. Georgia Factory: Southern Mutual Minute Book, January 6, 1851; January 8, 1852; January 15, 1852; August 28, 1852; January 8, 1853; October 12, 1855; October 19, 1855; November 19, 1858; March 23, 1860; April 12, 1861; January 24, 1862; April 10, 1863; March 25, 1864; April 21, 1865; September 27, 1867. Itemized descriptions of insured Georgia Factory property, Athens Fire Register, 5. Pioneer Paper Mill: Southern Mutual Directors Minutes, December 25, 1851; September 9, 1853; September 22, 1854; October 24, 1856; April 30, 1858; October 22, 1858; May 10, 1861; May 9, 1862; April 24, 1863; May 6, 1864; April 20, 1866; November 16, 1866; April 5, 1867; August 26, 1870; September 2, 1870. Athens Foundry: Southern Mutual Minute Book, March 31, 1851; September 8, 1854; January 15, 1858; April 13, 1860; July 11, 1862; July 18, 1862; April 10, 1863; June 26, 1863; July 17, 1863; March 25, 1864; November 17, 1865; August 10, 1866; August 17, 1866; April 24, 1868.

Factories in Greater Athens: Scull Shoals Factory: Southern Mutual Minute Book, March 20, 1849; June 6, 1879. Curtright Factory: Southern Mutual Minute Book, February 3, 1851; July 4, 1856; August 29, 1856. Greenesboro Factory: Southern Mutual Minute Book, January 16, 1851; February 5, 1852; February 26, 1852; February 13, 1863. High Shoals Factory: Southern Mutual Minute Book, November 4, 1853; October 26, 1854; October 28, 1858; October 28, 1859; December 16, 1859; November 16, 1860; October 25, 1861; October 31, 1862; November 14, 1862; October 23, 1863; October 5, 1866; September 27, 1867; March 10, 1876. Itemized descriptions of insured High Shoals Factory property, Athens Fire Register, 5.

Factories in Athens's Hinterlands: Rock Mills Factory (also known as Jewel's Factory): Southern Mutual Minute Book, July 21, 1854; January 29, 1858; January 10, 1862; November 9, 1866; November 7, 1879. Planters Factory (also known as Shoals of Ogeechee Factory): Southern Mutual Minute Book, March 31, 1851; June 7, 1855; June 14, 1855; and November 9, 1855. Hancock Factory (also known as Sparta Factory or Montour Factory): Southern Mutual Minute Book, May 18, 1852; May 25, 1852; June 1, 1852; June 18, 1853; June 9, 1854; June 14, 1855; June 21, 1855; July 12, 1855; February 22, 1856; December 25, 1857; October 1, 1858; August 17, 1860; August 24, 1860; June 7, 1864; June 27, 1873; July 18, 1873. Eatonton Factory: Southern Mutual Minute Book, January 16, 1851. Madison Steam Factory: Southern Mutual Minute Book, June 30, 1851. Newton Factory: Southern Mutual Minute Book, December 17, 1853; February 24, 1854;

December 23, 1859; December 21, 1860; December 27, 1861; December 26, 1862; April 24, 1863; July 10, 1863. White's Factory: Southern Mutual Minute Book, December 11, 1852; December 14, 1855; December 19, 1856; December 25, 1857; December 24, 1858; December 30, 1859; December 25, 1863. Cedar Shoals Factory (also known as Porterdale): Southern Mutual Minute Book, November 8, 1872. Anthony's Shoals Factory: Southern Mutual Minute Book, August 27, 1853; September 7, 1860; October 25, 1861; March 8, 1862; June 13, 1862; October 23, 1863.

Georgia factories: Sweet Water Factory (also known as New Manchester Mfg): Southern Mutual Minute Book, January 24, 1851; August 27, 1853; September 2, 1853; September 1, 1854; October 26, 1854; February 1, 1855; May 30, 1856; May 29, 1857; July 23, 1858; January 21, 1859; April 28, 1859; October 5, 1860; September 26, 1862; June 19, 1863. Nickajack Factory: Southern Mutual Minute Book, July 16, 1853. Roswell Factory: Southern Mutual Minute Book, April 8, 1852; August 7, 1852; October 16, 1852; October 26, 1852; May 28, 1853; October 28, 1853; November 7, 1853; January 6, 1854; March 10, 1854; May 19, 1854; May 26, 1854; August 18, 1854; August 25, 1854; September 29, 1854; July 26, 1855; August 23, 1855; September 6, 1855; May 9, 1856; March 27, 1857; July 3, 1857; January 29, 1858; July 20, 1860; August 3, 1860; July 17, 1863; August 14, 1863; January 25, 1867; June 17, 1870; October 15, 1875. Macon Factory: Southern Mutual Minute Book, April 7, 1851; April 14, 1851; May 18, 1852; March 10, 1854; March 15, 1861; March 1, 1862; June 7, 1864; February 22, 1867; March 29, 1867; June 17, 1870. Ocmulgee Factory: Southern Mutual Minute Book, December 25, 1857; September 23, 1859; September 27, 1861. Milledgeville Factory: Southern Mutual Minute Book, April 14, 1851; September 13, 1851; March 10, 1854; November 16, 1854; June 21, 1855; February 25, 1859; November 30, 1860; June 21, 1861; June 28, 1861; August 9, 1861; June 20, 1862; June 26, 1863; October 16, 1863; June 24, 1864; October 16, 1868; October 23, 1868; February 7, 1873; June 13, 1873; November 27, 1874. Troup Factory: Southern Mutual Minute Book, April 27, 1852; June 15, 1852; April 30, 1853; June 4, 1853; May 8, 1857; March 19, 1858; July 18, 1873. Lawrenceville Factory (also known as Gwinnett Manufacturing Company): Southern Mutual Minute Book, September 6, 1855; July 25, 1856; October 15, 1857; December 2, 1859; December 6, 1861; January 31, 1862; December 26, 1862; January 16, 1863; December 25, 1863; June 17, 1864; June 24, 1864. Bainbridge Steam Cotton Factory: Southern Mutual Minute Book, September 27, 1861; October 11, 1861; September 23, 1864. Waynmansville Factory: Southern Mutual Minute Book, December 17, 1858; November 17, 1871. Trion Factory: Southern Mutual Minute Book, July 14, 1854; February 1, 1855; February 12, 1855; January 23, 1857; February 21, 1857; January 22, 1858; January 28, 1859; January 27, 1860; May 25, 1860; January 25, 1861; January 24, 1862; January 23, 1863; January 22, 1864; April 20, 1866; February 8, 1867; February 22, 1867; December 13, 1867; July 17, 1874; December 3, 1875; December 8, /1876; February 21, 1879; December 5, 1879. Parson's Wool Factory: Southern Mutual Minute Book, October 31, 1851. Augusta Factory: Southern Mutual Minute Book, March 8, 1851; June 8, 1852; May 19, 1854; July 25, 1856; March 26, 1858; July 30, 1858; June 1, 1860; July 7, 1860; July 5, 1861; August 2, 1861; May 22, 1863; July 21, 1865; June 28, 1867; July 24, 1868; July 31, 1868; September 8, 1870; September 16, 1870; January 16, 1880 and March 5, 1880. Richmond Factory: Southern Mutual Minute Book, May 26, 1854; May 29, 1863; June 12, 1863; June 21, 1878. Belleville Factory (also known as Schley's Factory): Southern Mutual Minute Book, February 26, 1852; May 12, 1854; May 29, 1857; October 1, 1858; August 26, 1859; April 6,

1860; July 12, 1861; March 1, 1862; March 21, 1862. Muscogee Factory: Southern Mutual Minute Book, February 12, 1855; July 20, 1860; June 21, 1878. Carter's Factory: Southern Mutual Minute Book, May 19, 1851; August 1, 1851; January 24, 1862. Eagle Factory (also known as the Eagle & Phoenix Mills): Southern Mutual Minute Book, June 30, 1851; August 27, 1851; December 11, 1852; September 8, 1854; December 21, 1855; January 4, 1856; January 25, 1856; April 2, 1858; August 16, 1861; November 14, 1861; March 13, 1868; April 10, 1868; May 10, 1868; March 18, 1870; June 21, 1878; December 20, 1878; October 29, 1880. Howard Factory, see Southern Mutual Minute Book, July 26, 1851; December 21, 1855; July 25, 1856; April 5, 1861; December 8, 1861. Columbus Factory: Southern Mutual Minute Book, January 20, 1854; August 2, 1855; January 25, 1856; April 30, 1858; January 18, 1861; December 14, 1866; February 15, 1867; May 17, 1867; November 21, 1867; May 13, 1870; May 20, 1870; July 22, 1870. Coweta Falls Factory: Southern Mutual Minute Book, August 1, 1851; July 19, 1855; December 21, 1855.

South Carolina factories: Cotton factory near Spartanburg: Southern Mutual Minute Book, August 27, 1851 and August 27, 1851. Cotton and wool factories at Greenville: Southern Mutual Minute Book, June 30, 1851; August 27, 1851; October 30, 1852; February 22, 1855. Saluda Factory: Southern Mutual Minute Book, September 28, 1860; January 4, 1867; January 25, 1867. Graniteville Factory: Southern Mutual Minute Book, April 18, 1862; January 18, 1867; November 10, 1876; July 20, 1877.

Alabama factories: Troy Factory: Southern Mutual Minute Book, February 8, 1856. Dog River Factory: Southern Mutual Minute Book, July 26, 1851. Bell Factory: Southern Mutual Minute Book, March 1, 1851. Pratt's Factory: Southern Mutual Minute Book, March 11, 1852. Mallory's Cotton Factory: Southern Mutual Minute Book, July 14, 1852. For Montgomery Factory, see Southern Mutual Minute Book, May 8, 1851.

Tennessee factories: Robert James Factory, in Blount County: Southern Mutual Minute Book, March 19, 1853. Deevy & Brother's cotton factory near Winchester: Southern Mutual Minute Book, February 5, 1851; August 15, 1851. Metcalfe's spinning factory near Athens: Southern Mutual Minute Book, March 1, 1851.

North Carolina factories: McDonald's Steam Cotton Factory near Charlotte: Southern Mutual Minute Book, May 17, 1861, and August 23, 1861.

72. Either the local agent or the general agent might be assigned to renew the policy of a factory, depending on who was to receive the commission. Southern Mutual Minute Book, January 8, 1852; February 18, 1859; March 23, 1860; December 27, 1867; June 6, 1879.

Partial insurance by multiple companies: Southern Mutual Minute Book, May 18. 1852; June 1, 1852; August 28, 1852; January 20, 1854; May 26, 1854; September 29, 1854; December 21, 1855; July 25, 1856; October 15, 1857; June 28, 1861 and October 4, 1878; Also see Athens Agency Register, vol. 1: 5 for Georgia Factory, October 2, 1868; October 21, 1868, for Princeton Factory; October 23, 1868, for High Shoals Factory; November 18, 1868, for Princeton Factory. Steam engine rates: Southern Mutual Minute Book, July 12, 1849; February 26, 1852; September 2, 1853; July 12, 1861; April 20, 1866.

Watchman required: Southern Mutual Minute Book, July 25, 1856; September 23, 1859; January 10, 1862; January 3, 1868; August 6, 1869. Additional factory insurance requests: Southern Mutual Minute Book, September 13, 1851; July 14, 1854; September 29, 1854; January 25,

1856; February 21, 1857; April 30, 1858; April 28, 1859; August 3, 1860; October 5, 1860; July 5, 1861; August 2, 1861; September 27, 1861; September 26, 1862; October 3, 1862; June 19, 1863; March 29, 1867; December 5, 1879.

General Agent for settling: Southern Mutual Minute Book, January 22, 1852, and April 20, 1866. Examples of quick settlement of claims: Southern Mutual Minute Book: George Schley's Belleville Factory near Augusta was reported burned on March 1, 1862 and Southern Mutual paid its $10,000 claim on March 21, 1862; Enoch Steadman's Lawrenceville Factory (Gwinnett Manufacturing Company) was reported destroyed June 17, 1864, and Southern Mutual paid its $10,000 claim on June 24, 1864.

73. McGuire, "Athens and the Railroads," 21.

CHAPTER FIVE

1. *Southern Watchman,* January 7, 1862, "Wanted"; December 31, 1862, "Wanted." *Southern Banner,* January 7, 1863, "Wanted"; March 30, 1864, "Dogwood Poles Wanted."

2. Maurice Melton, "Major Military Industries of the Confederate Government," Atlanta: Emory University, Ph.D. diss., 1978, esp. 131–294.

3. Coleman, *Confederate Athens,* 97–99. *Athens Banner,* December 24, 1962, "Athens begins vital role in Confederacy"; *Athens Banner-Herald & Daily News,* January 5, 1969, 8-D, "How Athens Went to War." Charles J. Brockman Jr., "The Confederate Armory of Cook & Brother," *Gun Digest* 14 (1960): 74–75; Charles J. Brockman Jr. "A Rebel Secret Weapon," *American Rifleman,* August 1956. Charles J. Brockman Jr. . ed., "Obituary of Major F. W. C. Cook," *Georgia Historical Quarterly* 37 (December 1953): 351–54. Charles J. Brockman Jr., "The Confederate Armory of Cook & Brother," *Papers of the Athens Historical Society* (Athens, Ga.: Athens Historical Society, 1979), vol. 2: 85. Inventory of the armory, Mortgage Book "R," 198–218 , Real Estate Office, Office of the Superior Court Clerk, Clarke County Court House, Athens, Ga. Deed of Athens Manufacturing Company to Cook & Brother, December 3, 1862, Deed Book "W," 387; Deed of Hodgson & Brother to Ferdinand W. C. Cook, August 14, 1862; Deed of Athens Manufacturing Company to Cook & Brother, dated December 3, 1862; for deed of F. W. Lucas to Cook & Brother, dated January 2, 1863; and for deed of Stevens Thomas to Cook & Brother, dated October 3, 1863, all located in Deed Book "X," 244–47. Original of Deed of Hodgson & Brother to Ferdinand W. C. Cook can also be found in "Papers 1862" folder, box 11, Chicopee Manufacturing Company, Hargrett Library. Southern Mutual Minute Book, vol. 1, November 21, 1862; March 26, 1863. "Letters Received by the Confederate Secretary of War 1861–1865," microfilm series m437, roll 85, frames 438–509, National Archives. *Southern Banner,* March 27, 1863, "Athens Guns"; March 30, 1864, "Confederate States Armory"; January 18, 1864, "Notice to all Concerned."

4. *Southern Banner,* March 26, 1862, "Princeton Factory." The war production of the cotton factories of Georgia can be found in the National Archives, Record Group 109, entry 180, "Firms that Did Business with the Confederate Government" (commonly known as the "Citizen Files"), microfilm series m346, roll 27 for Athens Factory; roll 823 for Princeton Factory; roll 344 for Georgia Factory. When looking for a specific factory it helps to know all the possible variations of the company's name as well as the names of its superintendent or agent. A letter dated January 22, 1862, addressed to Maj. J. K. Ferguson in Richmond, Virginia, found in the Athens Factory

documents on roll 27 explains that the factory then produced goods for the "Georgia companies" on the coast, meaning the state defense forces guarding against seaborne invasion. I organized and tallied pay vouchers to determine the gross receipts of manufactured goods sold to the Confederate government.

For change in premium due to running the Athens Factory and the Princeton Factory at night, see Southern Mutual Minute Book, September 27, 1861. For corresponding premium change for factories in Columbus operating at night during the Civil War: Southern Mutual Minute Book, August 16, 1861. Wilson, *Confederate Industry*, discusses similar trends throughout Confederate suppliers of industrial goods.

5. Chicopee Minute Books, vol. 2, September 29, 1860; May 3, 1862; October 4, 1862; February 19, 1863; June 6, 1863; October 3, 1863; January 11, 1864; October 1, 1864; February 4, 1865; June 10, 1865; and October 2, 1865. *Southern Watchman*, January 28, 1863, "Increase of Stock"; July 15, 1863, "List of Stockholders."

6. A. P. Dearing to John J. Dearing, April 12, 1864, John J. Dearing (Covington, Ga.) Papers 1864–99, Perkins Library.

7. Chicopee Minute Books, vol. 2, June 4, 1863. *Southern Watchman*, June 3, 1863, "Cotton Mill Stock"; January 20, 1864, "George Memno." Linton, "Random Recollections," 55. *Southern Banner*, March 16, 1864, "Notice." Chicopee Minute Books, vol. 2, June 10, 1865.

8. Mary DeCredico, *Patriotism for Profit: Georgia's Urban Entrepreneurs and the Confederate War Effort* (Chapel Hill: University of North Carolina Press, 1990). Southern Mutual Minute Book, June 21, 1861; August 23, 1861; December 6, 1861. Southern Mutual appeared to consider these a patriotic duty, and a doubtful investment. See also "Confederate Treasury Department, Field Offices"—Entry 135, Athens, Ga., Incomplete Name Index to (box 14) Entry 136—Athens Bonds issued, Record Group 365, National Archives. Pleasant Stovall Letter (MS 1103), Athens, August 21, 1862, Hargrett Library. Chicopee Minute Books, vol. 2, February 4, 1865. *Historical Review of the National Bank of Athens from its founding to its Semi-Centennial Anniversary* (Athens, Ga.: National Bank of Athens, 1916), 9, 16–17.

9. *Southern Watchman*, January 15, 1862, "Some Things can be done as well as others"; March 26, 1862, "Southern Independence!"; December 31, 1862, "Notice to Weavers and Others," and "Reeds, Harness, &c"; January 20, 1864, "George Menno." Jeremy, *Transatlantic Industrial Revolution*, 290 and 292. *Southern Watchman*, January 7, 1862, "Wanted"; December 31, 1862, "Wanted." *Southern Banner*, March 30, 1864, "Dogwood Poles Wanted."

10. *Southern Banner*, October 15, 1862, "The Military Exemption Act"; October 12, 1864, "Wanted." Coleman, *Confederate Athens*, 99 and 169. Stegeman, *These Men She Gave*, 108. Hull, *Annals of Athens*, noted the efforts of Moses Meyers to avoid the draft and the hiring of more operatives than necessary at the factories.

11. John Nicholson's sworn statement, August 14, 1865, Petitions for Presidential Amnesty, microfilm m1003, roll 21, frames 1223–31, National Archives. *History of Newton County Georgia*, 225–26, 949. R. G. Dun, Georgia, vol. 25: 30 and 60. Southern Mutual Minute Book, vol. 1, December 29, 1859, and December 21, 1860. R. G. Dun, Georgia, vol. 16: 116. *History of Newton County*, 420. Southern Mutual Minute Book, vol. 1, January 16, 1863; December 25, 1863; June 24, 1864. 1862 Receipts for sale of salt, and letter of Bradford Ridley to Enoch Steadman, November 17, 1865, Enoch Steadman Papers, 1862–70, Perkins Library.

12. Kenneth Coleman, *Athens, 1861–1865: As Seen through Letters in the University of Georgia Libraries* (Athens: University of Georgia Press, 1969), 45, Lamar Cobb to Howell Cobb, May 27, 1862; 47, John S. Linton to Mary Ann Cobb, June 20, 1862; and 53–54, Mary Ann Cobb to Howell Cobb, April 27, 1863.

13. *Southern Banner,* October 22, 1862, "Athens Factory." *Southern Watchman,* June 24, 1863, "Notice"; August 12, 1863, "Cotton for Yarn." *Southern Banner,* September 23, 1863, "Notice!"; March 30, 1864, "Confederate States Armory," and "Dogwood Poles Wanted"; January 18, 1865, "Factory Notice."

14. Jonathan M. Bryant, "'A County Where Plenty Should Abound': Race, Law, and Markets in Greene County, Georgia, 1850–1885," Ph.D. diss., University of Georgia, 1992, 100. *Southern Banner,* October 15, 1862, "The Exemption Act." *Southern Watchman,* November 19, 1862, "Commendable Liberality"; December 10, 1862, "Exemplary Conduct."

15. *Southern Banner,* March 19, 1862, "Reduction in Prices" and "Cotton Manufacturers"; March 26, 1862, "Princeton Factory." *Southern Watchman,* March 26, 1862, "Spun Truck," "Princeton Factory," and "Cotton Manufactory." *Southern Banner,* October 22, 1862, "Athens Factory" and "Liberal"; January 13, 1864, "Notice"; May 11, 1864, "Notice." *Southern Watchman,* November 19, 1862, "Commendable Liberality."

16. *Southern Watchman,* March 26, 1862; *Southern Banner,* October 22, 1862, "Athens Factory"; February 25, 1863, "Liberal Donation"; May 20, 1863, "Cotton Spinner's Convention"; July 15, 1863, "Donation to Soldiers' Families."

17. *Southern Banner,* May 20, 1863, "Cotton Spinner's Convention." Inferior Court Minutes 1864–72, January 5, 1864, and March 1864 entries, Probate Court Office, Clarke County Court House, Athens, Ga. Coleman, *Confederate Athens,* 168.

18. *Southern Banner,* January 18, 1865, "Factory Notice"; August 2, 1865, "Gold, Yarns and Cloth." Southern Mutual Minute Book, March 17, March 31, April 28, June 2, and June 6, 1865. Fannie Atkinson to Marion Blackshear, September 2, 1866, Baber-Blackshear Collection, Hargrett Library, as cited in Gamble, "Athens: The Study of a Georgia Town," 50.

19. Wilson, *Confederate Industry.* Gen. K. Girrard to Gen. William T. Sherman, July 6, 1864, *War of the Rebellion: Official Records of the Union and Confederate Armies,* ser. 1, vol. 38, pt. 5—Correspondence, 68, as qtd. in Clarece Martin, *A History of Roswell Presbyterian Church* (Dallas, Ga.: Taylor Publishing Co., 1984), 40–41. R. G. Dun, Georgia, vol. 7: 236. Caroline Matheny Dillman, *The Roswell Mills and a Civil War Tragedy: Excerpts from Days Gone by in Alpharetta and Roswell, Georgia* (Roswell, Ga.: Chattahoochee Press, 1996), vol. 1. Ruth B. Cook, *North Across the River: A Civil War Trail of Tears* (Birmingham, Ala.: Crane Hill Publishers, 1998). Michael D. Hitt, *Charged with Treason: Ordeal of 400 Mill Workers during Military Operations in Roswell, Georgia, 1864–1865* (Monroe, N.Y.: Library Research Associates, 1992). John Lupold, Historical American Engineering Record Report on Columbus and Muscogee County, Georgia, Columbus State University Library Special Collections. Georgia Department of Agriculture, *Georgia Historical and Industrial* (Atlanta: Geo. W. Harrison, State Printer, 1901). R. G. Dun , Georgia, vol. 6: 90, 176, for the Athens Manufacturing Company; 93, 107 for the Georgia Factory; 91, 166E, 175, for Princeton Factory, all of Clarke County; Georgia, vol. 6: 93, 105, 139; Georgia, vol. 22: 179, 182, & 189; and Georgia, vol. 35: 45 and 91 for High Shoals Factory on the border of Clarke, Walton & Morgan counties; Georgia, vol. 15: 67, 71, 78G, and 108, and Georgia, vol. 26: 181 and 201, for Curtright

Factory, Georgia, vol. 6: 154, Georgia, vol. 15: 67, 82, and Georgia, vol. 25: 168, 169, 199, for Scull Shoals Factory, all of Greene County; Georgia, vol. 18: 49 for White's Factory in Jackson County; Georgia, vol. 22: 172 for Madison Steam Mill in Morgan County; Georgia, vol. 1B: 161, 287, 394, for Richmond Factory; 53 and 96 for Belleville Factory; 111, 126, 255, 385, for Augusta Factory; 359 for the Enterprise Factory; 362 and 363 for King Factory; 336 and 363 for Simmons Factory; 435 for Sibley Mills, all of Richmond County; Georgia, vol. 26: 188 for Eatonton Factory of Putnam County; Georgia, vol. 25: 30 and 60 for Newton Factory; 11, 12, 56, 57, 85, for Cedar Shoals/Porterdale Factory; 54 for Alcovy/White's Factory, all of Newton County; Georgia, vol. 7: 229 and 230, and Georgia, vol. 8: 61 and 64 for Sweetwater Factory, of Campbell (now Douglas) County; Georgia, vol. 7: 283 and 317 for Concorde Woolen Mill in Cobb County; Georgia, vol. 7: 218, 231, 283, for Roswell Factory; 298 and 313 for Willeo/Hansell Factory; 307 and 310 for Laurel Factory, all of Cobb (now Fulton) County; Georgia, vol. 16: 108 and 116 for Gwinnett/Lawrenceville Factory of Gwinnett County; Georgia, vol. 16: 178, 189, 193, 196L for Hancock/Montour Factory; 179 and 196A for Jewell's Factory, all of Hancock County.

20. Internal Revenue Assessment Lists for Georgia, 1865–66, microfilm series (m762), National Archives. District four, which included Athens, is located on roll 7.

21. Chicopee Minute Books, vol. 2, February 23, 1866, to October 8, 1870. R. G. Dun, Georgia, vol. 6: 90. Gamble, "Athens: The Study of a Georgia Town," 111. *Southern Watchman,* July 8, 1868, "Wool-Carding." *Southern Banner,* September 24, 1869, "Athens Factory"; June 30, 1871, "Athens Factory."

22. R. G. Dun, Georgia, vol. 6: 125. Affidavit of Dr. James Camak, August 1, 1870, Clarke County, Ga., Superior Court Minutes (henceforth Clarke Superior Court Minutes), microfilm 98/2, book 24, 1870–72, 14–15, Georgia Archives. Brockman, "The Confederate Armory of Cook & Brother," 85. U.S. v. Athens Armory, *Georgia Reports* 35: 344–64. *Southern Banner,* January 22, 1869, "Calling on Hercules." Arthur Cook & Samuel P. Thurmond v. Athens Manufacturing Company, Henry Hull, R. Bloomfield and B. H. Hill, "Bill for Cancellation of Sale & Relief"; request of S. P. Thurmond to dismiss case at his own cost, October 22, 1870, Chicopee Manufacturing Company, box 11, "Papers 1870" folder, Hargrett Library. "S. P. Thurmond v Athens Manufacturing Company, Et Al, Bill in Equity," Clarke Superior Court Minutes, book 24, 1870–72, 41. *Southern Banner,* March 4, 1870, "The Armory"; March 31, 1871, "The Old Armory"; June 30, 1871, "Athens Factory." *Southern Watchman,* March 9, 1870, "Sale of Cook's Armory." Statement of Henry Hull as president of Athens Mfg Company affirming capital stock increase, March 31, 1870, Chicopee Manufacturing Company, box 11, "Papers 1870" folder.

23. R. G. Dun, Georgia, vol. 6: 91 and 150, Princeton Factory entries for September 10, 1866, and August 23, 1867. *Southern Watchman,* April 28, 1869, "Our Cotton Factories." *Southern Banner,* April 30, 1869, "Princeton Factory Shoals"; September 10, 1869, "Progressive"; and June 23, 1871, "Princeton Factory." Gamble, "Athens: The Study of a Georgia Town," 109–10.

24. R. G. Dun, Georgia, vol. 6: 93, 107 and 114. Agreement between the Cobb firm and John White regarding a twenty-five-foot addition to the Georgia Factory, February 1869, Cobb Erwin Lamar Collection, box 21, folder 21:9, Business Papers 1860–69, Hargrett Library. *Southern Watchman,* April 28, 1869, "Our Cotton Factories." *Southern Banner,* September 10, 1869, "Progressive." Gamble, "Athens: The Study of a Georgia Town," 49. Huffman, "Old South, New South," 13, 143–44.

25. R. G. Dun, Georgia, vol. 22: 179, High Shoals Manufacturing Company entries for 1866. Samuel Cloyce Watters, "High Shoals, Georgia; Then—Now" (High Shoals, Ga.: Historical Society of High Shoals, 1979), 36–37. R. G. Dun, Georgia, vol. 6: 92, 112, 117, 159, and 180 for Nicholson and Reaves connections. *Southern Banner,* October 1, 1869, "Valuable Property." Report of Scull Shoals, 200–201 and 289. Letters of Rufus Reaves in possession of Rufus Reaves Paine of Athens, Ga.

26. R. G. Dun, Georgia, vol. 25: 168, December 1874, Fontenoy Mills entry;. 199, Powell's Mills entries. Report of Scull Shoals, 5, 255, 271–76, 284–85, 289, 299, and 318. Allen Stovall, "Scull Shoals: A Feasibility Study" (Athens: University of Georgia School of Environmental Design, 1984), 11. E. Merton Coulter, "Scull Shoals: An Extinct Georgia Manufacturing and Farming Community," *Georgia Historical Quarterly* 48 (1964): 45–49, 51–52.

27. R. G. Dun, Georgia, vol. 6: 99, Athens Foundry entries for November 12, 1866, and March 2, 1868; 134, entries for February 6, 1871, and June 1872. *Southern Banner,* November 15, 1865, "Athens Foundry." *Southern Watchman,* December 13, 1865, "Athens Foundry and Machine Works." Gamble, "Athens: The Study of a Georgia Town," 50 and 108.

28. R. G. Dun, Georgia, vol. 6: 94, Pioneer Paper entries for November 12, 1866; May 1, 1869; June 1, 1870. Southern Mutual Minute Book, vol. 1, November 16, 1866. Gamble, "Athens: The Study of a Georgia Town," 108–9. *Southern Banner,* April 30, 1869, "Paper Mill Machinery"; October 29, 1869, "Items"; June 23, 1871, "The Pioneer Paper Mill." *Southern Watchman,* May 4, 1870, "Pioneer Paper Mill"; July 17, 1867, "Another Old Citizen Gone!"

29. R. G. Dun, Georgia, vol. 6: 119. *Southern Watchman,* January 25, 1865, "To Rent." *Southern Banner,* October 1, 1869, "Valuable Property"; November 12, 1869, "The Rome Fair." Gamble, "Athens: The Study of a Georgia Town," 118–19.

30. Bobbin Mill Record Book 1867–1877 (MS 108), Hargrett Library.

31. Data extracted from *Manufactures of the United States in 1860,* 61–79, and from Walker, *The Statistics of the Wealth and Industry of the United States . . . of the Ninth Census,* 646–48.

32. Genovese, *The Political Economy of Slavery,* 180–81. Chad Morgan, *Planters' Progress: Modernizing Confederate Georgia* (Gainesville: University Press of Florida, 2005), adopted Genovese's approach. Beatty, *Alamance.* Evans, *The Conquest of Labor.* Downey, *Planting a Capitalist South.*

33. De Treville, "The Little New South," 232–33. R. G. Dun, Georgia, vol. 1B: 53, 96, 161, 287, 291, 394, 395. Southern Mutual Minute Book, vol. 1, 1848–1868, entries for February 26, 1852, and May 12, 1854. Charles C. Jones Jr., "Pioneer Manufacturing in Richmond County, Georgia," *Textile History Review* 5 (July 1964): 78–82. *Southern Banner,* December 22, 1838, "Nomination for Governor"; November 13, 1840, "Governor's Message." R. G. Dun, Georgia, vol. 7: 190, 229, 230; vol. 8: 61, 64. James E. Brittain, Historic American Engineering Record (HAER) Inventory of Historic Industrial & Engineering Sites in Georgia (compiled 1974 and 1975), "Sweetwater Manufacturing Company," in the possession of the School of History, Technology and Society, at the Georgia Institute of Technology, Atlanta. Monroe M. King, "Destruction of New Manchester Georgia: The Story Behind the Ruins at Sweetwater Creek State Park" (Douglasville, Ga.: Monroe King, 1982). Email correspondence received July 16, 1997, from Louis McDonald, descendent of Charles J. McDonald, confirms relationship between McDonald and Farish Carter. *Southern Banner,* December 24, 1841, "From the Columbus Times"; August 26, 1842, "Extracts from a Speech of the Hon. Mark A. Cooper, of Georgia, on the Tariff Bill"; August 28, 1845, "Georgia Iron";

May 24, 1849, "Good News, Glorious News." William Letcher Mitchell to Governor George W. Towns, November 1, 1849, William Letcher Mitchell Papers (MS 2983), folder 2 (1848–50), Southern Historical Collections, Manuscript Department, Williams Library Special Collections, University of North Carolina–Chapel Hill. Brittain, Georgia HAER Inventory, "Cooper Iron Furnace." Davis, *Cotton, Fire, and Dreams*. Compare the above industrial elite to someone from Athens who was truly out of sync with the rest of his society: Coulter, *John Jacobus Flournoy*.

34. Chicopee Minute Books, vol. 2, June 6, 1863. *Southern Banner*, October 4, 1834, "For Sale."

35. Richard H. Dana Jr., *Two Years before the Mast; and Twenty-four Years After* (New York: Collier, 1937). Skinner, ed., *The Autobiography of Henry Merrell*, 166–67, 181.

36. Gamble, "Athens: The Study of a Georgia Town," 87.

37. R. G. Dun, Georgia, vol. 6: 112, 166A, 166L, 168, and 180. Report of Scull Shoals, 200–201, 289, and 296. Clarke County Court House, Athens, Ga., Will of John W. Nicholson, Clarke County Will Book "F," 20–25, particularly items 13 (regarding sale of paper mill property) and 17 (regarding Powell's Mills at Scull Shoals), and repeated in Clarke County Will Book "E," 28–33; Deed of Henry Grady to John W. Nicholson, October 9, 1871, Clarke County Deed Book "Z," 236–37.

38. R. G. Dun, Georgia, vol. 6: 90, 100, 155, and 176. *Southern Banner*, February 7, 1850, "More Clothing"; March 16, 1854, "New Arrangement!"; October 15, 1862, "Notice" and "Work for All"; May 6, 1863, "Notice"; September 24, 1869, "Athens Factory"; June 2, 1871, "Correspondence"; June 30, 1871, "Athens Factory"; March 1, 1872, "Considerate." *Southern Watchman*, June 3, 1863, "Cotton Mill Stock"; April 28, 1869, "Our Cotton Mills." Kenneth Coleman, *Confederate Athens*, 101 and 108. Tax Digests, Ledgers for 1866 to 1875, Athens, Georgia City Records (MS 1633), box 2, sect. B, Hargrett Library. Letter from heirs of William Herring, March 3, 1869, "Papers 1869" folder, and Power of Attorney granted by William Herring, of Augusta, to Bloomfield to vote his 27 shares of stock, dated May 7, 1873, "Papers 1873" folder, box 11, Chicopee Manufacturing Company, Hargrett Library. Hull, *Annals of Athens*, 391–92.

39. Telephone conversation with James W. "Jimmy" Dudley, on February 25, 1994. The Dudley family owned 100 percent of the stock in Climax Hosiery Mill from 1920s to 1947. Climax owned 70 percent of stock of the Athens Manufacturing Company at the time of its sale to Chicopee in 1947.

40. Lucian Lamar Knight, *A Standard History of Georgia and Georgians* (New York: Lewis Publishing Co, 1917), vol. 3: 1781.

Bibliography

Manuscripts

Augusta State University, Reese Library Special Collections.

Georgia Railroad and Banking Company Collection, Directors Minutes.

Clarke County Court House, Athens, Ga.

Real Estate Office, Office of the Clerk of the Superior Court.

Deed Books.

Mortgage Books.

Probate Court.

Inferior Court Minutes.

Will Record Books.

Columbus State University Library, Special Collections.

John Lupold, Historical American Engineering Record Report on Columbus and Muscogee County, Georgia, Columbus, Georgia.

Duke University, Perkins Library Special Collections.

Benjamin C. Yancey Papers.

Edward Harden Collection.

John J. Dearing (Covington, Ga.) Papers, 1820–56.

Enoch Steadman Papers, 1862–70.

Emory University, Woodruff Library Special Collections.

Henry Grady Papers.

First Presbyterian Church, Athens, Ga.

"Report of Committee of W. H. Presbytery on Instruction of Col'd People" (ca. 1832) in typescript "History of First Presbyterian Church, Vol. I , 1820–1949."

Session Minutes.

Georgia Archives.

1850 Manuscript Census kept by Clarke County (Incomplete), Schedule 5: Prod ucts of Industry.

Clarke County Tax Digests.

Clarke County, Ga., Superior Court Minutes.

T. B. Rice Collection.

Wilkes County Tax Digests.

Georgia Historical Society, Savannah.

Jeremiah Evarts Diary.

John Sprague Papers.

Varner Family Papers.

Georgia Institute of Technology, School of History, Technology and Society.

James E. Brittain, Historic American Engineering Record (HAER) Inventory of Historic Industrial & Engineering Sites in Georgia. Compiled 1974 and 1975.

Harvard Business School, Baker Library Historical Collections.

R. G. Dun & Company Collection.

Marguerite Hodgson, Athens, Ga.

Hodgson Collection of papers related to White, Thomas, and Hodgson families of Athens.

Monroe King, Douglasville, Ga.

Photocopies of Fulton County Superior Court Records (Atlanta), Alexander S. Atkinson & others, Executors of Charles M. McDonald v. A. V. Brumby & William J. Russell.

Gilbert Milner, Athens, Ga.

James White, Jr., "Jim White's Story." Undated.

National Archives.

Case Files Of Applications From Former Confederates For Presidential Pardons (commonly known as "Amnesty Papers") 1865–1867, microfilm series m1003.

Record Group 29, Manuscript Census, Population Schedules.

Record Group 29, Records of Census Bureau, Entry 322, Schedules of Mines, Agriculture, Commerce, Manufactures, etc (1840)—Georgia.

Record Group 58, Internal Revenue Assessment Lists for Georgia, 1865–66, microfilm series m762.

Record Group 105, Bureau of Refugees, Freedmen, and Abandoned Lands.

Record Group 109, Letters Received by the Confederate Secretary of War 1861–65, microfilm series m437.

Record Group 109, entry 180, Confederate Papers Relating to Citizens and Business Firms (commonly known as the "Citizen Files"), microfilm series m346.

Record Group 365, Confederate Treasury Department, Field Offices.

Josephine and Rufus Reaves Paine, of Athens, Ga.

Letters regarding Reaves, Grady, and Nicholson families.

Southern Mutual Insurance Company, Athens, Ga.

Athens Agency Fire Registers.

Board of Directors Minute Books.

Letter Books.

Texas State Archives.
Maribeau B. Lamar Papers.
University of Georgia, Hargrett of Rare Books and Manuscript Library.
Athens, Ga., City Records, Tax Digests.
Athens Historical Society.
Biography Vertical Files: Elizur L. Newton File.
Bobbin Mill Record Book 1867–77.
Camak Collection.
Chicopee Manufacturing Company.
Clarke County Grange Records.
Clarke County Maps to 1900.
Cobb Erwin Lamar Collection.
Coulter Collections.
Josiah Daniel Almanac Diary.
Dearing Collection.
Dubose Family Papers.
C. D. Flanigen Collection.
Linton Family Papers.
Linton Gift.
Minutes of the Intendant and Wardens of the Town of Athens.
Municipal Vertical Files: Athens: Athens Steam Company file.
Municipal Vertical Files, Athens: Civil War Centennial Commission file.
Municipal Vertical Files, Athens: Confederate Armory file.
Municipal Vertical Files: Athens: Southern Mutual Insurance Company file.
Seaborn J. Mays Papers.
Elizur L. Newton Bible Transcript.
John William Nicholson Manuscript.
Pleasant Stovall Letter.
William Price Talmage Diary.
University of North Carolina–Chapel Hill, Southern Historical Collection.
John Nisbet Collection.
William Letcher Mitchell Papers.
Wake Forest University, Z. Smith Reynolds Library Special Collections.
Richard Worden Griffin Papers.

Newspapers

American Farmer (Baltimore) 1827–28.
American Railroad Journal and Advocate of Internal Improvements, March 29, 1834.
Athenian (Athens, Ga.) 1827–32.

Atlanta Constitution, Oct 17, 1898.

Central Georgian (Sandersville and Sparta, Ga.) 1855–59.

Gales & Seaton's Register of Debates in Congress (Washington, D.C.) 1832–33.

Macon Messenger (Macon, Ga.) 1836.

Niles' National Register (Baltimore) 1840.

Southern Banner (Athens, Ga.) 1832–70.

Southern Watchman (Athens, Ga.) 1859–71

Southern Whig (Athens, Ga.) 1845–53.

Dissertations, Theses, and Papers

Anthony, Thurston Lafayette. "The Public Career of Augustin Smith Clayton." Master's thesis, University of Georgia, 1939.

Bryant, Jonathan M. "'A County Where Plenty Should Abound': Race, Law, and Markets in Greene County, Georgia, 1850–1885." Ph.D. diss., University of Georgia, 1992.

Carey, Anthony G. "Parties and Politics in Antebellum Georgia." Ph.D. diss., Emory University, 1992.

De Treville, John Richard. "The Little New South: Origins of Industry in Georgia's Fall-Line Cities, 1840–1865." Ph.D. diss. University of North Carolina–Chapel Hill, 1986.

Galenson, Alice C. "The Migration of the Cotton Textile Industry from New England to the South: 1880–1930." Ph.D. diss., Cornell University, 1975.

Gamble, Robert S. "Athens: The Study of a Georgia Town during Reconstruction 1865–1872." Master's thesis, University of Georgia, 1967.

Gates, Frederick Beck. "An Imitative Enterprise: Canal Construction in Georgia, 1820–1860." Master's thesis, University of North Carolina at Charlotte, 1995.

Griffin, Richard W., and Harold S. Wilson, "The Ante-Bellum Textile Industry of Georgia, 1798–1865." Unpublished manuscript in possession of Tom Terrill, Columbia, South Carolina.

Hild, Matthew. "The Knights of Labor in Georgia." Master's thesis, University of Georgia, 1996.

Huffman, Frank Jackson. "Old South, New South: Continuity and Change in a Georgia County, 1850–1880." Ph.D. diss., Yale University, 1974.

Hunke, Jimmy Paul. "Fluvial Morphometry as a Tool in Rediscovering Historical Waterpowers: A Case Study on the Georgia Piedmont." Master's thesis, University of Georgia, 1983.

Jones, James Allison, "History of the First Presbyterian Church of Athens, Georgia." Master's thesis, University of Georgia, 1949.

Marshall, Charlotte Thomas. "Glimpses into the Antebellum History of the First

Baptist Church, Athens, Georgia, with Appendix." Lecture series presented at First Baptist Church (Athens, Ga.) in 1981. Copy in possession of the author.

Melton, Maurice. "Major Military Industries of the Confederate Government." Ph.D. diss. Emory University, 1978.

Sandlund, Vivien Elizabeth. "To Arouse and Awaken the American People: the Ideas and Strategies of the Gradual Emancipationists, 1800–1850." Ph.D. diss. Emory University, 1995.

Stokes, Allen Heath. "Black and White Labor and the Development of the Southern Textile Industry, 1800–1920." Ph.D. diss. University of South Carolina, 1977.

Ward, Judson C. "Internal Improvements in Georgia, 1817–1843." Master's thesis, Emory University, 1934.

Published Sources

Alvarez, Eugene. *Travel on Southern Antebellum Railroads, 1828–1860*. Tuscaloosa: University of Alabama Press, 1975.

Atherton, Lewis E. *Southern Country Store, 1800–1860*. Baton Rouge: Louisiana State University. Press, 1949.

Bailyn, Bernard. *The Ideological Origins of the American Revolution*. Cambridge, Mass.: Belknap Press, 1967.

Bateman, Fred, James Foust, and Thomas Weiss. "The Participation of Planters in Manufacturing in the Antebellum South." *Agricultural History* 48 (April 1974): 277–97.

Bateman, Fred, and Thomas Weiss. "Manufacturing in the Antebellum South." *Research in Economic History* 1 (1976): 1–44.

———. *A Deplorable Scarcity: The Failure of Industrialization in the Slave Economy*. Chapel Hill: University of North Carolina Press, 1981.

Beatty, Bess. *Alamance: The Holt Family and Industrialization in a North Carolina County, 1837–1900*. Baton Rouge: Louisiana State University Press, 1999.

———. "Lowells of the South; Northern Influences on the Nineteenth-Century North Carolina Textile Industry." *Journal of Southern History* 53 (February 1987): 37–62.

———. "The Edwin Holt Family: Nineteenth-Century Capitalists in North Carolina." *North Carolina Historical Review* 63 (October 1986): 511–35.

———. "Textile Labor in the North Carolina Piedmont: Mill Owner Images and Mill Worker Response, 1830–1900." *Labor History* 25 (Fall 1984): 485–503.

Beck, John J. "Building the New South: A Revolution from Above in a Piedmont County." *Journal of Southern History* 53 (August 1987): 441–70.

Belissary, Constantine G. "Industry and Industrial Philosophy in Tennessee, 1850–1860." (East Tennessee Historical Society) *Publications* 23 (1951): 23–55.

Bellows, Barbara L. *Benevolence Among Slaveholders: Assisting the Poor in Charleston, 1670–1860*. Baton Rouge: Louisiana State University Press, 1993.

Billings, Dwight B. "New Ways of Telling the New South Story: Numan Bartley on the *Creation of Modern Georgia*." *Georgia Historical Quarterly* 67 (Winter 1983): 480–88.

———. *Planters and the Making of a "New South": Class, Politics, and Development in North Carolina, 1865–1900*. Chapel Hill: University of North Carolina Press, 1979.

Bonner, James C. *A History of Georgia Agriculture 1732–1860*. Athens: University of Georgia Press, 1964.

Bradford, S. Sydney. "The Negro Ironworker in Ante Bellum Virginia." *Journal of Southern History* 25 (May 1959): 194–206.

Breyer, Stephen. "The Cherokee Indians and the Supreme Court." *Georgia Historical Quarterly* 87 (2003), 408–26.

Brockman, Charles J. Jr. "The Confederate Armory of Cook & Brother." *Gun Digest* 14 (1960): 74–75.

———. "The Confederate Armory of Cook & Brother." *Papers of the Athens Historical Society* 2 (1979): 85.

———, ed. "Obituary of Major F. W. C. Cook." *Georgia Historical Quarterly* 37 (December 1953): 351–54.

———. "A Rebel Secret Weapon." *American Rifleman*, August 1956.

Bryant, Jonathan M. *How Curious a Land: Conflict and Change in Green County, Georgia, 1850–1885*. Chapel Hill: University of North Carolina Press, 1996.

Buckingham, James Silk. *The Slaves States of America*. London: Fisher, Son & Co., 1843.

Byrne, Frank J. *Becoming Bourgeois: Merchant Culture in the South, 1820–1865*. Lexington: University Press of Kentucky, 2006.

Cade, John Brother. *Holsey—The Incomparable*. New York: Pageant Press, 1963.

Caramia, John A., Jr. "Teaching about the Local Community: Focus, Techniques, and Resources." *Georgia Social Science Journal* 12 (1981): 1–13.

Carey, Anthony Gene. *Parties, Slavery, and the Union in Antebellum Georgia*. Athens: University of Georgia Press, 1997.

Carlton, David L. "The Revolution from Above: The National Market and the Beginnings of Industrialization in North Carolina." *Journal of American History* 77 (September 1990): 445–75.

Carter, Hodding. "A Proud Struggle for Grace: Holly Springs, Mississippi." In Thomas C. Wheeler, ed., *A Vanishing America: The Life and Times of the Small Town*. New York: Holt, Rinehart and Winston, 1964.

Chandler, Alfred D. Jr. *The Visible Hand: The Managerial Revolution in American Business*. Cambridge, Mass.: Harvard University Press, 1977.

Clark, Christopher. "Household Economy, Market Exchange and the Rise of Capitalism in the Connecticut Valley, 1800–1860." *Journal of Social History* 13 (Winter 1979): 19–89.

Clark, Victor S. "Manufactures during the Ante-Bellum and War Periods." In *The South in the Building of the Nation; a history of the southern states designed to record the South's part in the making of the American nation; to portray the character and genius, to chronicle the achievements and progress and to illustrate the life,* ed. J. C. Ballagh, vol. 5: 313–35. Richmond, Va.: Southern Historical Publication Society, 1909.

Clayton, Phillip. *A Vindication of the Honorable Augustin S. Clayton against the Aspersions of George R. Gilmer, contained in his Sketches of Georgia.* Washington, D.C.: G. S. Gideon, Printer, 1855.

Cleveland, Frederick A., and Fred Wilbur Powell. *Railroad Promotion and Capitalization in the United States.* New York: Longmans, Green and Co., 1909.

Cleveland, Henry. *Alexander H. Stephens in Public and Private.* Atlanta: National Printing Co., 1866.

Cobb, James C. "Beyond Planters and Industrialists: A New Perspective of the New South." *Georgia Historical Quarterly* 54 (February 1988): 45–68.

———. *Industrialization and Southern Society, 1877–1984.* Lexington: University Press of Kentucky, 1984.

———. "Making Sense of Southern Economic History." *Georgia Historical Quarterly* 71 (Spring 1987): 53–74.

Coleman, Kenneth. *Athens, 1861–1865: As Seen through Letters in the University of Georgia Libraries.* University of Georgia Miscellanea Publications, No. 8. Athens: University of Georgia Press, 1969.

———. *Confederate Athens.* Athens: University of Georgia Press, 1967.

Collins, Herbert. "The Southern Industrial Gospel before 1860." *Journal of Southern History* 12 (August 1946): 386–402.

Compendium of the Enumeration of the Inhabitants and Statistics of the United States as Obtained at the Department of State, from the Returns of the 6th Census. 1841. Rpt. New York: Norman Ross Publishing Inc., 1990.

Cook, Ruth B. *North Across the River: A Civil War Trail of Tears.* Birmingham, Ala.: Crane Hill Publishers, 1998.

Coulter, E. Merton. "The Birth of a University, a Town, and a County." *Georgia Historical Quarterly* 46 (1962): 113–50.

———. *College Life in the Old South.* Athens: University of Georgia Press, 1951.

———. *Georgia Waters.* Athens: Georgia Historical Quarterly, 1965.

———. *John Jacobus Flournoy: Champion of the Common Man in the Antebellum South.* Savannah: Georgia Historical Society, 1942.

———. "A Note on a Georgia Paper Mill." *Georgia Historical Quarterly* 48 (1964): 239–42.

———. "Nullification Crisis in Georgia." *Georgia Historical Quarterly* 5 (1921): 5–39.

———. "Scull Shoals: An Extinct Georgia Manufacturing and Farming Community." *Georgia Historical Quarterly* 48 (1964): 33–63.

Cummings, Joseph B. *A History of the Georgia Railroad Company and Banking Company and its Corporate Affiliates 1833–1958.* Augusta: Georgia Railroad and Banking Co., 1958.

Cummings, Mary G. *Georgia Railroad & Banking Company 1833–1945.* Augusta, Ga.: n.p., 1945.

Dalzell, Robert. *Enterprising Elite: The Boston Associates and the World They Made.* Cambridge, Mass.: Harvard University Press, 1987.

Dana, Richard H., Jr. *Two Years Before the Mast; and Twenty-four Years After.* New York: Collier, 1937.

Davidson, Philip G. "Industrialism in the Ante-Bellum South." *South Atlantic Quarterly* 27 (1928): 405–25.

Davis, Robert S. *Cotton, Fire, & Dreams: The Robert Findlay Iron Works and Heavy Industry in Macon, Georgia 1839–1912.* Macon, Ga.: Mercer University Press, 1998.

———. "The First Golden Age of Georgia Industry, 1828–1860." *Georgia Historical Quarterly* 72 (1988): 699–711.

Davis, William Watson. "Ante-Bellum Southern Commercial Conventions." *Transactions of the Alabama Historical Society* 5 (1904): 156–65.

De Bow, James D. B. *The Industrial Resources, etc., of the Southern and Western States.* New Orleans: De Bow's Review, 1853.

———. *The Seventh Census of the United States: 1850.* 1853. Rpt. New York: Norman Ross Publishing, Inc., 1990.

DeCredico, Mary. *Patriotism for Profit: Georgia's Urban Entrepreneurs and the Confederate War Effort.* Chapel Hill: University of North Carolina Press, 1990.

Delfino, Susanna. "Antebellum East Tennessee Elites and Industrialization: The Examples of the Iron Industry and Internal Improvements." East Tennessee Historical Society *Publications* 56 and 57 (1984–85): 102–19.

———. "Many Souths: Changing Social Contexts and the Road to Industrialization in Antebellum Tennessee." *Southern Studies* 22 (Spring, 1983): 82–96.

———. "'To Maintain the Civil Rights of the People': The Tribulations of Duff Green, Iron Manufacturer in Civil War East Tennessee." *Journal of East Tennessee History* 72 (January 2000): 49–61.

Dew, Charles B. "Black Ironworkers and the Slave Insurrection Panic of 1856." *Journal of Southern History* 41 (August 1975): 325.

———. *Bond of Iron: Master and Slave at Buffalo Forge.* New York: W. W. Norton, 1994.

———. "David Ross and the Oxford Iron Works: A Study of Industrial Slavery in the Early Nineteenth-Century South." *William and Mary Quarterly*, 3rd ser., vol. 31 (1974): 189–224.

———. "Disciplining Slave Ironworkers in the Antebellum South: Coercion, Conciliation, and Accommodation." *American Historical Review* (1974): 393–418.

———. "Sam Williams, Forgeman: The Life of an Industrial Slave in the Old South." In *Region, Race and Reconstruction: Essays in Honor of C. Vann Woodward*, ed. J. Morgan Kousser and James M. McPherson. New York: Oxford University Press, 1982. 199–239.

———. "Slavery and Technology in the Antebellum Southern Iron Industry: The Case of Buffalo Forge." In *Science and Medicine in the Old South*, ed. Ronald L. Numbers and Todd L. Savitt, 107–26. Baton Rouge: Louisiana State University Press, 1989.

De Vorsey, Louis, Jr. "Early Water-powered Industries in Athens and Clarke County." *Papers of the Athens Historical Society* 2 (1979): 39–51.

Dillman, Caroline Matheny. *The Roswell Mills and a Civil War Tragedy: Excerpts from Days Gone by in Alpharetta and Roswell, Georgia*. Vol. 1. Roswell, Ga.: Chattahoochee Press, 1996.

Downey, Tom. *Planting a Capitalist South; Masters, Merchants, and Manufacturers in the Southern Interior, 1790–1860*. Baton Rouge: Louisiana State University Press, 2009.

———. "Riparian Rights and Manufacturing in Antebellum South Carolina: William Gregg and the Origins of the 'Industrial Mind.'" *Journal of Southern History* 65 (February 1999): 77–108.

Dublin, Thomas. *Women at Work: The Transformation of Work and Community in Lowell, Massachusetts, 1826–1860*. New York, Columbia University Press, 1979.

Dupre, Daniel. "Ambivalent Capitalists on the Cotton Frontier: Settlement and Development in the Tennessee Valley of Alabama." *Journal of Southern History* 106 (May 1990): 215–40.

Dyer, Thomas G. *The University of Georgia; A Bicentennial History, 1785–1985*. Athens: University of Georgia Press, 1985.

Eelman, Bruce W. *Entrepreneurs in the Southern Upcountry: Commercial Culture in Spartanburg, South Carolina, 1845–1880*. Athens: University of Georgia Press, 2008.

Ellis, Richard E. *The Union at Risk: Jacksonian Democracy, States' Rights, and the Nullification Crisis*. New York: Oxford University Press, 1987.

Evans, Curtis J. *The Conquest of Labor: Daniel Pratt and Southern Industrialization*. Baton Rouge: Louisiana State University Press, 2001.

Fishlow, Albert. *American Railroads and the Transformation of the Ante-Bellum Economy*. Cambridge, Mass.: Harvard University Press, 1965.

Fogel, Robert W., and Stanley L. Engerman. *Time on the Cross: The Economics of American Negro Slavery.* Boston: Little, Brown and Co., 1974

Foner, Eric. *Reconstruction: America's Unfinished Revolution, 1863–1877.* New York: Harper & Row, 1988.

Ford, Lacy K., Jr. *Origins of Southern Radicalism: The South Carolina Upcountry, 1800–1860.* New York: Oxford University Press, 1988.

Fox-Genovese, Elizabeth, and Eugene D. Genovese. *Fruits of Merchant Capital: Slavery and Bourgeois Property in the Rise and Expansion of Capitalism.* New York: Oxford University Press, 1983.

Freehling, William W. *Prelude to Civil War; The Nullification Controversy in South Carolina 1816–1836.* New York: Oxford University Press, 1965.

Garrison, Tim Alan. *The Legal Ideology of Removal; The Southern Judiciary and the Sovereignty of Native American Nations.* Athens: University of Georgia Press, 2002.

Genovese, Eugene D. *The Political Economy of Slavery: Studies in the Economy and Society of the Slave South.* New York: Random House, 1965.

———. *The Slaveholders' Dilemma: Freedom and Progress in Southern Conservative Thought, 1820–1860.* Columbia: University of South Carolina Press, 1992.

Georgia Department of Agriculture. *Georgia Historical and Industrial.* Atlanta: Geo. W. Harrison, State Printer, 1901.

Georgia General Assembly. *Acts of the General Assembly of the State of Georgia Passed in November and December, 1839.*

Georgia Railroad & Banking Company of Georgia. *150 Years: Railroad & Banking Company of Georgia, 1833–1983.* Augusta: Georgia Railroad & Banking Company of Georgia, 1983.

Gillespie, Michele. "Artisan Accommodation to the Slave South: The Case of William Talmage, A Blacksmith, 1834–1847." *Georgia Historical Quarterly* 81 (1997): 265–86.

———. *Free Labor in an Unfree World: White Artisans in Slaveholding Georgia, 1789–1860.* Athens: University of Georgia Press, 2000.

Gilmer, George R. *Sketches of Some of the First Settlers of Upper Georgia, of the Cherokees and the Author.* 1855. Rpt. Baltimore: Genealogical Pub. Co., 1965.

Goldfarb, Stephen J. "A Note on Limits to the Growth of the Cotton-Textile Industry in the Old South." *Journal of Southern History* 48 (November 1982): 545–58.

———. "Laws Governing the Incorporation of Manufacturing Companies Passed by Southern State Legislatures before the Civil War." *Southern Studies* 24 (Winter 1985): 407–16.

Goodrich, Carter. *Government Promotion of American Canals and Railroads 1800–1890.* New York: Columbia University Press, 1960.

Gorn, Elliott J. *The Manly Art: Bare-knuckle Prize Fighting in America.* Ithaca, N.Y.: Cornell University Press, 1986.

Griffin, Richard W. "Ante Bellum Industrial Foundations of the (Alleged) 'New South.'" *Textile History Review* 5 (April 1964): 33–43.

———. "The Augusta (Georgia) Manufacturing Company in Peace, War, and Reconstruction, 1847–1877." *Business History Review* 32 (Spring 1958): 60–73.

———. "The Cotton Mill Campaign in Florida, 1828–1863." *Florida Historical Quarterly* 40 (January 1962): 261–74.

———. "Cotton Manufacture in Alabama to 1865." *Alabama Historical Quarterly* 18 (Fall 1956): 289–307.

———. "Florence, Alabama: A Textile Manufacturing Center of the Old South, 1822–1871." (North Alabama Historical Association) *Bulletin* 2 (1957): 21–24.

———. "Manufacturing Interests of Alabama Planters, 1810–1830." *Journal of the Alabama Academy of Science* 30 (October 1958): 63–71.

———. "An Origin of the New South: The South Carolina Homespun Company, 1808–1815." *Business History Review* 35 (1961): 402–14.

———. "The Origins of the Industrial Revolution in Georgia: Cotton Textiles, 1810–1865." *Georgia Historical Quarterly* 42 (December 1958): 355–75.

———. "Origins of Southern Cotton Manufactures, 1807–1816." *Cotton History Review* 1 (January 1960): 5–11.

———. "Poor White Laborers in Southern Cotton Factories, 1789–1865." *South Carolina Historical Magazine* 61 (1960): 26–40.

———. "The Saluda Manufacturing Company, 1832–1865." *Cotton History Review* 2 (October 1961): 229–38.

———. "The Textile Industry in Greene County, Georgia, Before 1860." *Georgia Historical Quarterly* 48 (1964): 81–84.

Griffin, Richard W., and Diffee W. Standard. "The Cotton Textile Industry in Ante-Bellum North Carolina; Part 1: Origin and Growth to 1830." *North Carolina Historical Review* 34 (1957): 15–35.

———. "The Cotton Textile Industry in Ante-Bellum North Carolina; Part 2: An Era of Boom and Consolidation, 1830–1860." *North Carolina Historical Review* 34 (1957): 131–64.

Griffith, A. E. *History of the Southern Mutual Insurance Company: Athens, Georgia, 1848–1923*. Rev. ed. Athens: McGregor Co., 1931.

Habakkuk, H. J. *American and British Technology in the Nineteenth Century*. Cambridge, U.K.: University Press, 1962.

Hahn, Steven. *Roots of Southern Populism: Yeoman Farmers and the Transformation of the Georgia Upcountry, 1850–1890*. New York: Oxford University Press, 1983.

Hahn, Steven, and Jonathan Prude, eds. *The Countryside in the Age of Capitalist Transformation: Essays in the Social History of Rural America*. Chapel Hill: University of North Carolina Press, 1985.

Hall, Jacquelyn Dowd, James Leloudis, Robert Korstad, Mary Murphy, Lu Ann Jones, Christopher B. Daly. *Like A Family: The Making of a Southern Mill World*. Chapel Hill: University of North Carolina Press, 1987.

Hall, M. R. "Utilization of Southern Water Powers." In J. C. Ballagh, ed., *The South in the Building of the Nation; a History of the Southern States Designed to Record the South's Part in the Making of the American Nation; to Portray the Character and Genius, to Chronicle the Achievements and Progress and to Illustrate the Life*. Vol. 5: 580–86. Richmond: Southern Historical Publication Society, 1909.

Hammond, Seth. "The Ante-Bellum Kentucky Cotton Industry, 1790–1860." *Cotton History Review* 1 (April 1960): 47–55.

Handlin, Oscar, and Mary Flug Handlin. *Commonwealth: A Study of the Role of Government in the American Economy: Massachusetts, 1774–1861*. Cambridge, Mass.: Harvard University Press, 1969.

Heath, Milton Sydney. *Constructive Liberalism: The Role of the State in Economic Development in Georgia to 1860*. Cambridge, Mass.: Harvard University Press, 1954.

Henretta, James. "Families and Farms: Mentalité in Preindustrial America." *William and Mary Quarterly*, 3rd ser., vol. 35 (January 1978): 3–32.

Hild, Matthew. "Past the Myth: Confronting Real Issues about Southern Industrialization." *International Labor & Working-Class History* 61 (Spring 2002): 165–69.

Hillyer, Junius. *The Life and Times of Judge Junius Hillyer (From His Memoirs)*. Tignall, Ga.: Boyd Publishing Co., 1989.

Hillyer, Shaler G. *Reminiscences of Georgia Baptists*. Atlanta: Foote and Davies, 1902.

History of the Baptist Denomination in Georgia: with Biographical Compendium and portrait Gallery of Baptist Ministers and other Georgia Baptists. Compiled for the Christian Index. 1881. Rpt. Easley, S.C.: Southern Historical Press, n.d.

Hitt, Michael D. *Charged with Treason: Ordeal of 400 Mill Workers during Military Operations in Roswell, Georgia, 1864–1865*. Monroe, N.Y.: Library Research Associates, 1992.

Horwitz, Morton J. *The Transformation of American Law, 1780–1860*. Cambridge, Mass.: Harvard University Press, 1977.

Hull, Augustus Longstreet. *Annals of Athens, Georgia 1801–1901*. Athens, Ga.: Banner Job Office, 1906.

Hunt, Caroline C. "The Settlement, Development, and Decline of the Scull Shoals Community in Green and Oconee Counties, 1784–1920." A Historical Survey Report of Scull Shoals community, Greene County, Georgia, performed for the United States Department of Agriculture Forest Service Contract 38-3231 by Archeological Survey of Cobb-Fulton Counties. Lawrence W. Meier, Administrator. May 1980.

Hynds, Ernest C. *Antebellum Athens and Clarke County Georgia*. Athens: University of Georgia Press, 1974.

Index to the 1830 Census of Georgia, Baltimore: Genealogical Publishing Co., 1982.

Index to United States Census of Georgia for 1820. Savannah: Georgia Historical Quarterly, 1963.

Jeremy, David. *Transatlantic Industrial Revolution: The Diffusion of Textile Technologies Between Britain and America, 1790–1830s*. Cambridge: MIT Press, 1981.

Johnson, J. G. "Notes on Manufacturing in Ante-Bellum Georgia." *Georgia Historical Quarterly* 16 (1932): 214–31.

Johnson, Paul. *A Shopkeeper's Millennium: Society and Revivals in Rochester, New York, 1815–1837*. New York: Hill and Wang, 1978.

Johnson, Vicki Vaughn. *The Men and the Vision of the Southern Commercial Conventions, 1845–1871*. Columbia: University of Missouri Press, 1992.

Jones, Charles C. Jr. "Pioneer Manufacturing in Richmond County, Georgia." *Textile History Review* 5 (July 1964): 69–83.

Kennedy, Joseph C. G. *Abstract of the Statistics of Manufactures according to the returns of the Seventh Census*. Washington, D.C.: U.S. Government Document, 1859. Rpt. New York: Norman Ross Publishing Inc., 1990.

King, Monroe M. "Destruction of New Manchester Georgia: The Story Behind the Ruins at Sweetwater Creek State Park." Douglasville, Ga.: Monroe King, 1982.

Knight, Lucian Lamar. *A Standard History of Georgia and Georgians*. New York: Lewis Publishing Co, 1917.

Kulik, Gary. "Dams, Fish, and Farmers: Defense of Public Rights in Eighteenth-Century Rhode Island." In *The Countryside in the Age of Capitalist Transformation: Essays in the Social History of Rural America*, ed. Steven Hahn and Jonathan Prude. Chapel Hill: University of North Carolina Press, 1985. 193–241.

Kulikoff, Allan. *The Agrarian Origins of American Capitalism*. Charlottesville: University Press of Virginia, 1992.

———. "Households and Markets: Toward a New Synthesis of American Agrarian History." *William and Mary Quarterly*, 3rd ser., vol. 50, no. 2 (April 1993): 342–55.

———. "The Transition to Capitalism in Rural America." *William and Mary Quarterly*, 3rd ser., vol. 46, no. 1 (January 1989): 120–44.

Lander, Ernest M. Jr. "Ante-Bellum Milling in South Carolina." *South Carolina Historical Magazine* 51 (1950): 125–32.

———. "Charleston: Manufacturing Center of the Old South." *Journal of Southern History* 26 (August 1960): 330–51.

———. "The Development of Textiles in the South Carolina Piedmont Before 1860." *Cotton History Review* 1 (July 1960): 88–100.

———. "Slave Labor in South Carolina Cotton Mills." *Journal of Negro History* 38 (1953): 161–73.

———. *The Textile Industry in Antebellum South Carolina*. Baton Rouge: Louisiana State University Press, 1969.

Larkin, Jack. *The Reshaping of Everyday Life: 1790–1840*. New York: Harper & Row, 1988.

Larson, John Lauritz. *Internal Improvement: National Public Works and the Promise of Popular Government in the Early United States.* Chapel Hill: University of North Carolina Press. 2001.

Lee, Francis Bazley (editor). *Genealogical Memorial History of the State of New Jersey.* Volume II. New York: Lewis Historical Publishing Company, 1910.

Levine, Lawrence. *Highbrow/Lowbrow: the Emergence of Cultural Hierarchy in America.* Cambridge, Mass.: Harvard University Press, 1988.

Lewis, Ronald L. *Coal, Iron, and Slaves: Industrial Slavery in Maryland and Virginia, 1715–1865.* Contributions in Labor History Series. Westport, Conn.: Greenwood Press, 1979.

Lewis, W. David. "The Emergence of Birmingham as a Case Study of Continuity Between the Antebellum Planter Class and Industrialization in the 'New South.'" *Agricultural History* 68 (Spring 1994): 62–79.

Linden, Fabian. "Repercussions of Manufacturing in the Ante Bellum South." *North Carolina Historical Review* 17 (1940): 313.

Linton, Lucy. "Random Recollections or Leaves from the Linton Branch of the Hull Family Tree by the Last Leaf." *Papers of the Athens Historical Society* 1 (1964): 53–68.

Lozier, John William. *Taunton and Mason: Cotton Machinery and Locomotive Manufacture in Taunton, Massachusetts, 1811–1861.* New York: Garland, 1986.

Lupold , John S. and Thomas L. French, Jr. *Bridging Deep South Rivers: The Life and Legend of Horace King.* Athens: University of Georgia Press, with the Historic Chattahoochee Commission and the Troup County Historical Society. 2004.

Majewski, John. *A House Dividing: Economic Development in Pennsylvania and Virginia before the Civil War.* New York: Cambridge University Press, 2000.

———. *Modernizing a Slave Economy: The Economic Vision of the Confederate Nation.* Civil War America Series. Chapel Hill: University of North Carolina Press, 2009.

———. "Who Financed the Transportation Revolution? Regional Divergence and Internal Improvements in Antebellum Pennsylvania and Virginia." *Journal of Economic History* 56 (December 1996): 763–88.

Manufactures of the United States in 1860; Compiled from the original returns of the Eight Census. Washington, D.C.: Government Printing Office, 1865. Rpt. New York: Norman Ross Publishing Inc., 1990.

Marrs, Aaron W. *Railroads in the Old South: Pursuing Progress in a Slave Society.* Baltimore: Johns Hopkins University Press, 2009.

Marshall, Charlotte Thomas, ed. *Oconee Hill Cemetery; Tombstone Inscriptions for that Part of Cemetery West of Oconee River and Index to Records of Interments.* Athens, Ga.: Athens Historical Society, 1971.

———. *Historic Houses of Athens.* Athens, Ga.: Athens Historical Society, 1987.

Martin, Clarece. *A History of Roswell Presbyterian Church.* Dallas, Ga.: Taylor Publishing Co., 1984.

Martin, Thomas P. "The Advent of William Gregg and the Graniteville Company." *Journal of Southern History* 11 (August 1945): 402–13.

McCardell, John. *The Idea of a Southern Nation: Southern Nationalists and Southern Nationalism, 1830–1860.* New York: Norton, 1978.

McCarthy, J. Patrick, Jr. "Commercial Development and University Reform in Antebellum Athens: William Mitchell as Entrepreneur, Engineer, and Educator." *Georgia Historical Quarterly* 83 (Spring 1999): 3–28.

McCurry, Stephanie. *Masters of Small Worlds: Yeoman Households, Gender Relations, and the Political Culture of the Antebellum South Carolina Low Country.* New York: Oxford University Press, 1995.

McGaw, Judith. *Most Wonderful Machine: Mechanization and Social Change in Berkshire Paper Making, 1801–1885.* Princeton, N.J.: Princeton University Press, 1987.

McLoughlin, William G. *Cherokees and Missionaries, 1789–1839.* New Haven: Yale University Press, 1984.

McGuire, Peter S. "Athens and the Railroads: The Georgia and the Northeastern" Part 1, *Georgia Historical Quarterly* 16 (March 1934): 7.

Merrill, Michael. "Cash Is Good to Eat: Self-Sufficiency and Exchange in the Rural Economy of the United States." *Radical History Review* 4 (Winter 1977): 42–71.

Meyer, David R. *The Roots of American Industrialization.* Baltimore: Johns Hopkins University Press, 2003.

Miller, James David. *South by Southwest: Planter Emigration and Identity in the Slave South.* Charlottesville: University Press of Virginia, 2002.

Miller, Randall M. *The Cotton Mill Movement in Antebellum Alabama.* New York: Arno Press, 1978.

———. "Daniel Pratt's Industrial Urbanism: The Cotton Mill Town in Antebellum Alabama." *Alabama Historical Quarterly* 34 (Spring 1972): 5–36.

———. "The Fabric of Control: Slavery in Antebellum Southern Textile Mills." *Business History Review* 55 (Winter 1981): 471–90.

———. "Love of Labor: A Note on Daniel Pratt's Employment Practices." *Alabama Historical Quarterly* 37 (Summer 1975): 146–50.

Miller, Stephen F. *Bench and Bar of Georgia.* Philadelphia: J. B. Lippincott & Co., 1858.

Mintz, Steven. *Moralists and Modernizers: America's Pre-Civil War Reformers.* Baltimore: Johns Hopkins University Press, 1995.

Mitchell, Broadus. *The Rise of Cotton Mills in the South.* Gloucester, Mass.: Peter Smith, 1921.

———. *William Gregg; Factory Master of the Old South.* Chapel Hill: University of North Carolina Press, 1928. Rpt. New York: Octagon Books, 1966.

Moore, Barrington Jr., Social Origins of Dictatorship and Democracy; Lord and Peasant in the Making of the Modern World. Boston: Beacon Press, 1966.

Moore, John Hebron. "Mississippi's Ante-Bellum Textile Industry." *Journal of Mississippi History* 16 (1954): 81–98.

Morgan, Chad. *Planters' Progress: Modernizing Confederate Georgia.* Gainesville: University Press of Florida, 2005.

Morris, Michael. "Georgia and the Conversation over Indian Removal." *Georgia Historical Quarterly* 91 (2007): 403–23.

Morris, Sylvanus. *History of Athens and Clarke County.* Athens, Ga.: H. J. Rowe, 1923.

Murray, Paul. *The Whig Party in Georgia 1825–1853.* James Sprunt Studies in History and Political Science, vol. 29. Chapel Hill: University of North Carolina Press, 1948.

National Bank of Athens. *Historical Review of the National Bank of Athens from its founding to its Semi-Centennial Anniversary.* Athens, Ga.: National Bank of Athens, 1916.

Newton County Historical Society. *History of Newton County Georgia.* Covington, Ga.: Newton County Historical Society, 1988.

Norgren, Jill. "Lawyers and the Legal Business of the Cherokee Republic in Courts of the United States, 1829–1835." *Law and History Review* 10 (1992): 253–77.

Oakes, James. *Slavery and Freedom: an Interpretation of the Old South.* New York: Knopf, 1990.

Olliff, Martin T. "Life and Work in a Progressive Cotton Community: Prattville, Alabama, 1846–1860." *Agricultural History* 68 (Spring 1994): 51–61.

Olmsted, Frederick Law. *Journey through the Seaboard Slave States, with Remarks on their Economy.* New York: Dix & Edwards: 1856.

Owsley, Frank L. *Plain Folk of the Old South.* Baton Rouge: Louisiana State University Press, 1949

Perdue, Theda, and Michael D. Green, eds. *The Cherokee Removal: A Brief History with Documents.* Bedford Series in History and Culture. Boston: St. Martin's Press, 1995.

Phillips, Ulrich Bonnell. *Georgia and State Rights: A Study of the Political History of Georgia from the Revolution to the Civil War, with Particular Regard to Federal Relations.* 1902. Rpt. N.p.: Antioch Press, 1968.

———. *A History of Transportation in the Eastern Cotton Belt to 1860.* 1908. Rpt. New York: Octagon Books, 1968.

———, ed. *Plantation and Frontier Documents: 1649–1863, Illustrative of Industrial History in the Colonial & Ante-bellum South* (Cleveland: A. H. Clark Co., 1909.

Powell, Lawrence. "The Prussians Are Coming." *Georgia Historical Quarterly* 71 (Winter 1987): 638–67.

Pratt, Merrill. "Daniel Pratt: Alabama's First Industrialist." *Cotton History Review* 2 (January 1961): 18–29.

Preyer, Norris W. "The Historian, The Slave, and the Ante-Bellum Textile Industry." *Journal of Negro History* 46 (April 1961): 67–82.

———. "Why Did Industrialization Lag in the Old South?" *Georgia Historical Quarterly* 55 (1971): 378–96.

Prude, Jonathan. *The Coming of Industrial Order: Town and Factory Life in Rural Massachusetts, 1810–1860*. New York, Cambridge University Press, 1983.

Quinn, John F. *Father Mathew's Crusade: Temperance in Nineteenth Century Ireland and Irish America*. Amherst: University of Massachusetts Press, 2002.

Quist, John W. *Restless Visionaries: The Social Roots of Antebellum Reform in Alabama and Michigan*. Baton Rouge: Louisiana State University Press, 1998.

Rawick, George P., ed. *The American Slave: A Composite Autobiography* 12: *Georgia Narratives*, Parts 1 and 2. WPA Federal Writers' Project report, 1941. Rpt. Westport, Conn.: Greenwood Press, 1972.

Report on Manufacturing Industries in the United States at the Eleventh Census: 1890. Washington, D.C.: Government Printing Office, 1895.

Rodgers, Daniel T. "Republicanism: Career of a Concept." *Journal of American History* 79 (1992): 11–38.

The Rogers Locomotive Catalog, 1876. Newark: New Jersey Historical Society, 1983.

"The Rogers Locomotive 'Sandusky.'" (Railway and Locomotive Historical Society) *Bulletin* 44 (October 1937): 42–45.

Rorabaugh, W. J. *The Alcoholic Republic, an American Tradition*. New York: Oxford University Press, 1979.

Rosenberg, Charles E. *The Care of Strangers: The Rise of America's Hospital System*. New York: Basic Books, 1987.

Rozier, John, ed. *The Granite Farm Letters: The Civil War Correspondence of Edgeworth and Sallie Bird*. Athens: University of Georgia Press, 1988.

Rothman, David J. *The Discovery of the Asylum: Social Order and Disorder in the New Republic*. Boston: Little Brown & Co., 1971.

Russel, Robert Royal. *Economic Aspects of Southern Sectionalism, 1840–1861. University of Illinois Studies in the Social Sciences* 11 (March–June 1923). Urbana: University of Illinois, 1924.

Russell, James Michael. *Atlanta, 1847–1890: City Building in the Old South and the New*. Baton Rouge: Louisiana State University Press, 1988.

Ryan, Mary. *Cradle of the Middle Class: the Family in Oneida County, New York, 1790–1865*. New York: Cambridge University Press, 1981.

Schweikart, Larry. *Banking in the American South from the Age of Jackson to Reconstruction*. Baton Rouge: Louisiana State University Press, 1987.

Scott, Carole E. "Why the Cotton Textile Industry did not Develop in the South Sooner." *Agricultural History* 68 (Spring 1994): 105–21.

Scranton, Philip. *Proprietary Capitalism: The Textile Manufacture at Philadelphia, 1800–1885*. New York: Cambridge University Press, 1983.

Shelton, Cynthia J. *The Mills of Manayunk: Industrialization and Social Conflict in the Philadelphia Region, 1787–1837*. Baltimore: Johns Hopkins University Press, 1986.

Sheriff, Carol. *The Artificial River: The Erie Canal and the Paradox of Progress, 1817–1862*. New York: Hill & Wang, 1996.

Sherwood, Adiel. *A Gazetteer of the State of Georgia*. 1827. Rpt. Athens: University of Georgia Press, 1939.

Shryock, Richard H. "The Early Industrial Revolution in the Empire State." *Georgia Historical Quarterly* 11 (June 1927): 109–28.

Sisson, William A. "From Farm to Factory: Work Values and Discipline in Two Early Delaware and Maryland Textile Mills." *Delaware History* 21 (Spring 1984): 31–52.

Skinner, James L., ed. *The Autobiography of Henry Merrell: Industrial Missionary to the South*. Athens: University of Georgia Press, 1991.

Smith, Merritt Roe. *Harpers Ferry Armory and the New Technology: the Challenge of Change*. Ithaca: Cornell University Press, 1977.

Smith, Whitefoord. "A Discourse on the Occasion of the Death of the Hon. Augustin S. Clayton, delivered in the College Chapel, Athens, Ga., on the 23d June, 1839." Athens: n.p., 1839.

Sokoloff, Kenneth L. and David Dollar. "Agricultural Seasonality and the Organization of Manufacturing in Early Industrial Economies." *Journal of Economic History* 57 (June 1997): 288–322.

Sokoloff, Kenneth L. and Viken Tchakerian. "Manufacturing Where Agriculture Predominates: Evidence from the South and Midwest in 1860." *Explorations in Economic History* 34 (1997): 243–64.

Southern Business Directory. Charleston: Walker & James, 1854.

Southern Historical Association. *Memoirs of Georgia; containing historical accounts of the state's civil, military, industrial and professional interests, and personal sketches of many of its people*. Atlanta: Southern Historical Association, 1895.

Starobin, Robert. *Industrial Slavery in the Old South*. New York: Oxford University Press, 1970.

Steadman, Enoch. "A Brief Treatise on Manufacturing in the South." *Cotton History Review* 2 (April 1961): 103–18.

———. *The Southern Manufacturer*. Gallatin, Tenn.: Gray & Boyer, 1858.

Stegeman, John F. *These Men She Gave: Civil War Diary of Athens, Georgia*. Athens: University of Georgia Press, 1964.

Stewart, J. Adger. *The Webb and Allied Families consisting of the Manuscript of John Webb*. Louisville, Ky.: J. Adger Stewart, 1921.

Stovall, Allen. "Scull Shoals: A Feasibility Study." Athens: University of Georgia School of Environmental Design, 1984.

Stover, John F. *Iron Road to the West: American Railroads in the 1850s*. New York: Columbia University Press, 1978.

Tadman, Michael. *Speculators and Slaves: Masters, Traders, and Slaves in the Old South*. Madison: University of Wisconsin Press, 1989.

Tate, James H. *Keeper of the Flame: The Story of Atlanta Gas Light Company 1856–1985*. Atlanta: Atlanta Gas Light Co., 1985.

Tate, Susan B. "James Camak." In Kenneth Coleman and Charles Stephen Gurr, eds., *Dictionary of Georgia Biography*. Athens: University of Georgia Press, 1983. 154–55.

Taylor, George Rogers. *The Transportation Revolution, 1815–1865*. Vol. 4 of the *Economic History of the United States*. New York: Rinehart and Co., 1951.

Taylor, James H. "Manufactures in South Carolina." *Cotton History Review* 1 (July 1960): 131–37.

Tchakerian, Viken. "Productivity, Extent of Markets, and Manufacturing in the Late Antebellum South and Midwest." *Journal of Economic History* 54 (1994): 497–525.

Terrill, Tom. "Eager Hands: Labor for Southern Textiles, 1850–1860." *Journal of Economic History* 36 (March 1976): 84–101.

"Thomas Rogers." *Dictionary of American Biography* 16: 112–13.

Thorn, Cecelia Jean. "The Bell Factory: Early Pride of Huntsville." *The Alabama Review* 32 (January 1979): 28–37.

Thornton, J. Mills, III. *Politics and Power in a Slave Society: Alabama, 1800–1860*. Baton Rouge: Louisiana State University Press, 1978.

Thurmond, Michael. *A Story Untold: Black Men and Women in Athens History*. (Athens, Ga.: Clarke County School District, 1978.

Tyrrell, Ian R. "Drink and Temperance in the Antebellum South: An Overview and Interpretation." *Journal of Southern History* 48 (1982): 488–508.

U.S. Congress. "Documents relative to The Manufactures in the United States collected and transmitted To the House of Representatives in compliance with a resolution of January 19, 1832 by the Secretary of the Treasury" otherwise known as the "McLane Report" Volumes 3 and 4; reprinted New York: Burt Franklin, 1976.

———. "Message from the President of the United States in Answer to a Resolution of the House of the 5th of March last, Relative to Pardons and Property Seized as Enemies' Property, and Returned to Those Who Claimed to be the Original Owners." House Executive Document 99, 39th Congress, 1st session, Microprint Series 1236.

———. "Report of Lt. Col. S. H. Long, on a reconnaissance for railroads from Augusta, Georgia, to Memphis, Tennessee, in February, 1835."House Document 177, Appendix B, pp. 81–88, 23 Congress, 2nd session.

———. "Report of the Secretary of the Treasury." House Executive Document 6M, vol. 2, 29th Congress, 1st sess. Rpt. in "Walker Tariff Report 1846 . . . Circulars of the Secretary of the Treasury & abstract of Replies to them in regard to the Tariff." Senate Document 72, pt. 3, vol. 10, 62nd Congress, 1st sess., ser. 6088.

Walker, Francis A. *The Statistics of the Wealth and Industry of the United States . . . compiled from the original returns of the Ninth census.* Washington, D.C.: Government Printing Office, 1872. Rpt. New York: Norman Ross Publishing Inc., 1990.

Wallace, Anthony F. C. *Rockdale: The Growth of an American Village in the Early Industrial Revolution.* New York: Alfred A. Knopf, 1978.

Warren, Mary Bondurant. *The Hills of Wilkes County, Georgia and Allied Families.* Danielsville, Ga.: Heritage Papers, 1987.

Ward, James A. "Early Railroad Empire Builders, 1850–1873." *Railroad History* No. 160 (Summer 1989): 5–21.

———. "J. Edgar Thomson and the Georgia Railroad, 1834–1847." *Railroad History* No. 134 (Spring, 1976).

———. *J. Edgar Thomson: Master of the Pennsylvania.* Westport, Conn.: Greenwood Press, 1980.

———. "A New Look at Antebellum Southern Railroad Development." *Journal of Southern History* 39 (August 1973): 409–20.

———. "Promotional Wizardry: Rhetoric and Railroad Origins, 1820–1860." *Journal of the Early Republic* 11 (Spring 1991): 69–88.

———. *Railroads and the Character of America, 1820–1887.* Knoxville: University of Tennessee Press, 1986.

Watkins, James L. *King Cotton: A Historical and Statistical Review 1790–1908.* 1908. Rpt. New York: Negro Universities Press (Greenwood Publishing), 1969.

———. "Production and Price of Cotton for One Hundred Years." U.S. Department of Agriculture, Division of Statistics, Miscellaneous Series, *Bulletin* 9. Washington, D.C.: Government Printing Office, 1895.

Watters, Samuel Cloyce. "High Shoals, Georgia; Then—Now." High Shoals, Ga.: Historical Society of High Shoals, 1979.

Wells, Jonathan Daniel. *The Origins of the Southern Middle Class, 1800–1861.* Chapel Hill: University of North Carolina Press, 2004.

Wender, Herbert. *Southern Commercial Conventions, 1837–1859.* Baltimore: Johns Hopkins University Press, 1930.

White, George. *Statistics of the State of Georgia.* Savannah, Ga.: W. Thorne Williams, 1849.

———. *Historical Collections of Georgia.* New York: Pudney & Russell, 1854.

Whitman, T. Stephen. "Industrial Slavery at the Margin: The Maryland Chemical Works." *Journal of Southern History* 109 (February 1993): 31–62.

Wiener, Jonathan. *Social Origins of the New South: Alabama, 1860–1885*. Baton Rouge: Louisiana State University Press, 1978.

Wilentz, Sean. *Chants Democratic: New York City and the Rise of the American Working Class, 1788–1850*. New York: Oxford University Press, 1984.

Williams, Samuel C. "Ironworks in the Tennessee Country." *Tennessee Historical Quarterly* 6 (1947): 47.

Wilson, Harold S. *Confederate Industry: Manufacturers and Quartermasters in the Civil War*. Jackson: University Press of Mississippi, 2002.

Wood, Maude Talmage. *Once Apunce A Time*. Athens, Ga.: Classic Press, 1977.

Wood, Richard G. *Stephen Harriman Long 1784–1864: Army Engineer, Explorer, Inventor*. Glendale, Calif.: Arthur H. Clark Co., 1966.

Wood, W. K. "The Georgia Railroad and Banking Company." *Georgia Historical Quarterly* 57 (Winter 1973): 544–61.

Wright, Gavin. "Cheap Labor and Southern Textiles before 1880." *Journal of Economic History* 39 (September 1979): 655–80.

———. *Old South, New South; Revolutions in the Southern Economy since the Civil War*. New York: Basic Books Inc., 1986.

———. "Rethinking the Postbellum Southern Political Economy: A Review Essay." *Business History Review* 58 (Autumn 1984): 409–16.

———. "The Strange Career of the New Southern Economic History." *Reviews in American History* 10 (December 1982): 164–80.

Wyatt, Edward A. IV. "Rise of Industry in Ante-Bellum Petersburg." *William and Mary Quarterly*, 2d Series, 17 (January 1937): 1–36.

Wright, G. Richard, and Kenneth H. Wheeler. "New Men in the Old South: Joseph E. Brown and his Associates in Georgia's Etowah Valley." *Georgia Historical Quarterly* 93 (Winter 2009): 363–87.

York, Neil L. *Mechanical Metamorphosis: Technological Change in Revolutionary America*. Contributions in American Studies, vol. 78. Westport, Conn.: Greenwood Press, 1985.

Young, Mary. "The Exercise of Sovereignty in Cherokee Georgia." *Journal of the Early Republic* 10 (1990): 43–53.

Index